THE RED AND THE WHITE

THE RED AND THE WHITE
The Cinema of People's Poland

Paul Coates

WALLFLOWER PRESS
LONDON & NEW YORK

First published in Great Britain in 2005 by
Wallflower Press
4th Floor, 26 Shacklewell Lane, London E8 2EZ
www.wallflowerpress.co.uk

A catalogue for this book is available from the British Library

ISBN 1-904764-26-6 (pbk)
ISBN 1-904764-27-4 (hbk)

Book design by Elsa Mathern

Printed in Great Britain by Antony Rowe Ltd., Chippenham, Wiltshire

CONTENTS

In the introduction to his recent *Polish National Cinema*, Marek Haltof voiced a hope that 'more detailed and theoretically minded studies in English' would follow his survey work, which updates that done earlier by Bolesław Michałek in particular (Haltof 2002: xiii). The kind of work Haltof envisages is long overdue in a Film Studies that practises analytical overkill of American cinema and a few West European auteurs and neglects the many extraordinary film texts produced elsewhere in the world. The ignorance of the significance of the cinema of East Central Europe, for instance – in part the result of a definition of 'Europe' parochially anchored in temporary post-Yalta political arrangements – may be gauged by a leading publisher's late-1990s response to my proposal of a Polish film book for its national cinema series: its counter-proposal was a rolling of Czech, Slovak, Hungarian and Polish cinemas into one, rather than the necessary, and necessarily partial, inventory of the riches of any one of these remarkable national cinemas. One can only hope that growth of the European Union will both widen and deepen knowledge of these cinemas, among others. The rather generalised survey volumes publishers have been most eager to commission, however, succeed at the cost of selling short the remarkable filmmakers these cinemas have produced, the significance of the issues with which they grappled and the film-industrial structures that framed their efforts. I am, thus, deeply grateful to, and salute the imaginativeness of, Wallflower Press – and in particular Yoram Allon – for realising the significance of these national film cultures, and supporting this book. (My other acknowledgements will follow.) In the Polish context, the list of overdue studies includes ones of the oeuvres of Wojciech Has, Agnieszka Holland, Jerzy Kawalerowicz, Tadeusz Konwicki, Andrzej Munk, Jerzy Skolimowski and Krzysztof Zanussi in particular, and of such remarkable individual films as Gregorz Królikiewicz's astonishing *Na wylot* (*Through and Through*, 1973), Marek Piwowski's *Rejs* (*The Cruise*, 1970) or Witold Leszczyński's *Żywot Mateusza* (*Life of Matthew*, 1968).

The present book is an initial foray into this area, and forms a companion volume to *Lucid Dreams* – the volume on Kieślowski I edited for Flicks Books – and to my *Cinema, Religion and the Romantic Legacy*, in which Polish cinema figures prominently. My contention that any consideration of significant contributions to the dialogue of cinema and religion has to include works by Kieślowski and Zanussi among its primary objects of study indicates the resonance of these films well beyond the confines of any Slavists' ghetto. In particular, the works studied in this volume – products of the forty years of what called itself 'People's Poland' – dramatically pursue a dialectic of the political and the aesthetic, neither of which should be privileged, though of course individual works will swear stronger oaths to one or the other – sometimes, of course, under duress.

Although this book groups its close analyses of some key texts around several nodal points in Polish national identity, their intersections and overlaps indicate the validity of other constellations. Its other main task (pursued most intensively in the chapter on censorship, which could well have swollen to engulf the entire book) is to conduct a reconnaissance of some of the relevant archival holdings of the Warsaw Filmoteka narodowa (National Film Archive) and Archiwum Akt Nowych (Archive of Contemporary Files): mines of information barely tapped even by Polish scholars, most of whom are more interested in engaging with current non-Polish debates on digital media and postmodernity than in mapping these fundamental local resources. This reluctance to install oneself in the archive is partly understandable, as the informational mine can indeed be cramped and navigable only in a sweaty, laborious half-light. Moreover, prolonged immersion in Stalinist and post-Stalinist Newspeak can indeed seem to offer one's own sustaining blood to the hungry ghosts of a system most Poles are happy to have escaped; it is hardly surprising that the most sustained examination of its language – that pursued by Michał Głowiński in a series of volumes (for instance, in Głowiński 1991 and Głowiński 1993) – should have been itself an underground effort, written contemporaneously with the events reflected in its distorting mirror, and not in their aftermath.

It can seem superfluous to revisit what now, happily, lies in the past. However, quite apart from the relevance of Santayana's famous contention that a refusal to inspect the past condemns amnesiacs to relive it, there is also the opening chord of Christa Wolf's wonderfully richly orchestrated, tremendously important autobiographically-tinged novel *Kindheitsmuster* (*Patterns of Childhood*, 1976), which dissects the extent of a child's absorption of the National Socialism under which she was educated: 'the past is not past'. If National Socialism needed the reconsideration controversially named *Vergangenheitsbewältigung* (literally, 'mastering the past'), so does the other great totalitarianism of the twentieth century. Violent reactions against it may well strengthen its unconscious absent presence, granting it a determining force of taboo that limits the freedom in whose name the reaction is proclaimed (as if all looks backwards were as disastrous as that of Orpheus in the underworld). The willed neglect of history may even itself repeat that history itself, re-enacting the failed self-recreation that characterised a Stalinism that may well have been able to haunt 'People's Poland' only because of the premature issuing of its death certificate (ostensible date of demise, October 1956). 'Voluntarism' is all too human an ideological heresy, not an exclusively Marxist one.

It should be added that the fault lies also in part with the Polish authorities, which need to do much more to render these materials accessible, particularly within the Archiwum akt nowych, with its cumbersome rules of access, often restricted opening hours and exorbitant photocopying costs. For whatever reason, female researchers appear to have possessed more of the patience and meticulousness required to deal with this material: one thinks of the work of Marta Fik, Alina Madej and Ewa Gębicka in particular, though useful work has also been done by Krzysztof Kornacki. Publication of the stenograms of many of the various part-governmental, part-industry script- and film-scrutinising committees ought to be prioritised by any Polish government wishing to consolidate habits of democratic access, and the decline of the *Iluzjon* journal from a partial showcase for some of the files of the Filmoteka narodowa into little more than a film guide, deprived of the funds or scope to continue its project of publishing such materials, is deeply regrettable. Such inaccessibility starves Polish film culture of the essential resources of film history. It also hampers all scholars' efforts to define the socialist project in Poland, and investigate the complex causes of its failure.

It should be apparent from this that this book argues for a necessary interconnection of theory and history. Each pursues an unconscious, and each needs the other to guard against opposed temptations: history needing theory in order to escape the positivist drudgery of an unending accumulation of Gradgrindian facts; and theory requiring the historian's corrections of the potential narcissism and self-indulgence of speculation. Although it does not doubly expose its every scene as one of both theory and history (the ideal), this book nevertheless pursues a dialogue between them.

As noted above, I owe a good deal to a series of people and institutions. Apart from Yoram Allon and Wallflower Press, I must thank Jan Rek for access to copies of several key films; Film Polski, for access to others; the staff of the Filmoteka narodowa, headed by the omnicompetent Grzegorz Balski, for much help; the Arts and Humanities Research Board, for support of the six-month research leave that pulled together the book's primary thematic threads; the University of Aberdeen, for research leave during the first half of the year in question; and the Carnegie Trust for the Universities of Scotland, for funding a series of forays into the Warsaw archives.

It may surprise some readers to see a book primarily concerned with the cinema of People's Poland step outside the time and space of that socio-political formation in several important cases: those of *Pilatus und Andere* (*Pilate and Others*, 1972) and *Wielki Tydzień* (*Holy Week*, 1996) by Andrzej Wajda; of Agnieszka Holland's *Bittere Ernte* (*Angry Harvest*, 1985) and *Europa, Europa* (1991); and of Krzysztof Kieślowski's *Three Colours* Trilogy (1993/94). It does so in part because a boundary is better understood if considered from both sides. It also does so to emphasise that for all the rhetoric of the 'freedom shock' of 1989, a considerable degree of continuity characterises the work made just before and just after that date, a continuity further enhanced by the strength of these directors' authorial personalities. Kieślowski seems even to have believed that People's Poland could not be said to have died until those born within it had done so. The above-mentioned Wajda films are of particular interest to this book's project because one film – *Pilate and Others*, produced in West Germany – has to enter, and be dealt with by, a system run by officially atheistic authorities, while the other – *Holy Week* – forms a fascinating diptych with his most famous work, *Popiół i diament* (*Ashes and Diamonds*, 1958); for although each is based on a pre-People's Poland text by Jerzy Andrzejewski, whereas *Ashes and Diamonds* could be filmed there and then, *Holy Week* – despite various attempts – could not. Juxtaposition of these two Wajda films surprisingly suggests that if anything the religious theme was less sensitive than that of Polish-Jewish relations, perhaps because of the latter's uncanny closeness to an uncanny home, as significant swathes of Poland's populace were under the delusion that their socialist system rested upon a foundation of Jewish construction. Holland's *Angry Harvest* and *Europa, Europa* enhance that suspicion by dissecting the subject with an incisiveness unmatched by anything produced within Poland, before or after 1989. Meanwhile, Kieślowski's oeuvre further problematises the drawing of hermetically-sealed boundaries around 'People's Poland'. Since it has been described as developing 'outside People's Poland' long before that system's demise, even so apparently 'political' a film as *Bez końca* (*No End*, 1985) may exist 'outside it'. *Three Colours* then becomes its logical conclusion, as revolutionary political cinema both persists (the catchwords of the French Revolution organise the trilogy) and vanishes (those words are submerged in colour). The trilogy thus destabilises the notion that 'People's Poland' has a fixed 'inside' and 'outside'. After all, if chaos theory is correct and one butterfly can cause havoc on the far side of the globe, no phenomenon that has entered history can fail to leave some mark on later events. The theory should dispel all complacency about the ability of all-too-human humans to lay any past definitively to rest. And, understood thus, the butterfly, that stereotypical embodiment of the aesthetic, can provoke the chaos without which there is no revolution.

Drafts of portions of this book have appeared in various journals. A small portion of the chapter on *Ashes and Diamonds* first appeared in *Canadian Slavonic Papers* XXXVIII/2–4 (1996). The chapter on war and heroism incorporates an essay entitled 'Notes on Polish cinema, nationalism, and *Holy Week*' first published in *Cinema and Nation*, edited by Mette Hjort and Scott Mackenzie (2000). An earlier version of the chapter on Polish-Jewish relations appeared in *POLIN* 10 (1997), and the subsections on Konwicki and on Wajda's *Holy Week* were grafted from *Canadian Slavonic Papers* XLII/1–2 (2000). An earlier version of the second half of the Kieślowski chapter appeared in *Cinema Journal* 41/2 (2002). That final chapter also reworks material from reviews of *A Short Film About Killing* and *No End* first published in *Sight and Sound* 58/1 (1988–89) and *The Polish Review* 33/3 (1988) respectively, as well as developing some passages on *Blind Chance* first published in *Before the Wall Came Down*, edited by Ruth Dwyer and Graham Petrie (1990).

NOTES TOWARDS AN INTRODUCTION

A well-known joke from the period of People's Poland asked why the Poles were like radishes. Answer: they're red only on the surface. The joke is particularly good because the inside of the radish is white, and the Polish flag is half red and half white. One glance at that flag may have made Polish socialists blench and wonder whether their country was condemned to be only ever half-communist at most. Whether the glass of the national flag was perceived as half full or half empty would of course depend on the degree of true socialism – that is, optimism – of the socialist him- or herself. A non-Party member, conversely, may have been depressed by the notion that as much as half of the national identity might already have been ceded to socialism, and wonder whether the whiteness itself was a flag of surrender to the advancing, apparently historically privileged forces of the red. Might the combination of red and white on the flag even be most appropriate for the Poland of the twentieth century, and so require replacement after 1989? (A proposal as absurd and yet apposite as the actually proposed dynamiting of the Stalinist Palace of Culture at the heart of Warsaw.) Is the flag's duality the emblem of a split national consciousness? For a Soviet official, meanwhile, the split may well have recalled Stalin's likening of Poland's communisation to the saddling of a cow, or – alternatively – memories of a domestic civil war apparently long-since won but now returning, writ large, as a conflict within the body politic of the socialist fraternity itself. After all, red and white were the colours of the two sides in the conflict that accompanied the establishment of Bolshevik rule, and of the Soviet Union. The co-presence of red and white on the Polish flag may seem less like the optimistic joke about the colours of the radish (a little scraping suffices to remove what was only skin deep…) and more like a dark *jeu d'esprit* by a demonic deity known as History.

THE SPLIT SCREEN OF POLISH CINEMA: BETWEEN THE POLITICAL AND THE AESTHETIC

Between about 1948 and 1989 – the inception dates of the Polish Stalinism and capitalism that frame the period of primary interest to this book – Polish cinema is as much a split screen as the Polish flag: torn across, between politics and aesthetics, between – if one likes – 'the red and the white'. The two imperatives fuse perhaps in the allegory that retains political reference but also feeds the autonomy of the aesthetic. The implicit viewer or national subject of this cinema is split too, like the politico-aesthetic receptacle he/she may view as 'half full' or 'half empty', a matter of the half-truths that were either (a) the most particular artists could smuggle past the official gatekeepers or (b) the most that could be conveyed by any form of art, given the inherent mortgaging of the aesthetic to indirection. Metaphor may be the sheep to whose fleece escaping meaning clings, simulating absence, or it may be the metonymy of a pastoral outside a political sphere represented by the giant who checks everything for its right-mindedness. Surviving amidst contradictory and co-existing identities is the task continually laid upon a cinema that is never more than 'relatively autonomous' of the political: a task so unfulfillable as to render all its texts profoundly problematic and unsatisfactory, yet endlessly fascinating. It is because it may be deemed prototypical in this respect that Andrzej Wajda's *Popiół i diament* (*Ashes and Diamonds*, 1958) bulks so large in this book. Such texts are denied the complacency of closure: open wounds, they always remain open to us too.

EVOLUTION IN CAPTIVITY

The phrase 'evolution in captivity' may suggest the zoological, even the palaeontological: a story of how creatures revamp themselves and morph so nimbly as to sidestep the asteroids thrown through the bars of the cage known as Planet Earth, avoiding the fate that retrospectively defines others as dinosaurs. It may also be taken as alluding to the most penetrating and fascinating of analyses of the seductions of totalitarianism in general, and in Poland in particular: Czesław Miłosz's *Zniewolony umysł* (*The Captive Mind*, 1951). Is evolution held captive by the would-be totalitarian state, or does it occur even in captivity – for all the difficulty of breeding within the zoo whose name sometimes seem to summon the Greek word for 'life' only to mock it? Given the frequency with which Polish history between 1948 and 1989 was described as one of recurrent stasis and crisis, one might speak of a punctuated equilibrium: the moment of imminent catastrophe being one in which certain species manage rapidly to change spots or sprout new organs, or at least acquire new names, and so survive. If there is an evolutionary process at work even in captivity and under oppression – evolution within the human zoo – then perhaps Engels was right to invoke a dialectic of nature. Its leaps and transformational slides allow artists to become censors, socialist realists to become realists, and censors to become artists, even as all of them remain part of the species known as socialist. Just which of these life-forms should be deemed higher and which mere pond life may depend on the moment at which the metamorphosis occurs: on whether it is the mere unprincipled opportunism of a conscienceless life-force, or dictated by the higher imperatives that may threaten short-term survival but prove paradoxically useful in the long term. The question is, I suppose, one of the identity of the spectator to whose gaze the changes respond, be it real or ideal: Big Brother, the admonishing conscience, or one's real brothers and sisters. One of the main tasks of this book is to consider the interrelationships – and seek to suggest some of the laws of transformation – of these shifting identities.

SHIFTING BORDERS: THE IDEOLOGY OF 'EAST CENTRAL EUROPE'

Once upon a time, when even the war was cold, we used to speak of 'Eastern Europe'. For a while, however, in the mid-1980s, some of us began to speak of 'Central Europe'. Now we speak of 'East Central Europe', sometimes placing a hyphen between East and Central. What lies behind this shifting nomenclature? Does it show that despite legitimate postmodern – or merely commonsensical – scepticism regarding history's fabled pursuit of a Hegelian dialectic of opposites and final synthesisation, some such dialectic does indeed unfold in what was once described as the superstructural realm, that of terminology and ideology, with each generation self-consciously seeking to trump predecessors by ostentatiously redressing their mistakes and appropriating their achievements, adding 'Central' to 'East' to yield the synthetic 'East Central'? (Meanwhile, the gap or hyphen that separates 'East' and 'Central' recognises the synthesis as threatened, incomplete, as the two terms become potentially non-synonymous or even – as it were –'opposed synonyms'.)

The general acceptance of the term 'East Central', whatever else it may be, is of course the posthumous triumph of the historian Oskar Halecki, who first argued that Europe comprised a West Central Europe, which was Germanic, and a largely Slavic East Central Europe. 'East Central' may be less a synthesis than a compromise between the way 'the West' (another labile signifier) traditionally saw the countries in question (those of the former Warsaw Pact) as 'Eastern' and the way those countries' denizens defined themselves, at least during the period of their greatest unrest and hope for change, as 'Central'. Their countries' forty-year sojourn within the belly of the Soviet whale nursed a chronic fear that 'Eastern Europe' might indeed become the 'Western Asia' it was termed sardonically by Joseph Brodsky, and as it might have been described by neo-Marxists noting the paradoxical overlap between the Revolution's vanguard country and what Marx had defined as 'the Asiatic mode of production'. 'Central Europe' may have been a term steeped in utopianism – Mariola Jankun-Dopartowa, for instance, has described it as such (Jankun-Dopartowa 1990) – a sign of wishful thinking, or a banner strategically unfurled in the mid-1980s to persuade Western politicians that the realm they had consigned to a comfortable distance was nearer than they thought, and indeed central to the project of constructing a 'European' identity – by no means amenable to sweeping under the red carpet in the name of *détente*.

The recent general adoption of 'East Central' instead may in turn represent an Eastern assertion of difference from a 'Central Europe' that translates into the uncomfortably Germanic *Mitteleuropa*. The insistence on the new term may seek magically to banish fears of economic ingestion by a Germany whose first tottering eastward steps to absorb its own East might generate unstoppable momentum towards the malign old programme of the *Drang nach Osten*, in whose throat Eastern Europe would prefer to stick. The term is perturbingly unstable, and the compromise is not – *pace* Fukuyama – the end of history but a moment of balance within it, perhaps precarious but hopefully long. But will 'East Central' be treated as 'East' again – no real concern of ours – should a humiliated Russia seek to claw back its lost empire, in part or in full? What meanings and perhaps repressions and reservations underlie this phrase and its relation to previous names for this geo-political space? The designation appears to indicate an area that has overcome its past – in 1989, for instance – and yet somehow preserves it (the dialectic of *Aufhebung*). It functions both as a name and a confession of failure to name, the sign of a perception of the area as resistant to naming, transitional, suspended, perhaps permanently indeterminate, and thus a source of difficulty – future as well as past? (In reflection of this terminological undecidability, this book will not privilege any of the above-mentioned terms.)

A CALENDAR OF PAIN

In Polish, the months of the year are written beginning with small letters. In the national memory of most of the last two centuries, however (itself, one hopes, fading, becoming a memory), more than half of these small months are shadowed and overshadowed by larger sisters and brothers, swollen as it were with the burden of socio-political significance, with the weight of the historic surrounding year they have ingested. It is a broken calendar of pain, with some months missing, and a preponderance of the ones in which daylight is shortest. Say January – capital J – and the rebellion of 1863 flashes up; March is 1968, student protests and a state-sponsored anti-Semitic campaign; June has a double identity, though the primary one is 1956 (Poznań and the workers' revolt), there is also its anniversary, 1976 (state repression at Radom and Ursus of worker protests at price rises); August is 1980, the tumultuous birth-year of Solidarity; September – 1939, and cataclysmic invasion; October – 1956 again, and the installation of the then-popular Władysław Gomułka; November – 1830 (crushed rebellion); and December – 1970 and the shooting down of workers in Gdańsk. Each rises and falls against the calendar's dark sky, a flare of revolt against the occupation and oppression that prevailed almost unbrokenly between 1795, the date of Poland's final partitioning by its neighbours, and 1989, when communism again became the phantom it had been for the nineteenth century. The majority, alas, commemorate defeat: failed uprisings (1830 and 1863); the brutal truncheoning of the students in 1968; the crushing of worker protest in 1956, 1970 and 1976; the Nazi invasion of 1939. If memory attaches to months rather than days it is a sign of its oral, oppositional nature, and of the deep impact of the event, which impresses a wide crater around itself. One recalls what time of year it was, what sort of activities it interrupted (Sierpień, August, for instance, is the month of the sickle, the *sierp*). The authorities, those keepers of the calendar, prescribe precise dates for their ceremonies, and have them over and done with rapidly, to ensure a speedy return to work. An event associated with a month haunts week after week after week; it is a season, not a mere moment. And it is appropriate to speak of haunting, for these periods belong to the ghosts of the defeated, and almost every family has one or more. A single day would give the ghost a home; the month is the space in which it wanders homelessly, with the melancholy of the spectre. After all, for much of the two hundred years in question, where was the Polish soil in which a Polish body might rest? That is why the most remarkable single day of the Polish year is All Souls, and why it is the centre of the national drama, Adam Mickiewicz's *Dziady* (*Forefathers' Eve*, 1823–32). The nation visits the graves of its loved ones as one might a family member in hiding, to feed them, to dot their graves with the candles that hold back the night. The months of memory are mostly the ones when night is longest: one cannot act in the dark, only wait, and each night is a small image of the long winter. For much of modern Polish history has been locked in a long wait of hibernation, dreaming of release, seeing thaw after thaw conclude in a renewed freeze. This book concerns what may be called the darkness before the dawn, a darkness already greying – frayed at the edge – by the dawn's pressure; the long wait for liberation after the last war.

Not surprisingly, therefore, the commemoration of anniversaries played a large part in the production plans of the Polish Film industry. They were less the anniversaries that haunted popular consciousness, however, of which people needed no reminding, than those the PZPR (Polska Zjednoczona Partia Robotnicza – Polish United Workers' Party) sought to popularise, particularly the key dates in the history of the international worker's movement, the Soviet Union and the PZPR itself. When the dates haunting popular history are taken account of, it is so as both to steer their interpretation and to legitimate the authorities themselves by demonstrating their understanding of public feelings (arguably contradictory goals, as the reinterpretations invariably violated those feelings). Some proposals drawn up by the NZK (Naczelny Zarząd Kinematografii – Main Board of Cinematography) and presented at a meeting of the Presidium of the collegium of the Ministry of Culture and Art on 27 November 1979 offer representative examples. They begin as follows:

> 1982 sees the centenary of the Polish revolutionary and workers' movement and the fortieth anniversary of the foundation of the Polish Workers' Party. The importance of these two anniversaries, and their significance for socio-political education, is emphasised by the relevant resolution of the PZPR Central Committee of 1979.
>
> Bearing in mind the lengthy production cycle of a feature film, in the middle of 1979 the NZK began preparing the assumptions for these anniversaries, subsequently announcing a closed competition for film scripts devoted to them. In consultation with the Culture Section of the PZPR Central Committee, a list of over 70 authors was drawn up, to whom the NZK proposed participation in the closed competition. About forty authors responded positively to the invitation. (AAN, NZK 2/12)[1]

Doubtless mindful of the improbability of such films emerging spontaneously from the cinematic community itself (after all, only just over half of the likely candidates responded), the NZK guaranteed production to three to five of the best scripts. In an effort to demonstrate the project's feasibility, it mentions two relevant scripts already proposed for production, ironically originating in the two most restive film units of the period: a film based on Andrzej Strug's *Dzieje jednego pocisku* (*Story of a Bullet*, 1910) from the 'X' group (which became Agnieszka Holland's *Gorączka* [*Fever*, 1981]) and one about the affair in which the *fin-de-siècle* Polish socialist philosopher Stanisław Brzozowski was accused of spying for the Tsarist authorities (which emerged as Edward Żebrowski's *W biały dzień* [*In Broad Daylight*, 1981]). The decision to mark the Battle of Monte Cassino, and hence the exploits of non-socialist Polish forces fighting in Italy during World War Two, attempts to woo popular consciousness, though the proposed focus on a small unit suggests the officially approved formula of concentrating upon the rank-and-file and their suffering through the ill-conceived decisions of their leaders (thus discrediting the pre-war élite and – by association – their representatives in the still-extant Polish government-in-exile in London). The terms of commemoration of the Warsaw Ghetto Uprising are even more instructive – even aggressive:

> A statement is expected from Polish cinema concerning the struggle and martyrdom of the Jews, along with the help given them by Poles. This film should be a sincere statement that considers the issue from all sides – thereby giving the lie to the falsehoods of the American series 'Holocaust', which is widely … This film should have considerable promotional values, which could be secured through the possible engagement of a distinguished foreign actor. (AAN, NZK 2/12)

Even the anniversaries of apparently neutral figures could assume propagandistic dimensions: the commemoration of the birth of Copernicus in 1973, for instance, nationalistically emphasised his Polishness, implicitly underscoring the flimsiness of any West German (revanchist!) claims upon him.

ROMANTICISM, POLISHNESS AND THE IMAGINED COMMUNITY

Benedict Anderson has described 'the nation' as an 'imagined community' forged through a *visualisation* of like-minded others he deems deeply indebted to the dissemination of print vernaculars from the sixteenth century onwards, and involving the self-imagining of certain classes as well as nations: 'thus in world-historical terms bourgeoisies were the first classes to achieve solidarities on an essentially imagined basis' (Anderson 1983: 74). The national self-conceptualisation Anderson describes requires the generation of rhetorics of nationhood by small would-be élites seeking to persuade both themselves and others of their power, inspire self-confident action and intimidate prospective opposition. The nation may be defined as, as it were, the imaginary – phantasmal, non-existent – power-base of the bourgeois intelligentsia's contestation of aristocratic establishments (or – as we will see in the Polish case – of struc-tures imposed by foreign Powers). This imaginary, early-modern visual self-definition may be piquantly juxtaposed with the actually visual, late-modern national self-definition permitted by a technology as revolutionary as printing (perhaps, as Lenin would have wished, the 'most important' one for post-war Poland, albeit often with a non-Leninist message): that of the cinema. Socialism's claim to speak for 'the people' may prompt questions whether the use of real, rather than imaginary, visual images renders the process any more genuinely 'popular', or whether the struggle for the means of image-transmission remains one between élites. In the end however – at the end of *soi-disant* 'socialist' Poland – the socialist dream of a unity of populace and élite materialises ironically, if briefly, in its 'anti-socialist' nemesis, the Solidarity movement.

In the first instance, during the formation of 'nation-states', the two nouns' hyphenation both embodies and seeks to combat unease over its components' possible disjunctiveness. Whereas rulers could once imagine communities in terms of what they could realistically defend – or seize – from neighbours, regardless of the will of prospective new subjects, begin-ning in the early nineteenth century they may seek to legitimate such incorporations as the lib-eration of imagined fellows (speakers of the same language, members of the same 'race', fellow opponents of oppression). Linking the state to 'the nation' masks the alien features of a state that projects itself not as an apparatus but as the natural – organic – outgrowth of a particular people. The state may bring a unity of law, but the deeper, vaguer unities of 'culture', 'society', 'language' and – yes – 'nation' put flesh on its bones, serving as the naturalising disguise of the arbitrariness of state formations and as a block on the possibility of a fissiparous hatching of further 'nations' within them. If the state is perceived as alien, of course, this may be the con-sequence of either invasion or invasiveness, as its burgeoning bureaucratic centralisation and tax-gathering outreach into distant communities (feudal tithes to local lords being long gone) define it as inherently foreign. This sense of the state's alienness may of course also be the dis-sonant realisation of disempowered Romantic intellectuals' dreams of 'the nation' (the invis-ible addressee of their own work that idealises the market into a community). It may render bearable the lack of any immediate audience for their utopian, intensely subjective work, with the ideology of 'inspiration' emerging to combat the feared futility and arbitrariness of speech *vis-à-vis* a void, directed not to a known group – a class, one's peers – but to the purportedly classless nation. Writers take the existence of such communities on faith: faith in the existence of an audience for messages in bottles. Earlier rhetorics of 'the Sublime' are reconjugated into a 'beyond' which becomes this-worldly and yet unattainable, the invisible systems, networks and grids of which one knows oneself to be part stimulating both fear of encroachment and the Romantic longing for engulfment.

Internal exile in one state while communing with the nation in the dream of a different one, a *nation*-state; this Romantic condition is central, of course, to the self-conception of two centuries of Poles subjected to the invasions that absolutised a nation-state split that elsewhere was only partial, 'Polish' state apparatuses being by definition the creatures of alien rulers. Following the partitions of the late eighteenth century, in the early nineteenth century the voice of 'the nation' excluded from imposed state structures migrated mediumistically into singular individuals, the Romantic poets described as *wieszcze* ('seers'): Adam Mickiewicz, Juliusz Słowacki and Zygmunt Krasiński. Between the lines of their work 'the nation' (as represented by the *szlachta* ['gentry'] élite imagining a unity that belied its past chronic disunity) spoke to itself *sotto voce*, in the allegorically disguised, 'Aesopian' language that would typify two centuries of Polish cultural production. Such nationalism is as revolutionary as it is conservative.

In the second half of the twentieth century, meanwhile, in everyday Polish discourse the nation-state disjunction would be overlaid with one between 'Polska', the Slavic term designating Poland as geographical entity, and the 'Polonia', the appropriately deracinated Latin word for millions of émigré Poles. In a complex manoeuvre of compensation and self-castigation, those native Poles who looked to the Paris-based Instytut Literacki's publications for untainted exemplars of national culture often simultaneously sustained a sense of their own worthiness by deriding the linguistic incompetence of 'the Polonia' (usually Americans whose technological superiority was as embarrassing as their financial aid was welcome). Local intellectuals compelled to speak indirectly could disavow disempowerment by viewing themselves as descendants of Mickiewicz's Konrad Wallenrod, the apparent traitor who rose through enemy ranks so as to be able to lead them to their doom. More plausibly, they may have argued that at least they had their fingers on the pulse of events.

Within the sphere of Polish cultural production, meanwhile, there was a different status for different kinds of producers. Whereas writers still publishing only within Poland could be deemed compromisingly accomodating to the censor's demands, filmmakers dependent on local resources for both materials and sites of dissemination could expect greater understanding. In periods of extreme repression, their films may have been banned or – in the technologically advanced twilight of the Soviet empire – have suffered the distribution condition of books, circulating privately as *samizdat* videocassettes, or may even have taken the form of co-productions of restricted local relevance, but the cyclical thaws nourished hopes of eventual national distribution. One of the central concerns of this book, therefore will be whether or not a 'nationalist' discourse can be said to have existed in a public sphere monopolised by *soi-disant* socialist discourse (gentry-based Romantic 'classlessness' differing from worker-peasant 'classlessness').

'NATIONALISM', 'SOCIALISM', 'HEROISM'

After 1947, when carefully stage-managed elections returned the Soviet-sponsored PPR (Polska Partia Robotnicza – Polish Workers' Party) and Stanisław Mikołajczyk – the last significant pre-war Polish leader still on Polish soil – fled the country, discourses of nationalism became subject to ban in Poland. Władysław Gomułka, the first governing Party leader, who had pursued relatively independent policies for several years, was placed under house-arrest, not to recover power until the upheavals of 1956. In Jerzy Andrzejewski's 1947 novel *Popiół i diament* (*Ashes and Diamonds*), Maciek Chełmicki, the young AK (Armia Krajowa – Home Army) partisan who mistakenly assassinates workers rather than the newly installed Party leader he is charged with removing, is termed a 'fascist' by a grieving soldier. Under the binary mentality of the 'struggle for peace', 'he who is not with us is against us'. And yet, ten years later, after the 'Polish October' and Gomułka's reinstallation as Party First Secretary, Andrzej Wajda could film Andrzejewski's novel with a Chełmicki who was no 'fascist' but at worst misguided. The imprint of post-war Polish history's conjunctural freezes and thaws is apparent not only in the differences between Andrzejewski's 1947 text and the classic 1958 film he scripted with Wajda, but also in the disparity between that script and the various unfilmed versions of the intervening Stalinist period, all of which render Chełmicki a socialist realist 'positive hero' who undergoes an ideological change of heart.[2]

If the Soviet Union had found it possible to incorporate nationalist and even quasi-religious motifs into Stalinism, reconjugating Bolshevik internationalism into 'socialism within one country', no such latitude would be allowed the satellite states of its new empire. The Stalin who had annihilated the resolutely internationalist, Luxemburgist pre-war KPP (Komunistyczna Partia Polski – Polish Communist Party) would hardly extend leniency to Polish patriots who, after the defeat of National Socialism, deemed communism the new enemy. During Poland's Stalinisation the real-life Maciek Chełmickis were shot or jailed, regardless of whether they carried on fighting in forests or surrendered. And yet the nationalist discourse pilloried as 'fascist' had become paradoxically partly otiose, the pre-war nationalities question having been virtually 'solved' – appallingly – by Hitler's elimination of the one major minority, Stalin's annexation of another (the Ukrainians), and the Western Allies' 'transfer of the German populations and elements of German populations that remain in Poland' under Article 13 of the Potsdam Agreement. Within the Soviet empire as a whole, meanwhile, nationalism persisted in communities' sharp demarcations between themselves and immediate neighbours. Leading Poles' appearances in films by the Hungarians Miklós Jancsó, Karoly Makk and Marta Meszáros were less significant than their absence from those of the Czechs and Slovaks, those direct neighbours and practitioners of a realism so often qualified in Polish discourse by the dismissive adjective *mały* ('little'), while Wajda's only Soviet-bloc co-productions were with the former Yugoslavia, that black sheep of the socialist family. Equally pointedly, his adaptations of Russian literature were of nineteenth century, pre-Soviet texts, co-produced either in Yugoslavia (*Sibirska Ledi Magbet* [*Siberian Lady Macbeth*, 1961/62]) or France (*Les Possédés* [*The Possessed*, 1987]).

The ideological shifts of post-war Poland suggest that 'nationalism' is no unitary discourse but comprises various, possibly detachable components, some of which can go underground while others remain visible, abbreviated into metonymies or mere markers of the place of the buried, the repressed that will always return, albeit through upward leakages of varying strength. If socialism forbids some (patriotic emblems like the crowned eagle, for instance), and renders others unnecessary (the 'nationality question' having evaporated and in any case being taken off the agenda), others are compatible with it and persist. (Meanwhile, wartime instances of anti-Semitic nationalists aiding Jews because a local priest or New Testament ethics required helping one's neighbour indicate the complexity of nationalism's relationship with religion in Poland – a question to which I will return in the final section and which also suggests that none of us has a unified 'ideology'.) The primary element of nationalist discourse to survive into post-war Poland – perhaps because most politically neutral – was the idea of 'the heroic'. Thus, this book devotes a whole chapter to this question.

'DEMOCRACY, 'SOCIALISM' AND 'THE PEOPLE'S TRIBUNE': A BRIEF HISTORY OF TEMPTATION

In the early 1980s, the poet and academic Jacek Trznadel conducted a series of interviews with the Polish writers who had been most prominent in the years just after World War Two, inviting them to reflect – as he himself had done in his introduction – on the appeal Stalinism had held for them. It was an opportunity to confess sins of youth – indeed to have regrettable pasts reclassified as youthful indiscretions. Trznadel's book, one of the key ones of the 1980s, and the recipient of the Solidarity Committee of Independent Culture's award for 1986, described this period (in the vocabulary of a governess from the newly valued inter-war period?) as one of 'domestic disgrace' rather as characterised by the 'errors and distortions' that figured in the earlier, more diplomatic re-evaluations carried out in the mid-1950s. The autobiographical self-examinations of many of Trznadel's interlocutors are understandably defensive and hardly helpful, often resorting to metaphors of split personality and in one case defining the Russians as invaders from Mars (the Red Planet, of course!). They are reluctant to volunteer for the role of scapegoat the book seems to prepare for them: after all, Trznadel is far more willing to exonerate his own, slightly younger generation, and at one point cancels out one by one a number of factors potentially mitigating the earlier generation's choices. As he puts it:

> Today, as I write of that period in communist ideology, I can already attempt to view the generations previous to my own in a more distanced fashion. I think that here the situation becomes far more complex. So many of the above-mentioned factors prove unreliable. After all: the naïveté of the very young – does not apply. The lack of any great extent of reading, books and information – does not apply. The stress of war as life's first shock – does not apply in many cases. The first ideological crisis – also not a factor. One thing after another does not apply: so many factors seem not to have affected the generation that either led socialist realism, or accepted it mutely. (Trznadel 1990: 29)

This invalidation of various potential factors overlooks the degree to which the post-war system was able from the outset to employ the vagueness of several interlocked concepts to secure an assent that was itself correspondingly nebulous, founded upon the inevitably shifting sands of a sliding set of abstractions. The words in question could form substitutive chains precisely because of an original lack of clarity for which the Stalinists alone are hardly responsible. The first in the series is 'democracy', a fetish-word of all modernising societies: twentieth-century élites habitually seek power through the offer of modernisation, the technical progress that would liberate humanity from dependence upon nature, thus completing nature's transition from agent of patriarchal divine wrath to benign 'Mother Nature'. Even National Socialism practised modernisation under the cover of, and in tandem with, its nostalgic Nordic rhetoric, in a dialectic of consciousness that fused hypocrisy, self-delusion and misrecognition. Since 'democracy' was a keyword for both Solidarity activists and supporters of 'real existing socialism', awareness of its ambivalence should forestall self-righteousness. The extent of the lability of the idea of democracy is exemplified by its use in the self-descriptions of societies with both socialist and capitalist economies. The people's rule may be that of the popular, but might there not be cases in which the popular has been sold to them first by capitalists and so in fact serves the interests of an élite? This ambiguity of 'democracy' permits its slide into 'the popular'. Should one's choice between the two possible meanings of that term (opinion foisted on 'the people' from above, or arising spontaneously from below) light upon the latter and 'socialism', one may then follow further links in the substitutive chain and pass from that to 'communism' and even – *horribile dictu* – 'Stalinism': the present utopia, or at least the best of all worlds possible now, at this stage in the long march to communism.

The 'negative' counterpart of this 'positive' chain might find 'democracy' reconjugated into 'bourgeois' and 'capitalist', the economic jungle ruled by the survival not of the fittest but of the biggest and most brutal, though of course capitalism has no monopoly on the spells that transform the good of democracy into the evil of a general, all-pervading uncaringness. The socialism that can slide into Stalinism, becoming less abstract and more appalling in the process, can do likewise. Subscription to it becomes all the easier after Stalin's death and denunciation apparently reverses the slide; socialist counties now vie for the status of merriest barracks in the bloc, not least oppressed island in a gulag archipelago. Moreover, does not 'communism' claim to be internationalist and only accidentally (not essentially) Soviet? If Stalinists delude others is it because of the fatal facility of a self-delusion, cemented of course by the evident horror of National Socialism and its defeat by 'real socialism'? All this suggests that concepts pay for initial abstraction with a final discrediting by their attempted concretions. (The ironic result being a 'third way' of mixed economy of ideologies, vaguest of all because defined only by its double negation of the enclosing alternatives.) All diagnoses of the undoubted aberration that was the Polish People's Republic would be well advised to consider the ease with which a modern looseness of language (the possible concomitant of the colonial export of terms and ideals from their native contexts and of a pervasive valorisation of speed that blurs definition) facilitates a fall of which we ourselves may be guilty, albeit in a different direction.

Cinema, meanwhile, may seem to escape accusations of 'domestic disgrace', and no such interview book has been compiled for the Polish film industry. Indeed, the interview books that have proliferated in Poland in recent years are thick with often useful and/or entertaining directors' accounts of duels with the censor (of which more later in this book). Cinema's apparent exceptional status rests in part upon an awareness of the dilution of responsibility in an industry whose means of production are wielded collectively. Moreover, within the Polish system the cost of production, and the lengthiness of apprenticeships, generally precluded startling, meteoric débuts by young creators (the chief exception being Jerzy Skolimowski, whose unusual cunning planned his Film School exercises to permit their subsequent piecing together into a patchwork first feature, *Rysopis* (*Identification Marks: None*, 1965), though he may well have drawn confidence to assert himself in one medium from his prior success in another, that of poetry). The director who begins as a student and then becomes an apprentice assistant director, initially heading a second unit at best, resembles a writer with delayed access to pen and paper. That delay is also one in the advent of responsibility. Wajda may have placed his own name as putative assistant director on one of the imaginary socialist realist documentaries of director Burski in *Człowiek z marmuru* (*Man of Marble*, 1976), but the admission of responsibility is also an evasion. He is not to be fully identified with Burski, and the young firebrand director Agnieszka furnishes him with a second double: like Helmut Kohl, speaking on a different occasion, he might have mentioned the blessing of a late birth. That late birth is, I have suggested, the fate of all filmmakers, at least in the pre-Super 8 and pre-videocam era, who are denied access to the means of production during the very period of greatest susceptibility to the errors for which one otherwise has to seek the alibi of youth. Moreover, the dispersal of responsibility between the director and a production machine reduces the likelihood of later self-examination ever becoming as embarrassing or harrowing as it can be for the writer. So many censoring and shaping shadows fall between the filmic conception and the act that many directors can legitimately claim to have been less the work's author than the first formulator of a sentence subsequently released into an echo chamber of Chinese whispers. Thoroughgoing interventionism is Leninism's sincere but unwanted flattery of the art it deems 'the most important'.

Since Wajda himself often described himself as a 'socialist', and that term itself is highly unstable and controversial, anyone employing it ought to make a stab at determining just what it might mean in his case. After 1989, Wajda becomes apparently unwilling to endorse his past self-descriptions as a 'socialist' artist. Sensitive to the term's pejorative connotations in the new Polish context, which would override his possible classification via such venerable West European intellectual categories as 'humanist socialist' (for some socialists, and most Marxists, an oxymoron) or even 'Christian socialist' (an oxymoron for Poles), he would probably defend his own self-descriptions as 'socialist' as tactical ones needed to protect his filmmaking base within Poland, perhaps adding – for the benefit of native audiences – that in any case 'socialist' was not the same thing as (indeed, was manifestly less hard-line and supportive of the regime than) 'Marxist' and – for Western audiences – that 'socialism' was a movement of defence of the people. This last remark introduces a permanent element of Wajda's discourse which is continuous with the self-description as 'socialist', and which allows it to continue to stand: one relating to the idea of the popular and the artist as people's tribune. The position of such a tribune resonates, of course, with the nineteenth-century Polish Romantic tradition, in which artists preserved a sense of national identity through the masked, metaphorical speech of art when more direct speech was muzzled by the three partitioning powers. Not for nothing was the main organ of the PZPR entitled *Trybuna Ludu* ('The People's Tribune'); nor was it any surprise that Wajda's 1982 film version of Stanisława Przybyszewska's *Danton Case* shifted the sympathy from Robespierre to that genuinely popular tribune, Danton. Wajda's continual aim of producing works of popular resonance provides a rationale for the making of statements that enabled him to stay in Poland and so maintain the possibility of direct access to large swathes of the Polish people. Even an apparently avant-garde work like *Pilatus und andere – Ein Film für Karfreitag* (*Pilate and Others*, 1972) can be seen as partly motivated in these terms, with the Biblical reference a guarantor of popularity. Wajda's career-long fascination by the style and working methods of American cinema reflects his awareness of their popularity (rendering Hollywood – in a piquant paradox – to some extent 'socialistic', for all its horror of the term, which is of course why the 1920s Bolsheviks felt they had something to learn from it). What is more, even a character drama like *Panny z Wilka* (*The Young Ladies of Wilko*, 1979) can be linked to the politically popular works that precede and follow it in Wajda's filmography, through the clear *popularity* of two of its elements: the fashionability of the inter-war period in the late 1970s, which idealised it as the last era of Polish national freedom; and the canonical status of the author of the novella on which it is based, Jarosław Iwaszkiewicz, the uncrowned laureate of the late Gierek period. If the inter-war *uhlans* (lancers) also haunt Wajda's work, it is partly because their image was a popular one (one may recall how many commentators read the promotions of General Jaruzelski in 1981 as yardsticks of the unpopularity of a PZPR compelled to play the – popular – army card). If Wajda's 'socialism' is Pasolinian in its identification with 'the people', that 'people' is neither a Pasolinian *lumpenproletariat* nor the proletariat of the mainstream Marxist (Wajda's apparent flirtation with vulgar Marxism in *Ziemia obiecana* (*The Promised Land*, 1975) being one with a thumping stylistic vulgarity, not Marxist orthodoxy) but anyone opposed to the Soviet-sponsored rule of the PZPR, be they of the intelligentsia or the proletariat. It is more 'a people' (the nation) than 'the people' (a class). That is why the failure of students and proletariat to unite in the late 1960s is so crucially tragic in Wajda's *Człowiek z żelaza* (*Man of Iron*, 1981); it is a moment of a people's heart-rending failure of self-recognition.

SOCIALISM, CULTURE AND CENSORSHIP

Socialism's self-appointed brief of bringing culture to the masses defined art as inherently valuable. It was not a luxury but a crown-jewel in the freshly expropriated riches of the bourgeoisie (what the custodians of the German Democratic Republic would term the *Erbe* – the heritage). Of course, there were preferred varieties of art: 'socialist realist' and 'contemporary' in the first instance (capable of mobilising the masses), then simply 'realistic', as contemporary relevance became something the regime came to hope for rather than demand. Nevertheless, it was prepared to make a series of concessions, in some cases even tolerating explicitly oppositional work. This later state of affairs occurred twice in Poland, the most restive of the Warsaw Pact states: in the late 1970s, when Edward Gierek's regime sought to utilise a certain tolerance of oppositional work to feign a democratic legitimising openness to dialogue to a Western world to which it was heavily financially indebted, and then – after Gierek's fall – as a Party rocked back on its heels could only sit and watch as censorship was abolished and there emerged Wajda's *Man of Iron*, 1981, his celebration of the Gdańsk shipyard strikes. During this period, the oppositional filmmaking kick-started by *Man of Marble* – Wajda's critique of the persistence of Stalinism in mid-1970s Poland – had become so pervasive that the alternative would have been an embarrassing gagging of all the most talented directors. That desperate tactic would in fact be pursued by a different leader – Wojciech Jaruzelski – seeking legitimacy in the eyes of his Soviet paymasters, rather than of Polish society. However, the refusal of Polish society to knuckle under to martial law and accept Jaruzelski's 'normalisation' – the actors' boycott of State television, for instance – soon rendered the regime so desperate for any apparent participation by the creative community that it was prepared to fund an unparalleled evocation of the desolation of Polish society in the wake of martial law, Kieślowski's *Bez końca* (*No End*, 1985), and then to release his long-delayed *Przypadek* (*Blind Chance*, 1981; première 1987). The deep-seated schizophrenia that had funded works it then denied distribution persisted, however, as *No End* was shown only in out-of-the-way cinemas. This film demonstrates how the occasional conjunctures of guaranteed finance and weakened censorship gave directors the best and the worst of both worlds; in Kieślowski's case, this meant the freedom to alienate all possible constituencies, the Party disliking his film's bleak picture of post-martial law Poland, the Solidarity underground decrying its pessimism and the Church deploring its idiosyncratic metaphysics, respect for suicide and frank representation of sexuality. The occasional availability of such freedom made it no wonder that, come 1989, some directors felt a nostalgia for working conditions light years away from the early Stalinist, early 1950s demand for inspirational stories of life on the construction sites that metaphorically embodied the country's building of socialism. Whenever the periodic political thaws of almost all the Warsaw Pact countries yielded such micro-climates of freedom, artists' consciousness of the likelihood of a renewed freeze spurred their hectic, full use of them.

POLISH CINEMA, MODERNISM AND THE COMMUNICATIVENESS OF ART: À PROPOS HABERMAS

Polish cinema's relationship with the dominant art movement of the early nineteenth century – Romanticism – has been discussed frequently, even ad nauseam. Given cinema's emergence in the modernist period, however, and Polish cinema's flourishing at a time generally defined as one of transition between 'modernism' and 'postmodernism', it is not only appropriate but necessary to attempt to plot its position *vis-à-vis* these key categories of twentieth-century art and thought. This can be done fruitfully through a dialogue with the analysis of these categories executed by Jürgen Habermas in 'Modernity – An Incomplete Project' (Habermas 1998). It will be my contention that East Central European post-war art – and Polish cinema particularly forcefully – fulfils the desiderata he lays out, indicating that although they can be met under certain conditions, these conditions are not those of capitalism or democracy. Desiderata that can seem abstract, utopian, hypothetical and voluntarist in the post-war Western context – where Habermas finds no examples – assumed concrete, contemporary form there. In order to establish this, though, I need to reconstruct the stages of his argument.

For Habermas, a secret affinity links the modern and the classic; he does not give any examples, but one might think of James Joyce's *Ulysses* (1922) or T. S. Eliot's *The Waste Land* (1922). This affinity can be seen as an expression of what he terms (echoing Walter Benjamin) modernism's 'anarchistic intention of blowing up the continuity of history' (Habermas 1998: 3). Modernism's revolt against narrative tradition prompts it to range freely over the past, discovering family resemblances and anticipations in phenomena as temporally remote as, say, Expressionist paintings and medieval woodcuts. Thus the revolt against the past is no simple negation chained to a mechanical inversion of the anterior, but expressive of freedom. If such writers as Joyce and Eliot privilege affinity with the classical, other linkages are equally valid. As Habermas describes it, modernism is Baudelairean in its addiction to scandal, being 'fascinated with that horror which accompanies the act of profaning, and yet ... always in flight from the trivial effects of profanation' (Habermas 1998: 4) – a distinction between profanations that may suggest a basis for one between modernism and the postmodern.

Subsequently, however, Habermas will abandon a (Benjaminian and Adornian) definition of modernism in terms of the aesthetic in favour of one that focuses upon the Enlightenment separation of science, morality and art. Here the separation of artist from the public is no longer born of aesthetic provocation but rather of the specialisation and professionalisation of the expert. It is arguably because of the irrevocability of the gulf between the Baudelairean artist and the philistine that Habermas deems aesthetic modernism alienated from social life and seeks to recover an earlier modernism capable of fecundating that life. He goes behind aesthetic modernism to excavate one that is certainly anterior, possibly deeper, and, he hopes, possibly still viable in a late twentieth century in which modernism has (as Adorno put it) 'aged'. The cultural modernity of the Enlightenment bred hopes that an art that develops autonomy could feed back into everyday life: the aesthetic-expressive, the cognitive and the moral-practical must be re-injected into it to undo its reification. No single cultural sphere can have this effect or achieve such re-entry alone (art alone cannot free us), and 'the overextension of any one of these spheres into other domains' (Habermas 1998: 11) is linked to forms of terrorism. For Habermas, modernism is not yet a lost cause but must be liberated from 'extravagant programmes which have tried to negate modernity' (Habermas 1998: 11–12). One might wish to ask, though, why an aesthetic modernism usually deemed an outgrowth of the Enlightenment, with its autonomisation of art, should be deemed its extravagant negation and not its logical (if possibly lamentable) conclusion. Moreover, if the one truly does descend from the other, can the putatively unpolluted wellspring be cleared of the later detritus? Habermas may state that the expert's production of art as a set of solutions to internal artistic problems breaks down when issues of 'truth and justice' come into play 'as the aesthetic experience … is absorbed into ordinary life' (Habermas 1998: 12), but the raising of those issues has been the very thing that prevented its absorption. 'The reception of art by the layman' that – in words that may seem either euphemistic or mealy-mouthed – 'goes in a rather different direction from the reception of art by the professional critic' is in fact its rejection, usually on the grounds of its suspended referentiality or lack of evident or checkable congruence with 'reality' ('truth-value'). The process whereby those works are, as he puts it, 'related to life problems' (ibid.) is merely hypothetical, and it is telling that his only example is a description of an experience from 1937 found in the *Ästhetik des Widerstands* of Peter Weiss. His inability to cite any more recent examples is fatally disabling. And yet it could be argued that a glance beyond the sphere of Western capitalist culture might have furnished some. Examples of art receiving a popular reception that is cognitive, moral and practical as well as expressive-aesthetic pervade the East Central European artistic production of the post-war period: the specialisation of the artist was indeed a professional – State-sponsored – condition, but the aesthetic form permitted critique of the regime through symbol and allegory, and (during brief thaws, or formulated abroad) could even become near-direct. In either form, it had profound popular repercussions. When, in the 1980s, the Gdańsk shipyard workers erected a monument to their colleagues killed in the anti-government protests of 1970, they inscribed words from the exiled, Nobel Prize-winning poet Czesław Miłosz on its base. Similarly, the Cinema of Moral Anxiety (*kino moralnego pokoju*) can be seen as a midwife of Solidarity, and the Andrzej Wajda *Man of Marble* as a chief candidate for one of its parents.

It is possible, of course, that these possibilities of popular resonance depended upon a certain freezing of East Central European art in general, and Polish art in particular, in a mould that may be deemed 'pre-aesthetic'; for two hundred years, in the Polish case, art served less to furnish aesthetic delight – though it did that too – than to sustain the identity of a nation under occupation. (This freezing may not necessarily be a sign of historical outmodedness, but rather of the dialectic, described by Adorno, whereby certain apparently 'conservative' elements may anticipate a *future* utopia.) During this period, the cognitive and moral functions vied for primacy with the aesthetic one, and elaborate metaphor could gain a lease of popular life as camouflage from the censors. Whenever a liberation occurs, of course, the aesthetic assumes primacy, as occurred both in 1919 and in 1989, with modernism entering in the former case and, in the latter, a late capitalism of multi-nationalism and postmodern play. Although one is tempted to say that Polish art entered postmodernism (in this case, pastiche not so much of the past as of the West, in particular its hitman thrillers) without any primary passage through modernism, just as Russian socialism apparently skipped the advanced capitalist stage deemed its necessary precursor by Marx, in actuality the intermediate stages were not omitted but abbreviated, as historical developments truncated both the Polish modernism of the inter-war years (Gombrowicz, Schulz, Witkacy) and the pre-1917 nascent Russian capitalism.

CHAPTER ONE

ASHES AND DIAMONDS:
BETWEEN POLITICS AND AESTHETICS

Wajda's film perhaps shows the maximum amount of truth that is showable at the present time.
    – Maria Dąbrowska, diary entry after the opening of *Ashes and Diamonds*

It is fashionable today – I am writing at the end of October [1980] – to assign every-thing that appeared in Polish culture before August this year to a period that is over and done with and place it in a drawer labelled 'errors'. I speak of a fashion because I hope that it will pass and that good sense will prevail in this delicate area, so that we can see off the bad and retain and develop what is good. For one has to remember that cultural policies may be made by politicians, who ensure their execution, but that implementation is not their job. And however backward-looking or retrograde a policy might be, the people associated with culture act in line with their own views, language and understanding of the world. Otherwise one would have to say that Różewicz, Andrzejewski, Mrożek or Nowakowski 'collaborated' when they published their texts, that the authorities had Wajda and Zanussi on a string, or that Krall, Kapuściński and Bratkowski were time-servers.
    – Krzysztof Kieślowski, 'Deeper rather than broader', 1981

INTRODUCTION

Ashes and Diamonds has long been considered the most important of all Polish films. Its continued significance, even after 1989's earthquake in both cultural and political landscapes, can be gauged from its position at the head of the list of key Polish films in a 1995 critical poll conducted by the prestigious Polish *Kwartalnik filmowy* (*Film Quarterly*) and from its status as only one of two Polish films to feature in the BBC's 1995 'Cinema Century' list (the other being Kieślowski's *Krótki film o zabijaniu* [*A Short Film About Killing*, 1988]). Although made over forty years ago, in the heyday of the socio-political formation that flattered itself upon being 'People's Poland', it is particularly ripe for reconsideration now, following recent Polish-language work (possible only after 1989) on the earlier scripts of Andrzejewski's source novel, on the ways in which Wajda's project incorporated elements of other scripts he was unable to film, on the fate of the putative original of Maciek Chełmicki (Wajda's doomed hero, played by the charismatic Zbigniew Cybulski) and after Wajda's own post-1989 critique of the work in *Pierścionek z orłem w koronie* (*The Horse-Hair Ring/The Ring with the Crowned Eagle*, 1992). *Ashes and Diamonds* offers an unequalled test-case of the question of whether or not – to what extent, and in what ways – a work can elude the constraints of the political system sponsoring it. *The Horse-Hair Ring*, which at one point restages its most famous scene – the brief, impromptu vodka-glass wake for fallen comrades – may suggest that Wajda himself now views it as compromised, but the recent *mea culpa* is far less striking than the extraordinary, perhaps irrevocably tainted, original. Several varieties of historical falsification have been discerned in it and critiqued particularly trenchantly since 1989, when this could be done openly in the Polish domestic media. Tadeusz Konwicki, publishing abroad, stresses the disparity between the grey, emotionally withdrawn Home Army wartime resistance comrades of his own recollection and the glamorous neurotic spasms of the bejeaned Cybulski (Konwicki 1982: 35–6); Andrzej Werner denounces the film's distortion of the role and nature of the Home Army (AK) (Werner 1990: 23–7); and Waldemar Chołodowski (Lubelski 1992a: 157) criticises its isolation of Maciek and Andrzej to create the illusion of an absence of social support for the AK. Yet even as early as 1958 itself, when some spectators were granted the freedom of anonymity and polled on exiting the cinema, 14 out of 99 viewed it as 'too anti-AK' (Koźniewski 1958), while a (lunatic?) fringe of three – doubtless Party hard-liners – denounced its whitewashing of 'traitors to the Polish nation, who murdered for American dollars'. On the other hand, it exerted and continues to exert a purely aesthetic fascination: Sławomir Mrożek describes having emerged from his first viewing exhilarated that Polish film art could now hold its own in the world (Mrożek 1983: 33–41); Marek Hendrykowski laments various political agendas' capacity to dim awareness of its artistry (Hendrykowski 1984: 74); and Tadeusz Lubelski records its mythical impact upon him across repeated viewings (Lubelski 1992b: 20). Consequently, I will seek to do justice both to the work's poetics and politics, focusing stereoscopically on both the extraordinariness and the possible contamination – the double personality of a film in which 'art cinema' and 'political cinema' interlock as inextricably as 'message' and 'noise'. As is usual and necessary in matters Polish, however, I will begin with a certain amount of contextualisation.

THE POLISH SCHOOL:
THE MOVEMENT THAT DARED NOT SPEAK ITS NAME?

The term 'the Polish School' has become associated with the internationally recognised upsurge in Polish filmmaking after the 'Thaw' of October 1956 and before the 'small stabilisation' of the 1960s, which saw Władysław Gomułka – the onetime national hero of 1956, who returned to power as Party First Secretary and restrained Poland from an uprising that would doubtless have been suppressed as ruthlessly as the Hungarian one – denounce Poland's most creative filmmakers, helping precipitate the departures of Roman Polański and Jerzy Skolimowski in particular.

Andrzej Wajda's work is central to any account of 'the Polish school', and *Ashes and Diamonds* is its most renowned film. But although the term implies a movement with a shared aesthetic or goals, attempts to find a common denominator among its key directors have all foundered: images of World War Two and the Occupation, of national martyrdom and often ironically registered, failed revolt may pervade its internationally best-known works, but the diversity of the films underpinning it in fact undermines its identification with wartime themes.

Indeed, the common factor may be less a theme than the new production structure instituted in May 1955, allowing filmmakers to form Creative Film Units with considerable autonomy of project-generation, each headed by a filmmaker functioning as *primus inter pares*. Moreover, the term itself is neither used during the period it designates nor features in its directors' self-definitions. So how and why did it come to be employed? What, if anything, did and does it mean? And should one seek another term or terms to define the activities of Wajda, Andrzej Munk, Jerzy Kawalerowicz and Wojciech Has, among others, during this time?

Writing of an interview given to *Le Monde* in 1963 by Kazimierz Kutz, Philippe Hadiquet records his contention that 'Polish cinema is decentralised' and 'there is no School' (Hadiguet 1963: 5). The term 'school' does not feature either in Bolesław Michałek's influential *Sight and Sound* article, 'The Polish Drama' (Michałek 1960: 198–200), or in Jerzy Płażewski's report on Polish cinema for *Cahiers du cinema* in 1958, titled 'Le jeune cinéma polonais' (the common factor here is generational). Płażewski's primary point of reference, however, is Italian realism, the most significant European film movement of the recent past. He juxtaposes Munk's position with the 'faith in reality' of Cesare Zavattini, adding that Kawalerowicz, on the other hand, could not be suspected of allegiance to '"l'école italienne" polonaise' (Płażewski 1958: 21–33). Aleksander Jackiewicz wittily combines the Italian and Polish references by deriving Wajda's *Pokolenie* (*A Generation*, 1955) from neo-realism and titling his review 'Z ziemi włoskiej do Polski' (From the Italian lands to Poland), quoting the Polish national anthem's invocation of the dreamed-of, liberating arrival of Tadeusz Kościuszko's legions (Jackiewicz 1956: 148–53). Jackiewicz had advocated the creation of a 'Polish school of filmmaking' as early as 1954, yet neither he nor other late-1950s Polish critics utilised the term to describe what actually emerged. Jackiewicz notes the maturation of Wajda and his cameraman Jerzy Lipman during the heyday of neo-realism (Jackiewicz 1956: 148–53). Yet he highlights *A Generation*'s stylisation, a feature alien to the neo-realist programme. The ruined, stony aftermath of war that pervades Rossellini's films in particular may recur in those of Wajda and Munk, but 'the Polish School' differs from neo-realism as much as it recalls it. Whereas neo-realism programmatically pursued the unadorned recreation of reality, unencumbered by stars and sets, the Poles used professional actors and issued no manifestos. So what is the point of the comparison?

Its main purpose was surely to emphasise – as Płażewski later remarks – that 'one should – to the great profit of Art – submit more than one of our problems to the analysis of its reality' (this realism, unlike the Italian one, will not be neo-documentary)(Płażewski 1958: 33). As the last phrase suggests, the Polish school's common denominator is less a positive – a prototype to follow – than the massive negative of the socialist realism whose actually fantastic nature had precluded such analysis of reality.

'The Polish school' is a somewhat anomalous term, precipitated in part, I would suggest, by its directors' origins in another school, the Łódź Film School. Although the significant film movements have all arisen within single countries, fed by the debates and symbiosis of contemporaries and friends, their countries' names have never been part of their self-definition. Other countries' critics may have linked them to their point of origin and spoken of '*German* expressionism' or '*Italian* neo-realism', but in each case the national adjective easily falls away: all the more so because these movements can be seen to represent strong choices between the perennial alternatives of style and stylelessness. Why should 'Polishness' function as a self-definition? Once again, this may be seen as rejecting a socialist realism of non-Polish – Soviet

– provenance. Although one might then expect a movement pervaded by a certain national-ism, national motifs and socialist attitudes are intertwined within it. For what diplomatic code terms *raisons d'état*, however – the inadvisability of offending a Big Brother ever-ready to offer 'fraternal aid' – 'Polishness' cannot be highlighted in manifestos, lest it seem overtly to chal-lenge the 'socialist internationalism' of Soviet hegemony. The movement's namelessness, which torments categorising critics, is an incognito camouflage. War is not only a frequent theme but a simultaneous source of conspiratorial method. Meanwhile, inasmuch as the Polish school defines itself through *content* rather than form – unlike such movements as expressionism or neo-realism – its anonymity may also approach the despecified names of a later cinematic movement like the *Nouvelle vague*. The lack of a single worldview and style manifests anti-totalitarianism and tolerance. Resisting modernist urges to totalise, the very diversity teeming under the umbrella of 'the Polish school' might even tempt one to term it incipiently 'postmod-ernist' – at least in the Lyotardian sense of refusing grand narratives.

As noted above, the term 'Polish school' inevitably recalls the term 'Polish Film School' – and Poland's renown as the site of one of the world's leading film schools, the one at Łódź. Most importantly however, it reconjugates 'the Polish Film School' to argue implicitly 'we have a film school – but that is not enough'. The substitutability of terms is emphasised by Janusz Gazda, who himself rewrites 'Polska szkoła filmowa' as 'Polska sztuka filmowa' (Polish film *art*) (Gazda 1997: 17). Yet the term 'school' is worth preserving, however misleading, to highlight the idea of a common agenda of Poles in the mid-1950s: the aspiration to free-dom. The term 'school' proclaims solidarity long before the Solidarity movement's existence; unlike movements founded upon manifestos, it is eclectic and – as Marek Hendrykowski has stressed (Hendrykowski 1997b: 120–30) – *open*, excluding and excommunicating no one. No manifesto need be formulated, for the shared Polish aspiration goes without saying – as it has to. That is why its pre-eminent director should be Wajda, the one most deeply obsessed with Polish identity. Twenty years later there will be a real school, a formation with a master (Wajda) and pupils (primarily the 'X' film group). Nevertheless even after 1976 and the breakthrough effected by Wajda's *Man of Marble,* which paralleled the present with the putatively distant Stalinist past, a certain politic self-limitation and camouflage will be necessary; 'the Cinema of Moral Anxiety' is a name that intimates a programme rather than fully utters it – which is why some are happier to speak of a 'Cinema of Distrust' (Haltof 2002: 147–8). The 'movements that dare not speak their name' are in fact the self-limiting revolutions of those whose freedom is always relative; muted names and notes are the only ones the alien system will tolerate.

ANDRZEJEWSKI'S *ASHES AND DIAMONDS*

Wajda's film is widely and justly viewed as eclipsing Jerzy Andrzejewski's original novel; indeed, Andrzejewski himself wished he could insert into it the new dialogues of the screen-play. Nevertheless, the importance of the novel – a school set-book not only throughout the life of 'People's Poland', but even *after its demise,* running into almost thirty editions with a total print-run of almost three million copies – renders its independent consideration imperative. Only such comparative probing can help determine the degree to which its ideology persists into – and arguably poisons – the film. After all, eclipses entail a nearer, later phenomenon's *precise alignment* with the thing it obscures. The adaptation's status as critique of its origi-nal scotches the vexed question of fidelity but nevertheless mandates juxtaposition of the two works, for the one provides (for Polish audiences) the other's well-known, essential inter-text. The following synopsis of Andrzejewski's material is thus intended to aid assessment of Wajda's work upon it, while also acquainting non-Polish readers with a form of the narrative they probably do not know and may be unable easily to access.

Party District Committee secretary Podgórski travels through war-ravaged Ostrowiec with Party Provincial Secretary Szczuka and encounters the wife of judge Antoni Kossecki, his former superior. Podgórski learns of Kossecki's recent return from Gross-Rosen concentration camp, where Szczuka had also been imprisoned. Their jeep then encounters the aftermath of a shooting of two local cement-workers. Szczuka feels he and Podgórski were the intended victims: meeting Alicja Kossecka delayed them, saving their lives.

  In her ruined villa, Alicja finds that money is missing from her purse; she interrupts her 22-year-old son Andrzej's meeting with friends to discuss the 'botched job' and he offers her as much as 10,000 złoty. Her husband, who comes from a large petty bourgeois family and who has had to work hard for everything in life, seems indifferent to her wartime sufferings. Unsettling and fearful, he has no desire to see anyone, not even Podgórski.

  Podgórski deposits Szczuka at the hotel 'Monopol'. In the hallway Maciek Chełmicki lights Szczuka's cigarette. In his room, Szczuka reflects on his wife's death and then goes to the apartment of Staniewiczowa, his sister-in-law, where aristocrats are discussing emigration and Andrzej Kossecki and his Home Army commander plan Szczuka's assassination. Andrzej remains throughout Szczuka's visit. Szczuka cannot bring himself to tell Staniewiczowa of her sister's death. We then pick up Alek, Andrzej's 17-year-old brother, reflecting on his theft from his mother's purse of a sum intended to meet the demands of Janusz Szretter, his gang's leader. The gang meets in an abandoned cellar, where Szretter says the money is needed to buy a gun. A quarrel over contributions ends with Szretter shooting Janusz Kotowicz, who was carrying a large sum. One member, Marcin, leaves, objecting that 'we were supposed to fight for Poland'.

  Podgórski visits Kossecki and expatiates on the Party's difficulties: few trust the communists. Nevertheless, he is optimistic. Kossecki then discusses in the abstract how far people were prepared to go to survive in the camps. Podgórski says Szczcuka wants to see him.

  Drewnowski checks the preparations for a banquet in Szczuka's honour given by his own patron, Mayor Swięcki. He is buttonholed by Pieniążek, a former newspaper colleague of Swięcki, who drops hints of Swięcki's imminent promotion. Maciek flirts with the barmaid Krystyna as Drewnowski and Pieniążek get drunk. Andrzej Kossecki meets Maciek, who proposes that they do the same. Swięcki arrives at the banquet. On his way to it Szczcuka encounters a couple: since the girl's sister has just returned from Ravensbrück, he hopes she might know something about his own wife's death there. Back at the hotel, he discusses Kossecki with Podgórski, describing his moral failure in the camps as 'the bankruptcy of the petit bourgeois'. In the Monopol, Andrzej and Maciek recall past times. Maciek gets drunk and tries to attract Krystyna's attention. Various political conversations unfold during the banquet, including one between Szczuka and his pre-war socialist friend Kalicki, who worries about where the communists may be taking Poland.

  Meanwhile, Szretter's gang dispose of the body. Andrzej leaves the banquet, Alek Kossecki returns home, and Słomka seduces Stefka, the fiancée of one of the dead cement-workers, who has just learned of her fiancé's death. As the banquet proceeds, Staniewiczowa talks to Maciek and the drunken Pieniążek is locked in the toilet. During Szczuka's conversation with Kalicki, the latter describes the liberation as Russian imperialism. At the Kossecki villa, Andrzej contemplates a Russian in the neighbouring villa and wonders if this is really 'the enemy', Alek goes to bed weeping, and Antoni contemplates the meeting with Szczuka and the exposure of his wartime misdeeds.

As the banquet draws to its close, Pieniążek is joined in the toilet by Drewnowski, who is now out of favour. Maciek and Krystyna lie together, Maciek thinking how little she resembles all the other girls with whom he has slept. Although she had counted on an uncomplicated one-night-stand, they haltingly share their deeper feelings as Szczuka starts to pace next door. Maciek begins to ask himself why he has to kill him.

At dawn, the banquet ends with Kotowicz paring off the guests to dance to Chopin's A-minor polonaise. As Pieniążek follows them Kotowicz cries 'long live Poland'.

Kotowicz then goes innocently to Szretter to enquire about his son – and the money he was carrying. Szretter believably feigns ignorance. Szretter and another gang member, Felek, visit the impoverished Marcin, whom the killing had appalled and whose health has collapsed. Alek, whom they meet later, is fine however. At the riverside they pass Maciek and Krystyna.

As a radio announces details of the war's end, Maciek and Kryztyna talk in a café, Maciek saying he wishes to begin a normal life, study. Catching sight of Alek, he tells him to let Andrzej know he wants to see him. Alek and Szretter buy a gun; the dealer is accompanied by Drewnowski, who has now broken with the authorities. As Maciek and Krystyna part he freezes on seeing Szczuka emerge from his jeep.

Maciek runs into Andrzej. Discussing plans in Maciek's room, Andrzej informs him of his own imminent departure and asks if he needs help in killing Szczuka. Maciek confesses his love and wish to start a new, normal life, but Andrzej reminds him of his soldier's commitment. Maciek reluctantly agrees to kill Szczuka but calls it his last assignment. He writes to Krystyna to postpone his meeting with her.

Maciek then visits the cemetery where the cement-workers are to be interred. Walking among the graves, he sees one inscribed with Cyprian Norwid's verse asking whether what remains will be ashes or a starry diamond. The grave's occupant died in World War One aged 22 – his own age. Applying Norwid's words to himself, he wonders if only ash will remain of his life. The funeral procession arrives, bedecked with red flags. One mourner describes the dead as 'victims of fascist criminals'. Szczuka, towering above the crowd, gives a funeral oration describing 'our enemy' as 'the enemy of humanity' and praising the workers' deaths for humanity and fatherland. Szczuka leaves the cemetery on foot and visits the Szretters, where he hears from a former prisoner of his wife's courage in Ravensbrück. Maciek follows him to the Szretters' and kills him (the killing is not described) and then drops the gun in a toilet.

Kossecki leaves for his appointment with Szczuka. He tells Podgórski that whoever broke down in the abnormal conditions of war should be exonerated now normality has returned. He pales as Podgórski rings the Security chief.

Maciek checks out of the hotel. Thinking of Krystyna waiting at the station, he panics and runs when he sees three soldiers. When he fails to halt as ordered they shoot him. At the end a soldier leans over his body and asks 'man, why did you run away?'

It has been speculated that Andrzejewski's novel *Ashes and Diamonds* derives from a real incident, the fortuitous shooting of pre-war communist activist Jan Foremniak by Home Army soldiers responding to a break-in shortly after the Russian liberation of Ostrowiec (Kąkolewski

1998: 41–110). If this was indeed the case the real-life key was carefully buried by Andrzejewski, though the resemblance between the name Kossecki and that of the actual Home Army soldier – Stanisław Kosicki – offers a clue. Kosicki, unlike Maciek Chełmicki, survived: the killer's fictional fate, like the novel's reported capture of partisan leader Szary ('Grey') – in fact still at large as Andrzejewski wrote – suggests a partial authorial identification with the new authorities' wish-fulfilling fantasy, both being committed to artefacts of the imagination. Andrzejewski's larger ambition, however, was to promote national reconciliation, convincing members of the Home Army (now officially dissolved) of the futility of continued resistance and the authorities of the need for clemency to opponents. The story is set at a moment of transition. On 8 May, the last day of the war against the Germans, the uneven civil war between Soviet-sponsored Poles and those engaged in armed struggle against the newly imposed order does not end. Although on one level Andrzejewski validates the change effected by that day – the establishment of socialism in Poland – neither of his central characters survives it. It is clear that the new order has no place for Maciek, the Home Army fighter taking orders from the London-based government-in-exile, though one may wonder whether his accidental death (shot while fleeing soldiers who told him to halt) represents a judgement on him, as Jacek Trznadel argues (Trznadel 1988: 237),[1] or simply a fortunate solution to the political problem he embodies: after all, the novel's incorporation of a real collaborator with the Germans – Antoni Kossecki (the father of Andrzej Kossecki, the only member of his family to survive into Wajda's film) – allows one to compare the two figures and grasp the dubiousness of the Party rhetoric that pilloried such anti-Soviet Home Army members as Maciek as 'fascists'. But why should Szczuka, the weary exemplary communist, die too? May not his death be a logical extension of the fact, noted both by Trznadel and Czesław Miłosz (Trznadel 1988: 236; Miłosz 1981: 105), that he is never shown *doing* anything? Andrzejewski may seem to achieve the best of both worlds – the aesthetic and the political – by killing off both Maciek and Szczuka, both gaining a tragic conclusion and underlining the futility of continued armed struggle after Armistice Day, but Szczuka's death – prepared for by his often-voiced battle-weariness – can also indicate the unfeasibility of his ideals under the new order, rendering the book far more than a simple apologia for the new regime (something Andrzejewski may both want and not want, as the elusiveness of such implicit criticism allows him to appease both patriotic Poles and the Party, to which he can pretend no substantive criticism exists). In the novel's first drafts Szczuka appears as Utopian reconciler of opposites, a 'Christian without God', the projected ideal Communist (Chwin 1993: 185). Perhaps not surprisingly, Andrzejewski's inherently contradictory effort to reconcile Catholicism and Marxism left everyone dissatisfied (Chwin 1993: 188). Szczuka is not shown acting lest his signature on Home Army arrest and deportation lists dispel sympathy for him. Nor is his dependence on Soviet power openly conceded. Only archaic aristos looking West are beholden to foreign masters. They cynically pull rank while blackmailing the young honourably attached to military discipline to pursue doomed, 'fratricidal' activity.

Maciek Chełmicki and Szczuka match each other, contrasting images of the split within Andrzejewski himself. The gentry code of honour he mocks is as Conradian as his own novels, frequently wrapped in the solitude of the vast night. Aware perhaps of his own partial adherence to the code, he distils a 'good' form of it in Maciek, but then compensates by condemning him to ignominious death. The code of 'fidelity to self', meanwhile, may justify Kossecki's condemnation in a happy fusion of Marxism and the Conradian, but it omits the Christian forgiveness Andrzejewski also seeks. That omission nags him like a guilty conscience. The following tortuous statement attributed to Szczuka in an early draft vainly strives to still its nagging: 'did you never realise that people who get along without God in fact have no right to pity criminals? For what could they base that right on?' (Chwin 1993: 186) Meanwhile, mixed feelings about youth cause the novel to multiply categories and age-groups within it, some condemned outright, others in more qualified form.

The contradictions come to a head when Podgórski remarks that the war taught him both communism and patriotism, implying the compatability of motives most Poles would deem irreconcilable. A moment later they re-establish themselves as genuinely contradictory: Antoni Kossecki voices the implicit Polish reader's scepticism (the text's own dialogue with itself a substitute for dialogue with the reader) and asks 'simultaneously?' (Andrzejewski 1970: 114). Andrzejewski provocatively bifurcates his implicit reader, for the average Pole's assent to this remark is undercut by its attribution to Antoni, the weak-willed turncoat. Andrzejewski gives the voice of purely Polish patriotism enough rope to hang itself. But in killing off Szczuka, his copybook good Communist, and showing at the Monopol dinner how the dregs rise under the new order, he is himself as sceptical as Kossecki, to whom he is far closer than he might consciously admit: the evocations of Kossecki's drained solitude are among the best things in the book. Indeed, the fragments of Andrzejewski's diary that preface later Polish editions show the work's conception to have begun with Kossecki.

So shifting and ambivalent is his novel that Andrzejewski may have welcomed co-author-ship with Wajda as a way of diluting responsibility for its begetting. His claims to have reread in the mid-1950s only those portions of relevance to the screenplay gain in plausibility when one considers his possible reluctance to consider what he had done in the rest (Trznadel 1990: 83). When Podgórski tells Kossecki of 'the multitude of conflicts and contradictions one encounters at every step among us, which we certainly will not resolve either tomorrow or the day after' (Andrzejewski 1970: 113; Andrzejevski [sic] 1962: 78), it is fitting that the novel that both reflects and participates in them is never truly resolved either. Jerzy Krzyżanowski argues that comparison of the original 1948 edition and the third one of 1954 'proves that the author's work was not finished on 10 June 1947, although it is practically impossible to estab-lish how many changes were introduced in the publisher's or the censor's office' (Krzyżanowski 1971: 328). These changes to the novel reveal 'a certain pattern of down-grading the Polish Socialists and promoting the Communists … apparently to make it politically more acceptable' (Krzyżanowski 1971: 329–30). Aware that political pressures 'could have affected Ashes and Diamond [sic] in a much graver way' (Krzyżanowski 1971: 330), Krzyżanowski nevertheless concludes – generously but not entirely consistently – by praising Andrzejewski's integrity.

Much of Ashes and Diamonds concerns the question of whether or not a person can change. After falling in love with Krystyna, Maciek seeks to shed his mission to kill Szczuka, remarking to his immediate superior Andrzej 'can't you see that a man can change?' (Andrzejewski 1970: 309; Andrzejevski [sic] 1962: 214). If Maciek can change, perhaps he could be won over to the new order? In the end, however, Andrzejewski, perhaps himself excessively loyal to gentry codes of honour, deems change either impossible or treacherous. It is Kossecki who tries to justify his treachery by speaking of how circumstances change people, and Podgórski deems such survivalist malleability typically 'petty bourgeois'. The verdict could come back to haunt the Andrzejewski who later echoed Kossecki's claim that his own mistakes were conditioned by an abnormal period (Andrzejewski 1970: 339; Andrzejevski [sic] 1962: 234). What is more, does not Marxism itself deem the intellectual's position a petty-bourgeois one? Fortunately, reality is more merciful than the author who kills Maciek and has Kossecki awaiting sentence at the book's end: 1956 and Andrzej Wajda gave him a chance to present his work in a new light. Self-frustrated, speaking of reconciliation and pity for the killer one moment and a fascist Home Army the next, it was fated for revision.

ASHES AND DIAMONDS: THE FILM

Andrzej, Maciek and Drewnowski wait by a roadside chapel: when two men drive up they shoot them, then flee. Another two men arrive, Party officials Podgórski and Szczuka; the latter explains that they were the intended victims and tells workers that despite the war's end the political struggle continues. Andrzej, Maciek and Drewnowski are now in town. Andrzej and Maciek discuss Drewnowski's 'double game'. As Soviet soldiers walk past, Drewnowski supervises preparations for a banquet at the Monopol. Andrzej and Maciek meet its barmaid, Krystyna. As Andrzej phones Major Staniewicz to report success, Maciek interrupts to tell him of Szczuka's arrival at the hotel. The Major summons Andrzej to make new plans. Szczuka asks after the Staniewicz's and Maciek reserves another room in the hotel, ostensibly for a date. He checks into the room beside Szczuka's and sees a woman cursing the killers of her fiancé (one of his victims) at the opposite window. He loads his gun as Szczuka paces next door. Russian tanks roll by outside as Staniewicz reminds Andrzej of the importance of killing Szczuka. Elsewhere at the Staniewicz's, aristocrats discuss the uncertain new order and Szczuka comes to visit his sister-in-law, seeking news of his son, whom she brought up as 'a good patriot' after his wife's death. Andrzej leaves the apartment after Szczuka – Maciek is flirting with Krystyna when Andrzej returns. As Hanka Lewicka sings, Maciek and Andrzej recall fallen comrades. Maciek must kill Szczuka soon if he wishes to catch the 4.30am train with Andrzej. Maciek makes a date with Krystyna. Pieniążek battens on Drewnowski, seeking an entrée to the banquet. Mayor Święcki arrives and the banquet begins. Meanwhile, as Maciek checks his gun Krystyna knocks at his door: they talk. Drewnowski gets drunk and Pieniazek gatecrashes the banquet, which Święcki addresses. Maciek and Krystyna grow closer and make love. Wrona interrogates Home Army partisans. Maciek and Krystyna come downstairs and pass Szczuka; they walk and come to a ruined chapel, where Maciek voices his desire for normality and they find the bodies of the men he shot. Podgórski and Szczuka recall their own dead comrades, Szczuka adding that good times will return. As Maciek and Krzytyna part he tells her he might be able to stay, but his conversation with Andrzej ends with him accepting the assassination as his duty. Meanwhile, Drewnowski is finally disgraced and Wrona summons Szczuka to meet his partisan son. Szczuka walks alone and Maciek follows and kills him. As Kotowicz conducts a polonaise for the partygoers, Maciek tells Krystyna he has to leave. As he does so he sees Andrzej reject Drewnowski, who then runs after Maciek. Maciek flees, runs into three soldiers; as he carries on running they shoot him. While the polonaise plays inside and the hotel porter unfurls the Polish flag, Maciek dies on a rubbish heap.

Andrzejewski made the most of the thaw of 1956 to revise his story for public consumption. Some of the changes are doubtless mere side-effects of a novel's compression into a film, particularly one whose 24-hour time-span suggests classical tragedy and maximises ironic contrast. Others, however, appear more ideologically motivated. For instance, the elimination of

Kossecki, the Pole who becomes a kapo to survive in Gross-Rosen, may reflect Wajda's own unwillingness to show a collaborationist Pole (an unwillingness that colours his later *Eine Leibe in Deutschland* [*Love in Germany*, 1983], where the Pole prepared to accept Germanisation in Rolf Hochhuth's book of the same name becomes heroically intransigent), Andrzejewski's own awareness of the wider public's reluctance to confront the possibility of Polish cowardice, or be a simple side-effect of the focus on the symbolic parricide of the Szczuka-Maciek encounter. Certainly, the greater prominence the film accords Maciek accentuates and at least initially lends glamour to the active Polish resistance (unlike the novel, it begins with him, at the heart of the whirlwind of botched action). Some early 1950s critics had denounced Maciek as a fascist, and a soldier in the novel blames fascists for Szczuka's death. But is this Andrzejewski's view? He has Podgórski, Szczuka's companion, state that not all the young people hiding in the forests are fascists – though on the other hand the only conspiratorial group directly shown at work is the parodistic one (omitted from the film) of the Szretter group, that Gidean adolescent version of *The Possessed*. (A group the later Wajda, to whom Dostoevsky is very close, might well have included.) 'Youthful conspiracy' thus assumes two forms in the novel, one at either end of adolescence, with the younger one the scapegoat for the older. In the film, however, Szczuka is given a son, Marek, a Home Army fighter who is 17, exactly the same age as Andrzej's brother Alek, who is presented negatively in the novel. His name's echo of 'Maciek' emphasises the homogeneity of youth in the film – the identity between both the 22-year-olds and the 17-year-olds. Maciek's embrace of the Szczuka he kills suggests tragic Oedipal elements. As is usual in Eastern Europe, however, this Oedipus is non-Freudian, dispersed between real and symbolic sonhood, and any secret yearnings to murder the father or any suggestions of tainted father/son relations are displaced into the character assassination of those 'bad fathers', the aristos and the exiled former rulers in the West. That distant older generation is the real victim of the symbolic parricide of both Andrzejewski's novel and Wajda's film: as in Wajda's later restaging of elements of *Ashes and Diamonds* and *Krajobraz po bitwie* (*Landscape After a Battle*, 1970) (of which more later), the sympathy and fascination is with the cruel stories of youth. Oedipal overtones are also downplayed by the separation of sexuality and the maternal: Szczuka has no wife. And why kill the older generation when one has no hope of grasping their power – when they themselves are powerless? As they commemorate dead comrades Andrzej and Maciek evoke a past in which 'we knew what we wanted', a phrase instantaneously and tellingly reconjugated into 'we knew what they wanted of us'. The identity the army once bestowed and the unity of will of leaders and led has evaporated. All that remains is the split consciousness that doubts the validity of its own actions, though not so much because struggle has now become 'fratricidal' (as in the official propaganda that sought to render it morally repugnant) as because it is hopeless – for Russian armies swarm the streets, occupying the public space of 'Poland'.

Although many differences separate Andrzejewski's *Ashes and Diamonds* from the one he and Wajda crafted eleven years after the novel's first publication, one can generalise and subdivide them into four crucial areas: the two works' treatment of Maciek Chełmicki, their treatment of other characters, their narrative structure and their overall politics.

The most glaring change, with ramifications for the entire work, concerns the treatment of Maciek. A background figure for much of the novel – particularly its first half – he occupies centre-stage unremittingly from the very opening of the film. Foregrounded as he awaits the jeep, silhouetted against the horizon, he becomes the action's prime mover. Wajda's beginning, the cement-workers' shooting, displays the focus on action often deemed 'cinematic', starting with deeds rather than their aftermath. The elements of femininity and reflection so important for the novel – which begins with Alicja Kossecka and features much isolated meditation – wither away accordingly, as might be expected from the Wajda traditionally more interested in male struggle than in either the female or introspection. The erasure of Andrzejewski's hints of Home Army effeminacy – Maciek's 'girlish' eyelashes and the Major's 'almost feminine' hand – legitimates it as an agent of male contestation. Although Andrzej Kossecki survives the screenplay's decimation of the Kossecki family, he becomes secondary to the Maciek whose charisma is accentuated by the frequent light-points reflected in his dark glasses: their darkness spells intriguing enigma while the lights represent the eyes (soul, humanity) hidden behind them. The film's simultaneously melodramatic and tragic compression and deep focus nevertheless multiply ironies around Maciek, showing him trapped in space. The novel's Maciek sports a summer coat and brown hat as Szczuka checks in at the Monopol and ironically seems to have no initial knowledge of the latter's identity; obtaining the hotel room next to him is a matter of fortuity rather than planning. Szczuka's death, unseen in the book, is inserted here to carry a double irony as fireworks illuminate it and the dying man sinks in his killer's arms. The film is very much Maciek's story, focusing far more consistently ('cinematically'?) on the transforming power of romance underlined particularly emphatically in the stylistically anomalous love-making scene, with its tender dissolves, shadowy close-ups, Maciek's lack of glasses, sense of plenitude conveyed by the lovers' direct looks at the camera, and final daring (in terms of period conventions) camera-slide down Krystyna's bare back.

Various other characters undergo change in the film. Krystyna, divested of her continuing aristocratic connections, becomes a more ideal and floatingly attractive figure. First seen in a mirror (as Andrzejewski's own mother had been by *his* father), and hence isolated from the surrounding space, she is a figure of the imagination, like Daisy – the blonde in *Kanał* (*Kanal* 1956/57) – who also first appears thus. Less socially grounded than her counterpart in the novel, she inhabits an isolation that makes her well-matched with Maciek. And as she no longer joins the aristocrats at their tables, the gulf between youth and age deepens, reflecting late-1950s reality. Drewnowski is written into several of the early scenes (doubtless to make the most of the established interplay of Cybulski and Bogumił Kobiela, who had worked together in the Bim-Bom cabaret) and is shown playing a double game: in the novel he is merely a careerist, gravitating slightly towards the Home Army only after his disgrace (which is far more developed and comprehensive in the film). His family is omitted, as is that of Andrzej Kossecki, who loses father, mother and younger brother. Wajda's removal of families across the board both serves dramatic compression and accentuates the characters' existential isolation and glamour, subverting the sociological determinism of the book's more explicitly Marxist moments. The sympathy extended to Szczuka issues less from his ideology – which the film largely suppresses – than his limp, familial losses and nostalgia for fallen comrades: his reminiscences of Spain explicitly parallel, and so link him with, the young, as does his possession of a son who is a double for Maciek. The Spanish Civil War connection stemmed from Wajda, who suggested it in order to show that 'the people who went to Spain to fight did so for our and their freedom' (Wajda 1996/97: 16). The phrase 'for our freedom and yours', an age-old motto of the Polish *national* liberation struggle, is very significant: its application to Szczuka shows him as 'one of us', for all his drinking of tea from the saucer *à la russe*. Impoverishing the young, meanwhile, generates further sympathy for them, as they no longer splash money around as in the book – Andrzejewski's heavy gesture towards Western backing and black marketeering. Omitting the novel's keyword – *znużenie* ('weariness') – accentuates the identification with youthful vitalism and the sense of tragedy associated with its premature amputation.

The rearrangement of material, like the changes in characterisation, has both aesthetic and ideological effects. Beginning with Maciek and the Home Army, as I have noted, renders them – rather than the world-weary older generation (Kossecka, Szczuka) – the protagonists. Stefka's lament for her dead fiancé, the cement-worker Gawlik, is situated early in the film rather than the middle of the banquet. Her curse on the perpetrators thus enters the work's tragic framework as a form of fatality, the sign of inescapable doom. In having it witnessed by Maciek (the point-of-view zoom onto Stefka shows how closely it concerns him emotionally), Wajda lays the groundwork for his later crisis of conscience, which dawns more gradually and hence more plausibly. (As in this scene, looks and sounds often link scenes with simultaneous ones elsewhere, enhancing the compression.) Towards its end, the book showcases the workers' funeral in a cemetery where Maciek reads the Norwid verse alone; it thus functions as a possible curse. Its reading in Krystyna's presence in the film reinforces its stress on relationships, its eschewal of the book's real and metaphorical images of events taking place on the other side of a wall isolating individuals from them. Wajda taps film's tendency to tie characters to their immediate contexts. Having the verse read in Krystyna's presence renders her Norwid's diamond and emphasises Maciek's shyness and sense of tragic isolation as he swivels away from her after making the comparison. Unlike the book's, this Maciek knows both the source and the final line: sympathetic characters can now have the intelligentsia background socialist realism had proscribed. Andrzejewski's idealisation and homogenisation of the workers (at the funeral, they all look the same) may have anticipated socialist realism, but Wajda's heart clearly is not in the work's socialist realist elements: Szczuka's early speech to grief-stricken workers is horribly wooden. The book's emphasis is less on Norwid's 'diamond' than on the abyss threatening Maciek, as the word 'ashes' haunts him. Another change involves Wajda's combination of the vodka-glass scene with Hanka Lewicka's song, thereby doubling its quotient of nostalgic regret. The song is no longer about partisans but becomes one with pointed political connotations, 'The Poppies on Monte Cassino', commemorating the suffering and achievements of Polish armies under Western, not Soviet, control. It thus undermines the earlier caricature of Home Army aristocrats under orders from London.

And here one can move on to the changes in the treatment of politics. The above-mentioned alterations, of course, all have implicit political consequences, all serving to heighten sympathy for and identification with the Home Army. But the book also features various political discourses, only some of which are preserved in the film. Such omissions may flow excusably from Wajda's accentuation of action – kino as kinesis – but their effects require consideration. Two of the key discourses – indicative of the variety of positions within the left – are either attenuated or disappear. One is the hardline discourse best represented in the novel by Security Chief Wrona, who is preserved but only shown in action; this discourse is also echoed by the worker at the funeral who terms the dead men 'victims of fascist criminals'. In this discourse, to disagree with the communists is to become 'objectively fascist'. This discourse also pervades Szczuka's (deleted) funeral oration. The omission of the arguments of the pre-war socialist Kalicki, however, is perhaps even more significant. Kalicki is present only as a background banquet guest. The omission of his discourse demonstrates the degree to which film, as the Leninist's 'most important art', is likely to be more thoroughly censored than a novel. Andrzejewski's Kalicki is a positive figure who suffered for his socialist views during the 1930s. Yet while conversing with Szczuka he worries about where the communists will take Poland and speaks of a continuity of Russian imperialism. Although Szczuka disagrees, the moment was clearly too sensitive for filmic inclusion; certain things can be written – or said silently to oneself while reading – that would be inflammatory were they to issue into a public space, from screen or stage, as was the condemnation of Tsarist Russia in the prologue to Mickiewicz's *Forefathers' Eve* when spoken in 1968, a mere decade later: it ignited student protest. Andrzejewski may use Kalicki as a legitimating sign of his own realistic novelistic fidelity to life's variety and a demonstration of the bankruptcy of even 'non-fascist' opposition, but his novel does at least include the line about Russian imperialism, as Wajda's work could not. The most we are shown is Russian commissars arriving at the banquet and Russian soldiers singing in the street. Wajda's simplification of the range of political positions intensifies the dramatic chiaroscuro in line with the theory of tragedy Hegel derived from *Antigone* of Sophocles. As Wajda himself later put it in *Double Vision*, that book haunted by *Antigone*: 'Creon's reasons are only revealed through Antigone's, Szczuka's through Maciek Chełmicki' (Wajda 1989: 5).

Jerzy Andrzejewski's *Ashes and Diamonds* is a profoundly unsettling fusion of cunning and self-delusion. It maintains links with the author's pre-war work by invoking the ideal of fraternal reconciliation. At the same time, utilising the Christian prohibition of murder to legitimate a communist regime that was far from a simple victim of Home Army soldiers and other independence-fighters out of step with history and sadly wedded to outmoded pre-war notions of honour, it offers no hint that there might be legitimate, democratic, non-violent forms of opposition to the new Soviet order. It thus suppresses the two years that followed the war, a period of ostensible preparation for democratic elections whose actual Soviet manipulation drove all opposition underground – where it became necessarily violent – or abroad, as in the case of the main opposition leader, Stanisław Mikołajczyk, who fled Poland in 1947. Andrzejewski's collapsing of 1945 into 1947 conceals the Soviet Union's two-year violation of its own undertakings. Wajda accepts that conflation of dates but superimposes upon it the dilemmas and style of 1958 youth. Unlike Andrzejewski, however, he firmly supports the young, be their adolescence in the mid-1940s or the late 1950s. In omitting the final cry 'why did you run away?' after showing Home Army partisans under interrogation (an allusive metonymy for the torture that was their routine lot) he acknowledges Maciek's good reasons for so doing. He thus supports the thirst for freedom that made them so representative of the Poles of both periods. And although his derision of the Home Army leaders seems to chime with Andrzejewski's, it is not Marxist criticism from without but disappointed critique *from within*; himself a member of the Home Army, Wajda has described his generation's immediate post-war feeling of 'disappointment with pre-war Poland and with the occupation Poland created by the London government then by the AK. These forces were unable to play the decisive role that would have given them an influence on the outcome of this war. So we were left alone' (Wajda 1996/97: 11). In the name of Andrzej and Maciek, *Ashes and Diamonds* accuses the ruling older generation of having no other agenda for the young than their death for Poland. Their doubts of hard-bitten adherence to the cause were Wajda's own: 'all our later attempts to come to terms with the new system and contribute to the new reality were connected with the fact that after six years of war we could no longer go on waiting for something that was supposed to happen and which we knew very well now would not happen' (Wajda 1996/97: 12).

ROMANTICISM

Romanticism's presence in Wajda's work is often-noted and marks the film through the commitment to youth, the emotionality customarily associated with the term and the adoption of the position of national spokesman, a role into which many of Poland's artists were cast following its three-stage destruction as a nation-state in the late eighteenth century.

The commitment to emotion is apparent in the clangour of opposed images, becoming explicit in Wajda's statement that 'emotional values are the ones I rate most highly' and belief that 'the means must be emotional to be effective' (Mruklik 1969: 35). Wajda's consuming sense of political mission is squarely in the tradition of the Romantic artists nineteenth-century Poles termed *wieszcze* ('seers'), unofficially delegated to represent the nation following the abolition of representative bodies. Poetic speech could convey messages indirectly either between the lines or behind them, through an allegorical or fabular discourse termed 'Aesopian'. When Wajda gleefully notes the problems censors encounter when regulating images it is because of the implicitness of imagistic 'speech'. It is thus not surprising that Wajda clearly draws on one key work by one of the four great nineteenth-century poetic 'seers' – *The Wedding* (1900), by Stanisław Wyspiański – and has been seen to allude to two others (*Kordian* [1835], by Juliusz Słowacki – Poland's Shelley – and *Forefather's Eve Part III* [1832], by Adam Mickiewicz, the friend and contemporary of Pushkin).

Wyspiański's play dramatises an enfeebled intelligentsia's inability to discharge its responsibility and lead the peasantry into national revolt. Their failure is most glaring in the final scene, as all the wedding guests move in a circle at dawn to the tune of a Straw Man who came to life during the night's revelries. The peasant given a golden horn to mobilise revolt lost it while galloping to do so, and a hypnotic stupor envelops all. This scene is, of course, the prototype of the dawn-lit close of the Monopol banquet.

If Wyspiański's concern is with Polish Hamletism, an earlier form of it is dissected in Słowacki's *Kordian*, first linked to *Ashes and Diamonds* by Aleksander Jackiewicz (Jackiewicz 1983: 26–33). Kordian nurses fevered dreams of killing the Tsar, but when he stands outside his bedroom door he proves unable to complete the deed. Maciek, of course, would also prefer not to; he may accomplish his mission, but is arguably as close to unmanning by conscience as is Hamlet.

Barbara Mruklik, meanwhile, has paralleled the banquet with the Senator's Ball in Mickiewicz's dramatic poem *Forefather's Eve Part III*, a fierce denunciation of the Tsarist persecution of a Vilnius student literary society in which the poet saw the Polish national tragedy distilled (Mruklik 1969: 36). Both the Senator's Ball and the *Ashes and Diamonds* banquet show a Russian-sponsored power-figure surrounded by flattering rogues as a brave youthful opposition suffers behind-the-scenes torture. This torture, obsessively foregrounded by the Senator's cruel remarks in Miczkiewicz's work, is suggested in the film by the intercut moments of Home Army interrogation. Wajda and Andrzejewski can indicate Russian patronage through the arrival of commissars, but cannot afford Mickiewicz's explicitness, the *émigré's* bitter freedom of expression. Moreover, the comparison may both flatter and potentially devastate their work. After all, the Senator's brutal comments on the 'defective morality' of the young anticipate a strand of Andrzejewski's novel only partly cut in the film, which also draws a discreet silence over any links between Szczuka and the everyday process of interrogation. Making one partisan his son renders it well-nigh impossible to deem him in any way aware, approving or responsible with respect to the most unacceptable face of the establishment of communist power.

It may thus be safer to say that for all Wajda's indebtedness to the Romantic aesthetico-political ethos of emotionality and commitment, the reminiscence of *The Wedding* is the film's only unequivocal allusion to a Romantic work, and even that work may be read as critiquing Romanticism. The naming of Norwid in both book and film, meanwhile, is important inasmuch as he is the only great nineteenth-century Polish poet not to be preoccupied with revolt. His explicitly Christian preoccupation with moral work points away from the collective deed of revolution to the responsibility of the individual, that category Kierkegaard saw as being of Christian provenance. Norwid's Christianity is important to Andrzejewski as a sign of continuity with his own fiction of the 1930s. Ironically, a shelving of revolt is something both Andrzejewski and Maciek desire.

CYBULSKI

If Wajda's film has a double personality, split between heart and head, its protagonist is similarly riven. Descriptions of Cybulski's performance stress Maciek's bifurcation, for instance between brutality and tenderness (Jackiewicz 1958) or even masculinity and femininity (Afanasjew [1970] 1987: 136). The internal contradictions are produced by a process Cybulski himself described as 'seeking out the negative characteristics in the positive hero, and vice versa' (Anon 1959: 17). Cybulski himself gives two starting points for his performance. The first involved pre-film research into the behaviour of the young. As they lounged, hands in pockets, he asked them what they were doing. 'Waiting for something to happen', they replied. The felt need to study the young typifies the late beginning of Cybulski's career, delayed by war and various private false starts: he was 31 when called to play the 22-year-old Maciek. Later Cybulski would describe James Dean – whom he had not yet seen when making *Ashes and Diamonds* – as just such a youth, waiting for something to happen. Filming then began with the scene in the toilet. Nervous, feeling he lacked the key to the role, he remembered those youths, leant on the toilet door, rocked back and forth, and heard Wajda comment: 'That's how it should be done: rocking.' Maciek's rocking, Cybulski himself notes, is one between eras, the epochal moods of war and peace (Afanasjew [1970] 1987: 126). It had to be so because Maciek is neither here nor there. Wajda's association of Maciek with back and forth movement is stamped in one of his memories of the shoot: Cybulski standing in a doorway, this time at ease, shifting his weight from leg to leg (Wajda 1989: 35). Maciek's back and forth movement is one of self-offering and sudden withdrawal – the glass extended to Krystyna across the bar, then pulled away.

For Cybulski the film may have begun with research and the first scene, but viewers of course see a different beginning. The opening scene succinctly and comprehensively embodies Maciek's contradictions, what Wajda termed his 'sometimes exaggerated mobility and spontaneity' (Wajda 1989: 32). Maciek sprawls in the grass before the chapel, sunning himself. The call to action causes him to leap up, donning his glasses, cursing the ants on his gun. The movement from horizontality to the vertical also breaks up the static balance of the cross above the chapel. Action precipitates rapidly, explosively, from inaction, with Maciek's dark glasses the sign of an exterminating angel's trademark self-distancing from victims, eyes unseen, soul extinguished in virtual animality (beyond humanity one is both beast and god). Events charge the passive waiter with electricity; one feels the battery filling up, then its violent discharge.

And, as Konrad Eberhardt notes, 'the violent change the protagonist undergoes is also one in the object accompanying him' (Eberhardt 1976: 35). Eberhardt usefully stresses the role of such objects – the cigarette lit for Szczuka, the glass moved back and forth before Krystyna, the part of the pistol rolling on the hotel floor. An actor's props, they also mark the gap between Maciek and others, the nervous distraction and self-absorption of someone always elsewhere.

The most important of these props are the dark glasses, which play a double part. The instantly fashionable sign of late-1950s cool, they also protect the weak eyes of the underground fighter who cannot live above ground. The eyes they protect are also buffered from the full impact of what one is doing, permitting greater ferocity. They become the uniform of the civilian warrior making himself hard; not surprisingly, they vanish in the melting dissolves of the love scene. One viewer even saw the glasses' duality assume another form as they appeared sometimes with one eye, then the other, in plain glass. The dark glasses' cool is of course also expressive of boredom – of waiting for something to happen. That something is a violent discharge, bringing relief. That waiting mood is contemporary with the film, like Maciek's clothing, for – as Cybulski notes – outmoded dress would have rendered the protagonist laughable. The 1950s clothing, conversely, assured the spectator that the film concerned *him*, that the past had not gone away (Afanasjew [1970] 1987: 126). But it is also as if the prolongation of combat serves to banish (post-war, 1950s) boredom. Maciek's death may be caused less by adherence to an outdated ideological formation than by inability to adapt to peacetime (the logical conclusion of war's brutalisation of youth?). After all, Wajda's film – unlike Andrzejewski's book – sees him bid Krystyna a definitive farewell.

When given the part, Cybulski himself felt divided between delight and fear at the responsibility (Afanasjew [1970] 1987: 124). The fascination of his performance is that of quicksilver, the contradiction that founds stardom. Legends of stars' capriciousnesss surely reflect a sense of life's contamination by the contradictions of their personae. The contradictory figure is, of course, both the most representative, embodying opposed positions, and the least, for no one can long maintain the tension between them. No wonder the stars – those the gods love – die young. Cybulski would become the best-known of Polish actors, the only one to achieve international stardom, not only likened to Dean but ranked above him by *Films and Filming* and *L'Humanité*. But the role of Maciek would prove an ambiguous gift. The praise of Marlene Dietrich, an offer of the lead in an American network version of Tennessee Williams' *A Streetcar Named Desire* (1947) and the adulation of teenagers all may have been sweet, but a matching follow-up role to that of Maciek proved elusive. For only a star system would have provided scenarios that amplified the star's persona. In the Polish film industry, however, the production units' habits of literary adaptation theatrically subordinated actors to their roles, minimising the improvisation in which Cybulski revelled. After five years of insignificant roles, Cybulski's next major role, in Wojciech Has's *Jak być kochaną* (*How to Be Loved*, 1962), marked Maciek's supplantation by a boastful coward shielded from the German occupiers by a woman (indeed, Has would provide Cybulski with the highest springboards from which to attempt to leap over the shadow of Maciek, the other two being his roles in *Rękopis znaleziony w Saragossie* [*The Saragossa Manuscript*, 1964] and *Szyfry* [*Ciphers*, 1966]). Wajda later wrote that 'there is no way that anyone can censor Zbyszek Cybulski's performance. It is precisely the way he is that contains that certain "something" representing political obscenity' (Wajda 1989: 122). The actor's figure registered on celluloid could not be replaced by a white moving silhouette, but the system could indeed censor Maciek Chełmicki by ensuring that nothing remotely like him ever came into being again. Those five years before *How to Be Loved* may be taken as years of waiting to continue Maciek's story, followed by the resigned recognition of his death, or at best persistence in hiding, underground. Konrad Eberhardt comments that 'for a series of years Cybulski fought with the spectre of the role that had given him his position and ensured his popularity but at the same time had represented a continual reproach, a continual reminder of lost opportunities' (Eberhardt 1976: 12). Krzysztof Kąkolewski's description of the role of Maciek as a fate hanging over the actor may be melodramatic (Kąkolewski 1998: 36–7), but for all that those widespread comparisons with Dean (not Brando) may somehow have intuited the two actors' linkage in early, appalling death – in Cybulski's case, of course, under the wheels of a train.

STYLE

Ashes and Diamonds first pairs two key stylistic influences that would recur across Wajda's remaining career. They are of course those of Orson Welles' *Citizen Kane* (1941) (whose prismatic quest for the absent hero is the prototype for his most powerful works of the 1960s and 1970s, *Wszystko na sprzedaż* [*Everything for Sale*, 1968] and *Man of Marble* as well as the weaker, somewhat ragged *Man of Iron*) and the early, flamboyantly surrealist films of Luis Buñuel. Welles' presence is the most explicit and frequently noted, evident in the low angles (with the visible ceilings) and the virtuoso deep-focus compositions elaborately planned by Wajda and his cameraman Jerzy Wójcik. One often-noted, particularly striking example of composition in depth is the zig-zag layering of planes as Andrzej, front right, telephones the major to report the assassination's supposed success; Maciek, middle distance, lounges left of screen by the bar; and Szczuka, the ostensible corpse, enters in the centre, furthest from the camera. Another important one places Krystyna serving in the bar mid-screen in the background as Maciek stands by the window and reiterates to Andrzej that there's nothing to hold him in Ostrowiec. Such compositions are not simply 'Baroque' but imply that one has to *look well* before acting. Maciek's weak eyes, the legacy of his stint in the Warsaw sewers, may be the fatal hindrance preventing the last survivor of *Kanal*'s decimated platoon living long. Deep focus has the ironic edge typical of Polish art, leaving everything in view in order warily to survey the horizon for dangers. It is conceptual totalisation of a contradictory situation, not Welles' intoxicated theatrical clutch (a visual inebriation often matched by slightly slurred speech) of the regal orb of the whole world. Its rhetoric implies that the camera tells the whole truth of the scene: telling *the whole truth* (or at least seeming to do so) becomes the rationale for deep focus after 'the thaw' of 1956. And, of course, deep focus is appropriate in a political film – just as it was in *Citizen Kane* – precisely because the continual disparity in size between figures, some looming large in the foreground, others small in the background, incessantly dramatises power relations. Wajda seems to endorse the Bazinian contention that deep focus enables spectators to roam within the image and so propagates freedom (Bazin 1967: 31–7) (an argument that overlooks the composition's direction of the eye); its use suits a work seeking to exploit the greater freedom 'the thaw' had afforded. In the end, meanwhile, *Ashes and Diamonds* retraces *Citizen Kane*'s shift of emphasis from the clarity of depth-of-field composition to the evocative etching of shadows – in this case, by the final flooding in of dawn. Here, as in *Citizen Kane*, the silhouetted figures have become shadows of themselves. Nevertheless, Wajda's low angles are not simply

Wellesian: their iconising enhancement of the authority of Szczuka addressing the workers may recall socialist realism.

BUÑUEL, SYMBOLISM AND SURREALISM

As significant as the influence of Welles is that of Buñuel. After *Ashes and Diamonds*, Wajda went on record as admiring both the Buñuel Polish officialdom would deem more palatable, that of *Los Olvidados* (1950), and the one it could not stomach, the author of *L'Age d'Or* (1930) (Wajda 1967: 235). Surrealism is liberated in *Ashes and Diamonds*, however ineffectual the liberation of Poland itself. Eric Rhode rightly categorised the flames bursting from the back of the man falling into the chapel as Buñuelian (Rhode 1966: 181), but so is much else in the film (for Krzysztof Teodor Toeplitz, for instance, Maciek's death recalls *Los Olvidados*) (Toeplitz 1958), particularly the treatment of religion. It begins with the camera moving down from a chapel's cross into the fallen world of the assassins, lounging in the grass (a virtuoso move from the vertical to the horizontal). One does not look up at the cross but slides down from it, like a dying man; it offers no support. This moment is worth closer consideration, for the mixed emotions brewed within it set the tone for the whole film. It is significant that Wajda and Andrzejewski utilise the probable religious affiliations of many Polish spectators to turn them against the figures most likely to have religious sympathies: the members of the Home Army. The killing of the man at the chapel door drives a wedge down the middle of the term *Polak-Katolik*, the Polish term for the post-Romantic conflation of patriotism and religiosity, dislocating patriotism from the Home Army to facilitate its relocation in Szczuka. Wajda the surrealist relishes the Buñuelian image; Wajda the propagandist mobilises it against his lead character. In one of the film's key dualities, Wajda identifies with an areligiosity he simultaneously condemns. Thus it is hardly surprising that he should have declared 'it is my belief that the film is aimed against people of Maciek's type, even though I myself could have been just such a boy', the final 'boy' (*chłopiec*) then mitigating the condemnation (Wertenstein 2000: 23). His position may well be the common post-war 'identification with the aggressor' of the young bourgeois, whose hard-bitten embrace of history's verdict upon himself and his own class generates the air of national tragedy, projecting the fate of the patriotic intelligentsia as that of the nation and the collapse of a world. What Tadeusz Lubelski describes as 'the pain of separation from myth' pervading the film (Lubelski 1992b: 46) may be that of the condemned man granted the luxury of suicide. *Ashes and Diamonds* both destroys myth and laments its destruction.

The downward slides of this opening sequence are the film's most typical camera movements, preprogrammed in a sense by the insistent low-angle focus on ceilings. What is up has to fall as the camera drips down fatalistically to moments of unpalatable, unavoidable shock: to the inverted crucifix of the ruined church or the two dead bodies near its altar. Only once is a downward slide positive, when the camera moves down Krystyna's back as she makes love to Maciek; the transformation of this movement's customary meaning briefly emphasises the transforming potential of love. One from flame to diamond here, the movement is generally one from flame to the residue of ash. The flames leaping from the dying man's back are echoed when Maciek and Andrzej light vodka glasses in memory of dead colleagues and a shot from behind places the flames ironically at their backs also. Entertaining the end of one's life is playing with fire, as Andrzej realises when telling Maciek *'we're* still alive'. Their life is flickering, however, and it may well be that only darkness will follow. Wajda's existentialism and critical association of religion with a compromised older generation mean he has little time for it. The enormous inverted crucifix in the ruins, the lovers behind it in long shot, mordantly fuses the Wellesian and the Buñuelian. The man who lambastes Maciek for repairing Krystyna's heel on an altar does so because two dead men lie sheeted nearby, not out of religious piety. In effect Wajda drives a wedge between the cult of the dead and the Catholic religion later overlaid upon it. The audience may deem that cult a metonymy of the Catholicism that absorbed it, but Wajda's purpose seems rather to be to scrape away the encrustations of a religion once imposed on Poland to leave only the cult of the dead. It is that cult that Maciek practises, not Catholicism.

The surreal moments in *Ashes and Diamonds* include the train behind Maciek's head as he prepares to leave – a De Chirico image – and his clasping of the washing to his chest as blood blooms through it: if the circular Ogiński polonaise 'Adieu a la patrie' at the close echoes the ending of Wyspiański's *Wedding*, as noted above, so does this image, which makes of Maciek a paler version of the same play's Straw Man with roses for a heart. The final shots then translate verbal statement into image in the manner of surrealism's simulacrum of the dreamwork, as Maciek stumbles across a literalised rubbish heap of history. On one level the sequence jars, the excessive legibility of its allegory reeking of the sort of tendentiousness surrealism itself displays at its more explicitly psychoanalytically inspired moments, and there is smugness in Wajda's discovery of the best of both worlds in the fusion of existentialist imagery and Party-line meaning. Ironically, the fusion is only apparent, for Maciek the Home Army remnant on history's scrap-heap in 1948 (the year of Andrzejewski's novel) is also 'the Polish James Dean', the existential representative of every young 'homme revolté' in 1956. 'Dans le vrai' emotionally, he is intellectually wrong; and the same may be true of Wajda's film. On one level, the values of pre-1945 Poland (including gentry culture's Russophobia) are under attack; on another, the attack extends to those who had tried to inculcate love of Big Brother between 1948 and 1955. The film thus functions on incompatible levels, gaining in richness what it loses in coherence.

Thus its most successful, and richest, pairing of the aesthetically striking and the political is its least legible (that is, most surreal) image, that of the white horse – Wajda's version of the carriage passing through the salon in *L'Age d'Or*. A many-layered metaphor, it appears both in the painting at Staniewicz's house and in the background, in the street, as Szczuka arrives at the Monopol; its simultaneous linkage with the aristocratic interior and the street owned by alien armies suggests an inherent contradictoriness and omnipresence. Its usage embodies vulgar Marxist derision of those who expected liberation from 'General Anders on a white horse' (it is riderless here); summons up the country barracks of Wajda's own childhood (autobiography); symbolises Poland (horses are strongly present in the late nineteenth-century Polish art whose iconography haunted Wajda, the one-time art student); has religious overtones (which intertwine with the political ones), recalling the Book of Revelation; and is also surrealist, *inexplicable* in narrative terms. The polysemic *irrationality* is the sign of its genuine adherence to surrealism even though in *Ashes and Diamonds* the surrealism is tempered by other elements – as it was to be in most of the work of Buñuel himself.

Meanwhile the most pervasive symbolic complex – more than a matter of individual *images chocs* – radiates from the flame discussed in part in the previous sub-section. As noted, the downward movement of the camera enacts a degradation, flame's passage to ash. Similarly, as the fireworks explode in celebration of the armistice, Szczuka sinks into Maciek's arms and the camera slides down to their reflection in a puddle. Their consequent apparent *rising* is deeply mysterious, as they wriggle like starry spermatozoa, new life paradoxically pullulating in the moment of death. Yet they also resemble the water snakes of 'The Rime of the Ancient Mariner'; for although the association would hardly have occurred to Wajda himself, an artistic affinity links his image with Coleridge's, for comparison with the Mariner is apposite: both he and Maciek bear the stigma of death. Maciek stands locked in an unwanted embrace whose tableau-like quality reinforces the frozen essence of horror, as if for a moment he has stepped outside the time of film, and so the film itself must do likewise (as if killing has opened a door onto a bad eternity). In this most genuinely tragic and Shakespearean of the film's sequences, he then starts 'like a guilty thing', casting aside the tell-tale gun, as the fireworks illumine a crime so seemingly shrouded in darkness: it is as if in fact they do not mark combat's end but have been sent up like enemy flares – trained like searchlights – to render him visible (and hence vulnerable). They suggest an apotheosis and allegorical monumentalisation of the Oedipal moment at which the son seals his own fate by sealing the father's. The reluctance to let him slip to the ground disavows the fact of mortality; the realisation that the father's demise places the son next in line to encounter death. The holding up of the dead may also be read in Girardian terms, as an attempt to appease the spirit of the murdered scapegoat, for Szczuka's personality clearly renders him an innocent substitute for the new régime. For Christopher Caes, the murder of the father is the price to be paid in order to embrace a man (Caes 2003: 128–9). One could add that it therefore figures the embrace as taboo. Could murdering the father even be seen as a way of preventing his departure, or as indicative of guilt about his death during absence – his son's inability to protect him (Wajda's inability to hold and save his own father) becoming, as in a bad dream, tantamount to his killing, or that death itself representing the fulfilment of unacknowledged negative feelings about him? Here Maciek himself would become a scapegoat, in this case for the good son Marek, the doubling between the two preserving the untarnished image of the latter. The mid-sequence cut that immediately precedes the tableau with the fireworks may seem awkward but can also represent a shift in the gears of consciousness, down towards zero. The scene is the final haunting conjugation of the complex linking death, flame, degradation and water and seen earlier in the ironic mirroring of the initial chapel shooting by Drewnowski's drunken wielding of the fire-extinguisher at the celebratory banquet. Drewnowski's reversal of Maciek's opening action is complete: where the film's first shots spat fire, the extinguisher releases only water, the sign of the unheroic new order. The camera need no longer slide down from flame to ash, for the dregs are rising. As Szczuka dies, though, the social irony of the earlier scene becomes cosmic, and the rising fireworks briefly disclose an irrepressible universal creativity; loss dialectically generates recovery as life rebounds from rock bottom, as scenes reverse and mirror each other in a process that is never-ending. The work passes from the surrealist allegory of the unconscious and the political allegory of such elements as the white horse to the poetically unreadable unconscious, a mythical imagistic intimation of infinity.

THE SCREENPLAY, THE CENSORS AND THE POLITICS OF DISTRIBUTION

Prior to the Andrzejewski-Wajda version, two attempts had been made to film *Ashes and Diamonds* (Lubelski 1994: 17685; FN S-2541 and S-1103). One script was written by Erwin

Axer immediately after the novel's release; the other, by Antoni Bohdziewicz, close on the heels of Axer. The former follows the novel very closely in the main, even quoting its descriptions extensively, and resembles an abridgement, albeit with several major changes, particularly to the ending. Axer avoids tragedy by accentuating the possibility of Home Army conversion. He adds a minor character, Guzek, whom the initial failed assassination appals and persuades to leave the group. Later Szczuka will invite him to receive a portion of the land being divided among the peasants. Despite Guzek's guilty allusions to his work for the other side, Szczuka exonerates him, piously placing cleansing soil on his hands. More importantly, Axer's Maciek meets Szczuka in his hotel room, then shields him from Andrzej's bullets. Axer's scenario dwells on the virtues of political co-operation, particularly between the PPR (Polska Partia Robotnicza – Polish Worker's Party) and the PPS (Polska Partia Socjalistyczna – Polish Socialist Party), shortly to fuse into the PZPR (Polska Zjednoczona Partia Robotnicza – Polish United Workers' Party). Antoni Kossecki both features and is condemned, despite his freeing in Andrzejewski's 1948 version (things would be different in the 1954 revision). For all the air of possible reconciliation, the image of the enemy is retained.

The non-realisation of Axer's script doubtless reflects the politically sensitive nature of the material. Bohdziewicz's script, meanwhile, foundered after his condemnation at the Wisła conference of 1949, his ostracism overshadowing its exemplary Stalinism. Its relationship with the novel is so self-confessedly loose as to be one of self-distancing from it: not only is there a new title ('Po wojnie' – After the War), but a note preceding the script's third and final version announces that it 'diverges from the novel … at all important points' (sic). The script is highly detailed, containing many precise descriptions of proposed camera placements. Two of the work's three days begin in that hub of socialist realism, the factory. The first shows workers awaiting the return of Gawlik and Smolarski, whose joint trip anticipates the unification of their two parties, the PPS and the PPR. Their assassination is no accident; Szczuka has not yet arrived in Kielce. Day two begins with a factory speech by him rallying the workers to class warfare, and his consolation of one of the widows. Bohdziewicz's Maciek doubts the Home Army cause long before meeting Krystyna, and his plea for release from duty is moved from the work's ending to its beginning. He has already traded in his army boots, desires a normal life and questions the killing of Gawlik and Smolarski. Andrzej doubts the viability of a second assassination immediately after the first, the security services now being on high alert. His superior, Waga, however, realises its value for his own career and lovingly counts the dollars given him to finance it by his own commanding officer, Iks (X). Maciek is the hapless, merely expendable instrument of higher-level manipulations, and Andrzej will threaten him with execution should he pull out. Krystyna, meanwhile, is Maciek's old schoolfriend, and praises Szczuka, whom she knows from a camp in Bavaria; he persuaded almost all its detainees to return to Poland, which is by no means the cemetery others had described but teems with new initiatives. She leads a theatrical troupe on tour, reads Maciek's sullen silences as signs of 'a pact with the devil', and herself warns Szczuka of the underground's intentions. As in Axer's version, Maciek finally shields Szczuka from Andrzej. He, Szczuka and Krystyna stand reverently beside the dead workers' grave at the end. It goes without saying that a film of this version would hardly have confirmed Poland's importance on the world's cinematic map.

On 15 November 1957 Wajda sent Andrzejewski a letter outlining his proposed adaptation of *Ashes and Diamonds* and mentioning three major points arising from it (Wertenstein [1991] 2000: 24–7). It shows that Wajda has already virtually completed his editing of the novel (the major excision being that of all the Kosseckis, except Andrzej), though the script follows the book more closely than the film does (indeed '*jak w książce*' ['as in the book'] is a recurrent phrase). Drewnowski is not yet present in the opening scene, timed at 17 minutes; Krystyna's aristocratic descent is developed in a conversation about her; while her cousin Fred Teleżyński still discusses his career options with her. The dancer Seiffert and his partner Kochańska are still present at the Monopol banquet, Hanka Lewicka's song does not yet coincide with the moment at which (as the outline puts it) 'Andrzej and Maciek talk about the good old days', and Krystyna is shown awaiting the train after Maciek's death. The script ends with the Monopol polonaise reaching the market as 'Long live Poland!' is shouted (the end of the seventh chapter in Andrzejewski's ten-chapter novel here closes the story). As yet, Szczuka has a 'secret' but no son. Wajda then raises three key points:

1   SZCZUKA – What should this figure look like on screen? Who is he? What mission is he pursuing? What is his secret? It would obviously be best if his mission were linked to the fate of the persecutors (he fights for their lives and they kill him). Something of the sort. One might consider his personal affairs but that does not do away with the need to resolve the issues raised above.
2   LOVE – Maciek-Krystyna. Condensed into a few hours what course will it follow? For it has to motivate Maciek's hesitations, crises and decisions.
3   EPISODES – Apart from this trio (Szczuka, Maciek, Krystyna) all the figures automatically become incidental – but their function in the drama is not just to picture the attitudes, characters, everything that makes up the image of Poland contained in this night. These figures must also play a part in the main plot, which is the killing of Szczuka. (Wertenstein 2000: 26)

Of the three main plot-lines Wajda proposes – those of Szczuka, who has 'something he must achieve this night'; of Andrzej and Maciek, 'who aim to kill Szczuka'; and of the Security Service, 'which aims to uncover the killers and protect Szczuka' – the final one vanishes almost entirely from the film, reflecting perhaps a desire to intensify the bipolar dramatic conflict as well as the difficulty of persuading spectators to view Security Service officers sympathetically. Wajda's outline suggests that the subsequent co-operation involved some concessions on his own part; it begins like the film, with Andrzej and Maciek 'lying on the grass waiting. A third person is watching the road', but the screenplay lodged with the Filmoteka narodowa in Warsaw places this scene later (Lubelski 1994: 185). That screenplay (FN S-22143) differs from the filmed version in various ways (for instance, it begins with the repair of Szczuka's jeep, the cause of his delay). The most prominent additions are two lengthy scenes with Szczuka's son: the first, his interrogation by a sympathetic Wrona, culminating in his identification through his over-enthusiastic signing of a drawing made with a captured SS man's pencil Wrona has loaned him; the second, his rebellious dialogue with Szczuka and final leap from a balcony window, which he nevertheless survives, later agreeing to see Szczuka again. Szczuka is shot while walking to this meeting, though without the film's embrace of killer and victim. The screenplay frequently places Maciek before mirrors, expands the cigarette motif (giving Maciek a pistol-shaped lighter), and – like the novel – replaces the revolver in his pocket with the violets associated with Krystyna; whence the consternation of the soldiers who find only crumpled violets in it, not the revolver for which they thought he was reaching. These proposed metaphors and recurrent objects barely hint at the film's eventual density of theme and *mise-en-scène*. The spirit glasses as votive candles, the painting behind Waga as he answers the telephone, the white horse, or the lodging of the workers' corpses in the ruined church – all these will come later. If a single principle can be said to have governed the shooting itself, it is the elimination of the more tendentious political elements still preserved by the screenplay, allowing a tighter focus on the intertwined tragedies of Maciek, Szczuka and Krystyna.

Before *Ashes and Diamonds* could become a film, however, the script required scrutiny by the Commission for Screenplay Assessment (Anon 1994b: 188–94). Its discussion occurred on 17 January 1958 and began with comments from Aleksander Ścibor-Rylski, later to become internationally renowned through his screenplay for Wajda's two *Man of...* films, who adjudged it well-composed and providing the basis for an interesting film. Nevertheless, he bemoaned some of the omissions of material in the novel, stating that they impoverished Maciek Chełmicki, Andrzej Kossecki and Szczuka in particular: the screenplay places Chelmicki in a bad light, while the excision of several of Andrzej's scenes – particularly his conversation with his younger brother – renders him less sympathetic, more one-dimensional. Ścibor-Rylski's strongest fire however was reserved for the attribution of a Home Army son to Szczuka, which he called a mistake and a theatrical trick. He also described the opening's depiction of Home Army executions as a trivialisation of serious matters, found the action's concentration in the Monopol hotel suffocating, and deemed some of the conversations over-long.

The next speaker, Andrzej Braun – a writer and literary director of the *'Droga'* (Road) film unit – feared that the 1947 novel's material might seem anachronistic in 1958 and felt that the preservation of unity of place was rather artificial and theatrical. The portrayal of Chełmicki particularly troubled him, as the character seemed too nonchalant, viewing murder as an adventure. His emotional conversion through his relationship with Krystyna is unconvincing. In general, the characterisation is shallower than in the novel. Nevertheless, he recommended acceptance of the screenplay.

The important and independent-minded film critic Krzysztof Teodor Toeplitz commented that the work was neither historical nor anachronistic. He felt that the screenplay shaped up as a modern-day version of Wyspiański's *The Wedding* and that the depiction of Szczuka needed to be more precise. In a brief exchange with Ścibor-Rylski and Braun he defended the characterisation of Chełmicki, whom the Occupation would have habituated to killing.

Tadeusz Konwicki, one of the key and most original novelists of the post-war period, saw the construction as following logically from its isolation of the book's theme of the question of Poland.

The Commission's Chairman, Tadeusz Karpowski – once described as a 'sceptical, aestheticising libertine' (Zajiček 1992: 148) – said his reactions to Chełmicki resembled Ścibor-Rylski's, but that he had explained this as the result of viewing him too much in the terms of the book. The early part seems alarmingly undramatic, with the 'hunting' of Szczuka generating little tension. He contrasted the ideological positions of book and screenplay: the former warning the People's authorities and portraying the futility of Home Army activities, the latter showing that the sole positive figures die, with only the rogues remaining – though he felt he might have misread the authors' intentions. (Andrzejewski later interjected that they had not intended such a judgement.)

There followed an exchange focused on Szczuka, Ścibor-Rylski repeating his dislike of the addition of a son, Andrzejewski stating that to remove his family conflicts would make him a paper figure, and director Jerzy Kawalerowicz voicing his own preference for a sonless Szczuka and his sense that he is less attractive to spectators than the would-be assassins.

Further exchanges revolved around the final scene's recollection of the ending of *The Wedding*, which Andrzejewski described as ironic rather than a sign of meaninglessness. Karpowski reiterated his view that the screenplay constituted a serious depiction of 'the tragedy of the communist and the tragedy of the younger generation', but that it ended with the victory of the canaille – though since no one else shared his fears in this respect (Konwicki saying there was nothing to fear from the film and Toeplitz denying that there would be a total moral condemnation of the remaining characters) he conceded their possible groundlessness. Discussion of that issue could resume once the film had been made. In the final contribution, Andrzejewski remarked that the original intention had been to space events across two days, but that this conception had not worked; although Braun felt that the final accent should fall on Chełmicki's death, the chosen concept required the polonaise as an ending. Karpowski concluded by noting the Commission's vote for the screenplay's acceptance.

Wajda himself spoke only once in the whole meeting, interjecting 'but in this respect the whole arsenal of solutions can be massive' into the middle of the discussion of the changes to Szczuka's role.

The Wajda-Andrzejewski screenplay may streamline the novel, but the film's most pungent moments were improvised on the set, which became the site of creative freedom, away from the reach of censors. Tadeusz Lubelski lists the originators of several such moments: Szczuka's fall into Maciek's arms and Maciek's fumbling for his pistol's pin were Cybulski's suggestions, the spirit glasses' transformation into graveside candles came from Janusz Morgenstern, while Wajda himself – as might be expected – furnished such spectacularly 'Baroque' elements as the inverted crucifix, the white horse and the rubbish-dump death (Lubelski 1994: 186). For Wajda, Adam Pawlikowski's comment on the rushes – 'actors never played this fast in a Polish film' – reflects the energy crackling around its participants: 'we were never as effective as when we made *Ashes and Diamonds*' (Lubelski 1990: 22). The heat melted away such dross as Andrzejewski's final line – that 'most duplicitous of texts' (Wajda) – which was originally preserved and even shot but discarded during editing. Also deleted were Wrona's explanation of the Security Office's work and a meeting of the Party's Town Council (Lubelski 1994: 185). The majority of these cuts may be attributed to a combined 'cinematic' preference for action over verbalisation and suspicion of the ideology being verbalised, while the shrinkage of the role of Szczuka's son economically reflects his – and Wajda's – absorption by his twin, Maciek.

The next hurdles confronting the film concerned its release (Czeszejko-Sochacka 1981: 31–2). Initially there seemed to be no problems with its distribution, which was cleared by Tadeusz Zaorski of the Ministry of Culture and Art, which in 1957 had gained responsibility for Polish cinema (previously answerable to the Chairman of the Council of Ministers) as a result of the changes begun in 1956. Jerzy Lewiński, a high-ranking official in the Polish film establishment and later adviser to the Ministry of Culture and Art, described what happened next in the following terms:

> However, before an official première could be set, I received a phone call from the Minister of Culture and Art, Tadeusz Graliński. Somewhat uncomfortable, he said that various comments had come to his attention concerning the political message of *Ashes and Diamonds*. He felt that a screening should be arranged involving a wide range

of political and cultural activists and representatives of the film milieu, followed by a discussion. The screening took place with about forty people attending. The discussion was turbulent, though nobody denied the high artistic quality of Wajda's work. Several of the invited Party activists had something to say about what was then called 'the film's resonance'. But I recall that Włodzimierz Sikowski, Helena Jaworska, General Bednarz and Stefan Żółkiewski felt that the political message of *Ashes and Diamonds* essentially coincided with that of Andrzejewski's novel. After this screening, the official première took place in October 1958 and *Ashes and Diamonds* went into distribution without any problems. (Czeszejko-Sochacka 1981: 31)

Nevertheless, matters did not end there. Aleksander Ford, the grand old man of Polish cinema, said that the film could only create enemies of socialism (Zajiček 1992: 158). Wajda himself mentions Andrzejewski's mounting of a special screening to win over his artistic colleagues in the Party and counter the opposition of the likes of Ford, which either preceded the screening Lewiński mentions or constitutes a faulty recollection of who organised that screening itself. Wajda also mentions a last-minute anonymous telephone call from someone identifying himself as a censor and recommending that Wajda himself go to the projection booth of the 'Moskwa' cinema and cut Maciek's death-throes before they could be screened (Wajda 2000a: 105). And when the director of the Cannes festival requested its submission to the competition of 1959 and Lewiński recommended this to his superiors, they proposed several cuts, which Wajda refused to make. They particularly asked for a shortening of Maciek Chełmicki's death-spasms, arguing that their prolongation only generated sympathy for someone deserving of unequivocal condemnation. Lewiński adds that the interpretation of the deaths of Szczuka and Chełmicki as a 'shared social tragedy … was difficult for some representatives of the authorities to accept at that time' (Czeszejko-Sochacka 1981: 32). Permission to show at Cannes was refused, though Lewiński was allowed to take it to the Venice Biennale, for showing *hors concours*, the official Polish entry being Jerzy Kawalerowicz's *Pociąg* (*The Train*, 1959). *Ashes and Diamonds* received a great ovation, however, along with the FIPRESCI prize – and as head of the Polish delegation Lewiński had to explain to the nonplussed Polish authorities how a film not in competition could receive an award.

RECEPTION

In the early Polish reviews of Wajda's film, Marek Hendrykowski argues, awareness of its artistry is clouded by efforts to discern the nature of its final allegiance (Hendrykowski 1984: 74). And yet in actuality review after review displays a split personality, beginning with unabashed praise of the film's aesthetic achievement and the enumeration of successful (and one or two unsuccessful) scenes, only subsequently voicing misgivings about its ideology – or usual perceived lack of clear ideological positioning.

Unsurprisingly, the most arresting review is that of Zygmunt Kałużyński (1958), Poland's brilliant, erratic critical *enfant terrible*. Establishing one of the leitmotifs of the film's discussion, Kałużyński notes Maciek's centrality, then makes a move other critics would reject – attributing Maciek not to the Home Army but to the NSZ (Narodowe Siły Zbrojne – National Armed Forces), which Nicholas Bethell describes as 'a more right-wing, fascist-style group, some of whose members had collaborated with the Nazis' (Bethell 1972: 106). (Maciek's affiliation is, indeed, never spelled out, though his widespread attribution to the Home Army – the majority organisation – reflects his perceived representativeness and the sympathy he evokes.) Ironically, although Kałużyński laments the film's attachment to an outdated schematic view of the immediate post-war period, while 'today we can afford a deeper interpretation', this identification of Maciek's allegiance echoes Stalinist denunciations of his 'fascism'. For Kałużyński the film offers not historical reconstruction but a deliberately synthetic portrait of the entirety of disoriented post-war youth, fusing elements of 1945 with such mid-1950 anachronisms as Maciek's dark glasses and 'Juliette Gréco-style' sweater. Kałużyński notes Maciek's possession of the 'soft, sensuous, powerless charm' of Brando and Dean. Overall, the film combines two disparate elements: 'a simplified political motivation with a surrealistic refinement of the means of expression'.

Janusz Wilhelmi (1958) – later to become a hardline Minister of Culture in the late 1970s before dying in a plane crash – responds to Kałużyński by stressing the historical accuracy of such props as the sweater and dark glasses (the former being an English wartime one, the latter indeed the kind worn by persons with damaged eyesight) and contesting his ascription of Maciek to the NSZ. Wajda and Andrzejewski correctly show Maciek and Andrzej as 'victims, driven into a blind alley by politics and leaders, by a misconceived fidelity, by the moods of their milieu and moment'. He doubts that Szczuka defeats them. Viewers who think this is the case actually 'reach for arguments the work passes over in silence'. (Similar comments on the film's unwillingness or inability to fill in certain gaps appear in several reviews, as well as in analyses of Andrzejewski's original novel [Błoński 1978: 237–43].) Because 'Maciek does not say "my way is wrong" but "I no longer have the strength to go that way"' the clash of political stances remains unresolved. The work lacks historical contextualisation, omitting the communists' labour of reconstruction. It is thus 'not a national drama but only the initial sketch of one – and is perhaps incomplete because it is the first'.

Nevertheless, for Aleksander Jackiewicz (1958) – one of the most respected film critics of People's Poland – the work is indeed 'the fullest artistic vision of modern history since *The Wedding*', an example of art that is free but not devoid of ideology. Jackiewicz suggests that Wajda's first films constitute a trilogy by describing *Ashes and Diamonds* as the third act in a generational story: 'Wajda accuses nobody'; unlike Andrzej Munk, he does not even accuse history, for 'there is no distinction between history and the man'. Instead one has 'historical man', whom Wajda always shows 'in the hour of trial'. 'Maciek is probably the most complex figure in our contemporary art', largely because of his rapid shifts between such contradictory moods as cruelty and tenderness. Jackiewicz praises those moments in the film that resist description, such as the probably improvised ones of Andrzej and Maciek simply passing time together. He mentions criticisms of the relative artistic weakness of Szczuka but argues that any development of the figure would have overshadowed Maciek, who is the film's protagonist. He anticipates rewatching it and discerning further riches.

For Krzysztof Teodor Toeplitz (1958) – alongside Jackiewicz the other key critic of the formation known as People's Poland – *Ashes and Diamonds* represents a turning point, a rejection of the 'contemporary escapism' that imagines it can abandon 'the Polish question'. Toeplitz describes the work's project as rationalist, intending to bring dark matters into the light. Its sympathy for both camps creates a final impression of 'honesty and justice', devoid of 'false objectivism' precisely because 'although the sympathies are evenly distributed, the arguments are not': 'Maciek is wrong and Szczuka is right'. For while 'it is not hard to agree with a hero one loves; it is incomparably more difficult to deny that a dearly loved person is right'. Nevertheless, 'Wajda does not carry certain motifs to their conclusion', and has the somewhat simple belief that people get the fate they deserve. This both reduces the sense of tragedy and impels Wajda 'dangerously towards symbolism', which outweighs reality in the film's latter portions in particular; these fall below the level of its best elements (among which Toeplitz singles out the characterisation of Maciek, Andrzej and Krystyna). Wajda manages to tap Polish national traditions whilst avoiding their military kitsch.

'ART CINEMA' AND THE POLITICS OF OPEN-ENDEDNESS

At the beginning of his eloquent, influential article 'The Art Cinema as a Mode of Production' David Bordwell mentions two Polish films, *Ashes and Diamonds* and Roman Polański's *Nóż w wodzie* (*Knife in the Water*, 1961), alongside such other 'art films' as Federico Fellini's *La Strada* (1954), Ingmar Bergman's *Persona* (1966), François Truffaut's *Jules et Jim* (1962), Jean-Luc Godard's *Vivre sa vie* (1962) and Alain Resnais' *Muriel* (1963) (Bordwell 1979: 56). And yet the 'art cinema' category is surely inadequate for these Polish works, designating the mechanism of their Western distribution rather than their essence. *Within Poland*, Polish cinema was both 'art' and populist, reaching over the heads of self-proclaimedly socialist rulers to appeal to popular sentiment, using the Aesopian procedures that secreted meaning in invisible ink between the lines. Nevertheless, Bordwell may be partly right, as the work of Wajda – and many other East European directors – seems to offer the possibility of a political cinema that is less the enemy of 'art cinema' (as the historical-materialist film born of Brecht would be) than compatible with it. But how can the rhetorical suasion so characteristic of the one form (monologism?) be reconciled with the open-endedness (dialogism?) Bordwell deems characteristic of the other?

In art cinema, Bordwell notes, the spectator leaves the auditorium thinking. It is indeed a matter of *thinking* – a process – not the unwrapping of the single pre-determined meaning lodged between image one and image two by an Eisenstein, who may permit spectatorial activity in the sense of deduction of a third element – the idea – but assumes it will always arrive at the same conclusion. (As the legendary, perhaps mythical, 'Kuleshov effect' proclaims, the face of Mozhukin plus an empty plate simply means 'hunger'.) By short-circuiting such unanimity, an art cinema committed to ambiguity may be felt to preclude the political – and so be susceptible of denunciation by historical-materialist filmmakers. Hence it is worth considering how one early review of *Ashes and Diamonds* – not the work of one of Poland's most prominent critics, but useful precisely because it is not path-breaking but summarises and responds to the fortnight's debate following the film's release – seeks to justify the film's position outside the canons of socialist realist art whilst arguing that even though it permits us to decide (as in 'art cinema', Bordwell might say, though the term would be anachronistic) it nevertheless requires one particular decision (as obvious, say, as 'choose life' to all except the protagonists of *Trainspotting* [1996]). Thus this reviewer, Eugeniusz Boczek (1958) notes how hard it is to refuse sympathy to Maciek Chełmicki, even though he is 'on the wrong side'; 'The spectator has to decide for himself [but] despite emotional engagement on the side of the negative hero, he must withhold approval of the motives of his action.' In their avoidance of stereotypes the artists set themselves a harder task – and so achieve a greater triumph – than the creators of 'the gallery of repulsive types who frequented the screen earlier'. (The fact that the justified critique of socialist realist practices sits oddly alongside such a socialist realist phrase as 'the negative hero' indicates the contradictoriness of Boczek's position, one common among Party activists seeking to rationalise the film's appeal.) The measure of Wajda's and Andrzejewski's success is the fact that 'for all their sympathy for Maciek, no spectators will ascribe ideological correctness to his behaviour'. Similarly, those spectators who object that the depiction of the political struggle denies Szczuka decisive victory also miss the point, for 'it is not true – as some would have it – that the representatives of both camps, Maciek and Szczuka, have been defeated'. Whereas in Maciek's case both the man and his cause have lost, although Szczuka dies the ideas of the communist cause triumph. Boczek concludes: 'People filed out of the auditorium silent and thoughtful. Each had lived through the represented reality for himself, matched it against his own experience, classified the reasons. I am convinced that there need be no doubt about the result of this classification.'

Various PZPR activists were not so sure however (Gębicka 1998: 135), doubtless worried lest the concession of freedom to spectators undermine the Party's continued control. For in the East European case, at least the mystery of open-endedness was no merely existential or bourgeois mystification but rather the gift of freedom to the viewer. The open-ended work sustained dreams of freedom (in Bakhtin's terms, dialogism) even when those dreams were contradicted both by oppression without and by its own lip-service to oppression, its dues paid to Caesar. The repeated references in reviews of *Ashes and Diamonds* to the need for spectators to fill in gaps indicate a widespread perception of its open-endedness. And however aesthetically modern the effect of such irresolution, it was felt to be rooted in the impossibility of saying certain things – to be motivated more politically than aesthetically.

THE AFTERLIFE OF *ASHES AND DIAMONDS*

Ashes and Diamonds has a varied afterlife in Wajda's work, haunting it first as an unrepeatable, successful moment, then – after 1989 – as a compromised one. Successive Wajda films will revisit its iconography (*Lotna* [1959]), lead actor (*Everything for Sale*) and historical moment (*Landscape After a Battle*), before finally seemingly disowning it (*The Horse-Hair Ring*).

First the iconography. The white horse Wajda says merely wandered into the frame in *Ashes and Diamonds* (Douin 1981: 38) is firmly centered in *Lotna*, where it fatally kindles the mimetic desire of a group of *uhlans* during the rout of September 1939. Although it has been argued that both the swift horse ('Lotna' means 'the swift one') and the film's other symbols, unlike those of *Ashes and Diamonds*, are depressingly univocal (Helman 1959: 3), and although Wajda's own recurrent wish to reshoot this film casts it as a failure requiring reconfiguration, it cannot be dismissed so easily. However univocal or perversely paradoxical the film's other symbols (apples in a coffin, the emblematic Polish eagle in flames), the horse itself is as obscurely unreadable as it had been in the previous film. That unreadability may fascinate spectators almost as much as the horse did the *uhlans* who die on its receipt. The gift of death, it is no simple allegory of Poland.

Wajda's next return to *Ashes and Diamonds* would be in mourning for Zbigniew Cybulski. *Everything for Sale*, his most personal – and only personally scripted – film shudders with the aftershock of the actor's appalling death, constituting a guilty dream of an impossible film about a dead Actor who is the unnamed equivalent of Cybulski. In the early 1960s, when Wajda had ceased using Cybulski, the actor is rumoured to have said 'one day he'll yearn for me'. In *Everything for Sale*, Wajda seeks to console himself by adopting Daniel Olbrychski, who appears under his own name, as a new fetish. Whether or not the character Daniel participates in the Director's proposed film remains uncertain; after confirming the truth of the Actor's cynically doubted wartime experiences he announces that he will not participate, but nevertheless the next day he appears on the set – all the same, he flees the re-enactment of the Actor's accident in pursuit of a clutch of horses. The famous vodka-glass scene of *Ashes and Diamonds* is reprised: Daniel unwittingly enters a bar in the manner of the dead Actor, sporting a leather jacket over his pullover; indeed, the jacket the cloakroom attendant hands him had been the Actor's. He lights a vodka glass as the man beside him at the bar advising him to act in the dead Actor's style sings 'his pals aren't sorry he's gone'. Wajda's irony here – against both self and others – is biting, but Daniel's *unconscious* imitation of the Actor holds out the tantalising possibility of his spirit remaining, thereby justifying Wajda's decision to turn the camera on Daniel as he runs beside horses at the film's end.

After refusing to step directly into the shoes of Cybulski in *Everything for Sale*, Olbrychski ironically found himself partly insinuated into them in *Landscape After a Battle*, which filters elements of *Ashes and Diamonds* through a Lévi-Straussian mythical machine of inversion and transformation. Here too one has the immediate legacy of the war for the young: bespectacled intellectual Tadeusz (Olbrychski), now liberated from a concentration camp, is held with other Poles in a Displaced Persons camp run by the American military. Here he meets and falls in love with a Jewish girl emigrating from Poland. His remarks on the grotesqueness of surviving a war only to die immediately afterwards recall Maciek Chełmicki's fate. He is an anti-Chełmicki. Although he, like Maciek, behaves provocatively in a church (aggressively smelling the hair of the German girl praying there) the lines about a return to normal life and study are not his but the girl's, as if his utterance of them would rupture the taboo on donning Cybulski's shoes. This time it is the girl who dies sacrificially, accidentally shot by American soldiers. Not only is Tadeusz an anti-Maciek; the film is the verso of *Ashes and Diamonds*, dramatising the post-war encounter of Poles, Germans and Americans in the West, rather than Poles, Russians and Soviet-sponsored politicians in the East. The safe, easy caricature of the Americans, however, is as unsatisfactory as the Russians' shadowiness in *Ashes and Diamonds*, and – unfortunately – far more central.

After 1989 – ironically, like Andrzejewski after 1956 – Wajda himself would seem also to disown *Ashes and Diamonds* in *The Horse-Hair Ring*, based on a novel by Aleksander Ścibor Rylski – Wajda's scriptwriter on *Man of Marble* and *Man of Iron* – that had lain unpublished since the 1960s. It is as if it had become a narrative perhaps so compromised as to compromise all who tell and retell it. For it is tempting to describe *The Horse-Hair Ring* as a frustrated dreamwork upon *Ashes and Diamonds*. Warsaw Uprising officer cadet Marcin disbands his unit as the Red Army enters and in the process becomes separated from his girlfriend Wiśka, who gives him a ring with a crowned eagle, the emblem of fidelity to herself, the Home Army and inter-war Poland. Trying to serve Poland from within the new order, Marcin effectively suffers symbolic castration as a security officer files the crown from the eagle (as Freud noted often occurred among his patients, and as one might expect in a film from the Wajda who has always marginalised sexuality, the castration is 'displaced upwards'). Marcin watches helplessly as ex-Home Army fighters are rounded up and their leaders lured to negotiations that end in arrest. Near the film's end, Marcin and Janina, the nurse who tended his war wounds, wander into a bar. Across the room the famous *Ashes and Diamonds* scene in which Maciek and Andrzej commemorate lost comrades by lighting vodka glasses like candles is unfolding with lookalikes. The re-enactment is grotesque and excruciating, and not simply because the Cybulski impersonator replicates gestures whose animating spirit he lacks. Wajda's work is not to be deemed an exercise in self-criticism, however. He may describe it as his farewell to the Polish school ('B.J.' 1993: 2–3), but he also termed it 'nostalgic' and denies having carried out any *volte face vis-à-vis Ashes and Diamonds*. If post-Romantic Polish art's combination of an interest in self-division with political impulses is possibly confusing, throughout Wajda's career the potential problem has been scotched by a division of labour that gave full rein to the theme of self-division in the aesthetic sphere only (*Everything for Sale*) while explicitly political works accorded self-criticism a minor role (Wajda's own name as assistant director on the fictive piece of 1950s propaganda in *Man of Marble*). Wajda's telling of the story of Home Army persecution *Ashes and Diamonds* never told breathes a tragic sense of his, and his own muzzled generation's, past inability to tell it. For some Polish critics the re-enactment casts a searchlight into the earlier film, belatedly highlighting its pathetic inadequacy to the history it ostensibly figured, but it can also be seen to rescue it by allowing its representation by its most authentic moment: that of the mourning it prolongs in a new situation. Resurrecting the scene is less a *mea culpa* than another act of mourning. Janina and Marcin are present like the unseen conjured spirits of the vodka glasses, no more able to influence events than Wajda can the past, at whose scars he tears masochistically. Indeed Marcin has the dreamer's helplessness throughout, and Wiśka's final return is oneirically improbable. Seeing the ring uncrowned, she hurls it aside, and Marcin kills himself. This ending itself revises an earlier one in which Marcin simply disappeared in a crowd. For Wiktor Woroszylski, the revisions have the effect of removing the ambiguities of the book's close (Woroszylski 1993: 11). (Bożena Janicka, however, wonders if any ending would have been satisfying [Janicka 1993: 12–13].) The film is all the more potentially distressing for Wajda's inability to make the actors his own, as he once had Cybulski: Adrianna Biedrzyńska, Mirosław Baka and Wojciech Klata truly live for the present in Kieślowski's films, not this one. As if aware of this at some level, Wajda cannily re-enacts the vodka-glass scene, rather than quoting it directly, lest its reality denounce the artistic inadequacy of the new film. Apparently political, it is in fact deeply personal – as personal as a dream. And that dreamlike status, not its fatal attachment to a past jettisoned in 1989, was surely the main cause of its failure to find an audience. Jarosław Kajdański, writing in *Tygodnik Solidarność*, felt it had not been 'bought' either by those who viewed the entire nation as having collaborated in People's Poland or by those 'to whom the main protagonist's attitude had never been a close one' (Kajdański 1993). Ironically, the art of forgetting deemed so typical of totalitarianism by Milan Kundera flourishes more rapidly in once-totalitarian countries whose desperate eagerness to make up for lost time causes sweeping dismissals of the past. Romanticism and surrealism may liken artworks to dreams, but here as elsewhere analogy indicates crucial difference as well as similarity; dreams only ever enter the public sphere in mutilated form, bereft of the overwhelming sense of significance they possessed in the mind and eyes of the dreamer. *The Horse-Hair Ring* shows Wajda as helpless dreamer, not artist.

The extent to which *Ashes and Diamonds* haunts Polish cinema can be seen in its generation of two strong counter-statements: Wojciech Has's *How to be Loved* and Kazimierz Kutz's *Nikt nie woła* (*Nobody Calls*, 1960). Has's film is analysed later in this book, in connection with a discussion of the work of Zbigniew Cybulski, so the focus here will be upon Kutz's work.

Kutz's visually experimental film presents an alternative life for a figure in the same position as Maciek Chełmicki. Had he not killed Szczuka, he might have arrived in the Western territories known as the 'Recovered Lands', a displaced person travelling on the roof of a train, like Kutz's Bożek. Bożek pursues a sultry, on-off love affair with another refugee, Lucyna, fearing meanwhile lest the underground to which he belonged catch up with him and avenge his refusal to attack communists. With the appearance of Zygmunt, an ex-colleague in the resistance, his fears seem to have materialised, but – ironically – Zygmunt himself is ill and afraid of Bożek. Since both wish merely to live in peace, the text poises neatly between a restatement and a deconstruction of the official (Andrzejewski's *Ashes and Diamonds*) image of an underground whose internecine internal strife is merely the logical extension of its 'fratricidal' attack upon Polish communists; for all the backward glances of Bożek and Zygmunt, there is no sign of real pursuit or threat. *Nobody Calls* is haunted by the phantoms of half-grasped allegorical significance generated by its deliberate crafting as a counter-statement to a work that is itself profoundly ambiguous. Thus the story's half-repression of the Poles' sense of loss of their Eastern territories, evident in such details as Lucyna's preference for Ukrainian barszcz and Russian songs and dances, deepens an atmosphere of the cryptic intensified still further by the anticipations of the art cinema stagings of Antonioni, Bergman and even Tarkovsky (the many ruined walls). Bożek's lack of a 'pioneering instinct' (Iskierko *et al.* 1980: 107) breathes unspoken, unspeakable melancholy over that loss. As if he were Maciek justifying to the Polish people his refusal to 'shoot at reds' (as he puts it at the beginning), Bożek tells Lucyna that he is no hero and that she expects too much of him. His splitting between three women suggests a Maciek disoriented by his Oedipal flight from a destiny, and in the end he leaves town as he arrived, still fleeing the Erinnyes of national conscience that are invisible to anyone else. Since he departs without Lucyna, it is almost as if the nation will grant him his life, but will not allow him any reward for his choice. The demands of both Party and people are half-satisfied and half-frustrated.

CONCLUSION: DOUBLE PERSONALITY

If *Ashes and Diamonds* can seem to occupy two political positions simultaneously, this is very much in the tradition of Polish Romantic art. The motif of double personality recurs across the discourse of the Polish Romanticism inaugurated by Adam Mickiewicz, the greatest of Poland's Romantic poets, the theme in fact reflecting both politic political self-concealment and its corrosion of the self biding its time. Where the price of speaking out is silence, deferring speech until less drastic sanctions apply is indeed advisable. All the same, guilt over one's silence can cause irascible hypersensitivity to criticism from without, lest it reinforce the nagging inner voice of self-reproach and deepen self-division. That division could be approached through Sartrean dissection of the false outworks of selfhood behind which the true self is secreted. Such analysis has the advantage of sharing the anti-psychoanalytic premises of those Polish 'committed' artists for whom any admission of the possible reality of an unconscious would simply augment the external enemy with one within, making the self a divided house doomed to fall. It is thus hardly surprising, for instance, that the concept 'socialist realism' evaporated almost overnight after 1956: it belonged to a false self that could be dropped like the conspiratorial mask of Konrad Wallenrod, that Mickiewicz hero who joins his enemies' ranks to lead them to the slaughter at the appointed time.

After 1989 Wajda himself would seem to disown his film of *Ashes and Diamonds*. And yet, for all that Tadeusz Lubelski is surely right to argue that 'the things that are false about the film by no means determine the authorial position inscribed within it' (Lubelski 1992b: 21). *Ashes and Diamonds* may strike notes of both 'falsity' and 'truth', purveying both official satirical anti-Home Army propaganda through Eisensteinian montage and Wellesian *mise-en-scène* on the one hand, *and* Polish affection for the Home Army on the other – but it is not evenly divided between them. Rather its life is in its truth, that is, in the riveting presence of Cybulski-Chełmicki (the embodiment of the doomed Home Army and the touchstone of the reality of its commitments) and in its most arresting sequences, flung forth by the work's centrifuge – plucked as it were, like brands from the burning of official ideology. In other words – in the terms of the existentialism mentioned above – *Ashes and Diamonds* finally dispels its own bad faith, and its key sequences are a searing wind, dispersing the ash. What remains is the authentic, the diamond, or such diamonds as the deeply mysterious image of the falling fireworks *rising* in the puddle's reflection, the mourning beside the vodka glasses, or the white horse wandering in the rain. Such scenes represent art's power to generate myths from broken traditions: the bitter, Nietzschean consolation of the aesthetic in the face of political despair.

CHAPTER TWO

TYPICAL STORIES? (SOCIALIST? REALISM?)

POLITICS, AESTHETICS AND SOCIALIST REALISM

This book speaks of politics and aesthetics in the cinema of post-war Poland. If 'politics' comes first, this is partly because the political world always frames and interrupts the aesthetic, like the history that repeatedly frustrates the performance of 'Golfo the Shepherdess' in Theo Angelopoulos' *O Thiassos* (*The Travelling Players*, 1975), as air raids or members of one party pursuing cast-members of another disrupt it unceremoniously. It is also because within the Poland of the last two centuries, art itself generally functioned as a domain of disguised political argument within a public sphere of occupation and disenfranchisement of most Poles themselves. The binary opposition of politics and the aesthetic is deconstructed from the outset by the former's infiltration of the latter. It is also, as Walter Benjamin would have said, deconstructed by the overlaying of the former by the latter in the fascism that replaces debate with spectacle and history with the utopia of supposedly reconciled opposites, which may be said to be the case in both the 'red fascism' of Stalinism and the more obviously, indeed self-proclaimedly, black one; after all, the two colours were co-present on the roulette wheel used by all the gamblers on twentieth-century history. Meanwhile, both binaries are themselves fissiparous. The aesthetic, for instance, subdivides into the realistic and the fantastic. The realistic habitually presents itself as a *parti pris* for the political, usually the left: realism is close cousin to the materialism that derides metaphysics (but also – and here the theory of socialist realism encounters severe problems – to an oppositional spirit that resists standardisation and collectivisation). This realism also denies its own internal split between the descriptive and the melodramatic: since unadulterated description would be tedious, the spice of melodrama (primarily, of heroes and villains, which in this case means 'progressive' and 'regressive' forces) is indispensable. But the presence of the melodramatic is repressed, becoming the political unconscious of the text, lest it compromise the strategically crucial claim of realism, the effective, vote-winning simulation of veracity by verisimilitude. Few realist texts can dispense with either melodrama or fantasy. Even Vittorio De Sica's *Ladri di biciclette* (*Bicycle Thieves*, 1948), which approaches the squaring of the circle Bazin said it had achieved (Bazin 1972: 51) – that of an implicit politics – is realism with a *nero* ('flaw'), as the critics of neo-realism quipped: the suggestion of a demonisation of the lumpenproletariat partakes of melodrama and of a distinction between the 'deserving' and 'the undeserving' poor; the apparent and inexplicable fulfilment of La Santona's prophecy regarding the speed with which boy and father will find the thief is a dark, unexplored tunnel to the fantastic; and the evocations of a mysterious system are almost Kafkaesque. Most realism is even less disinterested, and if the lack of objectivity is clear and up-front in socialist realism's refusal to conceal its political allegiances, the very shrillness of its melodrama swamps the realism to the point of being the arguable source of the movement's falsity. The lack of concealment may also be an artlessness that denies not only art but the art of realism in particular, for which the classical dictum *ars est celare artem* ('true art is to conceal art') could well have been coined anachronistically. This is perhaps hardly surprising: a Marxism that declares the impossibility of objectivity amidst an absolute sovereignty of interests quickly dispels the shoots or residues of disinterestedness found in merely realistic description, deeming them accidental tourists on the battlefield of history; the Balzacian description of a door is stripped of its fascination by the sheer *haeccitas* of the object and the challenge of matching the relative abstraction of language with the materiality of the concrete – an operation that seeks to 'suspend polarities' in the same way as mist mediates between wet and dry – and becomes instead exclusively an array of labels. To utilise the terms of another, perhaps too-hallowed, ancient opposition: the potentialities of the poetic are overlaid with the certainties of prose, the symbol with a sign that always means one thing. The falsity of socialist realism in Poland is inherent not just in its status as an alien import (doubly alien, because originating both in the nineteenth century and the age-old enemy, the Slavic Big Brother) but in its own contradictoriness, allowing one to term it the utopia that dare not speak its name – the acme of politico-aesthetic bad faith. The historical linkage of realism and dissent makes of state realism a contradiction in terms.

In its original, Soviet version, 'socialist realism', as Edward Możejko has shown, had two pillars: Marx's eleventh thesis on Feuerbach, which stated that whereas the philosophers had merely explained the world, the task was to transform it; and Leninist reflection theory (Możejko 2001: 34). Since Marx's thesis postulates action to shape reality, while the latter privileges passivity with regards to reality, the practice of socialist realism was suffused with contradiction from the outset. One such contradiction is the ironic accusation directed against Polish socialist realist films: one of actual divergence from reality, a state of affairs Piotr Zwierzchowski attributes to the imperative that the work conform to the Marxist theoretical model of historical development (Zwierzchowski 2000a: 39–41). Quite apart from its silence regarding the way typicality was supposed to bridge the gap (become the key form of mediation) between work and reality, though, this critique begs the question of the relationship between 'reality' and all artworks, ignoring the status of every 'reality' as a variable 'image of reality' filtered through different systems of signs and belief. Given the differential framing of reality by artistic conventions, there is no a priori reason why a work's 'unreality' should cause the artistic failure widely associated with socialist realism: its products could, after all, be called successful fantasies or utopias. The unmentioned and genuinely fatal problems may be two: the vastness of the gap between the specificity of photographic representation and the abstract types the actors were to embody; and the refusal to admit utopian status. Moreover, whereas literature had a greater a priori chance of suspending disbelief in the theory's abstract agenda, its own signs being already partly abstract and drawing the addressee into co-creation and co-concretion of a world, cinema is far removed from the origin of theatre in mask, and the fact of its own abstraction is itself masked by the greater general (indexical) closeness of signifier to signified in film than in any other art-form. In film, socialist realist abstraction rides roughshod over the concretion of the individuals presented on screen: the attempted collectivisation of their individuality liquidates the particular actor, leaving only a label attached to a mobile hole in the air. It is ironic that socialist realist theory should have emerged only after the demise of silent cinema, as that cinema's acting practices frequently involved an exaggeration and stereotyping of emotion that pushed the individual actor's body in the direction of a univocal allegorical sign whose instant legibility may be described as the prerequisite for the rapid cutting of an Eisenstein, typicality being the bedfellow of typage. The Stalin era's chronic critical discontent with any and every example of a socialist realist film (Zwierzchowski 2000a: 48) nicely mirrors the films' own discontent with the concretion of a world to which the photograph adheres even after peeling off from it. No mere artwork could ever achieve the degree of generalisation of (the) theory. No wonder – as we will see later – that György Lukács takes a work of philosophy (Plato's *Symposium*) as the starting point of his discussion of artistic typicality.

One of the most interesting, if tantalisingly brief, discussions of socialist realism in recent years has been that of Lev Manovich:

> Socialist realism wanted to show the future in the present by projecting the perfect world of future socialist society onto a visual reality familiar to the viewer – the streets, interiors and faces of Russia in the middle of the twentieth century – tired and under-fed, scared and exhausted from fear, unkempt and gray. Socialist realism had to retain enough of then-everyday reality while showing how reality would look in the future when everybody's body would be healthy and muscular, every street modern, every face transformed by the spirituality of communist ideology. This is how socialist real-ism differs from pure science fiction, which does not have to carry any feature of today's reality into the future. In contrast, socialist realism had to superimpose the future on the present, projecting the communist ideal onto the very different reality familiar to viewers. (Manovich 2001: 203)

Manovich's evocation of grey, fearful faces may itself, of course, be seen as a dubious projection onto Soviet scenes of a Western – and/or late twentieth-century – reading, since self-preserva-tion would have precluded any Stalin-era artist from even hinting that ordinary citizens had genuine grounds to fear their immediate reality. If socialist realism can indeed be deemed truly realistic, as Manovich surprisingly suggests, the artist's registration of the colourlessness and fearfulness of the present could only have been unwitting, its meaning possibly decipher-able only from beyond the timespace of its parent culture. But although Manovich's analysis is compromised by unconsciousness of the sheer improbability of any Soviet artist courting accusations of a negative view of the present, it usefully pinpoints a double exposure effect rooted in what a truly Marxist analysis might term a contradiction: that between the ideal socialism these works displayed and a present 'real existing socialism' that was not yet ideal. Even if the one layer is manifest and the other latent, their co-presence may make one wonder which is which, and this may depend on the identity of the viewer. This double exposure can be described as a continual disavowal, a utopianism that dare not speak its name, lest the appearance of unreality in the ideal – however unavoidable – incriminate the artist as defeat-ist, or, worse still, 'objectively revisionist'. The problem lies in asserting both that the ideal has arrived and that history is a dialectical process of its perfection, a circle putatively squared by the historiosophy that posited a movement from socialism to communism: more of the same, only more so. The belief that defeating the underground saboteurs is a mere a mop-ping-up operation (the unwillingness to admit the real strength of opposition, or to eschew its satirical caricature as the work of bald or paunchily ageing enemy agents with petit bourgeois moustaches) drastically saps dramatic tension. The contradiction did not evaporate with the passing of socialist realism, as both socialism and realism continued to shape Polish cinema after 1956. The change 1956 effects lies in the recognition of the existence of a contradiction, of the degree to which Polish reality was not socialist: a disparity that generated genuine drama, not the pseudo-drama that undermined the meaningfulness of its own temporal unfolding by defining the ideal as already here. That recognition involved, among other things, a shifting of accents from pathos to irony.

IRONY AND PATHOS

Although the categories of irony and pathos have been used by Yvette Biró to model the psychic shift that took place in East Central European cinema between the late 1950s and the late 1960s (Biró 1983: 28–48), they may serve more legitimately to describe the movement from the monumentalist didacticism of the late 1940s and early 1950s to the more questioning, open aesthetics that emerged through the ice-holes after Stalin's death, in the various thaws of the post-Stalinist period. Whether or not epochs can be pigeonholed so neatly is, of course, dubious, and I will engage this issue later, arguing that various strands connect even the 'flagship socialist realist' *Piątka z ulicy Barskiej* (*Five Boys from Barska Street*, 1954), by Aleksander Ford, with Wajda's *Ashes and Diamonds*, and even works by Jerzy Skolimowski. The case for describing Stalinist aesthetics as based upon 'pathos' – again, in the European sense of something like 'high seriousness' – becomes all the more compelling when one considers the use made of the irony/pathos opposition by an earlier text that may well be Biró's unnamed source: Abram Tertz's classic polemical essay 'On Socialist Realism'. For Tertz, irony is 'the faithful companion of unbelief and doubt [which] vanishes as soon as there appears a faith that does not tolerate sacrilege' (Tertz 1960: 75). The thin outcrops of irony in a revolutionary poet like Mayakovski are, for Tertz, 'mostly from prerevolutionary times. Mayakovski soon found out what he could and what he could not laugh about' (ibid.), the new Leninist faith being, of course, sacrosanct. Tertz proceeds helpfully to qualify his argument by admitting that laughter persists nevertheless; he is neither so absolutist nor so absurd as to suggest that the features of an entire epoch freeze into a single expression. The laughter in question, however, is unlike the subversive one for which Mikhail Bakhtin yearned. After the October Revolution, Tertz notes:

> As in the eighteenth century, we became severe and serious. This does not mean that we forgot how to laugh; but laughter ceased to be indecent and disrespectful; it acquired a Purpose. It eliminates faults, corrects manners, keeps up the brave spirits of youth. It is laughter with a serious face and with a pointing finger: 'This is not the way to do things!' It is a laughter free from the acidity of irony.
>
> Irony was replaced by pathos, the emotional element of the positive hero. We ceased to fear high-sounding words and bombastic phrases; we were no longer ashamed to be virtuous. The solemn eloquence of the ode suited us. We became classicists. (Tertz 1960: 75–6)

The reference to eighteenth-century classicism is particularly suggestive, allowing one to conclude that if irony is opposed to pathos, and classicism to romanticism, then irony and Romanticism belong together. This coupling is worth holding on to, for although the German

Romantics wrote extensively of Romantic Irony, a widespread conception of Romanticism – one that focuses upon its links with eighteenth-century sentimentalism and valorisation of feeling – identifies it with pathos in both senses of the word: with tears and an elevated tone. Moreover, the anti-Romanticism of Milan Kundera has given widespread currency in East Central Europe to the identification of Romanticism and sentimentality. The Romantics, however, were well aware of the ironies of their extreme individualism, including that of individualist expression within the collective medium of language. The Romantics' irony reflected a consistent awareness of the inevitable defeat of all merely human or individual straining to encompass the ideal; and so was – dialectically – realist also (as were the great nineteenth-century novelists – perhaps no one more deeply and simultaneously realist and Romantic than Balzac). This is irony understood as in the Hegelian theorisation of tragedy, in which the unfettered, principled assertion of individuality generates not the best of all possible worlds – one of universal tolerance and free expression – but contradictions so unresolvable as to destroy their key representatives. And 'Romantic irony' is a term that is all the more valuable for its particular applicability to the post-Thaw Polish cinema known as 'the Polish School'.

THE POSITIVE HERO

For Tertz, 'socialist realism' is a contradiction in terms, because 'a purposeful, a religious, art cannot be produced with the literary method of the nineteenth century called "realism". And a really faithful representation of life cannot be achieved in a language based on teleological concepts' (Tertz 1960: 91). In the words of his earlier, biting aphorism: 'Socialist realism starts from an ideal image to which it adapts the living reality' (Tertz 1960: 76). The key ideal image is that of the positive hero, whom Tertz defines with withering wit:

> The positive hero is not simply a good man. He is a hero illuminated by the light of the most ideal of all ideals. Leonid Leonov called his positive hero 'a peak of all humanity from whose height the future can be seen'. He has either no faults at all or else but a few of them – for example, he sometimes loses his temper a little. These faults have a two-fold function. They help the hero to preserve a certain likeness to real men, and they provide something to overcome as he raises himself ever higher and higher on the ladder of political morality. However, these faults must be slight or else they would run counter to his basic qualities. It is not easy to enumerate these basic qualities of the positive hero: ideological conviction, courage, intelligence, will power, patriotism, respect for women, self-sacrifice, etc. etc. The most important, of course, are the clarity and directness with which he sees the Purpose and strives towards it. Hence the amazing precision of all his actions, thoughts, tastes, feelings and judgements. (Tertz 1960: 48–9)

The besetting contradiction of socialist realism may be defined as that between the teleology Tertz mentions and the positive hero so central to it. For Tertz, the result is 'neither psychology nor hero' (Tertz 1960: 90). Just why this should be the case needs more investigation, however. The contradiction between teleology and hero runs between time and space, or reality and the ideal: narrative time requires change, but the hero's sheer positivity renders him or her impervious to it. Thus the hero's status as 'slightly imperfect perfection', alluded to by Tertz, involves doubling, to allow him to exist both in time and outside it. If the hero can 'raise himself', as Tertz puts it, it is because his ideal form, located outside time, pulls up his temporal body. (This hero may be sexless and genderless, combining virtues culturally coded as 'masculine' – strength, independence – with others equally frequently coded as 'feminine', such as community-mindedness; and to the extent that it combined elements habitually separated by stereotype, socialist realism was genuinely utopian.) The socialist realist work may seem akin to a *Bildungsroman*, but – as Piotr Zwierzchowski acutely points out – it is really something rather like a western, with the officially prescribed ingredients of the positive hero corresponding very closely to the cowboy's 'Ten Commandments' laid down by Gene Autry (Zwierzchowski 2000a: 83–4). In his chivalric purity, and pure form, the hero is Shane, not Wayne: without the vein of bluff bitterness that salts the image of Wayne with the hints of inner conflict actually spelled out in John Ford's *The Searchers* (1956). The more interesting the work, the greater the number and depth of the impurities in the hero. They are coded, and officially acceptable, as the roughness of a diamond. In such cases, temporality and changelessness are reconciled through the former's definition as a process of arriving at something whose pre-existence is partly obscured, like that of the forms Michelangelo saw himself as liberating from the marble (thereby yielding the first 'men of marble'). Another corollary follows from this: the more interesting the work, the more multiple the hero. This may go beyond the roughness to be polished, the idealism to be tempered with wisdom, in which case the hero's duality really does generate two heroes: an older man, usually a Party member, and a fiery youth. It can, however, cause genuine multiplicity: in *Five Boys from Barska Street* 'the hero' becomes bearable through his dispersal across five youths and a Party mentor. The marble's surface – as well as its deep structure – is genuinely marbled.

The time that works upon the hero takes the form of other characters, whom the central, positive hero successfully confronts. In a sense, the confrontation is one between the register of 'the hero' and that of 'the protagonist', though a language like Polish confuses the matter by using the same word for both figures (*bohater*). This confusion may indeed have fed the mistaken belief in the reconcilability of real and ideal, that is, in the possible validity of 'socialist realism' per se. This reconciliation is one of 'spontaneity' and 'consciousness', as Geoffrey Hosking notes in his description of the template of socialist realist narratives: 'a hero appears from among the people, he is guided and matured by the Party, which tempers his "spontaneity" with its "consciousness", and then he leads his brethren to great victories over enemies and natural obstacles in the name of the Great Future which the Party is building' (Hosking 1980: 9). The usual suspects in this process are lined up authoritatively and characterised at greater length in Tadeusz Lubelski's typology of the master, the adept, the satellite and the enemy:

> At one pole: the master, the authority, the guarantor of the world's stability – the Party Secretary or Security Office (UB) [Urząd Bezpieczeństwa – Security Office, PC] functionary … At the other: the enemy, the hopeless case – the subversive, the spy, the kulak, the shirker, the social butterfly. Whereas in the middle is the main hero, the adept, inclined from the outset to find himself on the side of good but, due to certain circumstances (usually, he is inexperienced), initially incapable of demonstrating this disposition and doing so only in the course of the action. His transformation – the famous 'process of ideological maturation' – usually constitutes the film's central theme. The first part of the work places in the vicinity of 'the enemy' a 'satellite', a

wavering figure, usually 'burdened with the baggage of the intelligentsia'. At the film's end the 'satellite' generally gravitates to the pole of the good and also 'matures', though with greater difficulty. (Lubelski 1992a: 99)

One can add that the fault-line separating adept and satellite may be read as corresponding to the invisible one that bifurcates the word *bohater* ('hero'), locating it between fantasy and realism: the one closer to the ideal, the other to the real. Adept and satellite mediate between the poles of absolute opposition: those of the master and the enemy. Changelessness is located at either end of a spectrum, in these two fixed points of the work. Between them lies the realm of time and ideological conversion. As the work proceeds the inner flame of the adept lifts him to the good as all dross falls away to the pole of the enemy.

This conversion is possible, of course, because the youthfulness of what may be called the central identification figure renders him (and it usually is 'him') both malleable and not fully responsible as yet. The deep structure of the socialist realist narrative could bear the Eisensteinian title 'The Old and the New', with the youth of the convert-to-be also allowing him allegorically to represent that of a country still in the process of building socialism. Mistakes are not the 'errors and distortions' which would later be taken as characterising Stalinism, but part of the learning process. The hero's youth is matched and reinforced by the senescence of the opposition. Enemy and satellite are often of similar age – though where this occurs there may well be a duality in the satellite, with an older figure slated for destruction and a younger one for possible redemption, albeit 'by fire' and the skin of his teeth. Forces of opposition may persist into the present order, but mopping up operations are well underway. The resultant movement from realism to socialism is also a generic one, from realism to the utopia. (The problem may be the lack of any markers to indicate just when one passes from the one register to the other.) If the master and the enemy are usually older, they represent the positive and negative forms of age: the former, its wisdom and fatherly understanding; the latter, its possible blind, hidebound traditionalism. The understanding attitude of the former indicates the reconciliation of old and new within him, for although physically mature he also represents the liberating force of the new (the true form of maturity). In a sense, therefore, he is the most positive of heroes, though not available for the identificatory processes of a temporal art, as he has no need to change. Inasmuch as he is an unmoving icon, he is the true man of marble.

If socialist realism breaks down, it may well be because it represents an attempt by elite, avant garde and intellectual artists, capable of and even primed for production of great complexity, to generate simple, popular works. Such was the case with the pre-war START group, led by Aleksander Ford, that founded the post-war Polish film industry. The falsity of this effort is one of the faux naïf. This internal contradiction surely explains how and why the film industry they had founded so rapidly became capable of the complexity of the Polish School, after 1956. They simply reverted to the type against which they had struggled so vainly. Their earlier works are unconvincing because their hearts and heads were not in them, as they willed self-impairment in the name of a shibboleth of accessibility. Those earlier works may be taken as the product of a false, perhaps ideal self, the communist equivalent of the fascist false self adopted by Marcello Clerici in Bernardo Bertolucci's *Il Conformista* (*The Conformist*, 1970). Nevertheless, it is as if the attempted self-mutilation – like Clerici's identification with the blind – hamstrung their later efforts at identification with the Polish School, such as Ford's bombastic *Pierwszy dzień wolności* (*The First Day of Freedom*, 1965). Socialist realism is unreal because its implicit audience is a phantasm: an élite's projection of a working-class, mass audience, not one that ever really existed. If the work of Wajda is more durable than that of Ford it is because it permits the co-existence of complexity and popularity – often, in fascinating contradiction – rather than concealing the one, embarrassed, under the mask of the other. Ford's besetting stylistic bombast may well have been aimed, first and foremost, at convincing himself.

APORIAS OF A SOCIALIST (REALIST) AESTHETIC

There are, of course, more significant proponents of a socialist aesthetic than the largely anony-mous ones skewered by Tertz. The most prominent and serious proponent of an aesthetic that was both socialist and realist was the Hungarian Marxist György (Georg) Lukács. Lukács' early work was not Marxist, of course, and the neo-Marxist philosopher and critic Theodor Adorno has discerned a coarsening of thought in the work of the later Lukács, linking it to a maso-chistic subscription to the Party line (Adorno 1981: 251–80). Whether or not Lukács' later work in aesthetics eludes the constraints of a Stalinist Marxism with which it is in tortured, enforced dialogue remains a moot point. Beyond dispute, however, is its status as the most powerful and erudite Marxist aesthetic to emerge within the Soviet bloc, and its openness to writers uncongenial to the most hard-line of local critics: such figures as Thomas Mann and Solzhenitsyn. But can the 'critical realism' Lukács proposed avoid crumbling into a 'socialist realism' whose artistic fruits were lamentable? Does both models' strategic privileging of the notion of 'the typical' (a counterblast to the 'bourgeois' highlighting of individuals that had relegated the surrounding historical forces not just to the backstage, but to outer darkness) create an incompatability between the theory's two goals: adherence to canons of realism and analysis of the movement of the *Zeitgeist*? The issue can be pursued through an investiga-tion of Lukács' seminal 1936 essay *Die intellektuelle Physiognomie der künstlerischen Gestalten* ('The Intellectual Physiognomy of Artistic Figures') (Lukács 1977: 166–217), which argues for a notion of typical characterisation that not only registers the large shifts of history but is even (an ahistorical argument perhaps?) compatible with the creation of characters as haunting as Don Quixote, Hamlet and Lear.

Lukács' essay begins, somewhat surprisingly, by praising the characterisation in Plato's *The Symposium*. This initial move becomes less startling in the light of the argument it introduces, however: that a characterisation wishing to illuminate characters completely (*vollständig*) must include presentation of their worldviews. Later, Lukács will cite the number and quality of the soliloquies accorded Hamlet or Lear, arguing that these distinguish them from their doubling counterparts (Laertes and Gloucester), thereby rendering them central figures. The insist-ence that a character state his or her worldview elides the distinction between the Platonic philosophical dialogue and the novel. In socialist realism, this requirement becomes one for a declaration (or rise to awareness) of class consciousness, interest and allegiance. The charac-terisation it fosters is one-dimensional rather than rich, however. Not only is class identity not necessarily an individual's governing identity, as modern individuals are often the bearers of compacted elements of various worldviews, some of them the embedded shrapnel of exploded ones; it may even be the case that their stated views either do not accord precisely with their material (and class) interests, or contradict them completely (the syndrome registered in the satirical observation that 'all you need to be a surrealist is to come from a "good" family'). The ideal, intellectual superstructure is no simple, monotonous reflection of the material base, but can even oppose it radically, particularly when characters feel no need to employ their intellects to develop arguments in defense of their position in life but can take it so for granted as to use it for nebulous explorations, with no notion of a terminus (the fullest example surely being that of Ulrich, the protagonist of Robert Musil's novel *Der Mann ohne Eigenschaften* [*The Man Without Qualities*, 1930–43]).

Nevertheless, Lukács would seem to oppose such simplicity. After all, he echoes and reiterates Marx's critique of Schiller's characters for being 'mere mouthpieces of the *Zeitgeist*' (Lukács 1977: 169), even extending it to Racine. His critique of Racine and Schiller is of playwrights whose characters' views are abstract. The attack on the non-integration of their ideas and their social being is directed implicitly both against the possible threat it poses to a reflection theory of character, and to idealism in every sense. Lukács' advocacy of a unity of character he associated with Shakespeare and Tolstoy can thus be seen as a refusal to countenance characters who are split (which may, of course, mean 'modern'). His desiderata appear in motto-like form in the statement that 'the general, typical phenomena should at the same time be the particular actions and personal passions of concrete human beings' (Lukács 1977: 171). Here 'it is clear that the shaped figure's capacity for conceptual generalisation plays an enormous part' (Lukács 1977: 172); the privileging of the fully-conscious figure – and hence, of the intellectual or philosopher – persists. One might interject that this privileging indicates the utopian dimension of a realism so conceived, and that this matches that of socialist realism in particular. The dream of every individual's awakening to total self-awareness resembles Freud's enlightenment programme of 'where id was, there shall ego be', reconjugated by the pre-eminence of collectivism into 'where id and ego were, there shall super-ego be'.

Lukács contends that 'the generalisation only subsides into empty abstraction when the link between abstract concepts and the figure's personal experiences slips away' (Lukács 1977: 172). In a realism dominated by typicality, however, abstraction does indeed corrode lived experience by transforming the individual into the simple carrier of a single thought: in other words, into an allegory. Of course, a defense of allegory might argue that because sign-systems are always partly abstracted from what they designate, and hence implicitly generalising, the transformation of representation into sign is simply a logical conclusion of its development. To argue thus, though, is to repress a genuine dialectic in favour of one of its poles; the artistic image is never subsumed entirely into a regime of signification but is always partly in excess of conceptual meaning. (Susan Sontag's 'Against Interpretation' remains a necessary corrective for most critics, particularly those in pursuit of ideological analysis.)

Worse still, Lukácsian realism is further undermined by its formulation in terms that are a recipe for melodrama. Lukács declares that 'the deeper the poet's grasp of an epoch and its large issues, the less his representation can occupy the level of the everyday'. This is because at this level 'the great contradictions are blunted, appearing criss-crossed by indifferent, disconnected fortuities'. They can only achieve 'their pure and developed form' when conditions are such that 'every contradiction is driven to its most extreme consequences' (Lukács 1977: 176). Lukács the would-be realist may be said to come damagingly clean when he admits that typical figures are 'completely impossible in everyday life' (ibid.). It is thus that he describes Don Quixote, failing to grasp that the character's defining feature is less his impossibility than the fact that he was so possible at a particular time and place that it could easily have been said 'if he had not existed, he would have had to be invented' (as he was, by force of what may even be read in quasi-Marxist or Hegelian fashion as historical necessity). 'The extreme nature of the typical situation derives from the need to bring out the deepest and ultimate in human characters, including all the contradictions they contain' (Lukács 1977: 177). The conception of characterisation as a form of embodiment of extreme contradiction is a formula not for realism, however, but for melodrama, with its extreme polarisation of Good and Evil. Only when these polarities are laden with ambivalence – as in the Dostoevsky Lukács abominates as pathological – do they generate another level of realism: the psychological. Lukács' contradictions are vampires that suck the characters dry.

And where does cinema fit in here? Despite the arguments of Siegfried Kracauer or André Bazin, cinema is not necessarily realistic, committed to the real-time registration of wind-blown leaves or Nanook's patient waiting for the seal. Equally important is its capacity to shape and recreate reality: traditionally, through montage, but more recently through a manipulation of pixels that may be described as an extreme, microscopic form of 'montage within the frame'. But, like realism, the fantastic and fictional has its laws, the most fundamental of which dictate formal separation from reality (which can then reappear only in distorted, reworked, transposed, metaphorical form, like Kansas in Dorothy's Oz). To superimpose upon realism the fantastic law of radical character-opposition – the law of the fairytale whose optimism does not always survive into its modern descendant, melodrama – is not to analyse contradictions but to blur the distinction between them. Lukácsian 'critical realism' resembles socialist realism in its ironic ignorance of the degree to which contradictoriness figures not just in capitalist systems and bourgeois world-views but persists at the core of socialist aesthetics. For socialist realism, the key contradiction is one of apparent realism and a fantastic, optimistic fairytale ideal. For Lukács, it is that between the demand for an objective rendition of life in its totality and a didactic predetermination of reality's dialectic in favour of one of its extremes, the proletariat defined melodramatically as exclusive carrier of correctness. The privileging of realism in socialist aesthetics may thus be simply an accident of the predominance of the novel during the historical moment of their formulation. Their deep-seated preference for melodramatic scenarios renders the realism so paper-thin as to be virtually a veil. In the case of the artists themselves, meanwhile, it may be argued that a high degree of self-consciousness is incompatible with the creation of successful realistic works. (The level of fruitfulness of the work of a Wajda, for instance, surely corresponds – as I argue later in this book – to a frequent incoherence that limns it with the oneiric.) The artist compelled to attend Script Assessment Commission meetings cannot avoid such awareness, though of course he or she may have possessed it already. Does the individual event retain its true scale – its integrity and dimension of reality – when the artist knows it will be read as typical, and even deliberately crafts it to dovetail with such a form of interpretation? Do its integrity and coherence perhaps even depend upon suppression of any awareness of how it will be read, as one cannot concentrate upon meeting the inherent demands of the material while glancing continually in the direction of that external instance, the prospective viewer? Is such obsessive awareness a continual interruption of the creative process that can be justified – and successful – only as a modernist rupture of illusion, but proves ruinous to any art with aspirations to realism? Such questions cannot but haunt an aesthetics of creation in conditions of modernity, and become all the more pressing where those aesthetics – like socialist realism or its possibly fatally similar, more sophisticated sibling, the 'critical realism' of Lukács – become the prescriptive allies of power.

Lukács' critical realism, with its assumption of the continued vitality and viability of nineteenth-century fictional modes in conditions of modernity is like socialist realism inasmuch as it can be critiqued as ahistorical. In the case of socialist realism, the ahistoricity is more massive and glaring, whence the depth of the falsity of the works generated according to its prescriptions. Using the terms of Lukács' seminal early work *Die Theorie des Romans* (*The Theory of the Novel*, 1920), it is a confusion of the epic and the novelistic. The opposition has been summarised eloquently by Fredric Jameson:

> Where the epic hero represented a collectivity, formed part of a meaningful organic world, the hero of the novel is always a solitary subjectivity: he is problematical; that is to say, he must always stand in opposition to his setting, to nature or society, inasmuch as it is precisely his relationship to them, his integration into them, which is the issue at hand. Any reconciliation between the hero and his environment which was given from the beginning of the book and not painfully won in the course of it would stand as a kind of illicit presupposition, a kind of cheating with the form, in which the whole novel as process would be invalidated. The prototype of the novel's hero is therefore the madman or the criminal; the work is his biography, the story of his setting forth to 'prove his soul' in the emptiness of the world. But of course he can never really do so, for if genuine reconciliation were possible, then the novel as such would cease to exist, would once more give place to epic wholeness. (Jameson 1971: 172–3)

The alternative conclusion from the application to socialist realism of Lukács' historical typology of narrative forms is that here 'the novel as such' – the narrative of modern life – crumbles into a parody of epic wholeness. The conclusion may well be that a false aesthetic generates a false practice: typicality became stereotypicality, cliché. It is thus unlike the American genre system, whose heavy dependence upon stereotype nevertheless allowed enough free play for innovation, as the ideal product the market required combined the spice of novelty with the reassurance of the tried and pre-tested. The planned economy of the aesthetic, however, took account only of supply, not demand, and counted the audience out. No wonder it never won their hearts.

In the context of Lukácsian aesthetics, it is worth mentioning the argument that not only the critical realism he favours but even socialist realism can be likened to the *Bildungsroman* (Rek 2003: 15). Insofar as both are concerned with the education of the young, they do indeed overlap. Their conceptions of education are fundamentally different, however: in the *Bildungsroman* the focus is on the individual's passage through and subjective experience of the world, and the *Bildung* is unsystematic and usually not ideological; in socialist realism, the focus is on the system that educates the individual, and it inducts him/her into an ideology. The latter has no interest in the evocation of the random texture of individual experience pursued by the former. Where a *Bildungsroman* does privilege an educative system or group (as in the case of the Tower society in Goethe's *Wilhelm Meister*), it remains in the background, and is not foregrounded all the time, in the manner of socialist realism.

MŁODOŚĆ CHOPINA: ROMANTICISM AND THE REOPLE

For many critics and aestheticians of the early 1950s, Aleksander Ford's *Młodość Chopina* (*Chopin's Youth*, 1952) represented a near-flawless example of socialist realist art. Jerzy Toeplitz's article on the film in the leading Polish film periodical of the time – *Kwartalnik filmowy* – deemed it sufficiently exemplary to merit an exhaustive 44-page examination that extended even to the work of the set designers and make-up team. Particular emphasis was laid on its ideological soundness: on its variations on the theme of the Romantic artist's linkage to the people through his use of folk melodies, and on its stressing of the social dimension of art through continual contextualisation of Chopin's work within the patriotic and revolutionary struggles of 1825–30. The historian Joachim Lelewel is the work's mouthpiece when he remarks that 'the scholar and poet ought to have the deepest conviction that they are creatures that live for the community'. Toeplitz's extensive delineation of the work's ideology, however, leaves one aspect unsurprisingly unprobed, even though a Marxist might well have sensed the potential contradictoriness of the two adjectives bracketed together earlier, as they are in the film: 'patriotic' and 'revolutionary'. (A failure to note this contradiction is surely indicative of doublethink, a strategic momentary switching off of the dialectical machine.) For how can the revolutionary strains of Romanticism be extolled without that movement appearing as anti-Russian as it often was? After all, 17 years after Ford's film, the primary catalyst of the student March protests of 1968 would be the banning of a performance of *Forefather's Eve* by the Romantic national bard, Adam Mickiewicz – some of whose other works are praised in Ford's film. *Chopin's Youth* boldly and cunningly takes this particular bull – Mickiewicz – by the horns. This occurs during a significant coffee-house clash of the generations. Chopin and his friends have just burst in, provocatively singing the words of a love song learnt from his maid. His staid professors promptly lament the Romantic contamination of literature with folklore. One even denigrates the Polish vernacular, justifying his preference for French novels by asserting 'the inadequacy of our native tongue to render the delicate feelings of the game of love'. Lelewel then enters the room, and the fray, to support the young Romantics. Significantly, he quotes a Russian newspaper's praise of the poet: the wider world approves of what the professors disdain as incorrigibly parochial. As at the film's beginning, which raises the possibility of Poles joining a Russian revolution after the imminent death of the Tsar, following a Russian lead is defined as patriotically Polish (it is the professors' Western orientation that is dangerous, even treacherous). The professors may well seem discomfited momentarily, since they have in effect been rebuked by Stalin, and the implicit spectator's *Schadenfreude* over their position is identification with Big Brother: in essence, the masochist's 'identification with the aggressor'. One professor counters Lelewel, however: 'there are many Tartars in Crimean Russia [the place of Mickiewicz's exile] and perhaps they understand these Crimean – God have mercy! – sonnets [*Crimean sonnets* was the title of the collection Mickiewicz wrote during this period], but I don't and I won't read them'. A youth replies that 'one has to seek inspiration within one's own nation'. The implicitly pan-Slavic interchange effaces the contradiction between 'the Soviet' and 'the Polish', identifying the latter with the former. Russians approve Polish self-expression, a freedom opposed only by fuddy-duddies fixated upon a West they effetely ape.

For *Chopin's Youth*, as this demonstrates, Romanticism is primarily a social movement. If Chopin can be allowed to praise Paganini for showing what can be achieved without an orchestra – thus setting a precedent for himself – it is because 'he showed one could play the whole world on a single instrument'. Placing the entire world within the singular creator separates Romanticism from its individualistic idolatry of the genius: the artist is the microcosm within which the world is reflected. Romanticism is separated from individualism by its presentation as rooted in peasant works, and by showing this to be particularly true of Chopin's music. The leitmotif of its popular origins is laid out in the very early cut from a peasant woman's singing of a Christmas lullaby to Chopin's instrumental setting of the same melody in a salon concert. Moreover, Chopin's music might even be deemed preferable, purified of the song's religious content. As is to be expected, the film is firmly anti-clerical, mocking the ecclesiastical inspectors despatched to round up truant students on Sundays. Their press-ganging into attendance at edifying services is further compromised by its mandating by the Tsarist ruler of the Russian partition of Poland, Novosilcov. The way in which instrumental music empties the song of dubious content may be particularly important as a way of countering the argument that it in fact voids music of its social element, anticipating the later *Symboliste* 'de la musique avant toutes choses'. How is music to be refilled with appropriate social content?

Ford employs two means of doing this, each related to his predilection for lengthy, heavily epic panning shots. The tightening of the relationship between Chopin's music and Polish revolutionary impulses is rendered by both paralleling and contrasting sequences in which a pan links discrete spaces. The first we see of Chopin is at the piano, playing his version of the Christmas lullaby; the camera then pans rightwards, ironically registering society ladies' praise of his aristocratic features. The pan continues to the next room, where it picks up a conversation between Prince Jabłonowski and the Tsar's representative Novosilcov about the Tsar's possible death, before moving still further to the right, to a room where Polish army cadets are deliberating whether or not to join the Russian uprising that death would precipitate. The later, parallel passage shows Chopin arriving at a salon, where he is to meet Maurycy Mochnacki. He is kept waiting, however, as Polish political options are being debated fervently in the next room. This time Chopin is in a room that directly adjoins the site of Polish revolutionary debate. He is symbolically nearer to the revolution, and the music he plays while waiting becomes not only an accompaniment to the discussion but in a sense its prompter. In his extremely long analysis, Toeplitz gives especially high praise to the momentary foregrounding of the music in a significant pause in the discussion, before the intervention of Lelewel. It allows Lelewel's words to stand as the music's translation into political discourse (Toeplitz 1952: 138). His words may even represent a variety of recitative superimposed upon its groundswell, as he argues that any uprising must be accompanied by an abolition of serfdom. If not, he prophesies, it will fail for lack of peasant support.

Another means of imparting a social significance to Chopin's music also uses pans, this time across auditoria during his performances. The apparent 'contentlessness' of the panning shot doubles that of the music itself while also transforming it into a panorama of society. As in the case of Paganini, the singular performance is justified by its embrace of a world. As one would expect, given the Marxist context, this is a world built on contradictions (a word Ford himself employed in his declaration of intentions [Bocheńska *et al.* 1974: 244]): of high and low (animation in the Gods, stupor below); of upper and lower classes; of youth and age. It is nothing like the 'Family of Man' montage of faces found, for instance, in the overture section of Ingmar Bergman's *Trollflöjten* (*The Magic Flute*, 1975). Rather, it emphasises the co-presence of opposed elements within a single continuous space. The pan – like Chopin's music – is conceived as a virtuosity that is more than merely virtuoso, for it enfolds the bristling conflicts that shape a world. Consequently, individualism – and individual suffering – are swallowed up in the collectivity. The desolation of Konstancja during Chopin's farewell concert may be underlined by close-ups, but her suffering is only one element in a larger situation. As Toeplitz and others would aver, contrasting Ford's film with Hollywood versions of Chopin's life, there is no bourgeois focus on the merely individual. That is why the work's end is not Chopin's death but his marching shoulder-to-shoulder with French revolutionaries singing 'La Marseillaise'. Thus although Toeplitz would lament the way this ending severs the direct linkage between Chopin's music and revolutionary upsurge established earlier in the film (Toeplitz 1952: 129), Ford might have countered that his ending simply illustrated the expendability of the 'great man'. Once his work has fulfilled its historical function, others can take over with Chopin falling away like a spent booster-rocket. Not unexpectedly, the argument is that the artist has to be prepared to give way to the ideologue – much as occurred in the many socialist realist works that now, as a result, survive only as ghosts few have any mind to summon from the cinematic Hades known as the archive.

ANTI-GENRE AND GENRE

The question of the class of film to which *Chopin's Youth* belonged is particularly important in the light of its project of reconciling an apparently anti-generic Romanticism with a socialist realism obsessed with questions of genre. This obsession may be read as an academicising policing of art that seeks to control it through a neo-classical enforcement of rules. The socialism in socialist realism uses genre to check and discipline the possibly anarchistic openness and historic shapelessness of both Romanticism and realism. This policing is the aesthetic echo of political policing. Here, as in Hollywood, the paradoxical populist justification of neo-classicism lies in the need to meet codified audience expectations. Unlike the Hollywood generally termed 'classical', however, no tension between classical rules and narratives of Romantic rebellion energises this art; rather, form and content are stultifyingly unified. Unable to incorporate – co-opt – rebellion, as Hollywood can and does, socialist realism proves far less flexible and durable than the American genre system. Instead, its rigidity eventually precipitates the auteurist revolt against academic prescription known as 'the Polish School'. Hence both the plaudits and the (rare) brickbats addressed to Ford's film focus (implicitly or explicitly) upon the questions of generic allegiance that would continue to haunt Party-inspired criticism of Polish cinema, its primary victim among the Polish School films being the one in which the School's leading exponent – Andrzej Wajda – first faltered artistically: *Lotna* (Gawrak 1959). It is little wonder that Wajda met such a fate, as even so 'ideologically correct' a film as Ford's could be castigated for structural looseness. Jerzy Płażewski argued that its 'collection of scenes from Chopin's life has no coherent thread, no uniform, rising line of tension, culmination and release … Not for one moment does the spectator fear for Frederick's fate, but follows it with Olympian calm, more like the reader of an encyclopaedia than a witness to the drama of somebody's life' (Bocheńska *et al.* 1974: 245). One might imagine another critic lauding this sense of distance as a feature of the epic (Homeric rather than Brechtian: after all, although both a socialist and a realist, Brecht was no socialist realist), but drama remained the primary point of reference even for the film's defenders; as in classical Hollywood, film was measured pre-eminently against the genre it most clearly resembles, and most frequently taps. It could be counterargued though that its loose construction suits a representation of the unbridled Romantic era (ibid.), or – alternatively – that biography itself demanded such looseness. Jerzy Toeplitz fuses the two arguments, contending that 'the classical rules of dramatic construction are not appropriate for a biographical film, and still less for a film whose action is set in the era of Romanticism, a film steeped in the spirit of Romantic literature' (Toeplitz 1952: 129). Ford's film thus becomes 'a near-classic example of the Romantic "poetic drama"' (Toeplitz 1952: 130). The work's looseness is not defended as novelistic and realistic: partly because academicians deem drama and novel further apart than novel and film; partly because the novel itself threatens dissolution of the discourse of genre; and partly because the realism favoured in the Soviet bloc was a Lukácsian one subordinated to the narrator-controlled epic, rather than the unruly, dialogic, Dostoevskian one of a Bakhtin. (It is thus hardly surprising that whereas some Polish filmmakers, particularly those of the Cinema of Moral Anxiety, would later be drawn to Dostoevsky – either ignoring or overlooking his Polonophobia – they would bypass Tolstoy entirely.) Thus when Bolesław Lewicki ascribes a 'multiplanar, multi-generic' structure to the film (Bocheńska et al. 1974: 245), he quickly neutralises it as 'typical of the Romantic style'. Such defenses praise Ford for a Romanticism whose predictable historicist match with its subject displays not Romanticism but the academic pastiche characteristic of that movement's sworn enemy: neo-classicism.

The question of genre is also one of the degree of continuity between the cinema of socialist realism and the pre-war commercial one. If experience in Poland's pre-war cinema really did give older directors an initial advantage over such younger ones as Czesław Petelski, Witold Lesiewicz, Janusz Nasfater and even Andrzej Munk, as Marek Hendrykowski has contended (Hendrykowski 2002: 250), it was because of the centrality of genre to socialist realist aesthetics. If the acting styles of pre-war performers, based in generic typicality, to some extent 'met the demands of socialist realist typage' (Hendrykowski 2002: 251), it may be because of the intersection of its melodrama with the Eisensteinian learning of lessons from Dickens and Griffith. Nevertheless, one should note the need to bridge the definite gap between traditional professional acting and Eisenstein's typage, which was free to select figures largely according to physiognomy, for the silence of his films removed the need for actors to speak: the mediating link between traditional acting and typage being type-casting. Hendrykowski's statement of the usefulness of old practices to the new aesthetic may appear hard to reconcile with his later contention that the socialist realist valorisation of the new meant a passing over in silence of 'the traditions of art in the areas of style, genre, iconography, etc.' (Hendrykowski 2002: 255), but the point here lies in the word 'tradition': genres were defined not in terms of past examples but in relation to an ideal, Platonic essence the new works had to incarnate. The theoreticians' addiction to generic categorisation may well have responded to a sense of the potential over-capaciousness of a term such as realism, which usually appears – to revert to the policing metaphor used above – handcuffed to an adjective, attached to the hand of the relatively soft cop of 'critical realism' or the hard one of 'socialist realism', or with a placard around its neck specifying the conditions of its use. The modern notion of realism, built to attach a semblance of definition to the 'loose baggy monster' that was the novel, was linked to the pre-modern notion of genre. The result was a contradictory simultaneous retention and rejection of the past that might have sought an alibi as 'dialectical' but was in fact incoherent. The contradiction is sustained by a desire both to win a mass audience and to reform it, the former endeavour depending upon an appeal to existing tastes and habits, the latter upon their transformation. The resultant compromise formation may even be deemed 'half-Polish, half-Soviet', and it may not be too gross a caricature to state that new (Soviet-approved) content was to be poured into old Polish forms. No wonder the products frustrated both artists and ideologues.

BETWEEN GENRES: WAJDA, FORD AND *FIVE BOYS FROM BARSKA STREET*

An uneven, mongrel mix of socialist realism, neo-realism, Eisenstein, Riefenstahl, art cinema and tragedy (to mention only six of the elements hybridised within it…), Aleksander Ford's *Five Boys from Barska Street* does not entirely deserve the neglect into which it has fallen (it is totally absent, for instance, from a recent list in *Kwartalnik filmowy* of the best Polish films ever). After all, the six-part recipe I have described could (minus Riefenstahl) be deemed that of Andrzej Wajda's war trilogy, in particular the *Ashes and Diamonds* canonised as the most important of all Polish films in that very same *Kwartalnik filmowy* questionnaire (Anon 1997: 4). This is hardly surprising: it would be possible to describe the trilogy as a deliberate, Oedipal trumping of the earlier film, on which Wajda himself had worked as an assistant. Certain elements stand out as undergoing reconjugation: the socialist realist mentoring of the wayward young and Tadeusz Janczar's movement among the upper reaches of ruined buildings – low-angle shots emphasising their height – would find their echo in *A Generation*, while Ford's striking sewer-scenes and the motif of soldiers led astray by orders from the West would recur in *Kanal*. The strongest links, however, are with *Ashes and Diamonds*, a fact that becomes less surprising when one recalls the emergence of several proposed socialist realist screenplays based on Andrzejewski's novel, first published in the year in which Ford's film is set: 1947 (Lubelski 1994: 176–87). Of all these conjunctions, the most significant are those associated with Janczar's character – Kazek – and the blonde ZMP (Związek Młodzieży Polskiej – Union of Polish Youth) activist Hanka, which include one between the setting of one of their meetings and that of one meeting between Wajda's protagonists, Maciek and Krystyna.

Janczar's Kazek is one of five boys from Barska Street whom we first meet before a juvenile court facing two charges, one of theft and one of assault and battery. They confess to the former but deny the latter, as the witness to the incident has not appeared. They receive a two-year suspended sentence under the care of a probation-cum-welfare officer, who will find them work, keep them on the straight and narrow and help them develop their talents. This man – the gaunt bricklayer Wojciechowski – finds positions for two of them (Kazek and Marek) at his own workplace. Kazek learns to operate a digger, and falls in love with Hanka, a site draughtswoman who also inculcates literacy into the working class. However, like the other boys, Kazek is also involved with a Western-inspired 'fascist' subversive called Zenon, who issues orders near the film's end for them to dynamite the East-West Warsaw route upon whose construction Kazek and Marek have been working. Like the Maciek Chełmicki of *Ashes and Diamonds*, Kazek is under the military discipline of an anti-socialist conspiracy. Unlike him, however, his efforts at self-extrication are not simply ones to enter everyday life, but to develop the happy coincidence of love and socialist construction embodied in his building-site relationship with Hanka. The unity of the two strands is figured in the red tie another boy advises him not to wear to the New Year's Ball, lest it show Hanka just how much she means to him: after all, it knots together the reds of passion, communism and her own ZMP tie. The difficulty of achieving this goal is marked by his choice of another tie, its black-and-white as chequered as his own past and present. It is at the ball that anticipations of *Ashes and Diamonds* begin to pepper the work. First, there is the motif of significant cigarette-lighting and conspiracy, as a man whose face is at first hidden (and hence implicitly alarming) asks him for a light, then sets a time: 'tomorrow at eight'. It is Zenon. Hanka terms the chimes at midnight 'the time of confessions', but Kazek says she would be stunned by the one he might make to her. Like Maciek Chełmicki, he cannot reveal himself fully to his love. After dancing, the two go outside, kiss among ruins, and enter a church, where she says she wants to know everything about him. Wajda intertextually takes up, and trumps, this moment in his virtuoso scene with the inverted crucifix in the bombed-out church. They climb to the top of a building and he confesses 'I am lost', but the sight of a scrawled message from Zenon chokes the imminent self-revelation.

The combination of love and participation in the new post-war order, of which Wajda's Maciek only dreams, is of course partly enjoyed by Kazek. But it is also under threat, and the threats do not all emanate from the enemy agent of paranoid socialist realism. There is also his work-foreman, the fat and florid Macisz. Macisz is a dangerous, seemingly reckless figure. When Hanka stands her ground before his digger, protesting his failure to follow plans, he swings its arm shockingly close to her head. The low angle makes it seem about to hit her indeed, and the tension makes her dig her fingernails into her forearm. When the digger's excavations turn up an entrance to an underground cellar stuffed with vodka, Macisz leads the expedition to get drunk during work-time, a chaotic bacchanal halted only by foreman Nowak's hosing down of the inebriated participants. Later still, resentful of Kazek's public undertaking – on behalf of the diggers – to complete the East-West route by the public holiday of 22 July, he seeks to scapegoat his apprentice by pointing him out as a thief (I will say more of this important crowd-scene later). Macisz's opposition seems throughout to stem from simple human envy, officiousness, malice and sloth. His treatment by the narrative is particularly interesting, as his double appearance – initially, as simply malicious, but finally as part of the enemy conspiracy – preserves much of the text from the socialist realist paranoia that discerns sabotage in every work-glitch, even though any dispassionate observer of Macisz's behaviour might be tempted to argue that his consistent undermining of 'the socialist work-ethos' could hardly be coincidental. After all, he is suspiciously critical of work emulation (by associating a critique of it in the name of 'solid' work with him, the text seeks to discredit a very logical objection to it). But the film's refusal until its end to incorporate him into an enemy plot lets it breathe and achieve a degree of openness. Only at the end does it decisively lock itself into the world of a Soviet-style socialist realist discourse for which it is always 'no accident that…'. As it does so it becomes implausible in the extreme, virtually an unwitting parody of socialist realism. Openness persists even into the ending, however, which clips together a politically correct socialist realist revelation of conspiracy with an art cinema ambiguity regarding Kazek's fate. On the one hand, Macisz appears in the underground, brandishing a weapon and shooting Kazek. On the other, there is Hanka's anxious demand of the doctor whether Kazek will live. On the one hand, the legitimation of a socialist order requires the fulfilment of Hanka's dreams (in this reading, the off-screen closure is happy, but mutedly so). On the other, should Kazek not survive, however, he may indeed be another Maciek Chełmicki, unable to enter the new order: a tragic hero who has to die. Thus the ending is genuinely open and surprisingly anticipatory of art cinema. One may be able to spot the join that both connects Ford's artistic and his political ambitions and indicates their possible disconnection, but it holds, albeit in a 'now you see it, now you don't' fashion.

Part of that artistic ambition is manifested in Ford's moments of Eisensteinian shock, though he juxtaposes larger, heavier, clumsier and more pompously epic blocks than his Soviet mentor. The most powerful of these involve the death of Radziszewski, the inconvenient witness to the group's crime. Lutek (Tadeusz Łomnicki) – a go-between linking Zenon and the other five – relays Zenon's insistence that Radziszewski's silence be ensured. Marek lures him out of his flat, and he is bundled into an abandoned building. Lutek fights him, but, unable to achieve superiority, tries to fight dirty. Fleeing, Radziszewski falls to his death, and the camera's slide to his exquisitely twisted body anticipates the association of downward movement and death in *Ashes and Diamonds*. When Jacek, the group's diminutive, crippled comic relief, accuses Lutek of cheating at cards, the word he uses – '*świnia*' – brings to Lutek's mind Radziszewski's words shortly before his death: '*podła świnia*' ('low-down pig'). The depth of Lutek's traumatisation by the memory is shown by his violent overreaction to Jacek's accusation, and by the shockingly sudden resurgence upon the screen of the scene of the discovery of Radziszewski's corpse.

Lutek may be taken as a scapegoat figure whose function could be analysed in terms of a modified version of the theory of scapegoating and sacrifice developed by René Girard (1977). His status outside the five corresponds to his expendability, a defining feature of the scapegoat: it would be too painful to expel or destroy an integral element of the system. It is he who relays Zenon's orders to the five. When Wojciechowski introduces himself to the five, Lutek refuses his care. His position thus indicates that although the five comprise part of Zenon's underground army, they are also potentially separable from him. That underground force, of course, has the incoherence of the paranoid ideological construction embodied in the Stalinist use of the word 'hooligan': since the true enemy is the one who figures diabolically on two fronts, the apparently undisciplined 'hooligan' is really a controlled spearhead of external opposition. It is significant that Macisz also concentrates within himself the opposites – indiscipline, and active hostility – conjoined in this conception of 'hooliganism'. The political unconscious fuses enemies to ease the process of their confrontation, a round-up that already represents their defeat in the realm of the Imaginary. Their unification remains implausible, however (can these street-urchins really be soldiers?), and hints that the habit of interpreting all setbacks as the work of conspiracy is indeed paranoid.

Insofar as the film contains a moment of what Girard would term 'sacrificial crisis', it occurs at the works meeting where Kazek rashly declares the diggers' readiness in advance of his foreman, Macisz. The filming of the declarations of a series of individual mouthpieces for groups – architects, welders, engineers, draughtsmen, technicians and so on – is uncannily reminiscent of Leni Riefenstahl's *Triumph des Willens* (*Triumph of the Will*, 1934), with its rapid fire close-ups of faces of group representatives giving just such pledges to the Führer; a stylistic echo that may be read as a Freudian parapraxis betraying the proximity of Nazi and Stalinist worldviews. One may wonder whether its occurrence during the sacrificial crisis is an accident – to use the ominous Soviet locution. The sacrifice, however, is deferred. Macisz may identify Kazek as a former thief, but Marek – who has already won his stripes as a member of Wojciechowski's record-breaking brick-laying team – steps forward to identify himself as one too: his own achievements exemplify the possibility of reform. Whether or not his fellow-workers are convinced remains unclear, for the issue is left strangely unresolved, as the meeting's representation cuts out at this point, devoid of any conclusion. The crisis is suspended, though without suspense: the issue appears simply to have evaporated, its disappearance suggesting an irresolubility that requires its repression. Perhaps that is why the work has to end underground, in the place that is both the unconscious and the site of subversive political activity. Here too, though, the non-resolution persists, as it is left unclear whether or not Kazek will survive – and even, should he do so, whether he will be arraigned for his part in Radziszewski's death, as he was in the Kazimierz Koźniewski novel from which the film

derives. The suspension of the question of his death is of a piece with the simultaneous suggestion and suspension of tragedy. The mechanisms of scapegoating and tragedy, which converge
in classical tragedy, are separated here. The tragic hero is split between a set of scapegoats
(Zenon, Lutek, Macisz) who really *are* lost and a figure who may or may not be. This splitting
superimposes upon tragedy the Manichean oppositions of melodrama, which assigns good
and evil to separate figures rather than concentrating them in the single flawed but positive
tragic protagonist. Even if Kazek is 'lost' in the sense of perishing (tragedy), he is 'saved' for the
Cause (melodrama). One may well be relieved that Ford's materialism spares us any heavenly
choirs while wondering whether the openness of the ending represents less an incipience of
art cinema norms than the stark result of a deadlock of the opposed aesthetic systems of the
melodramatic and the tragic.

Describing the work as falling between genres, as I have done here, does not replicate the
socialist realist academicism, but rather retraces its process of formation as a patchwork of
categories that do not fuse – a disunity that may be deemed a defining feature of an aesthetic
that simply stitches together bits and pieces of the old, pouring the would-be new wine into
old bottles. Significantly, contemporary reviews did not see the category of tragedy as relevant.
Criticised by Zygmunt Kałużyński for sensationalism and ostensible lack of realism, Ford's
film was defended by Tadeusz Konwicki as a filmic poem that combines poetry and reportage.
Bourgeois individualistic judgement of a film's merits is displaced into a squabble over the
modalities of its classification. Ford himself weighed in with a muddy reference to its 'harsh
realistic Romanticism of style' (Bocheńska *et al.* 1974: 253), a phrase doubtless intended to end
all discussion through invocation of the socialist realist mantra that required both 'revolutionary romanticism' and, of course, 'realism' itself (that most slippery of desiderata). Given the
primacy of optimism, and the desire to avoid the apparent individualism of tragedy, the omission of the category is hardly surprising: *its* invocation might have raised the work's pedigree,
but at the price of suggesting a dubious defeatism. That darker tonality – including even the
24-hour time limit grafted onto Aristotle's requirements by Renaissance theorists – would be
the very element emphasised in Wajda's *Ashes and Diamonds*.

SOCIALIST REALISM AND COMEDY: *AN ADVENTURE AT MARIENSTADT*

As one commentator on the Polish cinema of the Stalinist period has noted, 'at the beginning of
the 1950s the issue of film comedy bristled with difficulties. Spectators weary of the monotony
of the repertoire of the time, comprising in the main films about production and "optimistic
dramas", cried out for entertainment. But countless obstacles blocked the way to the creation of
lighter films. There were contortions between socially mobilising satire and optimistic affirma-
tions of the achievements of the new regime' (Bocheńska *et al.* 1974: 239). If the author cites
even the highly popular *Przygoda na Mariensztacie* (*An Adventure in Marienstadt*, 1954) as an
example of the artistic inadequacies of the resultant comedies, the failing may lie in the way
it can be said to fall between stools: to translate this author's (Barbara Mruklik's) opposition
of satire and affirmation into the terms used by Piotr Zwierzchowski (to which I will return
later), to straddle 'the ideological' and 'the popular'. Yet the peculiar inadequacy of the period's
comedies ought to be surprising. It may seem as if the production of comedy should have
been the logical result of the positive view of history espoused by dialectical materialism, and
the official requirement for optimism in socialist realism. The lack of convincing comedies

becomes less surprising when one recalls that the production process had to answer to Party bureaucrats intent on ensuring that the class struggle was being taken seriously, while it is also arguable that no Polish Marxists could feel so sure of their ability to win over compatriots as to relax and extend the tolerance of foibles comedy demands. The favoured form would rather be that more aggressive, ideologically driven one: satire, as had been the case when Marxism was establishing itself in the Soviet Union, in the 1920s. Under the aegis of socialist realism, however, this satire was stripped of the hard edges, stylisation and formal innovation that had distinguished Soviet cultural production in its first decade, linking its satirical deformation of the human image to its truncation in modernism. Victory is not yet so secure as to allow the victors to banish all fleeting fears of its precariousness and of a fatal kinship between one's optimism and wishful thinking. It may even be that the state employment – and possible abuse – of the Marxist dialectic brings down upon its users the curse of paranoia (democratic anti-fascists, for instance, become 'objectively fascist' by propounding a democracy that goes hand in hand with capitalism…), causing a universal suspicion that all faces may be masks. The most likely form of merry-making becomes the sometimes sinister one known as carnival: the May Day parade teeming with parodistic masks of capitalist leaders. It is hardly surprising, therefore, that the authorities were suspicious of *An Adventure in Marienstadt*, a romantic comedy about a male and female bricklayer, or that its popular reception differed markedly from its official one.

It has long been a moot point whether *An Adventure in Marienstadt* is a socialist realist work whose continued popularity is a strange, inexplicable exception to the rule of that movement's general oblivion, or whether that popularity is easily explicable as rooted in its being simply a very traditional romantic comedy about the obstacles that defer the unity of country girl Hanka Ruczajówna and her bricklayer sweetheart, Janek Szarliński. The two possible readings are reflected in the clever strategy whereby Piotr Zwierzchowski offers alternative plot summaries, one of the work's 'ideological' interpretation, the other of its 'popular' reading. The exercise is so instructive as to merit quotation in full.

'Ideological' version: 1. New construction effectively does away with Warsaw's ruins; 2. A community centre singing troupe comes, colourfully costumed and full of song from Złocień to Warsaw, where it admires the rebuilt capital; 3. One of the trippers, Hanka Ruczajówna, meets girls from a brick-laying brigade, who are participating in Warsaw's reconstruction just like the men; 4. During a ball at Marienstadt, Hanka dances with a boy whose attractions are increased by the fact that he is a shock-worker who has achieved 312% of the norm; 5. Hanka travels to Warsaw to learn the building trade and work as a bricklayer; 6. An opponent of working women, foreman Ciepielewski, prevents her being employed at the building site; 7. The intervention of shock-worker Janek Szarliński gets Hanka the job, but Ciepielewski continues to seek to remove her; 8. Janek's productivity falls from 312% to 238%; 9. Hanka enlightens Ciepielewski's wife about the fact that her domestic labour is in fact the hardest; 10. Hanka joins the women's brigade; 11. The undertaking to carry out work-competition during the ceremonial handing over of the keys to new apartments; 13. The intervention of a wise Party secretary saves the face of the women's brigade; 14. As part of their undertaking the women's brigade builds a Bricklayer's House in their spare time and from materials saved by their economies; when need arises, everyone helps, including Ciepielewski and Dobrzyniec; 15. The opening of the House of the Bricklayer, which is attended by the minister himself, ends in a wonderful ball.

'Popular' version: 1. Hanka arrives in Warsaw together with a community centre singing troupe from Złocień; 2. During a stroll round the city there occurs an amusing meeting with a bricklayer the girl meets again during a dance at Marienstadt; 3. Hanka has to go home, the young people part; 4. In spring Hanka travels to Warsaw, where she studies, works and looks for the boy; 5. At the construction site Hanka meets the comic twosome of foreman Ciepielewski and plumber Dobrzyniec, fierce opponents of women at the workplace who are nevertheless amusing in their stubbornness; 6. By chance, Hanka finds the boy she is seeking, Janek; 7. Nocturnal dance of the two young people in Marienstadt, shared song; 8. Hanka and Janek work together, but something begins to go wrong between them; moreover, Ciepielewski continues to interfere; 9. Quarrel and parting of Hanka and Janek; 10. Ciepielewski and Dobrzyniec meet with comic adventures on the way to meet the director-in-chief: going to complain about women, they run into them continually, from female tram conductors to the lady director herself; 12. Hanka and Janek are reconciled, Ciepielewski and Dobrzyniec accept that women are good workers, and everything ends in a ball. (Zwierzchowski 2000b: 3–38)

Since each of the two intertwined strands isolated here solicits a different reading, does either one prevail? Although Zwierzchowski appears to favour the popular cultural reading, the witty symmetry of his summaries suggests an aporia, or at least the possible strength of arguments for the alternative position. Zwierzchowski rightly stresses the importance of the popular reading – after all, the work's popularity had surprised the authorities – but it seems to me that in the end the socialist realist model prevails. The problem with Zwierzchowski's analysis – paradoxically, given its awareness of the text's duality – is its assumption of its fundamental unity, and its refusal to consider the way in which it unfolds so as finally to privilege one model over the other. For much of its first hour the film is indeed cast almost entirely in the mode of romantic comedy. It begins to undergo transformation, however, when it comes to rest at that key locale of socialist realist narrative, the building site. As Hanka becomes a bricklayer, the narrative gradually shifts focus from the lovers' attempts to reach one another against a mobile set of backgrounds and begins instead to immure them in groups of which they are fixed and typical representatives. Less and less emphasis is placed upon their individual desires, more and more upon their emblematic placement within the two, rival groups of male and female bricklayers. This is the process of *generalisation* that governs socialist realist theory, as collective circles multiply, radiating outwards around the individual and then rebounding to efface his or her separate being. Each of the two central individual protagonists becomes a metonymy of his or her group, which then undergoes further generalisation and universalisation as it begins to metonymise the sexes. The move away from the individual is a collectivisation of desire that can be read either as its repression (see its reading by Wiesław Godzic 1991: 120–8) or as its sublimation (the favoured ideological reading).

In the end, therefore, *An Adventure in Marienstadt* is less about the unification of two individuals than about the historical power of the movement of women's liberation, which becomes so irresistible as to encompass even the diehard misogynist Ciepielowski. If Ciepielowski falls far short of the dignity and danger of the melodramatic villain favoured by socialist realism, this renders the work not less socialist realist but more so. It indicates the depth to which the optimistic Marxist vision of history pervades the work. As Artur Hutnikiewicz puts it in his summary of socialist realist aesthetics: 'optimism and pessimism are conceived not as psychic dispositions or as the cast of mind of an individual but as class categories. Optimism is simply the natural attitude of a young, victorious class. It is an optimism "founded upon rational premises and on the anticipation that that which is regressive will fall of necessity, sooner or later"' (Hutnikiewicz 1974: 254). Ciepielewski appears as always already overcome: the comic, because defeated, devil is an imp or gargoyle, embodying an old ideology that is less a threat than an absurdity, as is underlined by his comic pairing with the plumber Dobrzyniec. Scenes of their discomfiture dominate the film's final thirty minutes, underlining its didactic (socialist realist) purpose. Its relatively avuncular tolerance of Ciepielewski involves uncoupling him from any of the foreign centres of subversion that usually sustain the socialist realist villain and which are refreshingly absent here. *An Adventure in Marienstadt* knows no foreignness, only a gradual transformation of the country into the city that represents social advance for the former. Nothing is lost as Hanka sheds her country dress and moves to town. Not only does she find her love there; first and foremost, she finds a career. When she and her female workmates build a unisex Home of the Bricklayer in their spare time, country girls resembling her former self help lay the bricks on their visits to the city. And at the end Hanka herself is singing in a group, as she had at the outset, only this time sporting the red communist tie. *An Adventure in Marienstadt* may be described as a fading out of romantic comedy that sublimates it into a utopian social vision of the reconciliation – in a sense, marriage – of all members of the two sexes, a moment initiated when the men join the work to repair accidental damage to the women's House of the Bricklayer, and celebrated when they dance in couples as night falls over Marienstadt. But if its resemblance to classical Hollywood films extends to a final extinguishing of previously indulged, potentially dangerous elements, the ending is not the Hollywood couple's kiss but the collective celebration of the dance. As if the isolated couple represents a possible danger, the romantic comedy that could seduce the viewer into individualistic identification is finally downgraded by the elevation of the community. And that identification is socialist realist. Barbara Mruklik's diagnosis of the film's 'situational schematism, slogan statements and exaggeratedly idealised image of the Polish society of the 1950s' (Bocheńska *et al.* 1974: 241) skewers its last half-hour above all, for the sweetness of its first hour is that of a charming, somewhat naïve romantic comedy, not that of sweetly-sick propaganda. Romantic comedy and socialist realism may indeed overlap for much of *An Adventure at Marienstadt*, but it is the overlap of a slow-motion dissolve. It is almost as if the filmmakers wanted to leave a final impression of having done their duty. They may have had their rather Westernised ('bourgeois', 'pre-war') fun for two-thirds of the time, but a shift in emphasis that takes up another third can hardly be deemed so perfunctory as to merit castigation for the proverbial insincerity of the death-bed repentance.

Given what has been said so far, the film's reception at its first consideration by the Commission for Film and Script Assessment assumes particular interest: the commission's inability to determine precisely which conventions it follows may be linked to the duality described by Zwierzchowski, which might be called a 'bi-conventionality'. (The objections to the lack of a single clear convention were so intense as to call for the film's reworking and a second presentation to the Approving Commission later in the year.) The well-known poet Adam Ważyk, speaking first, was 'stunned by its unreality' and felt this 'could only be accepted as a de-realising convention'. Journalist Krystyna Żywulska objected to the way 'everything can be foreseen from the beginning', failing to note that this is a convention of much popular culture, though she did then propose terming it a fairytale. For the next speaker, Jerzy Pański, 'the whole film followed an inappropriate tone', and he proposed calling it a 'monumental comedy' (a new socialist realist generic category?). Interestingly enough, his objections mostly concerned scenes near the end, indicating a subliminal, inadmissible recognition of the unreality of the conventions of socialist realism: 'instead of a comedy it's turned into a sort of song of triumph, a pompous story', becoming 'unacceptable as of the scene at Muranów at which she [Hanka] speaks'. Pański felt that cuts were needed to rescue the film. Culture Minister Włodzimierz Sokorski applied the deadly label of a film with 'a petty bourgeois atmosphere' that was rubbish from start to finish. He could not understand how something so bad could have emerged from an approved screenplay, deeming one-third of it 'decidedly politically harmful'. In response, Jerzy Broszkiewicz posed the issue as a choice whether to rescue one of two things, 'an essentially bourgeois comedy' or 'a realistic comedy'. Aleksander Ford wanted to know what was politically harmful about the work, and felt it had followed the script. Ważyk responded – in a reaction that cannot but suggest the charitable conclusion of his tone-deafness to comedy – by describing the conversations between Ciepielewski and Dobrzyniec as 'essentially serious' and concluding 'I see nothing comic in them'. Żywulska attempted to redirect the discussion to the terms of debate proposed by Broszkiewicz: if the work is 'a realist comedy', it is absurd, 'but if we approach it as an optimistic fairytale in colour … we will have a different attitude to it'. Minister Wilczek argued that, judged in terms of its relation to reality, this could not be called a realist comedy. Somewhat more menacingly, he adds 'we saw this kind of film before the war, it is not ours but gives off a whiff of a cosmopolitan convention' ('cosmopolitan' being of course code for 'Jewish' in anti-Semitic Stalinist discourse). As part of this raising of the stakes that gives one clear answer to the question why there should be a shortage of socialist realist comedies, he demands 'can one make a comedy on the basis of the forging of a new man?' Ford commented further that if the film was a disaster, it involved all those present, for the film closely follows an approved script. He proposed an adjournment of the discussion, which then followed. Four months later, an amended version passed the second meeting of the commission, the two main points in its favour being the likelihood of a favourable audience reception and the value of the Polish film industry's move into colour comedy production (FN, KOFiS, A-214 poz. 24).

The divergences between the views of the film voiced by press and public that marked its wider reception offer further evidence of the split between the ideologised view of the élite and popular tastes and readings. Thus, a Party document listing 'General conclusions from discussion of the film *An Adventure at Marienstadt*' (FN, Miscellaneous, A-239 poz. 15, 1953a) notes that 'journalists were of the opinion that at present only very few individuals have a view of women's work like that of foreman Ciepielewski' and so such a film was not necessary, whereas 'the film's issues were judged differently in discussions among workers. It was stated during a discussion at the Young Worker's House in Mielec that the old attitude to women and the refusal to believe in the equal value of women's work is still alive in many workers' milieux. That is why such a film is very much needed.' A document attached to this added that 'despite the frequent critical comments by press reviewers, the film's attendance shows that it is very well received among viewers. By 30 June the film had been seen by 2,710,388 spectators in the towns, and in the countryside – despite receiving copies late and in a small number – 41,383. Comparison with other films (*Sprawa do załatwienia* [*A Matter to be Dealt With* (Rybkowski,

1953)], 2,374,642 in the towns, 472,644 in the countryside; and *Żołnierz zwycięstwa* [First series] [*Soldier of Victory* (Jakubowska, 1953)] – 1,855,168 in the towns and 683,587 spectators in the countryside) show this to be a record attendance' (FN, Miscellaneous, A-239 poz. 15, 1953b). Unfortunately, no one else seems to have drawn conclusions from the paper's pointed final remark: 'The attendance figures show how strongly the public yearn for comedies. Not even negative press judgements are able to discourage spectators and prevent them watching a film *en masse.*' In the case of comedy, in the early 1950s as throughout the history of the Polish People's Republic (c.f. official responses to Marek Piwowski's *Rejs* [*The Cruise*, 1970] [Łuczak 2002] or Stanisław Bareja's *Miś* [*Teddy Bear*, 1981]), the authorities' desire to reach the masses seems to have been checkmated by their fear of the potential subversiveness of laughter.

WAJDA, SKOLIMOWSKI AND THE AFTERLIVES OF SOCIALIST REALISM

It has often been stated that various of Wajda's works contain elements of socialist realism, and the degree of dialogue between some of the films in his trilogy and Aleksander Ford's *Five Boys from Barska Street* has been examined above. If it is unsurprising that socialist realism should be patchily present in *A Generation*, made before October 1956 and the evaporation of socialist realist paradigms, it is somewhat startling to discover it in *Man of Iron*, made in 1981 during the brief overground heyday of a Solidarity it celebrated, and combining Solidarity content with a callow political melodrama straight out of the socialist realist stable. Every now and then, sly, hostile commentators might apply the label to other works. Whereas the pro-regime critic Zygmunt Kałużyński would rightly apply it to *Man of Iron*, cunningly masking a political disagreement most readers would not share under an aesthetic objection many might, it is piquant to see it applied to *The Promised Land* in a review written under the pseudonym of SPODEK for the Cracow-based Catholic weekly *Tygodnik powszechny*. A censor's report contains the following extensive excerpt from the review, and a comment on its fate:

> Wajda's *The Promised Land* is a socialist realist film. National in form, socialist in content – just as I was taught at university. But on top of that it's also an excellent film. And that is what is most astonishing. Not the fact that Wajda has made a good film, for we've all grown accustomed to that, but that a realistic film about 'social changes', 'economic processes' with 'typical heroes' who are 'representative of their class', with an 'accentuation of the progressive role of the working class' and showing the moral 'disintegration of the owning class' presents a fascinating image. How is that possible, I asked myself, leaving the cinema after its lengthy, two-and-a-half-hour screening? After all, it was impossible to sit through even fifteen minutes of *Bright Fields*, which was so famous in the days of my generation ... It is perhaps not without significance for considerations of the socialist realism of *The Promised Land* that the content of Reymont's work fits the image of capitalism that was the subject of the analyses of Karl Marx. It coincides with it historically in the novel, but even more so in the film that is its 'national-social' analysis, both the truth about nineteenth-century Łódź and its contemporary, ideological interpretation.

And its fate? We learn this in the first words of the censor's report: 'In material entitled "In search of the Promised Land" SPODEK reviewed Wajda's film in an ironic manner. After deletions had been made, the editors withdrew the review, in which we read, among other things'– at which point the passage quoted above begins (AAN, GUPPiW, Pf-ZI-050/67/75). Ironically, the authorities clearly could not tolerate the linkage of a work they sought to promote as a modern Marxist classic with the aesthetic most widely associated with Marxism, the thoroughly compromised one of socialist realism. (The alternative, Brechtian version of 'Marxist form' never made any headway in Poland, partly due to the centrality of Romanticism to the country's theatrical tradition, partly because the simultaneously oppositional and official status of his Epic Theatre aroused the suspicions of both the Polish system and its critics, rendering it too 'formalist' for the former and too Marxist for the latter.)

Grasping the internal contradiction of *Man of Iron* – an even greater one than that discerned in *The Promised Land* by SPODEK – is hindered by the way the term 'socialist realism' functions as a virtual synonym for 'kitsch', an identification reflected in the widespread coinage 'socrealism', which mocks and mimics the Stalinist habits of neologism well-known from George Orwell's *Nineteen Eighty-Four* (1949). The classic instance of the terms' fusion is found in the novels of Milan Kundera. This unfortunate identification denies both the variability of the material subsumed under the term, and the historicity of the term itself, as each individual political conjuncture determines which of the elements loosely aggregated as 'socialist realism' are to be selected or stressed and inflected to meet the needs of a particular situation. The historicity is clearly apparent in post-war Poland's changing reflections of developments within Soviet culture (including its early 1960s 'youth literature', whose Polish equivalent is the early work of Skolimowski), right up to 1976 – the moment at which *Man of Marble* effected a radical separation between the logics of their progression. Geoffrey Hosking's description of post-Thaw Soviet prose recognises one paradoxical element of this historicity during the 1960s: 'Real, ascetic, struggling heroism returned to fashion again: indeed, there was a reversion to the early socialist realist prototypes of the 1920s and early 1930s' (Hosking 1980: 22). 'Socialist realism' could return to favour because the artist's real enemy was less the positive hero struggling against negative phenomena – a scenario that could always yield drama, and be tapped for the heightened melodrama of *Man of Iron* – than what Tertz usefully termed 'socialist classicism'. Here, 'eternal conflicts are no longer a matter of life and death because the chief battles have already been won. This is the aesthetic of a confident, powerful Empire' (Hosking 1980: 16). The favoured art-forms of that classicism are monumental, celebratory, like the statue of himself eyed quizzically and uncomprehendingly by Mateusz Birkut in *Man of Marble* (a moment of what Pański might have called 'monumental comedy'). This classicism opposes such key elements of realism as slang and dialect. The disparity between *Ashes and Diamonds* and 'socialist classicism' may have as much to do with its characters' rapid speech-rhythms as its content; and the early 1960s work of Skolimowski would install slang with a vengeance. In this context, it is intriguing to review the Script Assessment Commission's opinions of *Walkower* (*Walkover*, 1965), which combine a concern for authenticity and truth to youth culture with a desire for a 'positive hero', though that term had become too hackneyed – and tainted by association – for use. Clearly, 'socialist realism' was not a monolith, and some of its elements could survive its general shipwreck and seem relevant even to such an obviously non-melodramatic and avant garde work as Skolimowski's. It is intriguing to see Skolimowski himself, present at the meeting, going out of his way to address worries about the hero's positivity and to argue that the hero develops and 'purifies himself'. Of course, this may be lip-service to official values, intended to camouflage one kind of film as another in order to ensure its production, and to fend off such objections as one earlier speaker's damaging worry that the script's 'moral message is in my opinion extremely nebulous. We are dealing with the enigmatic psyches of people who have no clear idea what to do with their lives' (FN, KOS, A-214 poz. 310). And yet the film was made. Perhaps not surprisingly: for the Party, Skolimowski represented more than just the token talisman of connection with youth he had been for the Andrzej Wajda who hired him to script his own early 1960s youth film, *Niewinni czarodzieje* (*Innocent Sorcerers*, 1960). The actual moralism of his statements would have rendered him congenial to them, as would an emphasis on youth culture that can be seen as part of the afterlife of the youth themes of socialist realism. It is a deep, tragic irony that Skolimowski's most consistently morally engaged work – *Ręce do góry* (*Hands Up!*, 1967) – should have ended his career by adding a critique of Stalinism to that of the careerist survivors of the 1960s 'small stabilisation'.

CHAPTER THREE

CENSORSHIP IN A HALL OF MIRRORS

The modern Procrustes owns a mirror maze. A bed – and, worse still, a single one – is too primitive an instrument for transforming the text affixed to it: one can hear its cries of pain as it is stretched or amputated, and what comes out has clearly been crippled. The distorting mirror, however, alters the text painlessly, always allowing it to seem to remain whole, unchanged, in another dimension; to retain actual identity while losing it in the virtual sphere in which exchange begins. The mirrors are the various stages of vetting, of censorship: in one of them, a detail will dilate, be dwelled upon, become potentially controversial; in another (usually held by a higher instance, one less fearful of superiors' approval) it may shrink to a matter of little importance. As the text passes from one stage to another there is no single tyrant, no responsibility, only bureaucracy. One after another the mirrors massage the textual body, shape and reshape it, draw it in and out like a concertina. On its emergence, no one knows what changes it has undergone. They may not even have felt too painful to the author, whose censor may have worn a polite and solicitous air: this change, that change, will surely be for the best. With its use of mirrors, the whole operation has more of seduction than of violence. And yet it is as if the mirrors have indeed stolen the soul, and the changes have all taken place upon the inside.

FROM POLITICAL CENSORSHIP TO ECONOMIC CENSORSHIP

At the heart of the system that called itself 'real socialism' lay a series of interlocking institutions of political censorship and control. Replicating the Soviet model would have meant monitoring every stage of the production process. Often, however, East Central Europeans missed out one or more of the stages of invigilation. Scripts may have been keenly vetted before production, but in Poland, for instance, there was no on-set Soviet-style inspector to ensure congruence between the approved script and what was actually shot. And once a work had been filmed, it was always on the cards that it would be shown, though its venue might be a matter of controversy: it might be official, unofficial (as occurred in the 1980s, when smuggled videocassettes gave films the same variety of distribution as literature had enjoyed through samizdat) or even the strange mixture of 'official' and 'unofficial' bestowed upon controversial works by well-known directors, the directors being too famous for their suppression, the works too subversive for wide distribution. Moreover, some of the links in the monitoring chain could break off, as occurred in Poland when the Script Assessment Commission – the pre-shoot stage of vetting – was abolished in 1967. Meanwhile, even a work based on a vetted script could elude the state mechanisms of control: as Andrzej Wajda pointed out, the multivalence of metaphor meant that some of its meanings slipped through the fingers of the censor. When the counter-revolutionary Maciek Chełmicki stumbles to his death across a rubbish dump in Wajda's *Ashes and Diamonds*, his evident agony generates sympathy; he is not just a reactionary in an open-air version of the 'dustbin of history' to which Marxism consigned the forces of conservatism. In saying more than a thousand words could, pictures sidestepped the controls that were applied so sedulously to language and that rendered the images of East Central European television mere handmaidens of the ideological commentary, and television itself a form of illustrated radio. Its imagistic basis may be what rendered the *cinema* of East Central Europe its most vital conduit of national dissatisfaction. Moreover, as the literary theorist Mikhail Bakhtin might have said, the inherently *dialogic*, conflictual nature of drama (something of particular importance for the Marxist philosophy that professed a *dialectical* materialism) required air-time for the opposition and the perennial danger of the audience cheering the 'wrong' lines. In this respect, artistic discourse becomes the most effective opposition to the ruling political discourses that seek to spin the world exclusively in one direction. Only the ever-present temptation to self-censorship could effectively stifle such opposition. The most penetrating analysis of the strength of *that* temptation is provided by Miklós Haraszti, who sees the socialist artist less as potential dissident than as a variety of corporate man, employed by a State he piquantly likens to a Hollywood studio (Haraszti 1987: 68). The credo of the artist content to inhabit a 'velvet prison' is 'Art is more important to me than upholding the myth of art's autonomy' (Haraszti 1987: 72). Nevertheless, Haraszti himself concedes the possibly excessive pessimism of his model (Haraszti 1987: 160–2). After all, if it accounts well enough for the fully adjusted artist, it ignores the possibility of tactical adjustment pending the opportunity for more open expression. Though artists might differ on just when such opportunities arose, they can be perceived as coinciding with the periodic 'thaws' noted by political meteorologists.

THE MYTHICAL CENSOR AND THE REAL ONE

There is, alas, a myth of the obtuse censor. It has several sources. One is the propensity of artists to dine out on stories of what do indeed seem like manifestations of pettifogging idiocy, such as a filmmaker being told that his character's dream of entrapment in a falling lift inside Warsaw's Palace of Culture and Sciences – the Soviet Union's gift to Poland – should include a close-up of the plaque indicating the lift's manufacture in Sweden, lest the Eastern brothers take umbrage at the apparent slur on the reliability of their products. This can stand as just one example of the artist's propensity to recall the more colourful incidents and to colour those that are recalled, his or her primary intention being to create a strong narrative to divert the audience. The artist may also be more or less consciously aware that any hint of possible intelligence in the censor may alienate an audience inclined to view this as a flattering of the devil that also violates the norms for narratives on censorship in an unacceptable way. (In other words, the raconteur's performance itself is precensored by conventionally codified forms of audience expectation.) The myth is fed further by a confusion between the various instances within the institution known as 'censorship': for censorship was not just the comments pencilled in the margin by the anonymous drones of Mysia street; it was also the spluttering expostulations of the Minister chairing the Script Assessment Commission, or his colleagues in the Central Committee or even the Politburo, where the First Secretary blighted Roman Polański's career by condemning his first – and only – Polish feature, *Knife in the Water*. Very often, the more highly placed the source of the objection, the less coherent – less aesthetically pleasing, and even crude or brutal – the manner of its formulation. For the drones were often quite intelligent, as becomes apparent from the fascinating interview 'K-62' granted to *Tygodnik Solidarność* (Brumberg 1983: 252–62). I should know: a friend was approached by the censor with an offer of work after her very good graduation from the University of Warsaw Polish Literature department. She was more indignant about the slight upon her morality than the compliment to her intelligence, however. She – and the Critics' Union – might also have bridled at the implicit slight upon her ambition. For behind the offer there lay, among other things, the prejudice that deems the critic a failed, frustrated and would-be artist, eager (particularly if female) to exact revenge upon the true ones by castrating their works, or else afflicted with the graphomania so widespread in Poland (one fruit of the privilege artists acquired through the two hundred years of Poland's subjugation, when they represented the nation unofficially) and seeking some of the satisfaction of joint creation by refining the artist's expression. These two incarnations of the censor are of course siblings of the modern, Western form of censor known as the copy-editor, whose censorship – to the extent that it seeks to regularise an irregular prose – may be deemed 'economic'. What was pettifogging to the artist was meticulousness to the censor, who was usually by no means stupid (stupid ones did not last long in the job). These two views of the censor's work are, of course, equally valid, since in each case the search for the *mot juste* had a different motivation: the artist's, in the quest for the work's integrity, coherence and elegance; the censor's, to uncover points of possible ideological sensitivity. The duel is less often one of creativity and obtuseness than of the aesthetic and the ideological.

It is possible to speak of censorship, therefore, whenever any criteria other than the aesthetic dictate a change. As noted already, censorship occurred on a variety of levels: in the vertical hierarchy of a ladder whose feet rested in the humble workaday censor's office and ended (sometimes) in the clouds of the Politburo; and, horizontally, in all the other branches of the culture and information industry. It also, of course, took place in the heads of the artists themselves, who will have strangled at birth – or aired only as a café *tours de force* – stories they sensed had little or no chance of realisation.

Perhaps some examples will help. Since censorship was so pervasive an institution, I would argue that the passage to be discussed below is a very instructive instance of its microscopic workings, even though it was not penned by someone employed as a censor. It was attached to a letter written by Jerzy Wittlin, then newly appointed director of the Artistic and Film Publishers (Wydawnictwa artystyczne i filmowe – WAiF), dated September 1973, and addressed to Comrade Edmund Makuch, deputy head of the Culture Department of the PZPR Central Committee, and was adduced as a cardinal piece of evidence in Wittlin's indictment of the publisher's former management. It is a text from Jerzy Płażewski's *200 filmów tworzy najnowszą historię kina* (*200 Films Make Up the Most Recent History of Cinema*), with a proposed rewrite. Wittlin comments that 'the texts in Płażewski's coffee-table book … are the result of many months of editorial labour devoted almost exclusively to changing the tone and notes relating to the film industries of the socialist countries. The author's stubbornness … together with the insufficiently principled stance of the publishers mean that in effect the book continues to present the history of the cinema of the socialist countries in too simplified and one-sided a manner' (AAN, PZPR 923/2). Wittlin goes on to critique other aspects of WaiF's publishing performance (too many collections of reviews, too few serious monographs), lamenting in particular the fact that the cinema of socialist countries 'has seldom drawn the attention of writers'. He then presents two particularly offensive passages from Płażewski's book, arguing that their egregiousness will be mitigated considerably by the rewrites he proposes. The first passage runs as follows:

> The sudden fall in the number of films produced, the silence of the most authoritative artists, the near-total arrest in the recruitment of young cadres precipitated a flight from contemporary themes. Filmmakers restricted themselves to only a few genres, first and foremost among them the film biography, which outstripped and in fact replaced other genres. The Soviet tradition in film biography constituted a break with romantic distortions of the facts and an emphasis upon the real historical conflicts. At the beginning of the 1950s, these characteristics, unfortunately, were augmented by the hero's safe enclosure within a few approved quotations from his work and the adjustment of his convictions to current political needs. *Mussorgsky* [1950] was successful because [director Grigori] Roshal showed his hero not through quotations but through details of character, including the 'awkward' ones. He might indeed have extracted a good deal of drama from the tragic personal fate of the great composer, but he refrained from doing so. But he showed the truth about the sphere of his artistic work: the creative surge of the great genius, his admiration for folk art, the friendship among the members of the Mighty Handful of composers, his struggle against the Tsarist officials for culture.

Only one sentence (itself suggesting the imprint of early editorial coercion, or self-censorship – the one defining the Soviet tradition in film biography) survives unchanged into Wittlin's proposed rewrite, which runs as follows:

> The entire history of world cinema is a history of the successive rises and moments of weakening of the creative inventiveness of national cinemas. In the Soviet Union, the temporary reduction in the number of films produced did not favour the thematic variety of the works made. Screen biographies of famous people began to be dominant among the film genres. The Soviet tradition in film biography constituted a break with romantic distortions of the facts and an emphasis upon the real historical conflicts. But certain filmmakers began to simplify the narrative strands and characters of the protagonists, making use of well-known quotations from the life and works of the heroes. *Mussorgsky* became a success however because Roshal did not present the hero through quotation but through the truth of his personality. He might indeed have extracted a good deal of drama from the tragic personal fate of the great composer, but he chose a more difficult and more ambitious solution. He showed the truth in the sphere of his artistic work: the rapture of the creative genius, his admiration for folk art and friendship with the members of the Mighty Handful of composers, his struggle with the obtuseness of the Tsarist officials. (AAN, PZPR 923/2)

If Poland's cinema was its best-known international artistic ambassador, it was surely largely because celluloid already in the can, the cast disbanded, is far less amenable to such revision than the written word: the systematic inversion of meaning proposed here would be hard and expensive to achieve. Thus films often underwent relatively minimal cuts or – in more controversial cases – were shelved, often to be released whenever the country's periodic political cataclysms brought forth new leaders anxious to demonstrate their status as new brooms (the release of shelved films in the late 1980s paralleling the period's recurrent amnesties). After all, if Wittlin's revision is to be believed, any problems in Soviet cinematography were temporary and typical of all cinemas (not specific to the Soviet model), while an artist's failure to make the most of his opportunities can be praised as a sign of greater ambition. The Polish comrades are in many respects *plus religieux que le pape* (sensitised, doubtless, to Russian irascibility regarding outside criticism), protective even of the era of 'errors and distortions' Khrushchev had denounced. The passage displays the censor as most creative – as genuine co-author, muscling in on the original text. If author and co-author constitute a duo, though, it appears here in near-comic form, with the censor the almost laughably complete mangler of meaning (the Mrs Malaprop with a vengeance who knits beside the guillotine).

A SKETCH OF THE SCRIPT AND FILM VETTING SYSTEM

For much of the history of People's Poland, the two main pillars of the system for vetting scripts and completed films were the Commission for Script Assessment (Komisja Ocen Scenariuszy), which underwent several rejiggings of its name, and the Approving Commission (Komisja kolaudacyjna). In 1967, however, the former was abolished and replaced by Programme Councils (Rady programowe) attached to the individual Film Units. The Approving Commission remained as a bulwark of the film milieu's partial co-operation with the process of censorship. The Commission for Script Assessment and the Approving Commission would comprise members of various relevant milieux: politicians, sociologists, representatives of the young, for instance, alongside film critics, directors, the head of the film unit producing the film in question as a counsel for the defence, and the film's director himself (and, of course, it usually was a male), who would speak rather late in the proceedings, be it defiantly or strategically self-critically. One proposed list of prospective members of such a Commission dating from the late 1960s lists 41 names, beginning with three 'political activists', nine 'representatives of creative associations and social organisations', three 'critics' (i.e. film critics), thirteen 'artists and members of the film units', one 'specialist' (in this case, a sociologist), three 'representatives of the Main Board of Cinematography and other State offices' and seven slots for 'invited guests' (one of whom is identified as a censor) (AAN, NZK 1/34). This number would, of course, be a pool of potential committee members, and the largest attendance I have seen was for the Approving Commission considering Andrzej Wajda's *Man of Marble* – clearly a big draw – with 25 present (FN, KK, A-324 poz. 9). The more usual number of attendees was in the teens, though attendance seems to have fallen in the depressed and 'normalised' mid-1980s (see, for instance, AAN, NZK 5/22, 5/23 and 5/24).

The Script Assessment Commission would determine the political and artistic merits of a prospective work, usually demanding some changes, and sometimes a complete rewrite. It had very clear notions of what constituted a script, and was likely to describe the submissions of such figures as Jerzy Skolimowski or Wiesław Dymny as not really scripts at all, those of the former being deemed too short and those of the latter too like free-standing literary texts, swirling with the useless atmospherics of description. The Approving Commission would judge the completed film by the same criteria of artistic and political merit, with the political unsurprisingly accorded primacy. One example of the evaluative scale it employed assigns an initial score of up to 15 points for 'general political assessment', 15 extra points for 'general artistic assessment', five points for acting, three for camerawork, three for set design and costumes and three for sound quality (AAN, NZK 4/14). This division is found in a document of the late 1970s which also spells out the overall categories of merit. Category I merits 40 to 44 points and is 'distinguished'; category II, 34 to 39, is 'valuable'; category III, 27 to 33, 'average'; category IV, 19 to 26, 'weak'; and below 19 is 'bad'. This version of the assessment scale was introduced in 1969, and a document of the time compares how nine films measured by the previous scale would have fared under the new one. Zanussi's *Struktura kryształu* (*Structure of Crystal*, 1970), with 30.21 points, is category II under the old scale, and category III under the new one; while Kazimierz Kutz's *Sól ziemi czarnej* (*Salt of the Black Earth*, 1970), with 39.92 points, is a category I film under both systems. Interestingly, *Jarzębina czerwona* (*Red Sorb*, 1970) – a war film sponsored by the Ministry of National Defence and placed in category I under the previous system – slips to category II under the new one, with 39.10 points. Possibly worried about the disparity or the shortage of category I films under the new scale, or more probably simply wishing to promote a flagship film with strong perceived political merit, a handwritten note crosses out its possibly embarrassing category II and replaces it with category I, adding – by way of justification – 'over 39'. Of the nine films listed, under the old system two were category I, five in category II and two in category III. Under the new one (following the promotion of *Red Sorb*), two are in category I, only one in category II and one in category III (though another handwritten note possibly prompted by a worry about spread, promotes it to category II because it was over 33 [33.4]) (AAN, NZK 4/14).

The possibly clogging effects of intense bureaucratic review can be gauged by a letter dated 3 December1969 and sent to Zbigniew Pastuszko, director of the Zespół Programu i Rozpowszechnienia filmów (Unit for Film Programme and Distribution), by the director of the 'Zespole Filmowe' (Film Units) film production enterprise, Wiesław Bożym. He complains that the budget for paying reviewers is being stretched by the sheer number of them employed by the Zespół, over and above those of the film units themselves. The result can be that some scripts are reviewed over twenty times. He adds sarcastically that 'we would not have any reservations if all the reviews represented an assessment of the work in question. A consideration of the transcripts of the Script Assessment Commission meetings prompts certain doubts however' (AAN, NZK 4/14). A year later, Pastuszko himself will lament that 'certain members of the feature film Script Assessment Commission who do not speak out at the meeting itself, or are absent from it, sometimes submit written reviews several days after a decision has been made regarding the script in question'. He asks Czesław Wiśniewski, Deputy Minister of Culture and Art, to issue an instruction that only reviews submitted in time will be remunerated (AAN, NZK 4/14).

The scripts and film assessment process was clearly subject to the ineffectiveness and delays afflicting any bureaucratic system. The lack of certainty that one's script would be produced makes it hardly surprising that a Skolimowski would present something rather sketchy, or that a Dymny would submit something that – in the event of its rejection as a script – could be published unchanged as a literary text, more leeway being open to writers than to workers at the coalface of popular consciousness in 'the most important' – that is, most heavily vetted – art. One Script Assessment Commission member once voiced a worry that one day a writer would simply submit one of the great Polish literary classics in lieu of a script, saying that all the action and dialogue were already there. In the opinion of the writers though, for whom the economic really does seem to have been the 'ultimately determining instance' described in Party dogma, script shortages such as the one worried about in the late 1960s, and the perennial one relating to the commemoration of key anniversaries of the State and the Russian Revolution, reflected the low level of remuneration for screenplays. Of the two phases, of course, the Script Assessment one was potentially the most productive, and it has been argued that the filmmakers of the Polish People's Republic benefited from the need to have a clear conception of a project in order to defend it before peers and political taskmasters. This particular commission could be seen as sometimes co-shaping material, not just censoring it – though its capacity spectacularly to fulfil certain censoring functions is most notoriously apparent in its vetoing of Aleksander Ścibor-Rylski's first script for *Man of Marble* in 1963 (FN, KOS, A-214 poz. 338). Its role as 'good cop' to the Approving Commission's 'bad cop' was the reason why it could be replaced by the Programme Councils whose directors saw them as 'Script Assessment Commissions in miniature' (Zajiček 1992: 195).

A FOREIGN BODY? WAJDA'S *PILATE AND OTHERS*

During the period of the existence of People's Poland, Andrzej Wajda made several films abroad – some of them during his own creative crisis of the 1960s, others during the moribundity of the state itself in the 1980s. But only in the case of *Pilate and Others* was there an a priori likelihood of the Polish production and vetting system being unable to stomach the resultant work: after all, it was a West German production, derived from part of a controversial novel by Mikhail Bulgakov, and devoted to that subject of extreme sensitivity in the Eastern Bloc (and, of course, a different sensitivity elsewhere), religion – and, worse still, the Passion of the founder of the Christian Church that was the state's main rival for unswerving devotion. Moreover, it was the work of a director who, during the shoot, described himself to a *Frankfurter Allgemeine Zeitung* reporter, Brigitte Jeremias, as 'a Catholic, though not a practising one' (Jeremias 1971: 28). In the following section I will be concerned, among other things, with just what kind of film is likely to emerge from a person whose self-definition is that of 'a Catholic, though not a practising one': a contradictory statement itself possibly further contradicted by two of Wajda's other self-definitions, as socialist and as surrealist. Are these different self-definitions offered tactically and self-protectively to different audiences, or can Wajda really be all these things, becoming possibly all things to all men (though not necessarily, of course, to all women, a strain of misogyny being an often-noted feature of his work)? If the three self-definitions of Catholic, socialist and surrealist are split by their awareness – conscious or not – of the counter-definitions, could the resultant pullulating, possibly postmodern mass be termed 'six directors in search of an audience'? Of particular interest, in the context of this chapter, is the question whether Wajda's choice of Bulgakov's text may have stemmed in part from a sense that it provided a 'pre-censored version' of the sacred text, filtering it through an alternative version in order to reduce the likelihood of his film's non-distribution within Poland. May not the choice of a Soviet text have provided Wajda with useful camouflage, for all Bulgakov's problems in the Soviet Union? After all, who could object to a film version of a text whose Soviet provenance could seem not so much to hide as to cancel its reliance upon texts written by Christian authors? Thus the film raises in an acute form questions both of censorship and of the degree to which even for the socialist artist working abroad apparent creative freedom is shadowed by forms of self-censorship.

These introductory remarks are, of course, speculative and may be unfair. After all, had not Pier Paolo Pasolini's *Il Vangelo secondo Matteo* (*Gospel According to St Matthew*, 1964) demonstrated the possible compatability of socialist or even Marxist radicalism with a form of religiosity? Given Jesus' youth when he died, his life so appallingly curtailed, the interest in his life-story displayed by the young and student radicals of the late 1960s was predictable, though for many the Christ-like icons were posters of Che Guevara. That Guevara-like quality was of course the basis for Andrzej Wajda's interest in filming his 1972 version of Jesus' story, *Pilate and Others*:

> I once saw a newspaper photograph, which I cut out and filed away. It showed three Dutch 'provos', the one in the middle being the spitting image of Christ and his two companions the thieves. I even thought up the outlines of a script: a child is born in a garage somewhere in Berlin in 1945; thirty years later we see him as a hippie wandering around the country preaching some message. (Michałek 1973: 143)

In another interview, Wajda describes how the photograph showed

> three such lads walking along in American army battle-dress. It seemed to me that this was Christ, Saint Peter and Saint John walking along, and that was how I captioned the photograph. Later, I obtained a poster ... 'Wanted: Jesus Christ'. I thought one could make a film on this subject, I looked for a way to do so, and eventually came to the conclusion that the best text to use as a base was Bulgakov's story about Pilate in *The Master and Margarita*. (Wertenstein 2000: 80)

Critical opinion has not been kind to the resultant film, tending to deem *Pilate and Others* incoherent.[1] It transposes the version of the Passion story interspersed among the chapters of Bulgakov's novel into drama but also makes a series of imaginative, telling additions. For Klaus Eder, 'the link with Bulgakov's literary mythology means that the issue – the rediscovery of Christian mythology by the younger generation – is theatricalised rather than illuminated' (Eder *et al.* 1980: 176–7). More damaging, perhaps, given its apparent subject matter, is the conclusion of Bolesław Michałek: '*Pilate and Others* is not ... a work likely to leave much of a mark on faith, the Church or Christian philosophy' (Michałek 1973: 147). Michałek – whose close co-operations with Wajda make his judgement particularly telling – would be among the critics to term it 'incoherent' (Michałek & Turaj 1988: 150). This description may be motivated by a sense that Wajda's film both attempts too much and does so too obliquely. Its efforts to probe the fascination of Jesus for late 1960s hippies and 'Jesus people', to dissect the mechanisms of totalitarian power, and to do so for both German and Polish audiences, are arguably muted by its simultaneous aim of fidelity to Bulgakov's remarkable original. The result is a palimpsest whose layers I will probe, as it seems to me that its address to a multiplicity of audiences results in a failure to satisfy any one of them. In this sense the film could indeed be termed 'Six Directors in Search of an Audience'. (After all, if the meeting of two Poles proverbially yields four opinions, the joke-like encounter of the Catholic, the socialist and the surrealist should yield six.) Nevertheless, here – as in the case of Pasolini's *Gospel According to St Matthew* – the encounter between religion and one of post-war Europe's leading socialist directors has great intrinsic interest, despite Wajda's believable assertion that the spiritual aspect of the story did not interest him (Wertenstein 2000: 80). The prominence attributed both to the figure of Matthew and to the *St Matthew Passion* of Bach might even justify titling it – after Pasolini – *The Gospel According to St Matthew II*, a whimsical proposal underwritten nevertheless by Wajda's own statement that *The Master and Margarita* could only have been filmed in omnibus fashion – with the best director for its *Pilate* section being Pasolini (Wertenstein 2000: 80). Had it been filmed in Morocco, as first intended by ZDF, the result would of course have been even more Pasolinian, recalling his *Edipo re* (*Oedipus Rex*, 1967) or *Medea* (1969). And if, as Slavoj Žižek has argued in connection with Alfred Hitchcock's *The Trouble With Harry* (1955), a director's least typical work may be his or her key one (Žižek 2001: 27) – what Friedrich Hölderlin might have termed the 'eccentric centre' of an oeuvre – it is worth also recalling Michałek's additional statement that 'it is one which counts very highly in the contemporary cinema and artistic biography of Andrzej Wajda' (Michałek 1973: 147).

Wajda's contention that he has not added a line to Bulgakov (Wertenstein 2000: 80) may not be entirely true, but the dialogues do follow the original ones very closely. Nevertheless, he begins with an addition to Bulgakov, a scene pairing footage of lambs being led to slaughter with a chorale from the *Matthew Passion*. The sheep can only be Passover ones. The recollection of the death of the Passover lambs is underlined powerfully by intercut shots of the serried joints they will become. It insists metaphorically on the reality of the blood that flowed on Good Friday. Klaus Eder's argument that the film makes no connection between the Passion story and the National Socialism suggested by its setting (Eder *et al.* 1980, 176) seems to me wrong: after all, Wajda's prologue forges just such a link by allegorising questions of obedience, authority, victimage and guilt. The film's address of a German audience as much as a Polish one is established strikingly – and possibly forced – by intercutting the slaughter with an interview with the ram charged with leading the sheep to their death. With the voice of Franciszek Pieczka, he says he is only doing his job, that it eases the lambs' deaths, and in any case he is only following orders: echoes of the stereotypical excuses of participants in National Socialist atrocities. This is then emphasised by the cut to the enormous semi-ruined former Nazi stadium in Nuremberg for Pilate's interrogation of Yeshua (Jesus). Ironically, only a German word adequately designates Wajda's pointed comments about the German setting: *Schadenfreude*.

> One could start with the fact that making *Pilate* was for us – the whole Polish crew – a very interesting experience from what one might call the psychological point of view. As is already known, the film was made three years ago in West Germany. There was something peculiar about this, which we all felt: under commission from the Second programme of West German television, a Polish crew was shooting a film amid the ruins of the Third Reich. I chose Nuremberg because it seemed to me that there was something appealing about using for our own ends the stadium where Hitler had given speeches, that amazing edifice that was never completed. It stands today, half-ruined, and those who were to have been destroyed to enable such buildings to rule the world appear there to mock them, demonstrate their absurdity. (Wertenstein 2000: 79)

The *Schadenfreude* becomes amusing when Wajda recounts how a passer-by approached Andrzej Łapicki, who was sporting his secret serviceman's dark glasses, asked him to confirm that some Poles were shooting a film nearby, and then told Łapicki 'you keep an eye on them' (Wertenstein 2000: 83). It slides towards shallow self-righteousness and false mimicry of expected socialist positions, however, when he criticises a West 'soaked in technology and material affluence' (Wertenstein 2000: 82) for the indifference of drivers sailing blithely past a crucifixion: after all, the improbability of a modern crucifixion gives its viewers every reason for supposing it to be unreal (and perhaps – in the German context – part of such a Passion Play as the one at Oberammergau). Indeed, Wajda's tired generalisation is nicely complicated by Daniel Olbrychski's references to passers-by crying out 'Jesus, don't let them get you' (Wertenstein 1971: 14).

Eder's criticism of the film for ostensibly failing to link National Socialism and the Passion Play is significant, however, because it can be taken as typifying the position of most of the film's spectators, primed to respond only to a limited portion of the many elements with which it bristles. A socialist such as Zygmunt Kałużyński, meanwhile, the regular film critic of the generally liberal weekly *Polityka*, could even bring a perverse allegorical ingenuity to bear upon it, remarking of Wajda's prologue that 'anyone who wished to do so might see here a multi-directional allusion indeed (Lamb of God…) to the role that religion, and the fanaticism that grew from it, played *later* in history' (Kałużyński 1975a). Kałużyński inserts this film into the socialist project by describing it as a further stage in Wajda's life-long urge to dismantle myth. Wajda himself may well have hoped to attract a large audience, appealing to Polish believers, Polish socialists, socialists and believers in general, Germans and – of course – the international art-cinema audience. After all, as his interview on the film with Wanda Wertenstein states, it offered 'Variations on a Well-known Theme' (Wertenstein 2000: 84). Ironically, but perhaps unsurprisingly, the apparently potentially popular retelling of 'the Greatest Story Ever Told' became his least popular work. As Michałek noted:

> It was shown first on Good Friday, 29 March 1972. Unfortunately it has never been shown in movie theatres on a commercial basis. When this was tried in France, a distributor ran into many obstacles. Thanks to Wajda, one or two copies of the film were made available for art-theatre showings in Warsaw. (Michałek & Turaj 1988: 150).

The première Michałek mentions was of course on ZDF, the commissioning West German TV station. The Polish premiere came three years later, and the authorities were clearly reluctant to countenance the wide dissemination of a work on a religious theme by the country's most prominent director: a published censor's note from the time of release reads:

> 13 February 1975. One should not allow the publication of any material, reviews, discussions and articles on A. Wajda's film *Pilate and Others*, or demands for the wide distribution of this film. Only information about the fact of the screening of this film in a particular art cinema should be released. This recommendation does not affect the specialist film journals, from which only possible demands for the film's wide distribution would have to be removed. (Cancelled 10 June 1975.) (Wertenstein 2000: 89)

Not surprisingly, a censor's report in the Archiwum Akt Nowych mentions the particularly large number of censorial interventions into the reviews of this film, as of other Wajda productions.[2] One may wonder whether the film's final emergence at this time constituted a reward for the class consciousness displayed in *The Promised Land*, whose simultaneous release may have been intended to overshadow it, but I have not found any evidence of this.

The authorities surely hoped though that the panache of *The Promised Land* – the work of a, to them, unexpectedly socialist Wajda (Wertenstein 2000: 90) – would obscure the experimental work of the self-proclaimed (if non-practising…) Catholic. The official restriction on its distribution on the basis of a letter of protest by a Christian offers the oxymoronic, nauseatingly oleaginous spectacle of an anti-religious State simulating guardianship of the Church's reputation. The letter, assuming it ever existed, could of course have been – and probably was – the work of one of the Party stooges regularly commissioned to write such documents of 'popular support' for actions the Party was either unsure of, or had not yet taken (Wajda 2000b: 96).

The identity of the architectural styles of modernity and the classical world in the Nuremberg stadium in which the film begins is as important for its themes as its *mise-en-scène*, as it synthesises ancient and modern, the Roman amphitheatre and the site of twentieth-century totalitarianism. History becomes an Adornian marking of time, a nightmarish double-exposure of oppression across a modernity still soaked in the blood it projects self-servingly and self-deludingly onto myth. The mixed attire of the participants (part period costume, part modern dress) reinforces the setting's fusion of ancient and modern, importing into Bulgakov's story of Pilate the carnivalisation of history in his novel's masked ball of devils. As Andrzej Drawicz notes, 'Bulgakov permits – indeed, more than that, wants one to find – a modern meaning in the confusion of levels and orders, of the damned of all eras and nations, the devil's ball; and Andrzej Wajda has managed to grasp that' (Drawicz 1975: 6). Although Wajda's dialogue closely follows Bulgakov's, modernising changes are built into Yeshua's flashbacks: Matthew is now a former pimp, Yehudah (Judas) a smart, sleazy, white-suited man met at the Las Vegas bar, and the telephone disgorges coins (instant payment of the thirty pieces) as he denounces Yeshua. Particularly telling, following the state-sponsored anti-Semitic campaign of 1968, is the staging of Pilate's dialogue with Caiaphas. When Pilate threatens the Jews in general, the low-angle shot accentuates the menace, and the cowering Caiaphas diverges considerably from Bulgakov's fearlessly defiant one. The film thus extends the oblique reckoning with 1968 that veins the surface of such adjacent Wajda films *Landscape after a Battle*, *Wesele* (*The Wedding*, 1973) and – of course – *The Promised Land*. The Jews are not the anti-Semite's Christ-killers, their persecution legitimated by their Gospel calls to bear the curse of Jesus' death; they too are victims.

As events unfold in the amphitheatre, surreal spectacles dot the arches above the main drama: an elegant couple look down from a modern opera box, five blind people approach the brink of a ledge, a Fellinieseque clown shudders enigmatically. As so often in Wajda's work, surrealism's lightning flashes jaggedly across the narrative, a matter to which I will return later. But Wajda's stated studied fidelity to Bulgakov hides a shift in focalisation. Bulgakov filters three of his four relevant chapters through the tortured viewpoint of Pilate, whose head is throbbing. Wajda, however, alternates objectively between the two speakers with crisp shot/countershot movements, even placing the standing Yeshua above the seated Procurator as if to suggest the pre-eminence of the former. Moreover, any expressionist subjectivisation or disturbance of consciousness is located in Yeshua, as it is he who hallucinates, not Pilate: his anachronistic vision of a cross around Pilate's neck undergoes traumatic uncanny animation into his own image suffering convulsively upon it. When Yeshua mentions Pilate's pain-ridden thoughts and longing for his dog, the film prevents us knowing whether or not he is right, dissipating the moment's otherworldly frisson. Wajda's coolness towards the hypothesis of the supernatural is reflected in a style generally more akin to documentary than expressionism. His work's modernity thus involves a draining of supernaturalism, which may be deemed either 'Bultmannian' or a fruit of the socialism Wajda professed for much of his career. Bulgakov's story suggests both a bedrock of factuality for the Gospel account, and its compensatory embellishment by Matthew the scribe, the sole faithful follower of Yeshua, who later refers to Matthew's misrecording of his sayings. Wajda underlines the idea of Matthew the mythmaker particularly strongly near the work's end, when Matthew charcoals the rays of an aureole around the dead man's face imprinted on his T-shirt while removing Yeshua from the cross: it is Wajda's demythologisation of the legend of Veronica. Wajda makes no mention of the fact that in Bulgakov's novel this narrative is begun by a devilish figure who seems to be Satan himself, whose status as the Father of Lies may prompt doubts in the entire veracity of his own account, or that the Devil-figure Woland is doubled by the Master, the hero of *The Master and Margarita*, who originally wrote this story, then burned it. (Woland's W is the diabolic inversion of the master's M, and each has lost his name.) Since Satan may in fact have stolen the Master's story, it may be more simply a fiction than an uncanny putative eye-witness account.

Wajda's film may begin with a pointed interpellation of German spectators, but its West German overtones reconjugate as allegorical Polish ones. This occurs primarily through the camera's repeated reversion to Afranius, the secret service head. Bulgakov's text may have him frequently present as the sinister 'cowled figure', but cinema makes it possible to pull him out of anonymity and show him constantly tracking events, evoking the totalitarian post-war East European world so well-known to Wajda himself. No wonder that a review in the Catholic periodical *Więź* ended pointedly with a censor-evading reference to the fact that his modern dress 'is also of significance' (Smosarski 1975: 141). The double-speak whereby Pilate apparently requests protection for Yehudah while really ordering his murder is a particularly chilling example of totalitarian political discourse. Following the proclamation of doom upon Yeshua, the film will be a duel of focalisation, between the diabolical state forces embodied in Afranius and the impotent rebellion of Matthew, who can only fantasise of ending Yeshua's agony by a thrust with a stolen bread-knife. It is from Matthew's viewpoint that we follow him to Golgotha. After hallucinating the stabbing of Yeshua, he realises, crestfallen, that he has no knife and goes in search of one. The knife protruding from a loaf in a breadshop window becomes an allegorical allusion to Yeshua himself as the communion bread of life, always already pierced: the lamb slain from the foundation of the world. Matthew fails to breach the military cordon around the crucifixes; rebuffed, he cries 'turn the other cheek' – a possibly significant addition to Bulgakov's text, which contains no New Testament quotations – then runs across a motorway to take refuge in a burnt-out car, from which he implores God to kill Yeshua. He again pictures himself stabbing Yeshua through a fantastically high leap up to him hanging on the cross. As he sits in the car, he writes. Thus Wajda the activist establishes artistic expression, writing's memorialisation, as inherently tragic, the fruit of impotence. That memorialisation, however, will fuse permanently with fantasy as Matthew draws rays round the bloody face imprinted on his T-shirt. Matthew's redaction of Yeshua's story does indeed represent its partial fictionalisation, as Yeshua himself had stated. Discerning the origin of the sacred text in fabulation, of course, may be taken as lending fiction the most comprehensive of legitimations by transforming it into myth. In one key dialogue, Pilate asks Afranius if Yehudah will be resurrected. Afranius replies that this will occur at the last trump, when the awaited Messiah arrives. For Wajda, however, Matthew's drawing of the aureole around Yeshua's head shows that for him – a painter turned filmmaker – resurrection is the task of art: an art whose fantastic resurrection of the dead – both here, and in *Ashes and Diamonds* and *Everything for Sale* – is tainted by a bitter sense of futility. It is Matthew who first transforms the crucifixion into symbolic representation and re-enactment, as his pulling of a cross alongside the Autobahn at the film's end inaugurates the Imitation of Christ.

If the dark glasses sported in Wajda's earlier *Ashes and Diamonds* by Zbigniew Cybulski, the director's favourite actor, reappear here on the face of Afranius, the implication is one of the impossibility of revolt. In *Ashes and Diamonds*, Cybulski had played Maciek Chełmicki, the young rebel gunned down by representatives of the new, Soviet-sponsored order of 1945. The rubbish dump across which he stumbled to his death is surely echoed in the site of Yeshua's crucifixion, reflected in and cynically negated by Afranius's dark glasses. Similarly, in the moment of death Yeshua's body becomes its own photographic negative. The rubbish dump and dark glasses encode the director's continuing dialogue with his best-known, most haunting film, *Ashes and Diamonds*, since both are crucial to it.[3] The interface between the image of the moment of crucifixion and these two key elements of *Ashes and Diamonds* establishes that film retrospectively as a story of crucified youth. The blue jeans of both Yeshua and Matthew in a sense replace Cybulski's dark glasses. The casting of Daniel Olbrychski as Matthew further recalls that work, as Olbrychski had been asked to stand in for the dead Actor who represented Cybulski in *Everything for Sale*, Wajda's controversial tribute to the recently deceased star. Wajda's interest in the attraction exerted upon the young by Jesus becomes in fact a coded appendix to his life-long threnody for the war-time martyrdom of his own generation: in essence not a 'demythologisation' of Jesus, but a reading of the 1960s' mythologisation of youth as a perennial response to its recurrent suffering, the recurrent crushing of its quest for revolution. For Wajda, Christ is – as in the title of one of Ryszard Kapuściński's collections – 'Christ with a Rifle in His Hand'. His description of the film's genesis in the sight of a 'Wanted!' poster for Jesus – and the film's opening sequence was initially planned as depicting the manhunt for him (Abu 1972) – chimes with the generally agonistic tenor of his work, and with his admission that he could only conceive of the Gospels in a military context (Wertenstein 2000: 80): casting Olbrychski, his talismanic substitute for Cybulski, in the role of Matthew simply underlines Wajda's closeness to this character: to the man who dreams of holding a weapon, then finds himself holding a pen. That directorial proximity to Matthew may have motivated Wajda's bizarre statement that Pilate is more interested in Matthew than in Yeshua – surely a projection of his own preoccupations onto the Procurator of Judah (Wertenstein 2000: 81). Wajda then links Matthew's final inability to write, as he pushes his typewriter aside, to the impossibility of writing not based on personal experience (ibid.); in other words, only autobiography, not biography, is possible. The statement has an ironic ring in the context of his own film, an adaptation of another person's work. Yet self-reference saturates it, from the casting of Wajda himself as the ram's interviewer to Matthew's drawing of the aureole – a gesture Drawicz likens to that of *Everything for Sale*, Wajda's most ostentatiously personal film (Drawicz 1975: 7). The work's possible incoherence – the excess of ambivalent culturally and personally overdetermined echo around it – may indeed mean that for Wajda at least the other text which protectively conceals the personal also suffocates it in its folds.

THE CATHOLIC, THE SURREALIST AND THE SOCIALIST

Having posited three conflicting and conflicted identities within Wajda – the Catholic (which can also, on occasions, be the nationalist, as in *Polak-Katolik*), the surrealist and the socialist one – it is worth considering their interrelations more closely. Initial German reviews of *Pilate and Others* spoke of its failure to shock. The expectation of shock had, of course, been generated by the project of modernising the Passion story. That expectation lends particular significance to the fact that Wajda makes this film outside Poland: even as Wajda wishes to tap the undoubted passion for religion of a Polish populace driven by discontent into the arms of the Roman Catholic church, he wants simultaneously to avoid antagonising it. The Western capitalist declaration that all publicity is good might not apply *vis-à-vis* an audience of acute religious sensitivities, and might also threaten Wajda's patriotic credentials. After all, is this not a work made in West Germany, at the heart of the favourite Other not just of Wajda's own war-ravaged generation but of the socialist state itself? The perhaps mythical letter of protest by an outraged Christian cited by the authorities to justify the work's restricted screening could indeed represent genuine popular disquiet with it, and – for all his protests – one could imagine Wajda himself preferring to have it shown in art cinemas rather than evoke popular opposition, as it might have done. Could the treatment of religion by a self-proclaimed socialist and surrealist avoid accusations of a blasphemous intent the Polish state could mobilise either to discredit Wajda, or to shore up its own atheist project – or even both? Filming in West Germany may permit a surrealist freedom, but it is limited by its restriction to a foreign space. The film is thus riven by the aporia of modern art evoked at the start of Adorno's *Aesthetic Theory*: the artwork's inner freedom is given the lie by the prevailing unfreedom without (Adorno 1974: 9).

The state's attitude to filmic depictions of religion, as hinted above, swayed uneasily between ambivalence, self-contradiction, self-deluded wishful thinking, opportunism and anti-clerical militancy. Almost all of these emotions characterise the censors' memos describing the restriction of Polish exposure of such films as Ken Russell's *The Devils* (1971) or Pasolini's *Decameron* (1970) to the Konfrontacje (Confrontations) film festival alone as a tactic 'to remind certain Catholic circles what shocking and anti-clerical films are made and distributed in the West, whereas, despite the existence of a State network of cinemas, they are not distributed here' (Fik 1993/94: 181). Here, as so often, the State sought to derive capital from a reluctantly accepted necessity: its inability to persuade any gifted Polish filmmakers to direct similarly anti-clerical works. Equally importantly, the non-distribution of such films as Russell's and Pasolini's surely owed more to State opposition to pornography (a term whose elasticity is apparent from its application by Party First Secretary Edward Gierek to Wajda's *The Promised Land*) than to concern for the tender consciences of Catholic viewers: an opposition motivated partly by austere traditions of Party morality, partly by a desire to distinguish socialist cultural production from the capitalist one and partly by dislike of the pornographic elevation of couples and their private, backroom interchanges above collective activity within the controlled public space of factory or street. Meanwhile, any domestic film too apparently respectful of religion (Janusz Morgenstern's *Trzeba zabić tę miłość* [*Kill that Love*, 1972], Edward Żebrowski's *Ocalenie* [*Salvation*, 1972] [Fik 1993/94: 179] or Stanisław Różewicz's *Samotność we dwoje* [*Loneliness Tête à Tête* (sic), 1968] [Fik 1994: 222]) was firmly castigated. The depth of the contradictoriness that finally doomed Party policy to collapse may be gauged by the simultaneous promotion of genuine pornography whenever it could be deemed an irritant to the church: thus, despite initial, and even subsequent, Party rumblings of misgiving over Walerian Borowczyk's *Dzieje grzechu* (*Story of Sin*, 1975), the director reportedly gained official approval by going before the minister (of Culture) and stating 'I've just come out of a meeting with the bishop, and the Church opposes the making of this film' (Hollender & Turowska 2000: 60).

Although accusations of blasphemy dot the history of cinema, with some declaring the invention itself diabolical at birth, statements of blasphemous intent are considerably rarer. This is understandable; the significant outlays filming often entails renders filmmakers loath to alienate potential audiences, to say nothing of fearful of infringing the blasphemy laws most cultures possess and finding themselves in court or jail. Actual blasphemous intent being rare, where is it most likely to be found? Primarily among low-budget filmmakers, whose future filmmaking would not be threatened by any withdrawal of public approval. Many such filmmakers have never enjoyed such approval in any case, even relishing its absence and the concomitant lack of constraints. Untrammelled imagination flourishes on such non-approval, and *épater le bourgeois* has long been a motto of the avant garde. During the first century of cinema's existence, of course, the most enthusiastic advocates of unfettered imagination included the surrealists, who deemed the aesthetic task inherently revolutionary. But if blasphemous intent is most likely among low-budget filmmakers and/or ones with an anti-religious worldview, the two groups are not necessarily identical. Although surrealism may have propagated anti-religiosity, so did socialism. The canon of great anti-religious directors would include Buñuel, in the one camp, whose first works were resolutely low-budget, and Eisenstein, whose arsenal included the extensive financial resources of the Soviet Union. Surrealists and socialists have themselves been at loggerheads on occasions, with the surrealist tradition of free imagination being itself labelled 'bourgeois', in the sense of 'individualist' and 'formalist' by socialism, declared incapable of the necessary clear analysis of the contradictions of capitalism, while socialism itself, upon graduation into a state ideology, became open to surrealist critique as a state religion as oppressive as the clericalism it had displaced. Moreover, the painterly surrealist fixation upon the *image choc* can subvert the narrative intention most filmmakers pursue.

At various points in his career, Wajda mentioned the importance of surrealism for his work. Indeed, *Wajda mówi o sobie*, the compilation of materials which includes the fascinating interview I have quoted frequently here, begins by citing Buñuel. The interaction in Wajda's work of surrealism and the apparently non-surrealist, constraining practice of literary adaptation is intriguing, as the self-imposed imperative of 'fidelity' – that issue that has bedevilled literary adaptations – arguably diverts the director's inventiveness into such possibly trivial or decorative details as the odd assortment of figures watching Yeshua's interrogation by Pilate. For Wajda, surrealism serves various functions, providing an outlet for his painterliness and interest in extreme compositional contrast, an aesthetic adequate to the violence history has visited upon Poland and a source of allegorical images to baffle the censor. The censor in question, however, is as personal as it is political, as much within as without.

SURREALISM AND LITERARY ADAPTATION

Wajda's multiple intentions suggest a surrealist anti-intentionality, a dreamlike fragmentation of the self. *Pilate and Others* may be the limiting case of the mixed motives that flow through so many Wajda films – the classic instance being the double politics of *Ashes and Diamonds* – and here suggest a reason for his apparent extreme lack of understanding of his own film. The split, multiplied director is not just in search of an audience, as usual: he is groping in the dark both for an audience and for coherence of self.

A further source of non-intentionality in Wajda's works is the substitute status of so many of them, particularly the literary adaptations, of which, of course, *Pilate and Others* is an example. Stand-ins for scripts he was unable to film, they are cross-hatched with frustrated shadows of the unmade. Adaptations can be 'automatic writing' in the sense of simply giving the director work to do; to keep his hand in, manifest continued existence, and ward off the nihilistic self-doubts of unemployment. If the adaptation is also meant to function as a Trojan Horse, in some cases the horse's belly is sealed: from the outside, by the authorities; from the inside by the artist sensitive to their vigilant breathing nearby. The inside of the horse can become a womb that fails to come to term. Alternatively, the authorities may allow only one meaning to emerge, as when they asserted that the ending of *The Promised Land* demonstrated its Marxism. The blocked intentionality of *Pilate and Others*, meanwhile, is augmented by the confluence within it of the separate non-intentionalities of surrealism and literary adaptation. This is hardly surprising: after all, one of the four sections of *The Master and Margarita* appears as the dream of a poet in a mental asylum, and the final sentence folds the whole text vertiginously into a prophetic dream. No wonder that Michałek could term the film incoherent, or Wajda himself could muse 'whether, in the midst of the allusions, free associations and fantasy, I lost the main thread' (Wertenstein 2000: 84). His assumption that the story is so well-known that one can allow oneself certain 'variations on the theme' (ibid.) overlooks the fact that it is the Gospel story, not Bulgakov's, that has this status: variations upon Bulgakov's own variation may be less comprehensible. Could it be that the work also fails to reach an audience because, as Adorno puts it, 'after the European catastrophe [the war and the Holocaust] the surrealist shocks have become impotent' (Adorno 1975: 157–8). If this is so, the historical moment of the movement would indeed be the inter-war one, and post-war surrealism would fall easily into the kitsch with which it is already complicit in Salvador Dalí, and later in Wajda's own *Lotna*. Both the surrealist dream-text and the literary adaptation are substitute-texts, attenuated by their links to distant, wordless content. That content is the illegible, unattainable substratum of the palimpsest, the work of several directors at least, its multivalence rendering it both suspect and almost impossible to censor (hence the official choice of censorship by marginalisation, rather than overt intervention?).

Finally, as part of an exercise in contrast that breathes the irony few Polish filmmakers could escape, it is worth mentioning the official attitude to another Wajda work of this period that touches upon religion, but is even less well-known than *Pilate and Others*: *Scena zbiorowa ze świętym* (*Collective Scene with a Saint*, 1974), for which one will search in vain in existing Wajda filmographies. Unlike *Pilate and Others*, it was a work the authorities were happy to see broadcast, the high profile granted it by the early-evening Television Theatre series being further enhanced by its broadcast on the extremely important, solemn national holiday of All Souls' Night. It dealt with the death of Father Maksymilian Kolbe, the Catholic priest who volunteered to replace a man with wife and children who would otherwise have been killed in Auschwitz, and filtered the event through the memories of the man himself, Franciszek Gajowniczek. A censor's report notes the refusal to print a critical review in which St. Drozdowski and S. Rusinek 'accused Wajda of distorting historical truth, denying "the authentic motivation of the deed of Father Kolbe attested to by the process of beatification", and of dishonesty in his dealings with Franciszek Gajowniczek' (AAN, PF-ZI-050/60/75, 3).

Lambasting Wajda's 'demiurgic inclination to create his own reality', Drozdowski and Rusinek note his unwillingness to follow the practice of foreign crews and allow Gajowniczek to read the script beforehand. Interviewed by them, Gajowniczek states that had he done so he would never have accompanied Wajda to Auschwitz. Drozdowski and Rusinek draw attention to the film's cutting of Kolbe's crucial words 'I am a Catholic priest' when asked why he was willing to die for another, an excision against which Gajowniczek had protested to Wajda. Wajda had posed a series of questions, such as whether or not Kolbe had known Gajowniczek before the war or in which row Kolbe had stood, demanding a 'clinical exactitude in non-essentials', all with the aim of persuading television viewers 'that it was impossible to recreate the rescue scene of 2 August 1941, and thus questioning its authenticity in general'. His 'insistent, aggressive interrogation ... of an old man ... was tasteless'. The article, entitled 'Wajda contra Gajowniczek, or the Devil's Advocate on the Appelplatz' may well misread Wajda's modernist doubts about representation and historical recreation as a deliberate assault on religion, but Wajda's removal of Kolbe's statement motivating his deed through his Catholicism was surely grist to the authorities' mill, as he surely well knew, whatever *his* motive for excising it (a probable feeling that even were he to include this line, the censor would delete it?). As in the case of *The Promised Land* (see the final section of this chapter), there was a part of Wajda the authorities felt they could use. His prestige was such that they were determined to defend, to cling onto and play up the significance of, that part.

KIJOWICZ AND THE AESTHETICS AND POLITICS OF ANIMATION

Animation is a notoriously critically neglected cinematic form. Rudolph Arnheim may once have pronounced it pure filmmaking, but its very freedom of movement and often extremely oblique variety of referentiality rendered it suspect to film theorists for whom the apparent indexicality of the photograph caused them to project film primarily in terms of 'realism' (good) and its sibling 'illusionism' (usually bad). Preconception ghettoises animation in the playroom, as short films for little people with short attention spans. After all, how can major work be achieved in a form dominated by Walt Disney, many may ask? The prejudice, of course, overlooks the degree of interest displayed in Disney by Eisenstein, and the way the abstraction of the cartoon can foster a pithy, fabular discourse which values *Tom and Jerry* as an X-ray of the basic shape of political reality, shading over into the absurdism of such shorts as Polański's *Le Gros et le maigre* (*The Fat and the Lean*, 1961): the uneven and unresolved conflict of the large and the small. Not for nothing was the Polish art of the period likened to 'Aesopian' discourse, a term that renders that most explicitly Aesopian of forms, the cartoon, the most powerfully political (because best-concealed) form of film in the Polish People's Republic.

The cartoon itself, in all its usual aphoristic brevity, is of course, a representative of the small. The ease with which it manages to be ignored frees it not just from referentiality, but from many of the constraints of official discourse. This freedom was to be exploited eloquently in the Polish animation of the 1960s in particular. One of the most striking examples is a series of films made by Mirosław Kijowicz, upon whom I will focus precisely because his work is less well-known than that of others among his contemporaries, such as Jan Lenica and Walerian Borowczyk. It is also, I feel, more profoundly politicised. His works – stories of persecution – could even be analysed in terms of René Girard's discussion of the sacrificial crisis and the mechanisms of scapegoating. Perhaps the most obvious example is *Sztandar* (*The Banner*, 1965).

The Banner itself plays its own cat-and-mouse game with the idea – and possible official reproach – of subversiveness. Here the eleven identical people occupying all but one of twelve squares marked on a street extract blue flags from their hats. The blueness, of course, creates the illusion that the subsequent film could not possibly deal with the carriers of a red flag, even as the frequent opposition of blue and red in theorisations of colour renders it a hidden allusion to the red it seemingly ignores: the opposites issue a hidden summons to one another. When a twelfth person arrives it seems as if the twelve-square pattern will be completed and the group will move off in a phalanx. But the new arrival pulls something else from his hat: first roses (in a witty, political form of anti-politics, *transformed red*), then fruit, then other things emerge, including a caged yellow bird. As the canary escapes, is recaptured, loses its feathers, and is then incarcerated anew, it is hard not to think also of that paradigmatic Polish tale of the fate of the nonconformist, Jerzy Kosiński's *Malowany ptak* (*The Painted Bird*, 1965). The significant objects that pop out of the hat, under the alibi of surreal randomness, include an American Airlines bag. Since time is running out, one member of the group climbs a pole to hold back the hands of the clock and prevent the striking of midnight (or noon?), another moment of rich potential political allusiveness (the most obvious possible referent being the nuclear clock). Finally, the new arrival is turned upside down and scraps of blue fabric are discovered. They are pieced together into a flag. The group moves on...

The reading of this film given in *Historia Filmu Polskiego* (published before 1989) demonstrates both the film's polysemic nature and the way it allowed the officially appointed interpreters of People's Poland to neutralise the more dangerous meanings by describing such works as examples of a *nurt filozoficzno-refleksyjny* ('a current of philosophical reflection'). 'In *The Banner* Kijowicz addressed an important political issue. He attacked the lack of ideology that hides behind empty assertions that are not backed up' (Drozdowski *et al.* 1985: 157). Another, equally subversive film is depoliticised into sub-existential banality: '*Klatki* [*Cages*, 1966] makes a laconic statement about human loneliness, the isolation of particular individuals and the impossibility of understanding between them' (ibid.). This reading's width of the mark becomes patent when one considers this remarkable film more closely.

At the beginning of *Cages*, a policeman gives a prisoner a series of geometric shapes to play with. The prisoner arranges them in various ways. These arrangements dissatisfy the policeman, who breaks each one up before eventually removing the shapes. The prisoner then begins to think, starting – appropriately, and perhaps inevitably – with the Cartesian '*cogito*', and such names as Plato, Hegel and Sartre blossom on the walls. The policeman rounds up these thoughts, including the last one, 'Sinatra', which briefly appears as 'sin', then shrinks to a timid 's'. As with the American Airlines bag in *The Banner*, all things American are suspect. When the despairing prisoner begins to saw at the bars the policeman removes the saw and then leaves the cage. The moment he does so, however, another policeman appears in the cage beyond his, and takes away the saw – another policeman appears in the cage beyond – and so on, in a rapid, vertiginous regress. This melting montage of cages concludes the film. In doing so it draws the logical conclusion from the way the prisoner's cage has been filmed throughout: the fourth-wall perspective has combined with the policeman's periodic retreat behind the far set of bars to make it seem as if *he* is the one in the cage, literally 'behind bars'. Ironically, the prisoner – the man with imagination – is the freest in the whole series.

The investigation of the mechanisms of imprisonment continues in *Młyn* (*The Mill*, 1971). It begins with one man pulling another along using a chain draped round the other's neck: the continuity of the imagery with the Lucky-Pozzo relationship of Samuel Beckett's *En attend-ant Godot* (*Waiting for Godot*, 1952) is patent, but Kijowicz knows his audience will overlay the existential with the political. It is not the politics of self-satisfied dissidence, however, but something far more dark and ambiguous. As the man is dragged along, every now and then a third man peers over a wall or from behind a tree, apparently unwilling – or fearing – to become involved. At one point, the prisoner's owner gives him a flute to play, and he does so: as in *Cages*, the artist is enchained. Kijowicz's film, however, eschews any sentimental idealisation of the artist. Eventually, the prisoner's owner shuts him up for the night in a mill. Under cover of darkness, the third man breaks in and helps the prisoner escape: they run away together. The next morning sees the former prisoner bringing his liberator to the mill with a chain round *his* neck. As freedom becomes a dark utopia, and absurdism has the last laugh, one is tempted to state that the inevitable dialogism and two-sidedness of art cannot but undermine politi-cal discourse as most of us conceive it: as something that attributes right to one side alone. Its counter-politics become those enunciated in Adorno's Beckett essay: 'only the nausea of self-satiation, the spirit's taedium before itself, desires complete difference' (Adorno 1973: 170).

That nausea pervades what may well be the darkest of Kijowicz's films, *Droga* (*The Road*, 1971), in which the unevenness of political relations infiltrates and reshapes the very body of the individual. A man walks along a road until it forks. Unable to decide which way to go, he finds himself shuddering between self and anti-self, then splitting in two. One half goes right, the other left. After a while, the half that took the right-hand turning meets another fork. It thinks of its lost other half and goes left. Further on, the two roads do indeed meet again, and the two halves reunite. But they do not quite fit: the left-hand half is larger than the right-hand one. They move on – together, yet not together – as one ill-formed being: Adorno's 'two halves that do not add up to a whole' with a vengeance. Reconciliation is a utopia, and the effects of opposed choices can never be erased. Read politically, left and right are always bonded – and doubly bound – within a misshapen humankind.

Reviewing these films, one can only wonder again why they were not banned. The answer, of course, is that the cartoon's sketchiness, abstraction and Beckettian decontextualisation require the spectator to fill something in; that the unlabelled character of its metaphors makes it possible to insert various meanings, including the ones found in the *Historia Filmu Polskiego*; that the association of the cartoon and the childish can be felt to spike its protest; and that the politics are more genuinely – and negatively – dialectical than anything countenanced by the Party. The problem posed by such texts is nicely embodied in the censor's reactions to another cartoon, this time a single drawing by Jan Sakwa which was published in 1975 by one periodi-cal (*itd*), but rejected by another (*Student*). It showed a tunnel at whose end was the sign EXIT, with arrows pointing not sideways – as in an aircraft – but upwards. Its meanings are multiple, with perhaps the most damaging one, from the authorities' viewpoint, being the possible reli-gious one, which no censor mentions, perhaps not daring to, or perhaps because it went with-out saying. One censor's report on mistakes made by lower-level censors makes the following rueful and critical comment, ratifying the decision to ban made by the editors of *Student*: 'the multi-valence of the symbol of the tunnel, whose only (apparent) exit leads through the ceil-ing, ought to arouse reservations in the censor. The extreme disparity in the evaluation of the self-same material – the intervention in *Student,* and its passing in *itd* – provokes exceptionally unfortunate repercussions among our clients, along with comments on the inconsistency with which our institution acts' (AAN, GUKPPiW, ZI-134/1/75). It is a comment whose ironies the modern reader cannot but savour. This cartoon, like the ones of Kijowicz, may have been marginalised by its brevity, but only in the margins was light to be found. The centre of the page – all that was centralised by the official ideology and the stencils it imposed upon polysemic art – was darkened by print. In the autocratic world, only the licensed fool, the jester, regularly speaks the truth.

SUBVERSION AND THE DIALECTIC OF METAPHOR AND REALISM: FROM SKOLIMOWSKI TO THE 1970s

Towards the end of the 23-minute prologue he attached in 1981 to his *Hands Up!* – the film whose banning caused his departure from Poland – Jerzy Skolimowski remarks that his friends who remained there were able to say more through their visual art than he had managed to do through his films. Skolimowski is perhaps excessively self-deprecating. After all, the greater leeway allowed the visual arts reflected the localisation of the problem a visual artwork represents: it is held in the frame – and, if not, within the museum or gallery. If dynamite is packed into the visual image, it either lacks a detonator or its explosion is muted by the institution's soundproofed walls. It is not the 'most important art' as conceived by Lenin, able to fan out along the nation's roads to meet all the people. The localisation of the visual artwork is also a matter of class and élitism, and although the socialist state may have proclaimed its desire to take art to the people, art's ghettoisation was a good second best in cases where artists could not be persuaded to meet the state's pedagogical demands: the production of 'advanced' art in a socialist country could give the lie to all those malicious foreign accusations of totalitarianism. What Skolimowski seems to have envied in the visual artists, though he did not put it in these terms, was the ease with which they could achieve a dense metaphorisation and their relative independence of state control of the means of production (though not, of course, of exhibition). Where the metaphorisation was concerned, the possible length of time available for a spectator's contemplative reception would permit the unpeeling of all the onion rings of meaning. In *Hands Up!*, by way of contrast, the layers are exposed one by one by the film itself, rather like the bandages surrounding the head of the former medical student who is its first protagonist in a cabaret act. The layers, like that bandage, are not removed at contemplative leisure but flung aside or at us, most of them relating to the idea of the raised hand and all arguably reconjugating the work's scandalous central image, that of the four-eyed Stalin, whose raised hand singles out the viewer as pedagogue, accuser and executioner. Skolimowski's cinema practises an extreme form of the metaphorisation that was the primary form of subversion adopted by the Polish School; in it, the production of metaphor goes into overdrive. The number of layers within the metaphor was a yardstick of the depth and energy of Skolimowski's subversion. This might have alerted the authorities: so many smokescreens, so apparently frenzied a dance of the seven veils, must indeed have suggested that there was something to hide. Indeed, the possible danger of the metaphorisation of *Bariera* (*The Barrier*, 1966) causing misreadings was mentioned at its visit to the Approving Commission by Skolimowski's film unit head, Jerzy Bossak:

> As for the large number of metaphorical and symbolic scenes, I've talked a great deal with Skolimowski and we've literally discussed every scene. Though no one has said this, I was afraid that someone here would say that the film is multivalent, as such mul-

tiplicity of meaning was the greatest danger. We did not want the film to be viewed as one that winks in two different directions, and which presents political and psychological issues within a particular defined society. (FN, KK, A-216 poz. 92)

Of course Bossak's remarks can, and perhaps should, be read as a double bluff, protecting the text by describing those who saw anything subversive in it as poor readers.

The great German poet Friedrich Hölderlin once asked the purpose of poets in times of need or distress. One definition of a 'time of need', however, may be one in which only poetic statement may enter the public sphere. If metaphor is a Trojan Horse, meaning descends from it only in darkness. Transparency of writing, the Orwellian ideal, is dangerously readable, vulnerable to removal from official channels. In the times of greatest need, meanwhile, even the poet may be compelled to write for his drawer. The notion of a film written for the drawer approaches a contradiction in terms, of course, as celluloid quickly degrading in obscurity would disobey the imperative to circulate and return at least some of its costs, and it remains a contradiction even when the sponsor is a state more concerned with the film's yield of cultural capital than with its pecuniary success. It is, after all, unlikely consciously to promote its own subversion (though of course one Party faction may seek to undermine another by securing the partial release of troublesome work, or by damning certain elements of officially approved ones). Nevertheless, it is possible for the artist to assert a right of metaphorisation that is simultaneously in accordance with the state and subversive of it. Such metaphor may need to flee to the outer reaches of the poetic, exhibiting an extreme density and bordering on the surreal. Thus in the case of Skolimowski, the mannerist profusion of metaphor of *The Barrier* was acceptable, as was that of much of his subsequent film, *Hands Up!* What went beyond the pale, however, and caused the latter film's banning and excision from Skolimowski's Polish-produced filmographies, was the daring moment of transparent parody of Stalinism: the sequence in which the image of the four-eyed Stalin appears, its slow-motion rise that of a monstrous icon limned with the implicit religiosity of the cult of personality. Its script-margin description by Skolimowski himself defines it as momentary, doubtless seeking to veil its éclat and forestall the script's possible non-acceptance. As filmed, however, it fuses absurdism and the political sublime. If one of its unwitting creators flees before it in mock terror that disguises real terror, most directors would have trembled when filming it. Skolimowski's courage may well have been underpinned by the boy-wonder success that surely blurred his instinctive awareness of the precise location of the boundary of the acceptable. One may call it the Orson Welles syndrome, though Skolimowski was less fortunate than Welles (after all, the Polish state had a greater monopoly of distribution than did William Randolph Hearst): his film was denied distribution, and he himself went into exile.

Just over a decade later, however, a form of filmmaking would emerge that dialectically and successfully combined metaphor and transparency: it was known as the Cinema of Moral Anxiety. The ruse of its metaphorisation was a concealment of its own metaphorical status. As in Poe, the purloined letter was best hidden by being left out in the open. This concealment is particularly easy for film, which can present itself as simply realistic, and indeed often has done throughout its history. After all, did not film simply register precisely what was placed before it (the notorious 'pro-filmic event'), fulfilling the realist dream of art as reflection? The authorities adopted the canny line of attack of decrying these late 1970s works as mere exercises in journalism, lacking the subtlety of art, an attack that backfired: subtlety is no necessary element in the recipe for an artwork, as the authorities' memory of their own onetime championship of realism could have reminded them. And, for all their journalistic immediacy and polemicism, these films were indeed artworks, for they did not mean exactly what they seemed to say. They were arguably journalism at one level, art at another. Thus Agnieszka Holland's *Aktorzy prowincjonalni* (*Provincial Actors*, 1979) did not just give a realistic image of the aspirations and frustrations of artists cut off from the metropolitan centre, but represented a microcosm of the national macrocosm, reduced 'in a drop of water'. The careerist emcee of Feliks Falk's *Wodzirej* (*Top Dog*, 1978) is both a local blot on the landscape (realistic or 'journalistic' code) and a sign of the pervasiveness of corruption within the Polish body politic. Film's best alibi is its apparent concretion: its apparent welding to a single time and place. The realistic Trojan Horse conceals the soldiers of metaphor, however. Ironically, just as Solidarity can be seen as a revolt against 'real existing socialism' in the name of the ideals of socialism itself, so the Cinema of Moral Anxiety rejects socialist aesthetics in the name of the generalisation that is one of its central aspirations and keywords. Since the smaller situation mirrors the larger one, this cinema might even be taken as less a rejection than a reworking of 'reflection theory'. It is therefore piquant to note the frequency with which censors' notes for the first half of 1977 mention the excision from reviews of Krzysztof Zanussi's *Barwy ochronne* (*Camouflage*, 1977) of references to the wider (Polish, or even universal) relevance of the events it stages in an apparently narrow academic milieu (AAN, GUKPPiW, ZI-Pf-052/6/77).

Of course, the state was not so naïve as to fail to notice the presence of metaphor in these films. Nevertheless, in the 1970s their concealment of their metaphorical status beneath a veneer of realism (the repressed link between those two levels being a 'typicality' that had ceased to be a subject of aesthetic debate, but remained central to the public's reading habits) usefully allowed the authorities to pursue a good cop/bad cop dialectic of censorship; something that seemed to offer a sophisticated solution to all their problems, but in fact was symptomatic of confusion and wishful thinking before a real impasse. The dialectic worked as follows. Whenever artists – or Western powers – accused them of repressiveness, they could argue that their simultaneous awareness of these works' subversiveness and willingness to permit their making furnished the best possible proof of tolerance. Restrictions on distribution, meanwhile, if mentioned, could be justified by arguments well understood by capitalists and be described as the inevitable by-product of the minority nature of a certain artistic vocabulary. After all, do star vehicles and art cinema enjoy the same distribution in the capitalist West? (This argument, used against Wajda's *Pilate and Others*, of course, cynically jettisons the socialist aspiration to bring to the people 'the best that had been thought and read'.) This demonstration of tolerance governed a sphere of the visible implicitly defined as 'that which is visible from the West'. On the other hand, though, local articles pointing out the real meaning of a work can be thoroughly censored, particularly when it, or the artist in question, lacks an international reputation. These figures are 'invisible from the West' and so, *ipso facto,* their works' suppression does not exist. It, like them, has been 'disappeared'. The problem with the cunning of this dialectic, however, was that it overlooked the cunning of the history deified by the socialists themselves, which declares certain procedures 'too clever by half'. The policy that permitted the making of subversive works and then claimed they were not subversive (they would only subvert totalitarianism, but we are democratic, always consult with the people…) was simple schizophrenia, while restrictions on distribution and favourable reviewing ignored, first, the efficacy of word-of-mouth and, then, the emergence of the video cassette, which subverted the institution of cinema itself. All those rooms in which people watched video cassettes of Ryszard Bugajski's *Przesłuchanie* (*The Interrogation*, 1982) were anti-cinemas, as well as, for good measure, sub-versions of the official television broadcasts that were known to lie but whose hardware could carry alternative messages. The Polish authorities could, of course, have installed the Soviet television sets notorious for exploding in living rooms, and then claimed that the blasts had been those of Solidarity activists' bomb-making equipment, but this method of destroying both the medium and the message of opposition was perhaps too surreal to occur to them. Moreover, in their heart of hearts they prided themselves on greater efficiency than their over-bearing Eastern neighbours, and would probably have taken exploding sets as besmirching their progressiveness.

What I have described as a dialectic within Party reactions to these works may of course often, and even usually, have been simple service in bad faith that was surely the most wide-spread form of service within the Polish system after the mid-1970s. This seems to be borne out by Zanussi's contextualisation of the censorship of one of his statements:

> Once, in an interview during Gierek's period, I stated that the people who only see Poland from the windscreens of Mercedes cars do not know it. And it was passed. I asked the editors whether the censor had had reservations. He had had. But he let himself be convinced, for the authorities had switched to Peugeots. Did that mean the censor was stupid? No, but he was looking for a cover, and he didn't care about the cause. We forget too rapidly that in the PRL [Polska Rzeczpospolita ludowa – Polish People's Republic] people differed from one another not so much in their belief in a grand idea but in their readiness to serve it. But they usually did so insincerely. (Fik *et al.* 1996: 165)

The same could apply even to cuts ordered at the highest level. Note the parenthetical final sentence of Zanussi's instructive description of the cutting of one item from his *Iluminacja* (*Illumination*, 1973):

> In it I showed a small sequence from March [1968], after which my hero is thrown out of university, for he was with the students during the strike. The cutting of this scene was determined by a Central Committee Secretary, Mr. Jan Szydlak. I was summoned to a conversation with him and heard what for me was an irrefutable argument. The Secretary stated that it will be the politicians, not the artists, who decide when the time is ripe for a reassessment of March. If the authorities had allowed this allusion to it to remain in my film, activists would have taken it as a signal that something is changing at the top. And since that would be a false signal, the scene had to be cut. (In the end I managed to negotiate its cutting to a minimum, so at least some trace remained.) (Fik *et al.* 1996: 166)

THE *KORCZAK* AFFAIR

March 1968 was notorious, of course, for an anti-Semitic campaign launched in the first instance in a bid for power by Mieczysław Moczar. Among the more absurd of its vile conten-tions was the declaration that Poland was the victim of an international Zionist-West German plot. Its most prominent victim within Polish cinema was Aleksander Ford, who might be termed its Jewish patriarch, one of the filmic casualties being his planned work about Janusz Korczak. Elsewhere in this book I discuss Andrzej Wajda's film *Korczak*. One aspect of that work not discussed there, however, is just how extraordinary it is that his should have been the first Polish film about this revered educationalist and wartime martyr, particularly given the initial proposal for a film about him made as early as 1945, when Ludwik Starski submitted one to the Film Production Studio of the Polish Army (Zajiček 1992: 197–8). What was it that made Korczak, a nonbeliever and potential 'secular saint' who had chosen to accompany his orphanage's children to their death in a concentration camp, so potentially difficult a subject for the cinema of People's Poland? The nature of the difficulty can be gauged by perusing the minutes of the 1967 'Studio' film unit meeting that accepted a screenplay to be filmed by that cantankerous grand old man of Polish cinema, Ford, as a co-production with Artur Brauner. The meeting concluded by demanding various changes meant to bring the script – the work of a non-Pole, Aleksander Ramati – into line with Polish state ideology. Whether or not this could have been achieved may be doubted, as even the late, revised version lodged in the archives of the Filmoteka narodowa emphasises Jewish resistance in the manner favoured by the state of Israel but not by the Polish régime. The ability to film it may have offered Ford scant recompense for the exile with which he met after the anti-Semitic campaign of the very next year. A summary of a late version of the script will give some idea of the nature of the material considered at this meeting, even though it post-dates it, incorporating some of its suggestions (for instance, ending with Korczak's death).

Ramati's version of Korczak's story is highly melodramatic, making far less serious effort at historical verisimilitude than Agnieszka Holland's script for Wajda's film, though it too focuses on Korczak's well-documented last days in the Ghetto. It begins dramatically with the shooting after the curfew of a coal thief who could be twenty or sixty: ageless in his suffering, he is 'the symbol of the eternal Wandering Jew'. A young Jewish couple, Jacob and Ester, find the man nailed to a door and recognise him as Jankiel, from Dr Korczak's orphanage. They go to inform Korczak who, for lack of food, is feeding his children with dreams. Jacob accuses Korczak of escapism, and when Korczak replies that Jankiel was not the first Jew to be nailed to a tree Jacob replies that that was the Christian God of Steffa – Korczak's Polish assistant, who calls Korczak 'the only Christian left in this heathen world'. Hearing a noise, Steffa and Korczak descend to the cellar, where what they find is not the expected potato-thief but the Polish janitor, Piotr, hiding grenades for the Polish underground. Ramati's ecumenism is underlined by Steffa's references to the Jews as 'we' and Piotr's knowledge of Hebrew words. Korczak, who does not want his children living above a powder keg, dismisses Piotr. The next scene sees SS Colonel Krüger complaining to Czerniaków, head of the Warsaw Judenrat, about Jewish violations of the curfew. He threatens to shoot Czerniaków if he does not bring them into line. Of the people in the neighbouring waiting-room, only Korczak, who has come to scrounge food for his children, shows no fear of Krüger. Korczak argues before Czerniaków that providing food for the orphanage could solve the Judenrat's problem by reducing Jewish discontent and so curtailing support for the Ghetto fighters. After walking the streets without wearing the Jewish star, his fearless entry into a café teeming with SS finally wins some food for the orphanage from its owner. The scar-faced German who seizes Korczak there does so to protect him, however: it is Erwin Schneider, a former pupil of the orphanage. When Korczak asks what made him a Nazi, Erwin answers that 'the Party is the only family I have' and that he does not hate Jews. As Jacob and Ester quarrel due to the similarity between her ideas and Korczak's, Jacob catches sight of Erwin with Korczak; the latter prevents Jacob killing the SS man. Although his contemporary, Jacob does not recall Erwin, though the German recalls how the other called him 'a stinking kraut'. Korczak is sceptical about Jacob's reports of annihilation in the concentration camps, deeming even the Nazi mind 'incapable of such horror'. As he feeds his children, a group of Jewish fighters, among them Piotr, make bombs in the cellar. When the Gestapo confiscates a cart full of food for the orphanage, Korczak visits the Gestapo headquarters in his Polish officer's uniform decorated with the iron cross. Krüger, appalled by this desecration, slaps him, only for Korczak to turn the other cheek: 'An old Jewish trick. Imitating Christ', the German comments. Jailed, Korczak does not pray, saying that his prayer is to feed children. A Hassidic Jew in the same cell accuses him of playing God. Meanwhile, in Korczak's absence, the orphanage is without food, which Jacob obtains by blowing up and raiding a train. He surrenders to the Gestapo to preserve hostages from reprisals. He and Korczak, now cell-mates, are escorted to the woods by Erwin, who pretends to want to kill them personally, but then frees them, torn between loyalty to Korczak and to the Führer. While hiding in the woods, the two encounter some underground fighters disguised as a fake Nazi patrol, which escorts them safely back to the orphanage. When drafted with other Jews into constructing the Ghetto wall, Jacob leaves some bricks loose for smuggling and escape. An altercation between him and some Jewish policemen sees him taken before the Judenrat, where he mocks Czerniaków's belief that the Germans will keep the Jews alive as workers. Korczak, for his part, is awaiting Hitler's mistake, and thinks the opening of the Russian front is it. Continuing his hunt for food, he visits the well-fed Bula Schwarz, who employs children as smugglers: each cares for children in his own way. When Korczak decries his own failure as an educator, Schwarz replies: 'You educated us for a world of humanity. This is a world of bestiality. One has to be re-educated.' Shortly thereafter fighting between Germans and Jews prompts Erwin to tell Krüger that 'the cowardly old Jew belongs to the past'. He then spoils the aim of a soldier planning to shoot Ester. At night-time, he comes to warn Korczak of the Ghetto's imminent liquidation, and offers to save him. When Jacob proposes taking the children to the sewers to protect them from 'a death walk into a gas chamber', Korczak replies that 'it won't be a death walk. I'll take them on a picnic.' Jacob's contention that if the children are to die it should at least be for a cause persuades Korczak to let him have those aged over ten. He tells the smaller ones that all are going to the same picnic, instructing them to close their eyes as they march to the Umschlagplatz: 'Then you can see better the land of the sun.' Korczak again rejects Erwin's last-minute offer of personal safety, telling him not to wake the children, for 'they are already in another world'. Erwin salutes the departing train. As it leaves, from amidst the Ghetto smoke the Hatikvah is heard. 'Leaving all this, the train of Dr Korczak and his children travels towards the sun' (FN, S-11131).

The archives of the Filmoteka narodowa contain a protocol of the expanded meeting of the 'Studio' film unit's programme council that approved the co-production of an earlier (the fifth!) version of this script. The favourable decision seems to have been strongly determined by the forceful and extensive arguments of Ford, the prospective director, who guaranteed a work of the proper ideological tenor. Thus although several figures were perturbed by the idea of a West German co-production on this particular subject (Stanisław Trepczyński) – one with regard to which Poles were widely accused of 'joint guilt in the killing of Polish citizens of Jewish origin' (Stanisław Wroński) – Ford retorted that the film had first been proposed as a Swiss-Yugoslav co-production, to be shot in Yugoslavia by himself, and that Artur Brauner was not a West

German producer but one 'who makes films in many countries'. The final summary by Culture Minister Tadeusz Zaorski echoed a point made by Wroński – that the Germans had intensified their slaughter of Poles in the year in which the film would be set, 1943, emphasising that 'the threat of complete extermination' hung over both the Ghetto's inhabitants and the Poles outside it. Ford had argued that since the 25th anniversary of Korczak's death was approaching, and Brauner was determined to go ahead, Polish participation was imperative: 'If, in so important a year, we for our part say nothing, if we do not accentuate our place in the world, it means leaving the field open for enemy propaganda.' 'In my humble opinion', he added, 'if we want to strike a blow against Israeli nationalism, it will be easiest to do so through a film about Korczak.' Where other speakers had described Korczak's story as one of defeat, of withdrawal from politics, Ford countered that this withdrawal was based on a recognition that 'the adult world is one from which an honest person and humanist has to dissociate himself'. Korczak's notion that the child's inner light is 'corrupted by circumstances in later years' is, moreover, 'very close to the Marxist one'. One speaker, Trepczyński, had argued that Korczak's abandonment of leftist positions after 1905 had been an element of his life that required analysis; the analysis should not focus on the latter part of his life (the route Agnieszka Holland would take in her script for Wajda's film) but be 'a larger film' – not a tear-jerker. For Ford, Korczak's willingness to pay the highest price by giving his life meant one could not speak of defeat.

As well as stressing the similarity of the prospective fates of the Poles and the Jews, Zaorski's desiderata included changes to Erwin, of whom one speaker had felt the script made too much: after all, he had been in Korczak's care only briefly. Zaorski felt he was too good to be true. It was also important to scotch the widespread belief that the responsibility for the Ghetto's destruction was shared between the Gestapo on the one hand and such nationalities as the Latvians and Ukrainians on the other: tellingly, Zaorski remarked that 'we know this is the historical truth, but I'd be afraid of such scenes, as they create the impression that the Jews were killed by representatives of the various nations of Europe, and not by the Hitlerites, who were the sole murderers'. (As so often in the Eastern Bloc, the aesthetic and the political meet and clash over the issue of 'typicality' and, in the case of film in particular, the often obscurely intuited difficulty of mediating between the depiction of a concrete reality and a sociologically accurate, statistically grounded image of the most common behaviours.) One earlier speaker had suggested giving a greater role to the Wehrmacht, since stressing the role of the Gestapo could narrow the sense of the range of German responsibility. Zaorski takes this up and proposes that 'the participation of various German formations' be stressed. When Zaorski remarks that at a certain point the screenplay appears more interested in the Ghetto Fighters than in Korczak, and that this is inappropriate in a film of which he is the intended hero, this may be taken as a way of downplaying an element that would match Israeli tastes, though he does not say so. His failure to dot the 'i' may mean that it goes without saying, or that he himself is not fully aware of – or able to articulate – the grounds of his decisions. As so often in the critical evaluation of artistic works within People's Poland, a remark whose significance is seemingly simply aesthetic has political ramifications. Thus when Zaorski concludes with a statement of belief in Ford's ability to create a work 'that accords with the presuppositions of our cinema', it is also a vote of confidence in his ideological soundness (FN, RP, A-329 poz. 57).

In the end, after his departure from Poland after March 1968, Ford shot the film abroad. Mieczysław Moczar must have danced with glee upon learning that it was a West German/ Israeli co-production.

TEXTS AND SUB-TEXTS: ŻUŁAWSKI'S *THE DEVIL*

Although the terms of Poland's censorship regime envisaged the banning of works on grounds of indecency or offences against public morality, these grounds (the usual ones for censorship in non-socialist countries) were almost never invoked. The cases in which they were usually involved non-Polish productions and efforts by 'study cinemas' to obtain permission for one-off screenings of works lacking any licence for general exhibition (for instance, Walerian Borowczyk's *Contes immoraux* [*Immoral Tales*, 1974], which a national meeting of study cinemas wished to show in 1979), though similar grounds were invoked for a 1978 refusal to permit a television screening of Truffaut's *Deux Anglaises et le continent* (1971) (AAN, GUKPPiW, ZI-Pf-052/11/78, 21). The case of Andrzej Żuławski's *Diabeł* (*The Devil*, 1972) assumes particular significance as virtually the sole example of moral censorship of a Polish production. The strength of the state mechanisms of script approval designed to forestall the making of works that would arouse such objections renders the mere fact of its making piquant. It may be explained in part as one of the few problematic fruits of the abolition of the Script Assessment Commission in 1967. This change had been won by the film units' artistic directors, who had thought it would enhance their power. The nature of their mistake is well analysed by Edward Zajiček in his seminal, shrewd and wide-ranging (and consequently sometimes frustratingly perfunctory or anecdotal) book on the production context of post-war Polish cinema, *Poza ekranem* (*Beyond the Screen*):

> The artistic directors had thought that chairing their own mini-Script Commissions would enhance their authority. The outcome was a different one. Previously every film author and director had to take account of the opinion of the director, for he sat on the omnipotent Script Assessment Commission. Liquidating the commission reduced the directors' influence to the circle of their immediate fellow workers. The directors' intention in dissolving the Script Assessment Commission had been to prevent colleagues from interfering with their programmes. This too backfired. Their boss friends no longer had to risk reprisals by making open comments to the commission. They could now quietly subvert the work of other units and undermine their screenplays by whispering venomous judgements and forecasts of disaster in the minister's ear. The proposers of the mini-commissions intended them as an effective barrier against cheap and half-baked proposals. Meanwhile, the members of the programmatic councils soon came to share the view of the units directors that the main duty of the mini-commission was to commend and force through any and every doorstep. After all, what would be the point of depriving the unit of work and income when the minister was in any case programmed to say no? The minister, for his part, deprived of the consultative forum whose crossfire of opposed interests yielded objective assessments, set up on the side a group of trusted reviewers. Their confidential opinions determined the fate of the screenplays. It was a return to the *Vehmgericht* of the 1950s. (Zajiček 1992: 195)

Meanwhile, if the Party was willing to tolerate this proposed decentralisation, it was probably because it felt that the existing mechanisms of usually invisible self-censorship could be trusted to preserve the existing order of things.

Andrzej Żuławski's proposal for *The Devil* (originally to have been directed by Jan Rybkowski, not himself), however, represented a special case, as would the controversial director himself. Its treatment was discussed in 1968 by one of the new programmatic councils, that of the 'Rytm' film unit, which concluded by deciding to pass it for scripting. The discussion is particularly fascinating in its demonstration of the possibility of contrasting apologias for the proposal, one in terms of its generic designation as a popular horror film, the other in those of poetic art cinema. The co-existence of these apologias indicates the potential for confusion underlying the socialist production system's declaration of the equal importance of popularity and artistic value, which could engender the state of mind known as *wszystkoizm* ('everything-ism'): the belief that a single work not only could but indeed should do everything and satisfy everyone (something whose negative form was the paranoid fear of possible attack on any and every front). The argument for popularity emerges first, as Ryszard Frelek argues that 'the time is ripe for our own *Dracula*': there is a dearth of Polish films for people desirous of such generic pleasures as those of the western. Frelek mouth-wateringly reels off the attractions of a treatment that augurs well for a Polish *Dracula*: 'Dead bodies fall thick and fast – usually with the aid of a razor – there's a devil with all the external attributes, a touch of macabre eroticism, jugglers, drunken noblemen, a raped nun, madmen, corpses planted on chairs, fires, grave-mounds, and so on. The full arsenal required for the super-macabre, which will not permit the hairs standing up on the viewers' napes to drop for a single moment.' Perhaps sensing that his enthusiasm has got the better of him, he then wonders whether 'there isn't a little too much of the macabre', for the genre is most effective when interrupting an idyll. One of his objections is nicely comic: commenting on Eziachasz's rape of his sister-in-law, Frelek muses 'perhaps it would suffice if she was burned chained to the wall'. More importantly, he then considers the role of the political background. Whereas Mirosław Żuławski – Andrzej Żuławski's father – would later accentuate the value of the work's suggestion that 'the moment a state loses its independent existence, evil emerges', Frelek contends that the genre's unreality requires a downplaying of its historical setting in and after the Prussian partition of Poland: it would be preferable if the attack concerned a single castle, not the entire country.

The next speaker, however, Mojkowski, opposed investing time and energy in the macabre. The political allusions worried him too, but rather 'because that leads to a certain generalisation, to a subtext, and as we know we are all in a period of the deciphering of subtexts – and this is unnecessary in the case in question'. The subtext of this remark is, of course, that of the fall-out from Władysław Gomułka's condemnation of sympathisers with the Israeli victory in the Six-Day War, and a film industry terrorised by the individual interviews carried out with its members in late 1967. It is ironic that a work that, for Mojkowski, summons the spectre of a politically motivated shelving should finally be shelved on moral grounds (or was the censor's mention of morality a smoke-screen for political objections?). Hardly surprisingly in the context of Mojkowski's references to 'generalisation' – a keyword of socialist realist aesthetics that suggests a lingering sympathy with them – he can discern 'neither a social need for nor a social gain from a film of this kind'.

A far more sophisticated analysis is provided by the gifted film critic Jacek Fuksiewicz. It may be taken as teasing out some of the contradictions implicit in his description of the project as 'a horror film with deeper subtexts', that is; both a genre piece and the more ambitious 'poetic film' he sees it as also aspiring to be. It diverges from the horror format, however, in presenting events not through the eyes of a normal onlooker but a character 'so demonised and possessed as to belong to the world of phantoms'. Though Fuksiewicz does not put it thus, there is nothing to fear when the identification figure is already lost. The rule of a gradual build-up of horror is also flouted, as the continually maintained high note of the macabre threatens to evoke laughter ('a natural defence mechanism'). On the other hand, though, it lacks the suggestivity of poetry, as the literal presentation of Romantic corpses, vampires and worms in eye-sockets becomes grotesque. The terrifying thing about the script is a literalism that destroys the poetic.

Fuksiewicz's contention that the work's philosophical dimension promises more than it delivers could, of course, be less a sign of chaos than of suggestivity transposed to another level. Mirosław Żuławski, by way of contrast, finds it very coherent: interesting less for its evocation of horror – a genre whose psychological necessity he defends – than for its 'Polishness'. (His invocation of this term, despite its dubious associations with the chauvinism of a politician like Mieczysław Moczar and a second-rate film director such as Bohdan Poręba, is itself an interesting effort to reinject it with seriousness, though critics of Andrzej Żuławski's work in general might read the mobilisation of a patriotism that had fallen into bad odour as a tell-tale sign of his work's underlying meretriciousness.) Where Fuksiewicz mentions Romanticism in general, Żuławski talks of 'Polish Romanticism' – and that, of course, permits a coupling of the horror generally typical of Romanticism with the politics inevitably permeating the Polish context. Indeed, to extrapolate from his argument, the linkage may even be necessary: loss of statehood entails loss of self. Here the script assumes potential allegorical relevance to post-war Poland also (the incriminating subtext feared by Mojkowski?), and it is unlikely that Żuławski would have been unaware of this possible reading. After all, his description of the devil as an *agent provocateur* seducing a former conspirator into treachery would reinforce such an argument, while leaving it safely unspoken. An excision of political realities would remove the determining element of textual meaning, 'leaving only the macabre – as in other, Western films – and that macabre would then be insufferable'. Could this critique of capitalist production be a billowing smokescreen for one of the socialist state, delivered on behalf of the vampirised Polishness of its inhabitants?

The linkage to Polish Romanticism did not recommend the project to the Chairman, Jan Rybkowski himself: Polish Romanticism 'immediately entered a mystical phase and that was rather to the detriment than the benefit of our national life'. What saves the project for him is its greater proximity to the pre-Romantic, partition period, and hence to an ethos of masonry, for which mystery means secrets rather than (Christian) mysticism. In terms of contemporary reference, meanwhile, one of his remarks is particularly pregnant: 'if we pay attention to the element of the hunt, there is a subtext, since at certain moments the people who are running forget why they're doing so'.

For the next speaker, Jan Gerhard, the text relentlessly pursued the thesis that a good end cannot be prosecuted through evil means. He then moves on to the pragmatic issue of what tactics will help secure the text's acceptance by the Ministry of Culture. Frelek declares that production would involve choosing between an unreal Romantic story and one that is more historically grounded, but Żuławski retorts that the differences are the result of different analyses of one and the same material. (May the possibility of such divergences reflect not just the material's hybridity but its genuine possession of the polysemousness of poetry?) Żuławski subsequently defends his conception as not a work of horror but something akin to Polański's *Repulsion* (1965), 'which churns people up but also makes them think'. Wishing the poetic level to be clearly apparent, he opposes more concrete reference to the time of the partitions, but appeals for the committee to assume he has sufficient good taste to avoid excessive horror. Could it be that he fails to perceive the subtext of the earlier references to the importance of the setting being the Prussian partition, or is he rather concerned at this point with issues of aesthetics rather than politics? Given the doubts expressed about the value of horror, he fears possible similar objections in the Ministry of Culture and solicits advice on how to forestall them, conceding that his writing may have been clumsy. Frelek's subsequent proposal of the advisability of the text's restriction to the Prussian partition may serve in this context to indicate a way of heading off probable Ministry objections to the merest whiff of anti-Russian sentiments – critique of the Russian role in Poland's partitioning being a far more sensitive question. If this is not spelled out, it may be because it goes without saying, or because even at this level – well away from the Ministry – committee members may be loath to be so explicit at a minuted meeting. I have to say that I suspect the latter, there being evidence against the former: Żuławski's own failure to grasp the implications of Frelek's insistence. Gerhard – older, and probably more worldly – endorses Frelek's suggestion (implicitly underlining it later by advocating the insertion of German words into the dialogue), and Frelek himself tellingly adds that such a limitation will 'clarify the entire subtext'. The discussion then peters out in a series of brief exchanges concerning aesthetic matters, including how to avoid the putative boredom of Has's *Saragossa Manuscript*. The Chairman's primary closing recommendation is that Żuławski rethink the characterisation of the main protagonist. Since Żuławski justifies his protagonist's abnormality in terms of his lengthy isolation in prison, Gerhard's comparison between his experience and that of De Sade is perhaps the most interesting thing in these last pages, and presciently relevant to any evaluation of Żuławski's entire, controversial oeuvre. If, as Baudelaire argued, the Devil's greatest achievement is to convince the world of his non-existence, it is both appropriate and ironic that the Polish authorities should attempt a similar operation upon Żuławski's film: following a decree by Piotr Jaroszewicz, head of the Council of Ministers, the chief censors would instruct their subordinates to excise all mentions of the film, for 'as far as the Polish spectator and reader goes, *this film does not exist*' (Fik 1993/94: 182).

THE SUN REHEARSES ITS RISE:
HENRYK KLUBA, WIESŁAW DYMNY AND THE CENSOR

As the opening chapter on *Ashes and Diamonds* indicated, treatments of the first years of the installation of communist rule were highly sensitive. The film that suffered most spectacularly from this sensitivity, however, was not Wajda's but Henryk Kluba's *Słońce wschodzi raz na dzień* (*The Sun Rises Once Daily*, 1967; premiere 1972), produced by the Syrena Film Unit and scripted by Wiesław Dymny, which underwent multiple rewrites in an attempt to counter political misgivings.

In the form in which it finally circulated, and whose narrative I will now summarise, Kluba's film presents an often highly stylised account of the new communist authorities' attempts to win the hearts and minds of Beskidy mountaineers in 1945. Upon the arrival of representatives of the new authorities, the charismatic local peasant leader Haratyk (Franciszek Pieczka) refuses first to summon the villagers to hear an official policy announcement about various progressive changes, then to accept his appointment as head of the Peasants' Council. He says the peasants have no need of the new things on offer, such as nationalisation. What is more, when help was needed, the visitors were nowhere to be found. The resultant altercation culminates in the shooting of Czarny, one of the People's Army representatives. Subsequently, Haratyk independently organises the construction of a village brickworks and sawmill. Nevertheless, he can be seen as driven to such independent action by the way his quest for official permission finds the local authorities otherwise engaged – installing such symbols of the new regime as the uncrowned eagle, for instance – brushing him off by saying that the villagers will have to sort things out for themselves. Haratyk then leads an epic expedition of village carts to the newly recovered Western Territories, in search of the necessary machinery. During it his group discovers an abandoned concentration camp and burns the corpses. While returning, they are ambushed by Germans just after Haratyk had ordered the dumping of looted pianos they had been carrying for the cripple Koślawy, the initial source of information about the riches of the Western Territories. A subsequent altercation between the two ends with him shooting Haratyk, whom he thinks unarmed, then being killed himself.

Upon recovering from his wound, Haratyk begins construction of the sawmill, and is given permission to do so by the Party Secretary, though he has not requested it. Voted village elder, he is invited to a Peasants' Movement conference, where some delegates speak in outrage of the peasants killing representatives of the authorities, and Haratyk himself walks out, complaining that they politick while people have nothing to eat. On returning, he finds that members of the NSZ (Narodowe Siły Zbrojne – National Armed Forces) (a right-wing resistance movement that is not identified precisely in Dymny's text) have broken into his house and killed his wife. The scene's juxtaposition with the Peasant conference shows both sides' dissatisfaction with him. The village's next requirement is for a school, and no sooner has Haratyk said there will be one than we see the completed building awaiting its formal opening. Bishop and Party Secretary arrive simultaneously, but Haratyk's speech stresses that whatever the villagers possess will be achieved by their own hands, not given by the grace of Heaven or the authorities. Haratyk is then summoned to the Security Service headquarters and – in a remarkably long jump-cut dialogue – is ordered to hand over the sawmill; the authorities must ensure that all villages have the same things. He refuses, as the mill belongs to the people (already, one might say), and when the authorities come to arrest him he flees to the woods. Where the security services speak of a 'counter-revolutionary band' that needs to be chained up, the Party Secretary urges gentler methods. Meanwhile, Haratyk and his followers burn down the sawmill. Hunted down in the woods, Haratyk sets a trap for his pursuers, then rescues the Party Secretary from the tree precipitated onto him by the trap. While carrying him, he is betrayed to the security service by Gorniok, one of his men, who had once feuded with him. 'Perhaps I fought on the wrong side', he muses as he is taken. Returning in the rain to the village several years later, released from prison, he concedes that in the past 'we only thought of ourselves'. The Party Secretary, village elder in his absence, invites him to join in the work of the country's construction.

An inspection of the script's reception at separate meetings of the Script Assessment Commission gives some idea of the controversy that had been aroused by its first two versions, and which persisted even when the film was completed, for, despite the trailing of its imminent release in the press by Krzysztof Teodor Toeplitz, a respected critic who was also close to the centres of power, it was shelved almost immediately. If even the (relatively) sanitised version summarised above encountered problems, it is no surprise that the earlier versions debated by the Commission did so.

A quick calculation of the length of the stenogram of the first visit Dymny's screenplay paid to the Script Assessment Commission – 32 pages – suffices to show that it was not rubber-stamped by it. Indeed, it was obvious early on that it would not have an easy passage, as the first speaker – Jan Gerhard – appended to his praise of its Polishness and plasticity a worry about 'what leading idea would be taken away by the spectator, particularly the young' (a potentially serious worry, misdirection of the young being a particularly grave threat to future socialist construction; fortunately for Kluba and Dymny, this motif was not widely echoed by later speakers). Gerhard's particular fear was that 'our opponents – forest extremists', like Haratyk, would gain the aura of a Jánošik (a mountain Robin Hood well-known to Polish cinema, and resurrected recently by Agnieszka Holland). Gerhard notes that Haratyk fought the Germans before defying the communists; the unspoken rider is that the former conflict will legitimise the later one, and perhaps even suggest an equivalence between the two sets of intruders in his mountain redoubt. Haratyk finally emerges from prison 'neither re-educated, nor ridiculous' but 'tragic'. These remarks are followed by an intriguing, if somewhat irrelevant, dream of Polish cinema conquering the world through its form of the western – Polish goodies defeating Nazi baddies – and a side-swipe at the 'ambitious, deep, planetary experience of Mr Skolimowski' (the object of the previous week's discussion). He concludes nevertheless that the Dymny-Kluba collaboration could stimulate Polish cinema to 'enter a truly Polish road', in which hope he supports it.

Given the absence of representatives of the Party authorities noted by the next speaker, Ludwik Starski, it is interesting to see him too voice political doubts. Some of these mice will speak for the cat in absentia. Starski also likens Haratyk to a larger-than-life Polish legend – the Kmicic of Henryk Sienkiewicz's *Potop* (*The Deluge*, 1886), a novel about the seventeenth-century Swedish invasion – but fears that spectators 'will leave the cinema with the most hostile attitude possible regarding everything happening around us'. He disapproves of the script, which he feels requires changes so far-reaching that little would remain.

The next speaker's primary objection was to its violence (thirty odd Germans killed in the first few pages), though he also deemed it full of literary elements impossible to translate to the screen, as well as of naturalistic vulgarisms he would like to see cleaned up. Worse still, Haratyk is less reminiscent of a Jánošik than of Ogień ('Fire'), a post-war anti-communist resistance fighter. He too fears the film's effect on the young and is astonished at the Film Unit's failure to consider this. This opposition was shared by his successor, who doubted the validity 'of applying a legendary style to events that really took place and did so only twenty years ago': turning reality into legend is 'squaring the circle'. Moreover, the film could not possibly come in at the five million złoty at which it had been costed, though since this was not a proper script its feasibility could not be gauged; 'The content is dangerous' and Haratyk 'an anarchist'.

Finally the script was defended by Krzysztof Teodor Toeplitz, who stated that the Commission would criticise even a screenplay of *Tikhii Don* (*Quiet Flows the Don*, Mikhail Sholokhov's 1929–40 novel, filmed by Sergei Gerasimov in 1957) due to the anarchism of its protagonist. (Toeplitz is cannily aware of the rhetorical usefulness of comparison with an approved Soviet model.) Haratyk's anarchism can be read as simply part of the expected characterisation of a mountaineer, and so poses no danger (in other words: this feature need not be read politically). Toeplitz even argues that 'in essence, everything that the people's authorities put forward within reasonable limits matches the judgements and wishes of the simple people, but when the people's authorities distort their proposals, disparities arise between their spontaneous acceptance by society and the ideology and conception of socialism of the Polish people.' Where previous speakers stress Haratyk's obduracy, Toeplitz highlights the mistakes of the authorities, implicitly invoking the accepted notion of a period of 'errors and distortions'.

Czesław Petelski, however, contrasted *Quiet Flows the Don*, which presented the truth about an epoch, with Dymny's legend, which for him reflected the tragedy of a younger generation of writers presenting the post-Occupation years on the basis of second-hand knowledge. 'Representatives of the people's authorities are presented as complete idiots', and the script is forced and unconvincing.

Speaking for the Syrena unit itself, Jerzy Pomianowski compared this script favourably with Dymny's one for Kluba's debut, *Chudy i inni* (*Skinny and Others*, 1967), as it has a clear hero and a logical construction. Somewhat plaintively, he says he had hoped that the Commission would help decide which parts of the script to cut, as there are indeed thirty pages too many. He maintains that it 'follows our political line', without giving any specifics, and lauds its 'political ambitions': 'We are dealing with an outstanding revolutionary work and a young, committed writer who shows the people's reactions to the initial phases of the changes that occurred.'

Professor Stanisław Wohl then argued the merits of dangerous themes. After all, Petelski's own *Baza ludzi umarłych* (*Damned Roads*, 1959) – 'one of the most interesting films of this period' – had originated in a problematic text. Indeed, he goes so far as to say that 'good films arise only out of difficult works, ones with perils'. As for the reproach that this is less a screenplay than a novel, ideal screenplays are rare, and this one should not be rejected on such grounds. The script for *Quiet Flows the Don* had been rejected initially. This one is of value.

Speaking in Dymny's absence, Kluba stressed 'the need for a film of this kind': that is, one that is contemporary and political. After Starski had reiterated his firm rejection, Chairman and Culture Minister Tadeusz Zaorski summed up a situation he termed 'ambiguous'. The script has not been approved. In fact, is it even a script? Compared with *Quiet Flows the Don*, the film lacks representatives of the other side made of something more than 'paper'. Doubtless eager to distance himself from the language of 'the period of errors and distortions', he adds that 'this does not mean that only scripts with positive heroes who are Party members can be approved for production, for we can agree equally well to a negative hero – but we need situations that allow us to see the reasons for this negative hero'. Kluba's previous film had also fallen short in its representation of the Party: its Party activist 'was completely isolated much of the time', 'a freak'. With some irritation he notes the limitations of his Commission's power: 'We criticised the role of the Party activist when discussing the previous script, but despite that judgement he figured the same way in the film.' The current screenplay does not do justice to the principled attitudes of security service members in the immediate post-war period. Only a script that includes counter-arguments could go into production. When Petelski interjected, somewhat surprisingly, that the film was worth making for the sake of Haratyk alone, Zaorski reiterated 'the need for figures to set against this chieftain' (FN, KOS, A-214 poz. 431).

The script's second review occurred with a slightly different set of Commission members. Toeplitz argued that the only possible objections to the new version were compositional ones, particularly concerning 'the over-saccharine ending', in which 'the author tries too hard to convince us … that the hero is now capable of positive action', and which shows Haratyk's post-prison breakdown at monotonous length, while his killing by Kośławy is very unexpected. Wincenty Kraśko, absent from the previous meeting, had strong doubts about the script's politics, though much in it appealed to him. Ernst Bryll argued for the development of the figure of Mały, since he had supported socialism from the outset and would therefore be a good counterfoil to Haratyk, who had done so only in his old age. This would solve the political problems. Like several speakers at the first meeting, he had doubts about Dymny's version of the mountaineers' strong language. Starski remained strongly opposed, deeming Haratyk too blood-stained to be a hero or for his final *volte face* to be credible.

Coming to the script for the first time, novelist Jerzy Putrament found its politics unacceptable, particularly its presentation of the People's Army as a brutal organisation. A Haratyk, guilty of many murders, would not have been freed in October 1956. Only if it drops its suggestion that 'the bad authorities began a war with the peasants' can the script be salvaged. Tadeusz Karpowski felt that his earlier objections still stood, as even Haratyk's final commitment to building socialism is 'purely theoretical'. He would like to give the unit the benefit of the doubt, but the project is too risky. Maintaining the incompatibility of legend and a recent past everyone recalled, he even added that 'memory among a certain section of the spectators is an additional danger'. Jan Alfred Szczepański also echoed his own previous misgivings, objecting particularly strongly to the opening, as a recent reportage had shown the People's Army to be well-known among the mountaineers at the time. Too much of the script is unrealistic and cast in the mode of the grotesque.

Stanisław Trepczyński, the next speaker, was the first to mention the central issue of the devils, which 'alarmed' him. Given the legendary context, though, the script ought to be feasible. After all, the 'dramatic tensions [between] the people's authorities and the mountaineers ... ought not to be idealised'. The script has something of the 'ambitious western' and could yield 'a great film'; 'after all, viewers will realise that the majority were for socialism, and our reality is the proof of that'. Interestingly, he sees a danger in the strength of the contrast between the 1945–56 and the post-1956 period. Putrament vigorously restated his objections. What he calls 'the civil war in the Podhale ... wasn't caused by incompetent PPR agitators' but by 'the exceptional hostility of the populace'. Only if it addresses these political issues, particularly in its beginning and ending, is the script filmable.

The fact that Starski, Toeplitz and Bryll then spoke again to reiterate their positions indicates the degree of attraction and antipathy exerted by the script. When Professor Stanisław Wohl spoke for the film unit itself, he said that only 'risky decisions' yielded 'new and interesting things'. He proposed that further changes be made not to the script but through the working out of a shooting script between Kluba and Dymny, and expressed particular faith in Kluba's ability to remove all dubious points. Although his summing up was generally favourable, Minister Zaorski felt it would be going too far at this stage to devise a shooting script. A whole series of political issues needed to be addressed first, and the unit was advised to write to the Main Board of Cinematography (FN, KOS, A-214 poz. 440).

If the perceived anarchism of Haratyk drew particularly strong fire from the Script Assessment Commission at both its meetings, an examination of portions of some of the different versions shows that they could also have embraced both the author himself and the unruly polyvalence of his/the poetic. The poetic means far more here than just the stylised rhythmic folk chants and the Fool who acts as a chorus (his pumpkin head doubling metaphorically as the sun). More importantly, it also engenders a multivalent use of the idea of the Devil, since while Haratyk embodies a stubborn spirit of independence that hovers between a subsequently demonised pagan Slavonic spirit and a Nietzschean Superman (thus at one point in the film a screen split horizontally renders him enormous in the upper half as he bestrides the hills while tiny villagers work in the lower half), the Party members who enter his village at the outset are also aligned with folk devils. It may be more appropriate to speak of the dae-monic than the diabolic, as this Devil – also described in a folk chant by women as hovering over the world – seems to be 'beyond good and evil', and may even be queasily redolent of the (Heideggerian and Nazi) projection of a mountain spirit. The film, however, reduces the link-age between the Party members and the Devils to a mere hint: to the simultaneous appearance of three of each in the first shots. Even after the text's first revision, condensation and partial doctoring for politically sensitive material, there is a small but telling difference between the way text and film present their first encounter with the villagers. In Dymny's text (published in part at the time in *Ekran* [Dymny 1967: 8]), Moskala replies to Górniok's call to look who is coming by saying 'probably those devils from Ochodzita'; the three Party activists promptly appear. In the film, though, Moskala's reference to devils is followed directly by a cut to the three dancing folk devils, rather than to the Party members, whose metaphorical connection to them is removed (they simply follow these folk figures, laughing at the spectacle). Only the links between Haratyk and the diabolic remain, as he proclaims in an early scene that 'we'll set up a brickworks and a sawmill even if we have to get them from the Devil himself'.

Reviewing the completed film in the Catholic weekly *Tygodnik powszechny*, Jan Józef Szczepański (not to be confused with the Jan Alfred Szczepański who was a regular reviewer for the Party daily *Trybuna Ludu*) began by stating that 'for this parable Kluba has chosen a form that precludes the possibility of journalistic interpretations: that of a ballad steeped in motifs of the folk imagination' (Szczepański 1972). The script's tortuous passage through its committee stages, however, showed the authorities' refusal to deem the work apolitical. If Kluba and Dymny had thought that stylisation would protect them from censorship, or that a peasant theme would garner automatic official approval from a Party formed through a worker-peasant alliance, they were sadly disappointed, as the accounts of the Script Assessment Commission meetings amply illustrate.

As in the case of Aleksander Ścibor-Rylski's script for Wajda's *Man of Marble*, one source of the trouble Dymny and Kluba encountered was surely the combination of the close relation-ship between Polish literature and film and the disparity in the reception conditions of the two media. Not defined officially as a mass art, literature had a licence to investigate areas hedged about with taboo where film was concerned. A work might be published – as were the scripts by both Ścibor-Rylski and Dymny – long before it was filmed or, if filmed, released. So sensitive is the material of Dymny's script that even the excerpt published in *Ekran*, which corresponds to the version published later in book form, doctors the original script lodged in the Filmoteka narodowa, doubtless in part because of the Script Assessment Commission's comments on the excessive length of the original (125 pages), but also apparently in response to official criticism of its ideology, and of the opening in particular. Consider, for instance, the published version's transformation of the following two exchanges between the three People's Army soldiers who represent the Party. The first comes in the script's opening paragraph:

> – Damn these peasants. I'd teach them to think dialectically – *the third one spoke, waving his tommy gun about*
> – If needs be. For the moment we have to get through to them, not shoot them.
> – *the first laughed*
> – More's the pity – *grunted the other.* (FN, S-9089, 4)

The second appears after Haratyk refuses to order the peasants to assemble, as these three have requested:

– They're tough ones – *said the darkest of the arrivals*
– I'd soften them up with lead.
– Why make such a furore. They'll soften up of themselves.
– Those from lower down are easier to talk to.
– Less independent, already depraved. (FN, S-9089, 5)

In Dymny's revised script (FN, S-5933) the first dialogue vanishes from the opening paragraph and is fused with the second one. The elements that are retained thus appear at a slightly later stage, and the passage now reads:

– They're tough ones – *said the darkest of the arrivals*
– I'd soften them up with lead.
– If needs be. For the moment we have to get through to them, not shoot them.
– Damn these peasants and teach them to think dialectically!
– Various 'boys from the forest' are telling them various things.
– Those from further down are easier to talk to.
– Less independent, already depraved.

Dymny's most significant alteration suggests that the peasants are being misled by 'boys from the forest' (resistance fighters). (It is surely also significant that guns are no longer being waved about, with the suggestion of Party trigger-happiness.) At the same time, though, any implications of the mountain villagers' suggestibility are countered by the statement of their greater independence than villagers living lower down. Dymny may be determined immediately to counter whatever concessions he makes, or simply be following the dictates of a dialogue form that ironically itself issues an imperative to 'think dialectically'. The dialogue's transfer to a later point in the script may be intended to mitigate the negative initial impression of the Party criticised by the Script Assessment Commission. Since it certainly shows its activists' negativism not as a provocatively pre-existent attitude but as a reaction to the peasants' refusal to assemble, this explanation is highly probable. But it is arguable that it also seeks to protect sensitive material by removing it from the relative exposure of the opening. Although the latter possibility is particularly speculative, there is little doubt that the condensation responds both to complaints of excessive length and to political criticism. And yet not one of these versions survived into the eventual film: neither the patent attempt to clear censorship, nor the possible attempted disguise of contraband, had any success.

Although one speaker at the Script Assessment Commission had described Haratyk as a tragic figure, most of its speakers had defined the work generically in terms of a legend. It is thus potentially significant that tragedy should have been the genre that featured most strongly in critics' comments. One headlined his review 'On the scale of a Greek tragedy' (Żórawski 1972), while Stanisław Grzelecki, writing in the popular Warsaw daily *Życie Warszawy*, argued that Haratyk, the Party Secretary and the security service officer have 'defined motives which each of the three deems fully justified, yet all three make mistakes and become caught up in a tragic conflict' (Grzelecki 1972). This reading, of course, is firmly in the post-October tradition that defined the period of Poland's Stalinisation as one of 'errors and distortions', with no conscious malice on any side.

AFTERMATH: THE ESCAPE FROM THE CENSOR'S CINEMA

Part-way through Wojciech Marczewski's *Escape from the 'Liberty' Cinema* (*Ucieczka z Kina 'Wolność'*, 1990) the chief censor of a provincial Polish town (Janusz Gajos) learns that in the course of a film's screening its actors have refused to play their parts, have begun to demand other roles, and are scandalising the public with their behaviour and occasional bad language. 'People have stopped rebelling; it's the rebellion of matter', says the censor, by way of explanation. After all, it is the late 1980s – Marczewski's film was made in 1989 – and the authorities are seeking to persuade themselves that martial law has fully pacified the populace. The censor may even seem to be speaking for Marczewski himself, whose bitingly oppositional Solidarity-period film *Dreszcze* (*Shivers*, 1981) had been followed by nearly a decade of silence, and who had famously lambasted the major part of the Polish cinematic production of the 1980s as unnecessary. The censor's explanation is picked up and parroted later in the film by his assistant (Zbigniew Zamachowski). His boss responds by telling him to look outside. The assistant peers down from the balcony and sees a crowd besieging the cinema. The explanation is now cast in doubt, and its placement in the assistant's mouth may even be deemed a dream-like disavowal; after all, events are indeed pursuing the logic of a censor's worst nightmare. The milling crowds do indeed seem to be rebelling. Moreover, the crowd within the cinema itself is very lively, packed eagerly together with standing room only; children are launching missiles at the screen and spectators are talking back to the actors. Could it be that rebellion is becoming widespread, and that its embrace of the material might even be an overflow from audience dissatisfaction with the irrelevance of just such trite melodramas as the one being shown, something sufficient to transform even a banal work like *Escape from the 'Liberty' Cinema*'s film-within-a-film, 'Jutrzenka'? The decision to limit the damage by buying up the tickets for all the 45 scheduled screenings suggests a suspicion that even if the problem does not seem to originate in the audience, it is far from subjugated. The recurrent early shots of the censor looking through his window at newspapers billowing freely across the roofs would seem to suggest a generalised rebellion that encompasses matter as well as people. The authorities may think they have the populace under their thumb, but the whole system may be tottering. Barriers are breaking down both on-screen and off, as an actor is said to have lowered his trousers, while within the auditorium itself a nun laughs out loud at his bad language. If there is a rebellion of matter, however, it may well also be one of *mise-en-scène*, as the censor's office wall carries a poster for Andrei Tarkovsky's *Zerkalo* (*Mirror*, 1975), while a Solidarity poster figures fleetingly in the projectionist's booth.

As he views the crowd from his boss's balcony, the assistant asks 'what do they want?' 'They're waiting for a miracle' is the reply. One may wonder whether in fact what they desire is so incomprehensible to the authorities as to seem miraculous to the latter. Could it be that the strength of their desire has in fact generated a miracle, in the sense of a violation of all known norms and expectations: an event that may also be described as a revolution or as the resurrection that will become leitmotivic, through various characters' singing of the 'Mors stupebit et futura Cum resurget creatura' section of Mozart's 'Requiem' and the censor's own sloughing off of his existential death? The censor's life does indeed seem to have reached a nadir and be in need of resurrection. He is no longer a person, only a function: the film gives him no name. His ex-wife surveys him disdainfully as she parades her young lover through his flat, and one of the on-screen actors notes the censor's inebriation and comments, 'if I were a censor, I'd be drunk all day'. When the censor tells his assistant that the crowds are like the actors in the film and 'also long to change their lives', is it not in part his prophetic soul speaking of himself?

Insofar as he changes, it is under the influence of the on-screen actress Małgorzata (Teresa Marczewska), whom Piotr Lis likens to the Margarita of Bulgakov's *The Master and Margarita* (Lis 1998: 196–7), though she is also in a sense its Jesus, pitying that other beleaguered state official, Pontius Pilate. When her poster was put up outside the cinema, the bill-fixer had been told it should be large, so as to make life worth living. 'Like Anita Ekberg?', the man had replied – recalling both Fellini's *La Dolce Vita* (1960) and his contribution to *Boccaccio '70* (1962), in which a larger-than-life Ekberg stepped out of her poster and bestrode the streets like a giant goddess. Małgorzata's influence may be less spectacular, but it is arguably of similar significance. The censor tells her 'I shouldn't be a censor', and when Party officials consider arresting the possible contagion of freedom emanating from the film by burning it, he protests and calls it murder. Despite the local Party Secretary's protests, he steps into the screen. The passage to its other side is one of recovered self-respect and great courage, since his expression of solidarity with the actors involves possible death by fire – in other words, martyrdom. The censor then follows various characters to a strange, visionary rooftop limbo housing the discontented, alienated and eliminated characters of Polish cinema, including the cast of the dismal 'Jutrzenka' and actors the censor himself had ordered cut (the cutting of a Jew who refused to abjure his faith appallingly suggests an echo of the Holocaust in the persistence of anti-Semitism in Poland). In just one of several remarks that anticipate concerns that would fester throughout the decade after 1989, one character is incensed at the censor's apparent lack of punishment for his crimes, and he hounds him downstairs, back towards the edge of the screen and the reality he re-enters only just in time, as the screen goes blank a moment later. His passage into, then out of, the screen has been like the hero's journey to the underworld. He walks back home to draw the curtains, as if ending the brief magical continuum of theatrical and filmic performance that has shaped this film, as it did a work it quotes in homage, Woody Allen's *The Purple Rose of Cairo* (1985).

Allen's film, of course, had placed its accents differently. Marczewski augments its wit with a metaphysical *frisson*. Particularly haunting is the multivalent rooftop scene. Marczewski's fusion of political cinema and art cinema opens a box that cannot be closed again. It is the one labelled 'liberty', and doubtless would be described by the censor as Pandora's. At the outset we see him delivering a lecture on censorship, which he terms an art. It concludes: 'Let's for the moment skip all the clichés about the inquisition and democracy. I don't know if you're aware, ladies and gentlemen, that the moment censorship as an institution is abolished, the task of censorship will devolve upon you.' Such censorship is rendered all the harder by the multivalent work, which – as is indicated by the censor's remarks on the cartoon and Jerzy Bossak's comments on the stylistics of *The Barrier* (discussed above) – poses particular problems of interpretation. In the case of Marczewski's work, that multivalence is firmly inscribed in its title. The censor would probably read it as a gratifying sign of people's fear of freedom and incapacity for rebellion. Yet it is censorship and power themselves that flee the anarchist miracle of this particular cinema. The authorities themselves seem to have grounds to fear it, as the local Party Secretary involuntarily bursts into the passage of Mozart that issues from the mouths of one power-figure after another. Another twist of the title reveals the on-screen actors themselves as succeeding in fleeing both their film and the cinema, after the censor has warned them to do so. They finally enter a freedom that lies beyond all stories, in the rooftop realm in which they simply circulate. This ultimate freedom may be one none of us can endure, as we leave the cinema – the space of art and imagination – and return to our lives just like the censor himself, exiting the screen.

Speaking of Marczewski's film, Bolesław Michałek states that 'in 1989 it wasn't clear whether or not censorship still existed. For that reason, the film assumed various forms' (Hollender & Turowska 2000: 197). Those various forms are surely still present in the final work, whose multivalence imprints the shifting, intermediate conditions of its prospective reception. Ironically, its near-abortion was not the work of any political censorship but of the economic one embodied in the TOR film studio's head, Krzysztof Zanussi, who vetoed it on the grounds of the excessive size of the proposed wage-scale for its actors (Hollender & Turowska 2000: 196). Only a personal appeal to the Ministry by Marczewski himself secured a reversal of this decision, though Zanussi was sufficiently gracious to admit the greatness of the completed work, and to back it to the hilt thereafter (Hollender & Turowska 2000: 198).

THE DEATH AND REBIRTH OF CENSORSHIP

In the aftermath of the political earthquake of 1989 and the establishment of a capitalism founded upon shock therapy, for many Polish viewers the Wajda film of the greatest relevance became *The Promised Land*, that tale of the ruthless capitalism of the last decade of the previous century. The fact that one of the key films of the late 1990s was Krzysztof Krauze's *Dług* (*The Debt*, 1999), a story of entrepreneurs whose business plans go so horribly awry as to end in murder, only underlines the continued relevance of *The Promised Land*, justifying Wajda's decision to release a recut version. The re-release follows the Western trend of the 'director's cut', though a close inspection of the reworking ironically – and anomalously for the genre – yields a *shortened* one which suggests that the director had come round to the view of Edward Gierek, who had criticised the original as 'pornographic' (Tejchma 1991: 52). It is as if Wajda had decided belatedly to follow the advice of the *kolaudacja* and, among other things, remove the rambunctious love-making of one of its three heroes, the German Maks. Perhaps more surprising, and less obvious, is the continued relevance of another Wajda film of the early 1970s, whose initial release simultaneously with *The Promised Land* was apparently fortuitous: *Pilate and Others*. If the leading light of 1990s Polish cinema was no longer Wajda but a Kieślowski lauded for his spirituality, Wajda's only film on a religious topic generally tabooed by the PZPR assumes renewed relevance also, and all the more so at a time when a preoccupation with the sacred has begun to permeate more and more Polish films. It was not simply tendentiousness that motivated the film critic of the Catholic *Tygodnik powszechny* to state that the Gdynia festival of 2001 showed a Polish cinema preoccupied with the transcendent. After all, several of its key films (Lech J. Majewski's *Angelus*, Witold Leszczyński's *Requiem*, Michał Rosa's *Cisza* [*Silence*]) dramatised religious themes, while another, Robert Gliński's *Cześć, Tereska* (*Hi Teresa*) – unanimously voted the festival's best film – began in a church to which it returned, as a central point of reference, near its end.

It might also be a particularly revealing exercise to pair *The Promised Land* with *Pilate and Others*, discussed earlier. Apparent opposites – in aesthetic, reception, distribution and treatment by the regime – they tell a great deal both about the workings of the Polish film industry, but also about the dialectical range and lack of homogeneity of Wajda's work in general. The pairing reflects one made by the censors themselves, who wrote in one report among the films and plays that evoked 'undesirable currents' in the first quarter of 1975, 'a particular resonance was aroused in the milieu by the theatrical spectacles of *The Danton Affair* in the Teatr Powszechny and *The Wedding* in the National Theatre, and by two films: *Pilate and Others* and *The Promised Land*' (AAN, GUPPiW, ZI-Pf-052/1/75).

In the case of *The Promised Land*, however, the censor's objections were less to the film itself than to any negative reviews of what was promoted as a copybook demonstration of Marxist class analysis. A censor's report to which Wajda himself gained access indicates how that promotion was to proceed:

The international popularity of Wajda increases the propaganda value of his works. It would seem, therefore, that *The Promised Land* should be used for propaganda purposes, in two different ways.

First, it is not often that one is confronted with a Polish film that combines an effort to portray aspects of historical materialism on one hand with a high degree of aesthetic achievement on the other. And here, after all, Wajda has portrayed the exploitation of the working class, the solidarity of capital, and the ideals and dedication of the growing working-class movement. (It is noteworthy that he does not deal with the nationality of the worker activists, precursors of the class struggle.) Both for a younger viewer in this country, and for one abroad, for whom Wajda's name is an important recommendation, the film is a good lesson in our way of thinking.

Secondly, it should be cautiously emphasised that Wajda has made clear his class point of view.

Such a point of view, by reinforcing what has happened, may help to distance Wajda from those circles that are unwilling to see art as politically committed, and may bring him closer to our propaganda art circles.

It would seem useful to slowly quiet the discussion concerning this film, and not permit people to bring up the nationalist elements – which are essentially secondary – but to emphasise the class elements and perhaps the aesthetic elements. Exaggerated praise for Wajda should be avoided absolutely. It is the work that should be praised, not the author. Wajda must not be turned into the bard of Marxism, but the ideological, educational value of *The Promised Land* should be emphasised. (Leftwich Curry 1984: 413–14)

Wajda's own account of the film's reception speaks of the film unleashing 'a storm of polemics' and quotes a text referring to a 'censor's ban' which insisted that 'one should not allow for the publishing of critical opinions similar to the one presented in *Żołnierz Wolności* [*Solider of Freedom*] on 18 February' (Wajda 2000b: 116). Wajda's words do not reveal the censor's intention of nipping negative coverage in the bud. The *Żołnierz Wolności* article, which Wajda does not quote, concerns a meeting he and the actors held with the press on 13 January in the 'Warsaw' cinema. It reports various criticisms of the disparities between the film and Reymont's novel; for instance, making the Polish Borowiecki the least sympathetic of the three friends 'diverges from the historical truth'. The reviewer sarcastically wonders whether Wajda continually chewed chocolate to calm his nerves, and reports one audience-member asking why Wajda has greater artistic successes in historical films than in contemporary ones. It regrets 'that the writer [Reymont] had no say in the matter of whether he would wish to be buddies with Wajda, particularly on the basis the director proposes. One wonders whether this is not a simple makeover of Reymont's work', adding in a pointed postscript that 'the reproaches thrown up by this press conference were also raised at meetings with workers of the Łódź FSO [Small Car Factory]' ('Kryśka' 1975).

Wajda's work can be seen as responding to the Script Assessment Commission's evaluation of an earlier screenplay based on Władysław Reymont's novel – that by Jerzy Krysztoń, reviewed as early as 8 September 1961 (FN, KOS, A-214 poz. 227). That meeting had described Krysztoń's script as lacking in educational value, displaying poor characterisation, having little potential appeal to the young and being apparently anti-Jewish. Its Chairman, Culture Minister Tadeusz Zaorski, clearly felt somewhat bound by his own initially positive reaction to the first feelers sent out by the relevant film unit, but the final decision was negative, the Commission doubting that any proposed alterations would make the script possibly acceptable, and hence worth resubmitting. Wajda's *The Promised Land* seems to meet each objection in turn: offering an educational and class-conscious display of the outlandish palaces of the Łódź industrialists; mobilising a frank eroticism that would attract the young; and reworking the character of Moryc Welt, the Jewish member of the entrepreneurial trio, to render him sympathetic. It is hard to not assume that the changes were made with an eye to the grounds of the first proposal's rejection. By the time Wajda's script was entered, of course, the Script Assessment Commission had been abolished. He seems to have been particularly attuned to Jerzy Bossak's contribution to the earlier meeting, mentioning the potential usefulness to the filmmaker of the preservation in Łódź of 'many of the props of that period'. The *kolaudacja* of Wajda's film was marked by initial comment on the eloquently stunned silence that followed its viewing: the first speaker thanks Wajda fulsomely for his film. There may be a comment on the relative lack of detailed explanation of the industrialists' money-grubbing machinations, and a momentary worry from Jerzy Passendorfer that the film might be difficult and appeal to a narrow public, but such objections were quickly quashed by Jerzy Kawalerowicz's praise of the clarity of its message. (The simultaneous, and restricted, release of *Pilate and Others* would make it quite clear just what counted as 'narrow' – for all the lines round the block to see it…) One or two scenes may have been deemed overlong, and the chairman (Jerzy Bajdor) may have advised Wajda to cut the 'explicit scene with Seweryn in the room' (something Wajda would only do 25 years later), but the positivity of the response is remarkable in the context of the usual bureaucratic nit-picking of meetings that often felt a need to justify their own existence (FN, KK, A-324 poz. 7). Consequently, the authorities were extremely protective of a film embraced all the more relievedly and fervently in the context of the absence of correct class analysis from recent Polish films – or, worse still, the suggestion made by a film like Zanussi's *Życie rodzinne* (*Family Life*, 1971) that certain indispensable values might be sustained by the *rentier* classes History had sent the way of the dinosaur (FN, KK, A324 poz. 2; Toeplitz 1971: 71–3). The censor was particularly interested in eliminating opinions such as the one written for, but never run by, *Tygodnik powszechny* and describing the film as socialist realist, discussed at the end of the previous chapter.

If Edward Gierek had described *The Promised Land* as pornography, ironically, 25 years later Wajda seemed to have come round to Gierek's opinion, though some saw the cause as a desire to appease the Roman Catholic Church, as he recut the film to excise its most orgiastic scenes. One of his stated rationales for the removal of Borowiecki's love-making during a train journey is that 'nowadays everyone does scenes like this' (Lubelski 2000: 4); another was that he did this out of respect for the recently deceased actress involved, Kalina Jędrusik (Nurczyńska-Fidelska & Sitarski 2003: 159). In the former case, the interviewer does not press the issue but allows Wajda to expatiate on the film's contemporary relevance, the faster rhythm it now displays, the shifting of the old beginning to a later point, and the usefulness to the Polish cinema of revivals of the superproductions of the 1960s.

CHAPTER FOUR

HEROISM, MASCULINITY, 'FEMINISATION' AND 'THE POLISH SCHOOL'

MASCULINE/FEMININE

Questions of heroism and the nature of masculinity are, of course, deeply intertwined: the hero is traditionally male, a defender of hearth and home, an avenger of a lost honour that is often that of his spouse or of another female relative, or, if it is his own, 'feminises' him until vengeance can be exacted. In the context of the Polish history of the past two centuries, however, both heroism and masculinity suffer the enormous shocks of recurrent military defeat and the encounter with modernity. The fusion of these two forms of shock is crucial to Wajda's *Lotna*, to which I will revert later. The repeated military defeats and prolonged occupations of the nineteenth and twentieth centuries gradually consigned initially hopeful revolts to the status of merely symbolic actions with nugatory likelihood of success. Once reduced thus, almost the only positive status to accrue to them was that of the aesthetic, though the deed's dependence upon a regime of Beauty could itself be seen as involving feminisation. The slimness of the chance of such actions' success would be further reinforced by their dependence upon premodern technologies of warfare: not horsepower – that abstraction and multiplication of an older force – but the horse itself. Its beauty breathed outdatedness, as beauty perhaps always does. If defeat is virtually inevitable, the only psychic gain it can yield is the masochism so often associated with femininity by males who take it as concomitant to the receptive position prescribed by female biology.

If heroism is taken as the preserve of a male warrior caste, and Andrzej Wajda is the bittersweet poet of that caste's demise, his first abandonment of the realm of grand passions assumes particular interest. This is adumbrated in *Niewinni czarodzieje* (*Innocent Sorcerers*, 1960) but only occurs in full in his first would-be comedy, *Polowanie na muchy* (*Hunting Flies*, 1969) based upon a story by Janusz Głowacki. Here the question of masculinity recurs obsessively in the dialogue's continual use of the adjective '*męski*' ('masculine') and in a claustrophobic, medium close-up *mise-en-scène* that evokes a male loss of freedom and space for action. Early on in the film its protagonist, Włodek, is instructed by his wife to sort out an issue with the local co-operative; it is a '*męska sprawa*' ('male matter'), she says, even as her direction of him effectively deprives him of agency and castrates him. It is thus hardly surprising that he should then commence a romance with a younger girl, the pretentious Polish literature student Irena. Irena, however, has a will of iron, and frequently flashed 'shark teeth' to match. She too seeks to mould him, describing him as '*męski*' and frequently pairing the word with the adjective '*ostry*' ('harsh'). When a hapless pedestrian is beaten up by thugs, she chivvies him into going to the man's aid. She determines that he will attempt a career as a translator of Russian poetry, recovering the thread of the studies he lost when expelled from university in the grim last Stalinist year of 1955. If she dresses him in her own clothes, including a very prominent and feminine scarf, it is almost as if to transfer the masculine quality of agency located in herself. But the graft does not take. It may indeed be significant that the proposed career is that of a translator – someone with no words of their own, whose versions of the words of others can always be corrected (as they are, again and again, by Irena). When rejecting his translation, the female editor of *Myśli młodych* (*The Thoughts of Youth*) significantly prefaces her criticism by saying that she offers it '*po męsku*' ('man to man', as it were). The anti-heroism of a modern world obsessed with careerism is one in which masculinity no longer resides in biological males, who thereby undergo a Kafkaesque translation into metaphorical insects. Is it significant, moreover, that Włodek's quest for a new identity is through subordination to the language of the country that called the tune in post-war Poland? If so, the anti-heroism becomes all the more comprehensive.

HEROISM

The question of the possibility of heroism is central to the Polish School, of which Wajda was the best-known representative. The idea of 'the heroic' pervades that school precisely because it forms a link between the official post-war ideology of proletarian internationalism, and the underground persistence in Polish consciousness of pre-war habits of thought.

For the thoroughgoing socialist, heroism belonged to Labour and was of safe Soviet provenance. Literary theorist and Newspeak-analyst Michał Głowiński's argument that this conception of heroism typified a socialist realism that never put down Polish roots is apparently corroborated by its parody in *Man of Marble*, but *Man of Iron*'s recycling of the iconic Worker, albeit to different ends, qualifies Głowiński's generalisation. Like Solidarity whose activists' terminology sometimes echoed that of the Party they opposed – and when it did not, was threatened by the incoherence proverbially characteristic of Wałęsa – Wajda the *bricoleur* was constrained by the political language of his formative years: *Man of Marble*'s parody of socialist realism bespeaks near-affectionate youthful intimacy with it, awareness of how as well as close it is also distant and hence risible, almost camp.

For the nationalist, meanwhile, heroism involved Polish fidelity to the cause, often at great cost, and overlapped with Conradian, gentry codes of honour. Poles had of course undergone double inoculation against acceptance of the notion of nationalism's compatability with socialism: on the one hand, the words' conjuncture had characterised the German effort to eradicate Poland, while on the other, socialism had its source in the traditional enemy to the East (Stalinism's 'socialism in one country', meanwhile, itself piquantly seemed to paraphrase 'national socialism', and was ironically ultimately far more successfully imperialist than the early Bolshevism ambitious for world revolution). 'Heroism' here has the traditional epic and martial connotations, while the time-lag between the war's end and its realistic cinematic treatment testified both to deep-seated, slow-healing trauma and to the insuperable obstacles to its fair representation thrown up by Stalinism. In what came to be known as the Polish School (a term first proposed as an ideal in 1954 by Aleksander Jackiewicz, but not actualised until after 1956, following the return to power of the man identified with 'the Polish road to socialism') the discourse of heroism would be ironised, be it in the bitter, tragic mode of Wajda or the blackly comic one of Andrzej Munk (in particular in *Eroica* [1957]). Consideration of heroism's fatal cost is what renders this cinema apparently compatible with the official discourse of socialism. Nevertheless, its critique of heroism is no simplistic ideologically correct denunciation of a key element of nationalist discourse: here, as later, the finest Polish cinema would be ironic, dialectical, activating the ambiguity of the word *bohater*, which can designate both the morally positive 'hero' *and* modern narrative theory's morally neutral (and hence possibly blank or ambiguous) 'protagonist'. So deep was the ironic questioning of the traditional male epic hero that in some respects unalloyed heroism would be found only in women: just as Colonel Netzer, leader of the Warsaw Uprising's 'Kryśka' group, contrasted the heroism of 80 per cent of his male fighters with the total dedication of the girls, so Wajda's *Kanal* (a work whose title is usually untranslated – doubtless lest its meaning of 'Sewer' deter audiences) shows a girl dismissing her wound as 'nothing' before her stretcher blanket slips to reveal her loss of a leg. In Wajda's early, most influential, and probably best works, an ethos that identifies Poland's future with socialism grapples and clashes with one fascinated by the defeated, but perhaps not defunct gentry codes that inspired the Uprising's soldiers, as in *Kanal*, *Ashes and Diamonds* and *Lotna*. A nationalism complexly underlies and is interwoven with the socialism. Eric Rhode pinpoints the contradiction when he remarks that 'the Polonaise may be butchered by an indifferent pianist, yet it still remains Chopin's Polonaise' (Rhode 1966: 186). Conversely, Wajda's weakest works deem self-division and doubt incompatible with heroism, yielding the flat iconic heroes of *Man of Iron* or *A Love in Germany*, or the more academic recreations of the gentry's lost world (a polemical subbstrand of *Ashes and Diamonds*) found in *Brzezina* (*Birchwood*, 1970) or *The Young Ladies of Wilko*.

TWO SEPTEMBERS: 1939 AND 1944

Two events bulked particularly large in the representation of war in the Polish People's Republic, both of them moments of symbolic defeat: the September campaign of 1939 and the Warsaw Uprising of 1944. Of the two, the latter was the more sensitive, and so I will consider it first. The London-led Home Army's decision to mount an uprising to liberate Warsaw before the arrival of Soviet troops had great potential propaganda value as a demonstration of the folly of a leadership apparently so steeped in anti-Sovietism as to refuse even liberation at their hands. The danger of this subject, however, lay in the Polish awareness that the Soviet Union had brought not liberation but another, less febrile form of repression, justifying the London government's wariness; and that the Red Army had shown its true intentions by remaining on the left bank of the Vistula while the German forces picked off the Poles at agonising length on the other. The 'madness' of the Warsaw Uprising had been its attempt to defeat Polish history and geography. No wonder the Poles cherished its memory, and in particular that of the courageous young people who died fighting in it. Bearing this in mind, its representation in the official media had to assume a form that would pay homage to the young foot soldiers of the struggle, compromise the leadership, and avoid even the slightest whiff of reference to Soviet treachery. The first two desiderata, of course, accorded well with a class analysis of the army, while the final one satisfied the ally who stood in the vanguard of the working class. The template for their fulfilment can be found in the war stories of Jerzy Stawiński, and its durability can be gauged by its use in a film from the 1950s, Wajda's *Kanal*, and one from the 1970s, Janusz Morgenstern's *Godzina W* (*'W' Hour*), based on works from the same volume (Morgenstern had also worked on *Kanal*, in a minor capacity). If Wajda's film overshadows Morgenstern's, it is not just because of Wajda's superior talent, but also because its focus upon soldiers' flight through the sewers generates images of a nightmarish underworld whose surrealism and tragic poignancy almost obscure the ideological framework. Nevertheless, the framework is there.

Kanal might indeed be criticised for its evasive image of the Warsaw Uprising. Wajda himself remarked of it:

> the only thing that may strike one is the absence of one element, namely 'force of circumstances' (let us leave it at that, in inverted commas) which precipitated the drama; but I can see no way of presenting this on screen until the problem has first been sorted out by the historians on the basis of the evidence. (Michałek 1973: 32)

This very guarded statement may begin as self-criticism but rapidly modulates into a coded self-defence: obviously Wajda could not depict the reasons for the inopportune launch of the Uprising (a desire to pre-empt Soviet liberation of Warsaw), for self-preservation and 'raison d'état' (another code term) precluded both that and any discussion of the Red Army's wait beyond the Vistula as the Uprising was suppressed. The sympathy *Kanal* extends to the soldiers in the sewers depends on defining them as victims of their high command and removing all hints of their possible identification with its goals. Indeed, Lieutenant Zadra, the battalion's immediate commander, is the one most critical of the orders of his superiors, commenting bitterly that the fighters have to go with pistols against the German bombers and tanks. (The relationship between the size of a weapon and feminisation becomes apparent when Halinka complains of the smallness of the pistol Mądry offers her.) Zadra is overwrought with the burden of knowledge of the slimness of the survival prospects of men and women he himself has recruited and with the effort to hide this from them. His position of apparent authority is that of 'the man between' who is virtually the fall-guy for his commanders: the split tragic hero. At first, he is even tempted to disobey the order to descend into the sewers. Setting the film in a late stage of the Uprising justifies its fatalism and erases any memory of its ever having had a purpose: there is no longer any mention of taking any of the Germans' positions (as occurs near the beginning of Stawiński's story), only of seeking to evade their attacks. The vision of the bearded corpse of a former colonel drifting, dead, in the water emblematises the failure and degradation of the higher command, while on two occasions (once above ground, just before the descent into the sewers, one below) mothers berate the fighters for deserting them. This Uprising is not the Romantic rebellion cherished in popular memory but a nightmare of abandonment, one of the 'crimes and follies' of Gibbon's vision of history. The nation does not pull together under pressure but disintegrates.

Isolation and breakdown are of course the governing formal and thematic principles of *Kanal*, as groups subdivide into smaller and smaller units until individuals finally wade through the eerily echoing waters of Avernus. The images of the soldiers trudging through these sewers have the power usually associated with World War One poetry: the sewers themselves, like the trenches, are part of the underground, made all the more deathly and vault-like by the walling off of the sky. After all, the opening voice-over tells us as the camera pans the characters, these are the last hours of the group. The film's formal development is a tour de force of stunningly virtuoso, deadly irony, from the freedom of movement embodied in the long and frequent pans and tracks of its first half, through the constrained passage through the sewers, to the entrapment of Jacek and Daisy by the bars separating them from the Vistula and Zadra's renewed descent into the sewers upon learning that his platoon is no longer behind him. The moment the fighters move underground the camera loses its freedom to roam: the claustrophobia is emphasised when they now move past it, rather than vice versa. (And when the pan returns, it is stripped of any connotations of freedom, moving from Mądry, now above ground, past the captured company, to the pile of dead bodies to which he and they will doubtless soon be added.) The musician's quotation of Dante sets the tone for this section very early on and is virtually equivalent to Dante's own reading of the injunction to abandon hope upon entering the Inferno. Close-ups and medium close-ups – justified by the poor visibility – enhance the claustrophobia, intensify identification, and strengthen the sense of breakdown of group cohesion, and the consequent growing disorientation of its members. Simultaneously, the drifting, atmospheric score distils a mood of directionlessness, dark enchantment (note the effect of the isolated celesta notes, recalling their use in some of the symphonies of Shostakovitch) and an uncanny, echoing sound-space in which unexpected threats and bizarre phenomena lurk beyond almost every corner or just outside the pitifully short reach of the torch. The group's breakdown rapidly causes the mental disintegration of its members, Jacek rambling feverishly, the musician wandering in a daze, Zadra laughing hysterically. The speed of the collapse suggests that the sewers in fact function as history's torture chamber.

Wajda stated that when making *Kanal* he had counted on the persistence of popular memory of the Uprising (Wajda 2000b: 18). Thus he doubtless felt he had done enough, or as much as was possible, by not condemning its foot soldiers, only its leaders (Zadra's final 'they've lost me my men' brands those superior officers as irresponsible). Nevertheless, Wajda's declaration of intention may be deemed partly disingenuous. After all, the film shows mothers berating the soldiers for abandoning them, something that hardly chimes with the popular support the Uprising enjoyed. The choice of a period in its latter part, when bitterness was more likely to appear, is also significant (Toeplitz 1973: 72). Meanwhile, if Zadra's company is lost it is arguably the result of his own misguided decision to allow Daisy (the best guide to the sewers) to bring up the rear with Jacek. Consequently, the controversy surrounding the film was not one between 'the political facts of life and folk consciousness', as Bolesław Michałek argues (Michałek 1973: 31), but rather between popular memory of events and an extreme selectiveness in the presentation of the political facts. Popular memory would recall, for instance: Moscow Radio's 19 July call for Warsaw to rise – issued twelve days before the Uprising; the arrest and deportation to Siberia of Home Army units that had greeted the Soviet Army as liberators in Vilnius and Volhynia, which of course validated the London government's distrust of its putative liberators; the initial successes of the Uprising; and, politically most sensitive of all, the Soviet Army's encampment beyond the Vistula, apparently held there by a Stalin content to let the Nazis do the dirty work of eliminating the Polish military élite for him, apparently indifferent, as the Uprising was crushed. The non-presentation of the Soviet Army on the other side of the Vistula (no sight or hint of them when Jacek and Daisy look through the sewer bars towards it) may be understandable, while the absence of any images of their self-proclaimed attempts to cross the river is even praiseworthy (if possibly due to Wajda's unwillingness to alienate his audience and desire to intensify the work's claustrophobia), but the omissions may have rankled so with spectators as to jaundice their view of the film. That spectatorial reaction, both irrational and comprehensible, depends in part on the issue of the typicality of the filmed events: a question that haunts all realistic theories of art, and probably all popular reactions to art, and so plagued the Soviet-influenced aesthetics of socialist Poland also. It becomes particularly acute in films, whose concretion gives representation a fragmentary and partial quality that may also be perceived as 'partial' in the unwanted sense of selective and prejudiced. Wajda's restriction of his story to one small and dwindling group may be taken as seeking to avoid the pitfalls of an attempt at synthetic vision, but the more intense the work and the process of identification it evoked, the more urgent the question of the representativeness of this group's experience. The negative reaction the film encountered may have been particularly strong because of its status both as the first about the Uprising and its emergence in the immediate aftermath of the 'Thaw' of 1956. *Kanal* is indeed remarkable for revealing more of the truth than had been disclosed earlier; as a half-truth, though, it fell mockingly, bitterly short of audience hopes, however irrational they may have been. Perhaps that is why it received the unwanted compliment of commendation by the Central Committee's Secretariat as one of a group of only three late-1950s films singled out for their 'positive, albeit sometimes one-sided ideological resonance' (Anon 1994a: 28), unlike other works castigated because they 'rarely … contain a clear and correct political assessment of the events of the war and the occupation' (Anon 1994a: 27).

Morgenstern's somewhat mediocre '*W*' *Hour*, for its part, treats the Uprising as the work of adolescents and young, fresh-faced adults. This renders it both more forgivable, and might also implicitly render even more unpardonable their older commanders' decision to launch it, though no reference is made to them. This emphasis is underlined at the end, where the lady of the flat in which a unit has been planning its assault on the Nazis' 'nest' exclaims 'but they're all so young!' A moment later they burst out of the building's doorway, many of them momentarily held in the freeze-frame associated with imminent death in a shoot-out in George Roy Hill's *Butch Cassidy and the Sundance Kid* (1969). Even when these young people seem open to criticism, such criticism proves unjustified. Sowa, a member of one subsection, may seem to have committed the heinous offence of drunkenness, but in actuality his unsteady navigation of the courtyard follows his wounding by a German soldier while obtaining a precious machine-gun. The bespectacled Andrzej may indeed seem to be the proverbial mother's boy, and may be criticised for failure to make the subsections' rendezvous, but this is because he is already dead, shot after lobbing two grenades at Germans pursuing a carriage bearing the wounded Sowa and his superior, Jacek. There may be talk of groups being infiltrated, but we see neither real traitors nor even weak links. These young patriots can only be pitied and admired. This is partly because their patriotism undergoes thorough depoliticisation: despite mentions of the extent of the Russian advance towards Warsaw, there are no anti-Russian comments, while the Uprising's actual rationale – to forestall a Soviet takeover – is passed over in silence. Consequently, the most frequent oppositional, patriotic terms for the Red Army, 'Bolsheviks' and 'Soviets', are discredited at the film's outset, where they figure in Nazi propaganda announcements; the young people simply call them 'Russians'. Their fate is lent greater poignancy by the dawning awareness of her pregnancy in Teresa (the group's courier and the girlfriend of its commander, Czarny) and through the presentation of the partings between quite a few of them and families within which they are the only sons or daughters. Their action is twice criticised as madness, but these two moments do not suggest a negative view of them. The first such criticism is undercut by its origin in the fat young Wacek, who guzzles soup as the unit installs itself in his aunt's apartment, the planned starting-point of their action. The second such utterance, meanwhile, comes from that aunt and immediately precedes her lament of their fate. It is thus less a criticism than a cry of woe from a figure one might term an incarnation of the 'Polish Mother' (Matka Polka) (Ostrowska 1998: 419–35). The fate of this one group, of course, becomes a microcosm of that of the entire Uprising. Focusing on one platoon, on the opening moments of the Uprising, and on the young people's assumption that the fighting will be all over by the next morning, Morgenstern renders the vast subject manageable dramatically and sparks a tragically ironic awareness of just how long, bitter and ruinous the struggle would finally prove. The film mobilises a portion of audience knowledge about the Uprising – concerning its length and bloodiness – while striving to cancel any prior knowledge of its rationale. The new rationale becomes the burning idealism of the young, their impatient unwillingness to, as Czarny puts it, 'watch quietly as they [the Germans] run from the Russians'. 'The hour of revenge has struck', he tells his platoon. The focus on one small group of very young people and their motives allows the filmmakers to present an image of the Uprising shot through with sympathy and hence acceptable to the Polish audience. The precondition of that sympathy, however, is a depoliticisation of the event that amounts to a distortion and an ascription of agency to them that ignores their superiors. We too weep for the young, the film says. But what one hand gives the other whisks away, overlaying real memories of the event with a new, politically anodyne myth.

Even that, though, was insufficient for more hardline reviewers, who branded it as sharing the failings of all the radio and television events commemorative of the Uprising in 1980:

> However, what was missing ... was a discussion of the political reasons for the issuing of the order to begin combat imposed upon the population of Warsaw, with the aim of seizing power, by the delegation to Poland of the London Government, before the entry of Polish and Soviet units. Above all, it was not explained how it came about that battle was joined at the least opportune moment, when – for strategic reasons – one could not count on support from the far side of the Vistula ... In the film 'W' Hour, Janusz Morgenstern also avoided touching on this problem. ('js' 1980)

One notes the careful mention of 'Polish and Soviet units', and the placement of 'Polish' before 'Soviet', in an effort to dispel the blame usually laid at the door of the Soviet Union.

Other, less charged images of tragic defeat are those of September 1939. I will shortly be looking at those of Wajda's Lotna, then those of the films of other directors, in particular Stanisław Różewicz's Westerplatte (1967) and Świadectwo urodzenia (Birth Certificate, 1961). As in Kanal, here the focus is upon figures in isolation: that is, on the effects of the break-up and scattering of the Polish forces – something that facilitates identification with small, separate groups or individuals but that also (significantly, and perhaps fatally) raises the question of the degree of their typicality.

KITSCH AND DEATH IN LOTNA

The spectacular nature and popular theme of Lotna (cavalrymen during the September 1939 campaign), along with the authorship of Wajda, ensured both a wide audience and, for political reasons, a controversial reception. All the same, irrespective of its position vis-à-vis various national and nationalist ideologies, the spectacle offered by the genre to which it belongs – the war film – can never be unproblematic, deriving as it does as much from destruction as ostentation (a term itself self-defined as problematic in the puritanical mind's eye, or eye critiqued by that mind). Wajda's film therefore offers a near-Syberbergian conceptualisation of 'kitsch' (the popular) as 'a fragment of myth' – in this case, the nationalist myths of military virtue – which it both ironises and perpetuates, positioning itself *beyond* high/low binarisms. The film has been almost universally deemed kitschy and unsuccessful (I have found only one exception to this widespread verdict, the recent opinion of Mariola Jankun-Dopartowa [1996a: 43–4]). Conceding the work's status as failure, Wajda himself has often voiced a wish that he could remake it.

Lotna's reviews repeatedly allege cheapness or vulgarity of symbolisation, indicating the relevance of the category of kitsch, which applies class judgements to forms of the aesthetic that are often mass-produced and described as simplified (the issue of simplification will return later [Broch 1955a: 346]). Since such terms discount the class whose aesthetic preferences kitsch ostensibly reflects – 'the vulgar' – their persistence in the criticism of a *soi-disant* socialist society itself piquantly and symptomatically displays that society's failure to eradicate its own class distinctions. Does this make the Wajda who sees himself as a spokesman for popular discontents inevitably the purveyor of kitsch?

Wajda's subject matter is indeed of a kind many reviewers would associate with kitsch. Reviewing Wajda's previous film, *Ashes and Diamonds*, the influential Krzysztof Teodor Toeplitz had praised its ability to tap Polish artistic traditions without succumbing to kitsch about 'hussars and a girl by a well' (Toeplitz 1958: 7). One may almost suspect Toeplitz of tempting fate, for the later film recklessly courts the danger the earlier one skirts. May the problem also involve *Lotna's* hermetic detachment from the present that, for all its period setting (1945), had entered *Ashes and Diamonds* through the fevered, 'existential' contemporaneity of Zbigniew Cybulski's performance?

The question is worth asking because Hermann Broch has linked kitsch to the historical novel. One may even say that for him kitsch falls under the double curse Plato pronounces upon art, being doubly imitative because mimetic of fantasy rather than reality. Furthermore, he deems it able to imitate only the simplest of forms, the most primitive aspects aspects of the prototypical artworks (Broch 1955a: 345–6). One may link this simplification (leading towards the rationalising streamlining – and hence the kitsch? – of Art Nouveau) to the pervasive leaning towards history, that homeland of spectacle, in late nineteenth-century art. Because our perceptions of historical reality lack the check of its grainy immediate presence, they slide seductively easily into fantasy or wish-fulfilment. The historical novelist's or art director's assiduous archival research yields an apparent visual simulacrum really at odds with other elements of the work, such as contemporary faces, gestures or stances. Wajda's own contention that there are no historical films is a truism (however great one's doubt whether many texts necessarily rework their present as simply allegorically as many Film Studies analyses have presumed), but it also fulfils a compensatory function, denying the bad faith perceived by onlookers sceptical of how the making of historical films demonstrates commitment to the here-and-now. One should add, of course, that Polish state control of the arts often did indeed render historical work the only option left for filmmakers once their contemporary projects had been blocked (official calls for works engaged with the present solicited only conformist views of it).

Lotna may be seen as a work of post-1956, post-Stalinist resistance and rehabilitation of the cavalry units whose legendary charge against German tanks the socialist state read as typifying the outdatedness of a pre-war regime it had rightfully replaced. Since Wajda grew up near a cavalry barracks, recalls his own father's career in the wartime infantry (Ratschewa 1980: 63) and himself served in the Home Army, such may indeed have been his intention. Yet, paradoxically, he would encounter official criticism for putative mockery of those units by showing the terrible mismatch of that legendary charge. ('*C'est magnifique, mais c'est pas la guerre*' Napoleon had reportedly remarked of an earlier ill-starred Polish cavalry assault, the one at Samosierra dramatised in Wajda's later *Popioły* [*Ashes*, 1965]. The magnificence renders it an irresistibly tempting subject for representation.) The allegation of mockery reflects the authorities' cynical appropriation of nationalism to discredit a director whose war trilogy had given him the aura of opposition. The line they cunningly accuse him of propagating was in fact their own.

Questions of history and resisting memory dominate Wajda's work, both here and in general. If one of several reviews in *Ekran* sees it suspended uneasily between such genres as the epic, the tale of heroes, the tragic lyrical rhapsody and the satirical study of manners (Gawrak 1959: 5), another, more important one – by Adam Horoszczyk – addresses its relation to history (Horoszczyk 1959: 5). For Horoszczyk, *Lotna* revives the pathos-laden, marytrological images of September 1939 cherished by those who may have participated in it but who have forgotten its reality. As he puts it, Wojciech Żukrowski's screenplay offered 'opportunities for relativisation of the uniform tone, for its enrichment with political reflection', but Wajda preferred 'another element of the work, one devoid of rationalist scruples, of psychology and sociology' (ibid.). Horoszczyk, like Alicja Helman, lambastes a symbolism he deems 'cheap', but reserves most of his fire for Wajda's 'possible lack of the courage needed to show that September as it was – "autumn-gold", yet grey with dust on the ground, blood, ashes and the smell of burning' (ibid.).

For all the underhand tendentiousness of this critique, its suggestion of the fallibility of participant memory is apposite. Consider, for example, for purposes of comparison, English memories of the coming of the self-same war. In a process Tom Harrison terms 'glossification', many who had lived through the period retrospectively realigned the personal memories recorded in their diaries with stereotypical official ones: one girl who was playing the piano as Chamberlain announced the war, and so missed his words, later 'recalled' her family sitting round the wireless as he spoke (Harrison 1978: 323). Whether analogous processes may be operative here is, of course, debatable, since in People's Poland the official view of September 1939 was countered by cherished oral memories of elements that view suppressed. Thus Horoszczyk's demand that a film about 1939 be also a settling of accounts implicitly prescribes the official scapegoating of the pre-war government.

The official socialist critique of the world that met its brutal end in 1939 was one of ostensible unreality, of fatal unpreparedness to counter German military threats. For all Horoszczak's complaints of Wajda's indifference to sociology, one is clearly implicit in sections of *Lotna*. For instance, refugees struggle through mud as the *uhlans* ride by, apparently insulated in their chivalric world, attuned only to the toy soldier bugles on the soundtrack. Beautiful but indeed unreal, they are poetically detached from the world of prose, and the juxtaposition of the lyrical and the prosaic helps justify the generic hovering the other reviewer decried. (The two may, of course, be united by terming the work 'balladic' – perhaps lyrically balladic, as in Wordsworth.) But is the *uhlans'* unreality also a feature of Wajda's own mode of presentation, perhaps as generally detail-free with fatal consequences as it is kitsch?

The possible unreality of Wajda's film may situate it closer to another genre not mentioned hitherto: that of the fantastic – specifically, of the form of the fantastic known as the uncanny. After the *uhlans* have marvelled at a riderless grey-white horse's charge across open ground amidst explosions, they proceed to a deserted house. On entering this site of the uncanny, they hear a recurrent incongruous sound, the surreally displaced aural image of a horse's hooves indoors. The air of the mysterious then generates the classic uncanny motif of the animation of the inanimate, as two white horses racing together as porcelain statues appear left of screen just before the *uhlans* open a door and see Lotna. The statues are white and pure, and some of their whiteness may be transferred to her, as the captain later describes her as white. The *uhlans*' passing of a statue as they approached the manor house, followed by the camera's discovery of statues indoors, blurs inner/outer boundaries in a manner befitting the fantastic. When first glimpsed through the door Lotna is shot as if no one else is present, as alluring an ownerless spectacle as at the outset: in another spatial blurring, house and stable become one. Only afterwards does the camera's rightward shift disclose the bed-ridden hand from which she is eating, identifying her apparent unreality as the result of her imaging by the entranced *uhlans* and replacing her in a reality (one defined in quasi-Brechtian terms as the place of revelation of the preconditions of eating). Thus the *uhlans* appear from the outset as denizens of a dream-world and the horse becomes the dream's embodiment. For despite critical condemnation of the unequivocality of the work's symbols (which may perhaps more accurately be termed allegories) (Helman 1959: 3), Lotna herself is ambiguous. On one level she may indeed belong in the allegorical world and figure as Poland (Polska – note the same vowels and number of syllables and the shared 'l'), but she also resists conceptualisation, possessing an oneirically wide hinterland of latent content. If she is death, she is also death fused with the maiden, for instance. Her femininity (note the name's feminine suffix) displaces other females for all but one of the *uhlans*, her passage among them suggesting the homosociality (yet also, for she is not a 'real girl', repressed homeroticism) of the group (Caes 2003: 120). The doom she transmits may not just be that awaiting pre-war Poland but also reflect the biological impossibility of a single-sex group's self-propagation. The horse's multivalence, her activation of surrealist dreamwork, may be the main thing – even the sole thing – that renders Wajda's work more artwork (albeit flawed) than kitschwork. The purity and menace of whiteness may even recall the 'Whiteness of the Whale' chapter of Herman Melville's *Moby Dick* (1851). Insofar as her whiteness suggests a screen that first solicits then outlives all human projections, it may even be profoundly cinematic.

Lotna is uncanny, a generator of delusion. Her introduction is both romantic and ironic, as an admiring comment on her gallop ('*leci w powietrzu*' – 'she flies through the air') is followed immediately by the bursting of shells around her. This word-image conjunction suggests that not only does she fly through the air but she might 'fly into the air' (the unspoken '*wyleci w powietrze*'), i.e. be blown up; it is as if, as in myth, words of admiration inevitably trigger disaster, with the bearer of the camera's invisible Gaze doubling as the evil eye. The syllables *leci* (flies) function as a hinge, and the ambiguity indicates at the outset that signifying procedures analogous to the dreamwork will influence the text. (The narrative rambling identified by Bolesław Michałek may also be called associative [Michałek 1973: 49].) Whatever flight there may be is linked to destruction, as in the cavalry charge whose first run is glorious, full of low angles and with *uhlans* shot against the sky, but whose second one, against tanks, is dark and catastrophic, focusing on the earth where the riders fall. Subsequently, within the manor, Lotna's disembodied hoof-beats echo continually before she is seen again, suggesting a luring sprite mocking the soldiers with her ungraspable presence. On first sight, the captain had described her as a grey. Once the manor's owner has transferred her to him, stating 'let her carry you to victory', he refers to her as white: language, implicitly symbolic, has draped the real horse with a significance that renders her even more dangerous, even more visible, than the grey would have been (thus her camouflaging with a coat to protect her rider, discussed briefly by the Officer Cadet and the Lieutenant, becomes extremely unlikely). Here Wajda figures tradition – literally 'handing on' – as entry into a delusion, rather as he had mocked religion when an iteration of the Lord's Prayer had seemed to summon down an instantaneous hail of bullets on the person praying. The fact that the hostess is later seen at prayer identifies this particular delusion with class elevation.

But if *Lotna* critiques the upper ranks of the officer class, it sees little attraction in the possible alternative to it, particularly as represented by the lowest-ranking of the four primary protagonists, the sergeant major. It is through him that the potential for conflict within the group first surfaces, as he reacts to the captain's account of his dream of his own death by starting forward and beginning to blurt out 'and what if...', obviously nursing – and then suppressing – hopes of taking over the horse in such an event. The captain resolves the issue by offering matchsticks to only the Officer Cadet and the Lieutenant, pointedly ignoring the sergeant major, whose baldness and pudgy stockiness breathe the disqualifying vulgarity of class otherness. But although class conflict may seem to simmer beneath the bland surface of apparent officer unanimity, with Lotna herself the apple of discord, the very blandness dulls the awareness of – and ability to thematise – the conflict, as it is unclear where one class ends and another begins. Is the sergeant major from 'outside' or 'inside'? Indeed, at one point he is possibly even more truly 'inside', truer to the code of honour than the Lieutenant, whose order to abandon the wounded he questions. Wajda's inability to determine whether or not he is 'inside' – 'one of us', in the Conradian sense – blurs the focus of his image. He is in fact the most complex figure in a film unable to handle complexity of character. In any case, his final possession of Lotna is no Marxist liberation but an almost Buñuelian marker of chaos and decline from an age of gold to one of bronze, like the elevation of the beggars in their banquet in Buñuel's *Viridiana* (1961), though bitterness and despair pervade Wajda's framing of what Buñuel would have viewed with cool objectivity. Is the sergeant major's lifting of the reins from the prone Lieutenant's hands an appropriation justified by his immobility and apparent death, or is it a simple theft? The Lieutenant gets up and orders the other man to stop, but the sergeant major's ride ends in an injury to Lotna that causes violent recriminations between the men and necessitates the horse's shooting. The desire for communal ritual highlighted as a central element in Wajda's work by Tadeusz Lubelski (2003: 45) may unite the two men briefly in commemoration of Lotna's death, but they then separate, as if in recognition of the divisions within and between classes, and within one character in particular, that run through the text, echoing and arguably deriving from the tutor-division within Wajda himself, between the modernist practitioner of shock (and member of the intelligentsia) and the people's tribune, whose work comes closest to kitsch when seeking to speak directly for people and nation, as in parts of *Lotna* and *Man of Iron* (most signally so in the ones involving romance and its ceremonies of communal ritual: Wajda lacks Wyspiański's sense for class conflict at the heart of a wedding, acquiring it only briefly and by association through his filming of Wyspiański's great play of the same name). *Lotna* may be a great film in its images of devastation, particularly its ending, which is haunted by the windmill of Don Quixote, but much of it is little more than an embarrassing daydream. Wajda's self-image may unite his two primary personae in a programme of shock therapy, but the notions of shock and of therapy may seem so contradictory as to arouse calls for the torturer-physician to heal himself, as they have done throughout his career.

Hermann Broch's critique of the procedures of kitsch included that of a rhythm he described as one of mere repetition, a drum rhythm or basic syntax of 'monotonous vocables of reality' (Broch 1955a: 346). If Wajda's film certainly has a simple structure, it is partly due to its derivation from a short story by Żukrowski, which may also precondition its lack of real detail. The structure is, of course, one of repetition: one owner of Lotna dies, another inherits her, he dies, and so on. *Its* drum rhythm is that of a funeral march in autumnal sunlight, a continually interrupted, continually resumed elegy for pre-war Poland.

Just how personal a project *Lotna* was for Wajda can be gauged by the extent of the divergences between Żukrowski's story and his film: divergences that are all the more noteworthy because the original is no novel necessarily requiring editing to fit a film's two-hour format, but a fifty-page novella, the kind of text that can easily be transposed *in toto*. The kinetic outdoor images of the *uhlans* in the field and masses in motion; the arrival at the manor-house, with its undertones of time-travel; the uncanny introduction of Lotna inside it: this entire opening passage is Wajda's addition. Żukrowski begins much later, with the *uhlans* already inside, joshing one another about their girlfriends. He also begins with a first person narrator, and Wajda's jettisoning of this device may enhance the sense of the group's solidarity and Lotna's pre-eminence, but the removal of a point of focus and identification may have contributed to the work's failure. Żukrowski's narrator may enthuse about Lotna, but he does so to veil his thoughts of his girlfriend Maria and avoid group teasing: beginning to say 'there is no other...', he adds 'like Lotna' so his colleagues will think he means the horse. The others are quick to second his praise of her merits though. The differences between Wajda and Żukrowski are ideological as well as aesthetic, and Zbigniew Załuski's contention that Wajda derides the inter-war cavalry can be refuted by considering a couple of the changes. In Żukrowski's text, during the wedding the major is happy to allow his soldiers' horses to trample oats underfoot, despite the farmer's protest at the destruction: 'To waste such a good crop! ... As if there wouldn't be a Poland after you.' And when Wajda takes a trick performed by Żukrowski's captain – riding while holding a coin between his knee and the horse's flank – and gives it to a priest, he echoes the venerable Polish image, central to Mickiewicz's *Pan Tadeusz* (1834), of the fighting padre. The personnel of this church are far from the uselessness ascribed to them by the state and so the work is not entirely mocking of religion (and perhaps, therefore, not entirely coherent?).

WESTERPLATTE

Stanisław Różewicz's *Westerplatte* garnered such fulsome praise upon release that any account of the discourse surrounding it may appear foredoomed to monotony and brevity. Within the discussions of the isolated, dogged resistance to the Nazi invasion offered by the defenders of Westerplatte, however, various controversies simmer subcutaneously. Much praise was lavished upon the work's sobriety and quasi-documentary modesty, some of it pointedly directed against what could be deemed the 'Baroque' self-promotion of other directors, in particular Wajda. Praise of the defenders' courage, meanwhile, could not sidestep the issue controversially raised in the mid-1960s by Zbigniew Załuski: that of the cost of a putative Polish propensity for *bohaterszczyzna* ('empty heroics') rather than heroism. Thus it is interesting to see how much time the Script Assessment Commission devoted to considering whether or not the soldiers should have fought on beyond the twelve hours originally required by their superiors (FN, KOS, A-214 poz. 393). Something close to uproar arose when director Jan Rybkowski, speaking for the absent Różewicz, suggested that 'in a normal army, strictly adhering to orders received, [the major] ought to be punished, for overstepping them' (the stenogram records '*poruszenie*' ['commotion'] in the room at this point). Krzysztof Teodor Toeplitz mentioned a recent questionnaire indicating that over half of the population felt shame in connection with September 1939, and hoped that the film might counteract this feeling. That sentiment would be echoed by one of Różewicz's own interview statements (Różewicz 1967), though it is significant that other commission members – and later reviewers – stress the atypicality of the event. Deeming it typical, of course, might seem to help rehabilitate the pre-war government that presided over Poland's horribly rapid collapse, and so have reduced the claims to legitimacy of the socialist regime that succeeded it. It is significant that the *Historia kina polskiego* describes its reception in terms that indicate reviewers' desire to avoid a problem by deeming it neither typical (thus angering the authorities) nor atypical (thus irritating readers) but as '*osobne*' ('set apart'), as it were *sui generis* (Drozdowski *et al.* 1985: 37). Rybkowski mentions the role contemporary radio greetings to the defenders had played in creating the legend of Westerplatte, and the commission members' ongoing reflections on the causes of the men's continued resistance often express bafflement, wondering whether they were correct to fight on when their doggedness made no difference to Poland's overall military position. Some of the most interesting and controversial remarks concern the moment of surrender. The consistently hard-headed Party representative Wincenty Kraśko is sceptical that the Germans would really have treated the defeated men so respectfully (a newspaper report goes some way towards meeting and correcting this stereotypical scepticism by mentioning the German officers' rapid silencing of the taunts that broke out among their own troops), and is particularly worried by Major Sucharski's final fainting in the moment of surrender, finding it distinctly unheroic, even distasteful. In terms of the central issues of this chapter, the vague distaste may be one for 'feminisation', and the moment itself becomes pregnantly Kleistian: indeed, one could picture Sucharski as almost a Kleistian hero, a patriot who disobeys orders and who faints. In the teeth of his knowledge of the work's deliberately documentary thrust (something Jerzy Putrament saw as of particular propaganda value in winning over blasé youth), Kraśko's disavowal even goes so far as to doubt the historicity of this moment. (Its absence from the completed film is probably significant.) All these concerns are riders of an issue that haunts socialist aesthetics, and, consequently, this book: that of the degree to which a single event can be presented legitimately as a form of generalisation, allegorically typical of a whole from which it is separated and which it can never encompass. Further worries – not reflected in the reviews – concerned the film's possible arousal of a generalised hatred of the Germans (an issue of close concern to Party members mindful of the importance of good relations with the 'good Germany' that now existed, the GDR). Yet again, the question is one of the degree of typicality an event receives from audience reaction and the event's filtering through the symbolising aesthetic procedures. After all, events assume legendary status by condensing behaviour deemed both unusual and worthy of repetition, like the legend itself. If the authorities fund a depiction of this event, thereby endorsing the social legend, are they also underwriting a stubbornness of resistance whose most powerful (taboo) embodiment is the Warsaw Uprising?

Not that the Uprising passed completely unmentioned in reviews. The undesirable association is made when *Życie Warszawy* states that 'the domestic resistance movement, the heroic
deeds of the soldiers fighting abroad in Narvik, Tobruk, Monte Cassino, the Battle of Britain,
Lenino, Kołobrzeg, Budziszyn, and finally the Warsaw Uprising, were demonstrations of the
same moral attitude, the selfsame will to struggle for independence' (Grzelecki 1967). A small
subversion, the sentence lists multiple actions by soldiers fighting in the West before coming
– rather late – to Lenino and the Polish People's Army, while the final mention of the Warsaw
Uprising is definitely 'last but not least'. Assuming that the censor grasped its implications, it
may be speculated that it was permitted on the basis of the paper's need to address its local,
Warsaw constituency, and of its limitation to it. The many veterans' meetings held around
the film may not simply have reflected the force of the legend but have sought to forestall a
nationwide noting of the symmetry between the Westerplatte resistance at the war's beginning
and the Warsaw one near its end by stressing the uniqueness of the earlier event. It is piquant
to note Polish correspondents' reports of foreign – particularly Soviet – reaction to the film:
where Westerners could not comprehend why the Poles fought on, Russian viewers failed to
grasp why they did not fight to the death. Seen in the terms of this opposition, the film's foreign
reception ironically and even poignantly replays the scenario of Poland's isolation in 1939.

The harrowing nature of the experience of the 182 Westerplatte defenders is measured by
the contrast between two troop-reviews, one at the film's beginning, the other near its end. The
intervening events are a sobering induction into the truth of Poland's situation. At the beginning, Colonel Sobociński tells the crisply uniformed men that in the event of an attack they
will not be left alone. At the end, their commander Major Sucharski informs them that he can
no longer risk their lives, and praises their honourable defence. The men are battered and one
– a lieutenant – feels betrayed by the surrender. They have had no support: no paratroopers,
none of the English whose arrival they expected any moment. The film interprets Sucharski's
surrender as courageous, not just the pragmatic good sense many reviewers felt had spoken
through him, though there is indeed little cause to continue fighting when one's ammunition is
all-but-spent and the conditions for one's wounded are appalling. The counter-argument reiterated throughout by Captain Dąbrowski – that the fight should continue as an example to the
rest of Poland – no longer carries such weight. 'Your blood will be useful to Poland', Sucharski
tells the men: it needs preservation, not shedding. But this is no mere victory of 'Positivism'
over reckless 'Romanticism', but is itself defined as bravery, as Sucharski had ended one conversation with Dąbrowski by stating, 'I don't have the courage to say "enough"'. Taking the
decision in his own name, without the consultations he has held with other officers throughout
the siege, Sucharski has the courage to assume responsibility. In the end, 'was it worth it to fight
so long?' is asked by the German commander who accepts Sucharski's surrender (his shaking
of his hand a moment whose suggestion of the conclusion of a game prosecuted according to
the rules of fair play had worried at least one member of the Script Assessment Commission).
The question hangs in the air, unanswered, but with the accompanying implication that only
a foreigner or outsider, one who has not shared the men's experience, could pose it. Since we
have shared their experience, we may find the question unnecessary – and not just because the
Poles were more than holding their own against the invaders before their ammunition began
to run out. The German's question may be as foreign to the film as the period footage of the
Schleswig-Holstein battleship and the Stuka divebombers inserted into it. For although contemporary viewers praised these inserts as seamless, the inevitable slight dislocation imparts a

sense of foreignness that intensifies their menace: the first shots of the ship and the Stukas in particular are sublime and terrifying, suggesting an invasion from outer space, by something as foreign to the human order, or to Różewicz's 1967 film – which seems to buckle under them, reality's ground shifting beneath it – as it had been to the Westerplatte of 1939.

WAJDA AND BEYOND: HAS, MUNK, RÓŻEWICZ

For the directors of the Polish School, heroism is ironised by its mortgaging to the visual image, the requirement that the hero look the part, that theme of Andrzej Munk's *Zezowate szczęście* (*Bad Luck*, 1959). The heroes of *Lotna* look the part to an absurdly callow extent. The irony surrounding the hero's appearance issues in a doubling whose richest focus may well be found in the work of Zbigniew Cybulski. In Wojciech Has's *How to Be Loved*, for instance, he plays Wiktor, the ironically-named generally-believed assassin of a German occupier, whom the Gestapo hunt and a woman, Felicja, conceals. Her love for him causes her to sleep with German soldiers to buy their silence while he lies concealed in the next room: the hero is compelled unheroically to tolerate abuse of the female he traditionally exists to defend. Felicja's is the true, hidden heroism, and Has pointedly contrasts it with the image of heroism Wiktor later purveys. As a girl sings 'The Poppies of Monte Cassino' (the song that accompanied the commemoration of dead fellow partisans in *Ashes and Diamonds*) Felicja enters the bar as he boastfully retails wartime exploits to a quietly mocking, incredulous young audience. Neither has found the love they sought in different ways. In *Ashes and Diamonds*, on which Has's film comments, Cybulski had been called Maciek and doubled by a young resistance fighter called Marek, who appears in a defiant cameo. Marek's single-minded heroism renders him less interesting, however, than the tragic hero Maciek, torn between budding love and the code of honour that enforces assassination of a Communist leader. A decade after *Ashes and Diamonds* Wajda would resurrect Cybulski and his heroism under the sign of absence, for *Everything for Sale* was precipitated by the death of the actor, which haunts it. In this film-about-a-film, a director seeks a substitute for the dead actor (the unnamed Cybulski) and thinks he has found one in Daniel Olbrychski. But Olbrychski refuses to assume Cybulski's mantle, becoming himself heroic in his refusal; as if in dialogue with *How to be Loved*, Daniel verifies the legends surrounding his predecessor: the story of a wartime excursion for Berlin to find better roses proves true. He then accuses the director, Wajda's own stand-in, of opposing the dead actor. If Cybulski represents both fantasist and hero, self-mythologiser and living legend, *How to Be Loved* insists on the fantasy while the *de mortuis nil nisi bonum* of *Everything for Sale* underwrites the legend. Apparently defunct heroism persists, transformed, in Olbrychski's fiery-eyed integrity: no wonder he would shortly play the lead in Jerzy Hoffman's film of Sienkiewicz's patriotic *Potop* (*The Deluge*, 1974). In one episode of *Eroica*, by Wajda's great counterpart Andrzej Munk, POWs' morale is upheld by the legend of the man who escaped. We then see him concealed by men who feed him and the sustaining legend. Munk's irony concerns heroism less than it does the need for heroic images: after all, the man who consents to this living death is extraordinary, his self-sacrifice perhaps the greatest – because unobtrusive – heroism. In a dialectic of the visible and the invisible, these films inculcate distrust of their own medium, the image: the hero always has a double, is always as dead as alive, giving blood transfusions to an image that may be either unofficial, oral legend (*Eroica*) or official visual icon (the statues and posters of shock-worker Birkut in Wajda's *Man of Marble*).

If a dialectic of heroism and anti-heroism pervades the Polish School, however, it is in part also because the directors themselves know their works to be both betrayals of and homages to the past. The betrayal lies in the impossibility of naming the Home Army, which took its orders from the Polish wartime Government-in-exile in London and was the majority resistance organisation within Poland itself, as the main source of heroic action. Ideological considerations demanded the upgrading of the Soviet-sponsored People's Army (the *Armia Ludowa* or AL). Nevertheless, denigration of the Home Army was not simply ideologically motivated. It also voiced visceral disillusionment with the pre-war Polish régime, whose bluffs of power had been called by the National Socialists, and an Oedipal struggle with the father. Wajda's *Lotna* is his weakest war film because it mystifies army defeats into and through the mythical curse of the enchanted horse. The metaphors of Polish School films do not just smuggle truth, as Wajda was to argue, but also garble it, turning history into a set of Chinese whispers ironically less accurate than that transmitted by actual oral history. The result is a persistence of traumatised consciousness whose most remarkable product is Wojciech Has's *Ciphers*.

Ciphers tells the story of the return to Poland from Britain of Tadeusz, who fought in the war and is seeking to discover the fate of his youngest son, Jędrek, rumoured killed in 1944 but also supposedly sighted later in Italy. Met at Cracow station by his older son, Maciek, Tadeusz gathers conflicting reports from a variety of sources, each one directing him to a further stage and delaying the possible revelation of truth. Upon reaching the woodsman who may know details of Jędrek's putative forest execution, for instance, he hears of the boy's transfer from the woods to a monastery. The trail goes cold at the monastery, while just before his departure for Britain someone phones him at his hotel. The line goes dead however. Since he subsequently receives a call from his former wife Zofia, who has gone into hospital with psychological problems, perhaps it was she who rang? As the camera lingers on his room's phone after his departure, though, there is a suggestion that someone else may yet ring.

On arriving from abroad, Tadeusz is reproached by Maciek with a failure to comprehend war's effect upon Poland. This war was not like the classical warfare in which Tadeusz participated but, Maciek asserts, 'entered the heart of life itself'. Maciek's station meeting with Tadeusz in a sense recapitulates that between Szczuka and that other Maciek in *Ashes and Diamonds*, something underlined by the identity of names, the casting of Cybulski in both roles, and the way he greets his father as if a stranger, and just as Maciek encounters Szczuka, in the lighting of a cigarette. Maciek's sense of inferiority and abandonment find expression in compensatory statements of bitter, superior knowledge. This casts Tadeusz as in a sense a child, and the Jędrek who haunts his dreamlike visions is in part his double, an image of what he might have experienced had he remained. The anachronism and even fantastic nature of his heroism is suggested by the World War One helmet he wears in these visions, as if he was not in World War Two at all, and both his quest for truth and impotent inability to locate it are childlike. (The helmet may be seen as anticipating that of the central narrator-son figure in Has's later *Sanatorium pod klepsydrą* [*The Hour-Glass Sanatorium*, 1973].) His visions correspond to the dreamlike unreadability of the reality through which he wanders. It seems that Jędrek, unhinged by the war, stalked Resistance-fighter Marian – who was staying with, and the lover of, Tadeusz's wife – threatened to reveal the arms cache held in their apartment and accidentally caused Marian's death. He himself then seems to have been executed in reprisal by the underground. If all this is supposition, what is clear is the compromising of the image of the hero. Tadeusz's departure to fight for Poland is experienced not as heroism but as paternal abandonment, and those who remained – the helpless children – lost their dignity. Unsurprisingly, therefore, the compromising of Tadeusz is matched by one of the domestic Polish resistance, the *nasi* ('our boys'), who are suspected of killing Jędrek. Tadeusz himself, meanwhile, decries the unknown, untraceable underground leader who is supposed to have ordered that killing, whose actions belied the heroic pseudonym he assumed. Kijowski's script and Has's film reinforce official Party ideology by suggesting that the underground – read Home Army – was murky and heroic both at home and abroad, but at the same time they hold back from that ideology by eschewing mention of the Party-approved, 'heroic' underground, the AL. Similarly ambiguous is the attitude to the Holocaust, as the assimilation of Jędrek in Tadeusz's mind to the famous photograph of the Jewish child arrested, with hands upheld, overlooks the specific horror of the fate that awaited Jewish children. (Anne Guérin-Castell's defence of the moment at which Tadeusz views this image in a photo album argues that its juxtaposition with a shot of Polish trench-diggers interrogates the Polish onlookers of the Holocaust in the manner of Claude Lanzmann's *Shoah* [1985] [Guérin-Castell 2000: 46–7; 52 n.19]; though it may be countered that the association with Lanzmann is anachronistic and that – more importantly – Has's intentions are more enigmatic.) Kijowski and Has suggest that a miasma of unknowing still envelops Poland, ironising all the claims to know and vocabulary of knowledge that pervade the film. The madness that befell Zofia during the war, the doctor maintains, was a reflex of the madness of reality itself. Since the disturbance persists, the implication is that reality itself still remains troubled also. Wartime trauma and political censorship overdetermine the impossibility of grasping the truth afflicting both characters and artists. The distance that might give access to truth actually frustrates it by clouding its object. Zofia declares herself uncertain whether someone looking after Jędrek said '*nic, nic*' ('nothing') or '*nie chce*' ('he doesn't want to'); similarly, Maciek claims to have seen Jędrek taken in a cart to the forest, but adds that he did not recognise him at the time, realising only afterwards who it must have been. A secondhand bookseller tells Tadeusz that Zofia's hope is due to those words 'which she didn't quite hear and whose meaning reached her only later'. His words have a dreamlike illogicality, as in fact hope is rooted in the way the word's indeterminacy *prevents* a crystallisation of meaning. That absence of a probably bitter truth leaves hope alive, as Jędrek may possibly be. Tadeusz clutches at the slim hope embodied in the uncertainty of those moments, even though others have concluded that Jędrek is dead. If the war is a labyrinth in which Poles are still trapped, Tadeusz's apparent ability to depart it breeds envy and resentment. The film as a whole can be taken as diagnosing the sickness of which it is itself a symptom: the impossibility, before 1989, of telling the full truth about the war. The half-truths of metaphor may be better than nothing, but they are not the unambiguous statements of truth Wajda claimed to have made in *Ashes and Diamonds*, but later implicitly admitted to be half-truths when he revisited this area in his post-1989 *The Horse-Hair Ring*, replacing the Home Army assassin of Communist fantasy with the Home Army victims of reality. Has's work, remarkably, knows itself to be a half-truth, a trauma-laden cipher whose meaning cannot be read off in easy, allegorical fashion. The prominence it accords its dream-sequences underlines the presence of un-analysed, unresolved material at the heart of Polish reality. They are themselves a form of the indeterminate words and images that nourish hope. *Ciphers* knows itself to inhabit a labyrinth still, using allusions to *Ashes and Diamonds* (in particular, Cybulski and the white horses that dot the visionary interpolations) to suggest that Wajda's work is in no better a state. If Maciek is still living below himself, as he claims, even 22 years after the war, so is everyone else in Poland – its artists not excluded. Has's work is no last gasp of the Polish School but a postmortem on its inability to name and dispel trauma.

Eroica and *Ciphers* represent only two of the alternatives to the position of Wajda. The most unjustly neglected may well be that of Stanisław Różewicz, whose work may bypass questions of heroism entirely, concentrating instead simply upon victims. (It is well worth comparing with *Ciphers*, which is also preoccupied with the fate of the child.) Różewicz's position, one of consistent understatement, accords with his ability to make one of the most remarkable, haunting films of the Polish School period, *Birth Certificate*, the only Polish war film to focus entirely upon the perspective of children. Children are, of course, by definition unable to fight back, and Różewicz's muted style evokes their depressed awareness of this fact. *Birth Certificate* comprises three novellas that move through different stages of the war, closer and closer to the heart of darkness that is the experience of the Jews. Most relevant in this context is the first, from which they are absent, which unfolds in the midst of the chaos of the Polish defeat of September 1939, and is called 'Na drodze' ('On the Road').

If, as Bolesław Michałek has argued, the specificity of the Polish School lay in combining neo-realism and literature (Michałek 1981: 122–5), the two figure particularly eloquently in Różewicz's film, which privileges children in the neo-realist manner and was co-scripted by the director's brother, the poet Tadeusz Różewicz. And just as De Sica's *Bicycle Thieves* had associated male disempowerment with the premature elevation and cruelly forced growth of the child Bruno, who walked beside the adult Antonio as the reflection of his inner distress, so the first section of *Birth Certificate* places Polish adult and child on a single plane. The short-trousered, dark Jacek even resembles Bruno. Adult and child are in fact even closer than Antonio and Bruno, as the latter no longer has to hurry to keep up with his self-absorbed, agonised father, and the camera no longer has to move up and down to register both man and child close up. Initially, however, we see Jacek alone on an empty road. We will later learn that he is travelling East, away from Warsaw, in search of his mother and brother, from whom he has been separated. When a German motorcycle and sidecar approach, the surrounding desolation drives home the evaporation of the adult world that ought to have shielded the child from the invader. Before and after this encounter, Jacek is filmed face-on, from his eye-level; during it, however, telling point-of-view shots look up at the German and down at Jacek, mapping the disparity in height between adult and child onto the inequality of invading soldier and civilian. The fact that the German can look down on Jacek – that the latter poses no threat – is emphasised by the former's gift of a bar of chocolate. The equation linking height and invader-status is then reinforced by Jacek's placement on the same level as the adult Pole (Józef) by his self-concealment at the back of the cart the adult is driving. The adult who uncovers the boy does not look down on him but encounters him at his eye-level, something that both lends dignity to the child and reinforces the adult's helplessness. Each addresses the other in first-name terms that suggest both comradeship and similarity. Józef does his best to shield Jacek from the appalling scenes they encounter, gently pulling him away from a peasant girl who has gone mad and burying his head in his chest to blot out the sight of a German execution of a group of peasants, but Jacek is already well-acquainted with the disasters of war. Before meeting Józef he has seen a train of adults move past, depressed and taciturn, on carts, the only sound to come from them being the shriek of a bandaged soldier, which takes him aback. While he and Józef pass through a depopulated small town, he encounters an adult taping his windows against bomb-blasts, and comments, 'I taped them too and they all flew out'. And in the end Jacek is alone again. As they travel together, Jacek asks Józef how many Germans he has killed; 'who can count them?' is the evasive reply. He asks Józef which way they ought to go, and his answer, 'I don't know', could have furnished the end of this short film. It does not end here, though, but in the forest. Shortly after they halt there Jacek sees Józef burning the military secrets he is carrying. What are they? 'Mobilisation orders. Without them you can't set off to war.' The pointed shot of their burning that follows underlines the impossibility of an effective counter-attack. The resistance Józef offers is brave but completely quixotic. Seeing some German vehicles trundle through the woods, and doubtless recalling both the sight of the peasants' execution and his own earlier slightly embarrassed response to Jacek's enquiry about his military exploits, he fires a rifle at the convoy. A tank immediately veers from the road and towards him. He tells Jacek to run, and the boy does. The final shot – an overhead one of Jacek amid the trees – reconjugates the film's preoccupation with high/low relations, reinstating him as small and vulnerable. It is both poignant and telling that even the peasant Józef has done as his superiors did and pursued a beautiful, futile resistance that once again leaves the child alone. That shared helplessness of adult and child before the new German ruthlessness will then be the theme of the work's second section, 'List z obozu' ('A Letter from the Camp'), as a boy looking after his younger siblings while his mother is away, procuring food, and his father is in a POW camp learns that the Geneva conventions for prisoners' treatment will no longer be observed.

PEOPLE ON THE WARTIME TRAIN

Trains bulk large in a Polish post-war cinema reflective of a system that frustrated individualist dreams of private transport, and are of course of particular relevance to the experience of war and occupation. They appear at the outset of Wajda's work, associated with daring and disaster: boys leap onto a goods train at the start of *A Generation*, seeking to filch coal from a Nazi transport; one of them is shot as he crouches on the huge chunks of coal. The Wajda film in which the train is most prominent also links it to disaster, as *Everything for Sale* obsessively re-enacts Zbigniew Cybulski's death beneath a train's wheels. If Wajda does not take one inside trains, it is because his cinematic kinesis is that of living in tumultuous motion – the running human, the horse – and the rhythm of the machine is alien. It is also because his films trace the rise and truncation of the life-force of individuals. In train films, by way of contrast, ordeals are as collective, the individual's movement constrained. The passenger sits tensely awaiting inspection, squirming under the real or imagined scrutiny of fellow passengers, one of whom may be a blackmailer (the Jewish experience in the last section of Różewicz's *Birth Certificate*). All passengers are likely to be ordered out at the same time. And, in the end, many of them will be herded together, helpless, in another train: the freight train drawing inhumanly packed cattle-cars to a labour or concentration camp. The individual's constraint, and the likelihood of fellow travellers suffering summary reprisals for any act of heroic defiance, raises questions of collective responsibility, questioning deeply just what heroism may be. Such is the case in two vastly contrasting films of the 1960s, each of which offers a different perspective from Wajda's: Kazimierz Kutz's *Ludzie z pociągu* (*The People from the Train*, 1961) and Jerzy Skolimowski's *Hands Up!*

Kutz's film is in many respects a conventional one, perhaps accurately damned with faint praise in its widespread description as realistic, sober and mature. The early 1960s governmental preoccupation with the possible forgetting of past values by a younger generation raised in relative comfort is reflected in the story station-master Kaliński recounts to a young female assistant bored with the humdrum of their provincial station of Kurjanty. A modest man, Kaliński only tells it because the throwing of a bouquet from a passing train requires an explanation. Refusing to be sidetracked, the film does not even toy with the notion that it may come from an admirer of the pretty new assistant but links it to an event from 1943, when the last two carriages of a train were discovered to be defective and its passengers unloaded to await transfer. Kaliński suggests to the German station policeman that the passengers be shipped on by the next goods train. When the German, a stickler for order, retorts that goods trains are not for people, Kaliński (who knows otherwise) mutters 'not always'. As the passengers wait, various small dramas play out between them. The most significant involve Piotr, a young Resistance member annoyed to find his girlfriend tagging along, and a boy carrying a puppy in a basket who befriends a young Jewish girl travelling under the name 'Marylka'. Piotr and his girlfriend bicker about love and commitment as the boy walks 'Marylka' outside the station, where she shows him the constricted movements that are all she has been able to learn of dance when hidden behind the wardrobe. A blackmailer compels the war widow who is caring for 'Marylka' to buy his silence with her two wedding rings – her own, and that of her dead husband. Meanwhile, other passengers play cards, chat, or demand when the next train will come. Some of them also drink, making the mistake of drawing in the German policeman to secure his inattention to their smuggling. The policeman, however, takes offence at a harmonica tune played ostentatiously before him and accuses everyone of being a partisan. He phones a drunken report to H.Q., though his inebriation precludes him identifying the station. Because the goods train is on its way, the film hangs in suspense over whether it will precede the alerted Germans. Kaliński frantically searches for a German-speaker to allay the suspicions of the H.Q., but cannot find the male necessary to impersonate the policeman.

The Germans arrive first, of course. On finding a machine gun in the waiting room, they demand to know its owner, threatening to punish silence by killing every fifth passenger. 'Marylka' is one of those counted to come forward, but the widow steps forward instead. Piotr does nothing when his girlfriend joins her. Marylka's friend steps forward and declares it is his. All the time the puffing of the waiting goods train measures each unforgiving second, charging it with suspense. As German soldiers brutally pummel the small, fresh-faced boy, Kutz makes his most daring move, lifting the film above conventionality: the suspense and earnestness receive a rude admixture of farce, as Kaliński pulls the drunken policeman towards the station, with grotesque music on the soundtrack. The juxtaposition of high tension and farce is near-Shakespearean, recalling the aspect of Kutz's aesthetic expressed in the title of one study of his work: 'Things look different from below.' The perspective is not that of Wajda – *The People from the Train* being in fact the third in Kutz's anti-Wajda war trilogy – but approximates that of Czech cinema; of Jiří Menzel's *Ostře sledované vlaky* (*Closely Observed Trains*, 1966). The crestfallen policeman reclaims his lost machine-gun, receives a dressing down, and the passengers are reprieved. There is heroism, says Kutz, but it is not where you would expect it. It is not in Piotr, whose girlfriend stands frostily beside him at the film's end, but in the boy lying bruised on a bench, Marylka smiling at him in a big, rewarding close-up. He explains that he stepped forward because he did not belong to any organisation, and so could not have betrayed anyone (he leaves 'if tortured' unspoken). Kaliński's story, told from his modest point of view, identifies the boy as the hero. Only the continued anonymity of the thrower of the bouquet indicates that someone deemed him heroic also. Collective responsibility is identified with the totalitarian German perspective, which sees all Poles as alike. If the policeman and the commander say as much, the film undermines them by depicting a sheer, pullulating human variety that is not just Polish but obtains among Germans too: with his photographs of wife and family and his lost limb, the policeman is very human. Collective responsibility banishes justice; no wonder that the departing soldiers shoot the most innocent of victims, the poor mongrel the boy had tended. The lesson is not just that heroism sprouts in the unlikeliest places (the closing shot from behind, of Kaliński resolutely performing his duty, underlines this) but also that the unlikeliest places are fascinating. The waiting room and its multiple mini-dramas fascinate Kutz just as much as the larger matter of life and death interwoven with them.

Death and symbolic death hang in the air from the very outset of Skolimowski's *Hands Up!* A figure whose face is invisible below bandages proclaims that he has to determine who lives and dies in his vicinity: the person fifteen kilometres away to one side, or the one twenty away on the other. This may be a performance before an audience pumping the air with their arms, but the urgently pulsing jazz and the symbolic import and menace of the bandages impart a nervous, thrusting seriousness, and when the man waves the microphone stand to shatter two of the many lightbulbs hanging down on long flexes, it is like an anticipation of an execution; as if his paralysis over which of two persons to help causes the death of both. The hands raised from the dance-floor seem almost to volunteer for the death this figure says people want at times. When we think about it, with the retrospective understanding that is the only one possible in this stunning film, we may realise that the suicide this person attempted a decade ago is still lurking within him: he too may be a man who wants to die. When his performance concludes and he asks a girl if she recognises him and remembers saving his life, we do not yet know in what circumstances, or that he had attempted to kill himself, but it becomes clear that the death that hangs in the air, like those lightbulbs, is more than symbolic. The death is not just his but the wartime deaths that haunt modern Poland so deeply that their ghosts penetrate even the partying reunion of rich, careerist doctors, perhaps through the spectre at the feast who is their mummified, outcast ex-colleague, throwing off his bandages. As the film proceeds, its obsession with this haunting will generate a metaphorical multiple exposure of the title, which itself is molested by all its other meanings. The hands are raised in the ritualised motions of a dance; white-gloved hands are thrust towards us (those of a doctor, but also a performer); they volunteer for death; they rise in confession of various careerist sins; they hold up the car keys that are the fruit of that careerism; and they are raised as if about to point at someone, war-poster style, in the image of the Stalin whose botched creation with four eyes has been the central comic-tragedy of the main characters' lives.

Hands Up! unfolds during a class reunion of medical students, just over a decade after their graduation. During the celebrations five close friends peel off and bribe a railway guard to grant them entry to a nearby, stationary boxcar, where they continue to party on alcohol and what they think is speed. A statement one makes upon entry sets the theme: 'They say our generation is incapable of heroism.' Subsequent events endorse the accusation. Where wartime heroes once used such pseudonyms as Eagle and Tiger, they bear the names of their cars: (Opel) Rekord, Wartburg, Alfa Romeo (the couple that share this car can then be split wittily between [Mrs] Alfa and [Mr] Romeo). The possibility of maintaining such heroic wartime identities is undermined completely when one scratches just such a name on the boxcar wall: 'Jaguar', however, is now the name of a car. The social failure of the fifth group member

– underlined by his possession of a clapped-out Zastava – followed his expulsion from the academy after he was blamed for the group's botched assembly of a portrait of Stalin as their ZMP (Związek Mlodzieży Polskiej – Union of Polish Youth) project. All the poster's elements were duplicated to provide replacements in case of damage, and consequently Stalin received two pairs of eyes. The raising of his image, wind blowing, is a monstrous epiphany from which Wartburg flees in consternation, running towards the camera, the telephoto lens flattening him into the background to emphasise an inability to escape it that reflects both its infernal magic and his own corpulence. (Wartburg's playing by Bogumił Kobiela renders this moment also a parody of the same actor's grotesquely alarmed run towards the camera after the failed assassination that inaugurates *Ashes and Diamonds*, establishing a jokey rhyme between these two 'anti-socialist' acts.) This scene is one of a series of olive-tinted flashbacks to the 1950s. They culminate in Zastava's suicide attempt, from which his then girlfriend, Alfa, contemptuously rescues him. The official inquest is particularly telling, as all five try to shuffle off the blame, though even Rekord's claim to have dozed off is no exoneration: the enemy is so watchful, the voices of the unseen committee aver, that lack of vigilance is reprehensible. Alfa proposes collective responsibility, but the blame alights on Zastava.

Collective responsibility on the one hand, scapegoating on the other: these become the reinforcing mutual poles of a culture of stigmatisation and blame. Being herded together has different consequences in different eras, however. The penalty exacted by 1950s totalitarianism – relegation to the provinces and unremunerating toil as a vet – pales beside the wartime one also evoked by the work. The characters imagine their packing together in a cattle truck bound for a concentration camp; but the plaster with which they have mummified the prone Wartburg is very different from that stuffed in the mouth of wartime execution victims of the Nazis. In the film's most awesome and vertiginous moment, the camera pulls back to expand the cattle car and its few candles into a vast space whose multitudinous candles burn as pinpricks in the darkness like those of a Polish cemetery on All Souls' Day. The vision of naked bodies intertwined on the ground measures the distance between the railway smoke that penetrates the boxcar and the Zyklon gas it recalls, all the more so as the scene is shot in solemn slow motion and in negative, to mournful organ music. These visionary metaphors are the realities traduced by the games. Such images of past trauma, like the olive-toned flashbacks, are not tied to the consciousness of any one character, a sign that not one is able to confront them. The malign dialectic of collective responsibility and scapegoating in the early 1950s becomes collective irresponsibility in the 1960s. It is thus fitting that later (in 1991) Skolimowski would film a version of Witold Gombrowicz's 1937 novel *Ferdydurke*: like Gombrowicz, he excoriates an infantilised nation. Unlike him, however, he defines that infantility as memory's failure to grasp the cataclysmically real wartime suffering that still lay in the future when Gombrowicz wrote. Thus, in the end Skolimowski resembles Gombrowicz less than he does the great *fin-de-siècle* dramatist Stanisław Wyspiański. The film's haunting by the compromises of the past, by memories of war and by its own protagonists' impotence, renders it deeply akin to Wyspiański's *The Wedding*, which it recalls in many ways: in the obsession with 'deeds' voiced by one character; in another's statement that this speaker has forgotten everything, recalling a famous quotation from *The Wedding*, '*Myśmy wszystko zapomnieli*' ('We have forgotten everything'); in the allusions to past carnage; in the use of the alcohol as a truth-drug releasing inhibitions and disavowed phantoms; and in the final helplessness of its characters as they emerge into dawn's bleak light. Like Wyspiański, Skolimowski challenges us to catch the shrapnel of information which erupts all round us, showering us in the metaphors that seem to have wounded the man with the bandaged head: he challenges us to understand why he should have tried to kill himself, and the reasons for his generation's thinly veiled awareness of the hollowness of its existence.

AFTER THE BATTLE

As war draws to a close, heroism can come to seem an ideology. As the end approaches, soldiers will think more intensely of loved ones they may soon see again, and strengthen their efforts to survive, using methods that may not only seem unheroic but involve desertion. With the adversary virtually defeated, the sense of parity – or even of being an underdog – will evaporate, and may extinguish the sense that one's struggle is heroic. Seen at close quarters, the enemy is no longer an overwhelming, dehumanised shadow, nor do any of the now often-bedraggled individuals one encounters quite fit the stereotype. Moreover, one's new-found superiority may spur one to pursue a revenge whose grim gathering of spoils may involve the rape and humiliation of female members of the enemy nation. Elements of all these last-day scenarios float through the three important films to be considered in this section: Wajda's *Landscape After a Battle*, Witold Lesiewicz's *Kwiecień* (*April*, 1961) and Aleksander Ford's *The First Day of Freedom*.

Of all post-war Polish writers, the most aggressively (and hence in a sense paradoxically) anti-heroic is Tadeusz Borowski (Miron Białoszewski, author of *Pamiętnik z Powstania Warszawskiego* [*Memoirs of the Warsaw Uprising*, 1970], represents a more whimsical, picaresquely *lumpen* anti-heroism). Interviewed during the making of *Landscape After a Battle*, whose organising structure derives from its primary source, Borowski's short story 'The Battle of Grunwald', Wajda mentioned the possibility of a different structure, that of a man searching desperately for a private place to commit suicide:

> A few days ago, I thought I knew how to narrate the whole matter, that I had found the dramaturgical spit on which to turn the story. In the very first scene we see a young man looking for a secluded spot behind the barbed wire in these SS barracks. But there are people everywhere. He shuts himself in the toilet, and straight away someone bangs on the door; he hides in the attic, and there is somebody there; and so on. In the end he finds a spot where no one can see him and places a noose round his neck – and then somebody disturbs him. The film would be the bitter story of a man who tries to commit suicide but does not succeed. So from the very outset we would be waiting for his death…

Wajda subsequently rejected this idea, however:

> I quickly sobered up. After all, this would be painting black on black. As if it were not enough that the entire background has this character, on top of that the hero would be defined straight off as a suicide. Apart from all other considerations – it was a purely formal idea. But at first it was an illumination for me. But I managed to construct – in theory – the following argument: I cannot do a suicide, for I don't have all the motives. Moreover, the final suicide does not ricochet back to the film's beginning and explain

it. But if one were to suppose that the hero keeps on trying to take his own life, one would not have to motivate it in detail. For the motive could stem from the fact that at the outset he began behind one barbed wire fence, and now he's behind another. Time has passed, something has happened, but the freedom he has received is an illusion, something completely different from what he expected. And that is why he wants to kill himself. This argument is correct and logical, except that in this context it's completely false. (Wertenstein 2000: 68)

Surprisingly, Wajda omits one of the most cogent and obvious reasons for raising the question of suicide in this context: the suicide of Borowski himself in 1951. Such an identification of the writer with his fictional persona of 'Tadeusz' would, of course, have been deeply problematic, and not just because the behaviour of this cynical survivor-figure diverges dramatically from that of Borowski himself within the camps, but it remains true that the post-camp lives of the best writers to survive them raises the question of the possibility of healing the damage inflicted upon them. The suicides of Borowski, Paul Celan or Primo Levi cannot be attributed simply to an identification (however momentary or belated) with the will of the (Nazi) aggressor they once seemed to have escaped, but their wounding may have been decisive, and the question is as unavoidable as it is unanswerable. It is cognate with that of the degree to which, on the scale of collective rather than individual behaviours, the post-war fashionability of existentialism, with its possibly dialectically interrelated themes of suicide and agency, corresponds to a crisis of self-worth in individuals humiliated by Occupation and unable to reconcile their self-images with the compromises they had made. If, in terms of cultural stereotypes, they had indeed been 'feminised', the intensity of Borowski's identification with the position of Nina in his 'Battle of Grunwald' achieves a significance enhanced still further by her Jewishness (after all, the frequency with which the wartime helplessness of the Jews has caused their image to be aligned with that of both the female and the child has been noted by Judith Doneson [1978: 11–13; 18]).

Earlier in his interview, Wajda speaks of including flashbacks to concentration camp life within the film. In the end, all we see of the camps is the opening sequence, based on Borowski's terrifying three-page sketch 'Silence', whose title may well have given Wajda the idea of switching off the natural sound and accompanying the action with Vivaldi's *Four Seasons* in a manner initially expressive of the inmates' elation upon release, but then disturbingly incongruous as they vengefully trample an ex-kapo into the mud. It is as if the fantasy of destroying the entire camp, expressed metaphorically in the shattering of the windows whose reflections represent it, necessarily involved one of its sound-world also. Nevertheless, the concentration camp proves inescapable, reborn as the displaced persons camp presided over by the American military. Wajda's eschewal of flashbacks is of a piece with his rejection of the quest for suicide as a leitmotif, as the former could have served to motivate and explain the latter. His unwillingness to 'paint black on black' itself raises several issues. In the context of this book, the most important concern the nature of the relationship between literature and film and the degree of compatability between his own worldview and that of Borowski.

Firstly, the question of literature-film relations. Reviewing Wajda's film, Krzysztof Teodor Toeplitz contrasted the Polish films about the camps made immediately after the war with later ones. Whereas the former showed individuals of pure character, the latter present torn, disturbed, even animalistic ones (Toeplitz 1974: 281–2). The disparity demonstrates both the difficulty of immediate assimilation of the full extent of the camps' defacement of the human image, and, equally importantly, the need for film to 'catch up' with literature. Borowski, for instance, published his stories directly after the war's end. This need to 'catch up' is indicative not of any inherent 'inferiority' in film, but rather marks the stages of a process whereby what had once been accessible to the consciousness of a single individual, working in a financially undemanding medium, becomes sufficiently widespread to be able to manifest itself in an art-form whose financial demands require wider appeal. It is also a question of the move from a less strictly censored medium to a more rigorously managed one, the Polish authorities having taken to heart Lenin's assertion of the singular importance of film. Indeed, some of the issues touched on in Borowski's story would never penetrate the cinema of People's Poland: 'Katyń', named early on in his text, would remain a blank spot on its ideological maps, even though it was of particular significance to Wajda himself, whose father was murdered there, and was a theme of which he once – during the first Script Assessment Meeting to discuss the first screenplay for *Man of Marble* – suggested he had no fear (FN, KOS, A-214 poz. 338). Thus although Wajda's decision to adapt Borowski implies that such a moment may have arrived, the completed film demonstrates the prematurity of the attempt. One can see why he may have believed in the possibility of an intersection between his own worldview and that of this particular Borowski text: after all, Tadeusz defines himself as a Polish artist, and decides to return to Poland, unlike Nina, who wishes to go west. Their dialogue about the possibility of departure has an electrifying subtext – like that of Zbigniew Herbert's allegorical poem about returning to Caesar's court – as it externalises thoughts that may well have plagued Wajda himself. On the other hand though, Wajda takes Tadeusz's declared Polishness as an excuse to imbue him with an obsession with German wrongdoing that privileges collective identity in a manner that regresses from the position of his Polish School films, towards the sort of 'pseudo-Polish School' work represented by Aleksander Ford's *First Day of Freedom* (Drozdowski *et al.* 1985: 60–1): towards another form of the chauvinism that so appalled Borowski's Tadeusz. Wajda's Tadeusz speaks bitterly of the solid German work invested in the camp tattoo on his arm, of the hair of his female SS interrogator and of the oak as a German tree. He describes Germans seen in the woods as rats (the irony of this echo of the Nazi discourse about the Jews is not activated) and writes a poem about killing a German. Where Wajda's mockery of the older generation's God-bothering jingoism lambastes its falsity, but does not attack patriotism per se, Borowski does. This is, of course, one reason why Borowski became the unambiguous Marxist Wajda could never be. Nina's dream of shedding both Jewishness and Polishness is Borowski's own, reflecting his belief that the patriotic prioritisation of ethnic identity issues automatically in the grotesque, robotic militarism of the individual called 'Batalion' (as if he is no longer an individual), whose appearances frame the story. For Toeplitz, Borowski's is a 'dream of a world of disinterested, broad humanism, and certainly of a world without armies, perhaps one without states and fatherlands' (Toeplitz 1974: 279): in other words, a utopia. Toeplitz overlooks Borowski's acrid awareness of its utopian status, however; the destruction of Nina, the dream's carrier, allegorises that of the dream itself. Borowski mocks the bombastic allegorical use of the feminine in the Grunwald pageant as his own allegory is very different, infused with realism. Wajda's work, on the other hand, becomes incoherent in its split view of patriotism: the distinction between Daniel and the camp officers is one of generation, ideology and privilege; the latter are as caricaturally anti-Communist as the aristocrats of *Ashes and Diamonds*. The quarrel between them, though, is indeed really infighting between members of the same camp. The genuine alternative is Nina's view. It would be inaccessible to Wajda's generation of Polish filmmakers, and first enters Polish cinema through Polański. The Jewishness and the departure from Poland of both the fictional character and the real director are hardly accidental.

Witold Lesiewicz's *April* (widely greeted by critics as a novelty, because of its interest in the Eastern front and in Polish victory rather than defeat [Kałużyński 1966: 238]) is often described as offering a 'common soldier's perspective' on the war that contrasts with the dramatic engagement with the heroic ethos in Wajda's films. One can see why: the very first image after the credits is that of a peasant soldier (Ankliewicz, the début role of Franciszek Pieczka) standing for a portrait by an officer. The officer may indeed sketch all the other troops and nurses, but placing the peasant first has particular significance. When the attack is launched the next day, Ankliewicz will seek to stay behind and guard coats rather than risk death and a failure to return home to his village to plant his potatoes. Ironically, he is then almost executed on the spot for desertion by Colonel Czapran, and his fate hangs in the balance thereafter. Much of the work, though, is concerned with an Oedipally-tinged conflict between Czapran and the ensign he has slapped for disobeying orders, and who wishes to fight a duel over it. The orders involved preparations for the attack: in the last days of war, the ensign cannot see its necessity and does all he can to undermine the colonel. At the same time, though, he does so by invoking pre-war codes of honour: one officer must answer for slapping another. The scene of the slap is one of the most pregnant in Lesiewicz's admirably lean, laconic work. The ensign turns up the radio to drown out the orders. Significantly, it is playing a slow foxtrot from Warsaw. Its playing in the capital city – from which there have already been reports of such returns to normality as the opening of a soda water plant – suggests the absurdity of any fighting elsewhere: it can be deemed unnecessary, as can the colonel's planned offensive, which seeks to raise the prestige of the Polish forces. The peace that enters the room with the music is simultaneously elsewhere, though: it is both present and absent. The point is reinforced when Jasiek, the batman of the prosecutor, Captain Hyrny, switches on the radio and hears waltz music from a liberated Vienna. Here too peace is both reality and mirage. If the batman can act unprompted on the captain's behalf in love matters and a peasant appear first in the film, there is clearly a doubling between levels of the social hierarchy that both reflects the particular weight anti-heroism acquires at a specific historical moment and anticipates the social revolutions that cascaded across Europe immediately after World War Two, as they had after World War One. The duplication is more than the traditional shadowing of plot by subplot, for the previously subordinate element in the social hierarchy has ceased merely to echo a primary one; both are of equal importance. That is why a thick-set man with an unflattering girth and the 'traditional attributes of the peasant hero' (Iskierko *et al.* 1980: 116) can be a colonel; why the garrulous cow-tending peasant can quote Wyspiański's '*chłop potęgą jest i basta*' ('the peasantry is a power') and even play Chopin; and why Ankliewicz and the colonel can die heroic deaths together and rest side by side on stored corn. In the end, therefore, there appears to be a male solidarity in heroism. Consequently, as the film nears its end the anti-heroic argument is shifted to its traditional enunciator, the woman: to the nurse who, on hearing that the war will probably last another week, asks '*a nasi ciągle będą się bić?*' ('and our boys will still go on fighting?'). Hyrny accepts as a necessity something she questions. In the end, as so often, anti-heroism's questioning of heroism is itself questioned by its gendering.

Aleksander Ford's *The First Day of Freedom*, meanwhile, has been described as 'a faithful adaptation' of the Leon Kruczkowski play upon which it is based (Drozdowski *et al.* 1985: 60). Careful comparison of the two works reveals fundamental differences, however.

Ford's film begins with a group of Polish POWs whose camp will shortly be vacated by the Germans and liberated by Soviet forces. Upon liberation, they make their way to a nearby German town, requisitioning an empty flat. There they encounter a local doctor, whose eldest daughter Inge has been raped by former prisoners (something Ford shows, but Kruczkowski has the doctor recount using indirection). Jan, the socialist in the group, suggests that the doctor move his three daughters into the requisitioned quarters to protect them. The doctor agrees, but leaves to hold his surgery; as the only local doctor, he may well be needed in the last days of war and first days of peace. The truth of this is borne out as numerous ex-prisoners shuffle into his surgery. Meanwhile, relations develop between the soldiers and the two eldest daughters (Ford's film, unlike Kruczkowski's play, gives no dialogue to the youngest, a difference that reflects both film's general preference for potential love-interests and the lack of child actors in the Polish theatre from which Polish cinema drew its actors). Inge talks with Jan, and her younger sister Luzzi (the nicely irritating Elżbieta Czyżewska is the film's best piece of casting) makes love to his friend Michał, who has lost his entire family to the Germans. Jan defends Inge against other comrades-in-arms who return from town drunk and wish to appropriate her as part of the spoils of victory; offended by this, the others leave. A studious ex-camp inmate called Anzelm, who found freedom in the camp but now feels he has lost it, also seeks and is granted shelter in the flat. Meanwhile, SS man Otto, who is linked to Inge, orders the doctor to tell Inge to join him in the church clocktower. The doctor in fact tells her of Otto's return but warns her not to join him. Meanwhile, remnants of SS forces mount an attack on the town. Inge, who feels that however much she hates the past it remains hers – because she is German – joins Otto in the tower. Otto rapes her, fires on the liberating soldiers and, when himself shot, compels Inge to fire the gun herself. She is then shot from the ground by a Jan unconscious of the gunner's identity. On climbing the clocktower and discovering the truth, he despairingly strikes the bell with his machine gun.

The First Day of Freedom might well have been filmed by Andrzej Wajda – in which case comparison with *Landscape After a Battle* and *Ashes and Diamonds* would have been not only piquant but mandatory. Kruczkowski's play was not just one of the many materials Wajda virtually optioned but ended up not using – as Tadeusz Konwicki has reported was so often the case, though he gallantly passes over the fact that his own novel *Sennik współczesny* (*A Contemporary Dreambook*, 1963) was once part of the Kamera film unit's production plan, with Wajda to direct. Wajda's proposed version of Kruczkowski's work actually went as far as the scripting stage, and so joins his versions of Stefan Żeromski's *Przedwiośnie* (*Pre-Spring*, 1924) and Aleksander Ścibor-Rylski's *Man of Marble* among his 1960s projects vetoed by the Script Assessment Commission. The reasons were almost bizarre: the dialogue was felt to be uncinematic, and there were doubts whether Kruczkowski would write new dialogues for his own play or approve new ones by someone else (Wajda's own, quasi-American proposed solution). The meeting closed with this issue unresolved, and Wajda himself pledging to approach Kruczkowski (FN, KOS, A-214 poz. 186). Obviously, nothing came of this. It is both appropriate and ironic that the work should finally have been shot by that other *Thematenfresser* – as Tadeusz Lubelski rightly terms him (Lubelski 1992a: 129) – Aleksander Ford. Kruczkowski's death in 1962 may be said to have paralysed Wajda's project but resolved the problem for subsequent adapters by removing the likely authorial veto on any very free adaptation. Ford himself summarises the history of the attempted filming as follows:

> When Kruczkowski wrote this text, he proposed that I film it. At first I thought it was completely impossible and it seemed to me to be a hellishly difficult undertaking. So I advised Kruczkowski to talk to somebody else and suggested Wajda's name, which aroused his enthusiasm. Unfortunately, nothing came of this co-operation, for Wajda had other projects or perhaps didn't know Kruczkowski sufficiently well.

In the meantime, he had come to see the task as achievable, and even as a debt to be paid to the author, who had been a friend (FN, KOS, A-214 poz. 343).

Somewhat surprisingly, therefore, Bohdan Czeszko's screenplay for Ford's film rearranges the play almost as systematically as Charles Marowitz's collage of *Hamlet*. It is as if it has been dynamited, blasting its larger and smaller elements of texture and dialogue into different locations within a structure misleadingly similar to that of the original. This retention of so many of the play's elements does it a disservice, however, by concealing the extent of the film's divergence: there is no such open declaration of independence as legitimates such great adaptations as those of Akira Kurosawa or Bernardo Bertolucci. Instead, there is an insidious suggestion of fidelity that can mislead even acute critics, a delusion which may have begun in the self-delusion of Czeszko and Ford themselves. The impression made by the one clear signal of fundamental divergence – the addition of the key character of Otto – is doubtless overridden for most spectators by the frequent partial quotations, even though some of them have their meaning inverted by their attribution to different characters (Luzzi's casual exchanges with Jan become part of an intense sequence with Michał, who is given Jan's words). The simulation of closeness can seem to mock the play even more thoroughly than would its blatant flouting. Take the ending, for instance. In Kruczkowski's work, Jan does indeed shoot Inge, who is firing from the tower. But in his play she is alone, and Jan is aware of the gunner's identity: she has spoken earlier of visiting the church. The film shows Inge terrorised into firing by Otto and Jan who shoots an unknown enemy. The change reflects a switch from Kruczkowski's sense of a tragic internal human division to an easy, melodramatic dualism between characters who are all all-of-a-piece, with the one exception of Inge. This melodrama conceives character extremely stereotypically. Unsurprisingly, Otto – for whom Czeszko and Ford are entirely responsible – is the worst example of sterotypicality: he parrots his Führer's belief in the worthlessness of a nation unable to win victory and so epitomises the 'bad German' as to force sex upon Inge in a manner staged to recall the earlier rape (represented by the ripping of clothing from her breasts). The melodrama is strongest in the domain of the political, an area untouched by Kruczkowski. Czeszko and Ford identify Jan as a pre-war socialist, and his least sympathetic companion mocks him as such when Jan frustrates his attempted sport with Inge. Perhaps the key omission is Jan's reference to his fear of himself: 'At times it seems to me that within each and every one of us there stands, alongside the person we see in the mirror when shaving, another entity we do not know closely, the one bred over there, behind the barbed wire' (Kruczkowski 1984; 79). Michał's jeering rejoinder that this entity is 'dangerous for the environment' may be taken as defensive. The dangerous self belongs to the camp, war and collectivity and is implicitly defined as bestial: Luzzi had described seeing the prisoners behind the barbed wire and feeling that zoo creatures were less animalistic. The film reconjugates the beast metaphor into the platitudinously accusatory: the doctor terms the rapists beasts (the play's doctor struggles to understand them) and the Poles shoot back the unanswerable question about who made them so. Sensitivity about the possible identity of the rapists runs through the film. When they enter, they use German and French monosyllables to indicate their hunger and cannot be identified. When the Poles ask the doctor if they were Polish, he retorts by asking whether they think Poles incapable of such things. Unlike the play's doctor, he aggressively casts the issue in terms of nationality. The film's characterisation of Jan and his companions suggests an absurd, different reply to his question: it might be possible for some Poles (older, boorish reactionaries), but not for inherently sensitive socialists.

Kruczkowski argues for the partial post-war persistence of the dehumanised self, identifying it with the blind execution of collective imperatives. He shows Jan returning to the flat just before the ending shows him respond to the firing from the clocktower by going out and shooting the gunner. As Jan enters the flat, Luzzi finds his appearance disturbing. It is as if he is already, tragically, succumbing to the old self, the one sustained by the 'solidarity' horribly resuscitated by the soldiers' renewed battle with the Germans. This relapse is tragic because, for much of the play, Jan has attempted to recover individuality and freedom of choice (a choice denied during five years of imprisonment) by performing an act that is unexpected because it goes against collective interests: by sheltering Germans. In Czeszko's screenplay, however, self-division persists only within Inge; Jan becomes an uncomplicatedly sympathetic figure of identification, betrayed not by his bestial and collective wartime second-self but by the gunner's anonymity and Inge's suicidal allegiance to her own past. The play's Jan is far more complex: those readers who deemed his killing of Inge difficult to interpret may have been reacting to the overdetermination of an act that was partly pre-individualised, unconscious. Having acted against the collective interests, is he now likely to act equally unpredictably and self-destructively by going against his own? Could the scene that shows the ex-prisoners dancing with naked female mannequins not just indicate a tendency to use women as the kind of sex object Inge became in the hands of the rapists, but an incapacity to relate healthily to women at all? No wonder the play's last line is the doctor's agonised question why Jan shot and why *he* had to be the one who did so. In the film, though, it is Inge alone who fails to elude the past and who tells her father that although hated it is nevertheless still hers, part of the nation to which she belongs. Czeszko and Ford take this as a simple example of stubborn German self-submergence in the national ethos, not as possibly simultaneously partly motivated by the suicidal self-contempt generated by her rape, and partly by revenge. Moreover, they cannot conceive of her deciding to attack on her own or being anything other than traumatised by firing, as stereotype dictates women must be.

The hard labour Kruczkowski's Jan invests in constructing a new identity indicates its fragility. In the film, however, the only person trapped in the resurgent past is the chauvinistically conceived, excessively 'German' German, the Valkyrie girl who is faithful unto death and is therefore – ironically, for all her traumatisation by her lover and by the machine-gun's unrelenting salvoes – as much the SS man's fitting partner in Götterdämmerung as his victim. (In a further irony, the Script Assessment Commission also saw Inge's loyalty to the lost cause as stereotypical, though in this case stereotypically Polish and Romantic.) Czeszko's reworking of Kruczkowski's play seeks to 'cinematise' it by opening it up (as if the chamber drama of mid-1960s Bergman were not also 'cinema'), for instance through frequent trips beyond the closed room and depictions of battle action. Ford's primary visual strategy for a similar intra-scenic 'opening up' stretches space through near-obsessive zooming. But the final upshot of film and play is radically different. Kruczkowski's play is a thoughtful dialogue with existentialism, pairing a Sartrean thematics of individuation through freedom of choice with a tragic pessimism about the viability of the Sartrean project. Its pessimism may reflect his willingness to admit into his play a figure like Anzelm (based upon a man he had met), whose argument that only loss of everything brings true freedom bespeaks an absurdity that is more Beckettian than Sartrean, and who suggests a sibling or even double of Borowski's Tadeusz. With its strains of chauvinism and nationalism, however, the film, for all its anti-Nazism, could be classified sarcastically as a form of 'national socialism'. Whatever its authors' intentions, this travesty of Kruczkowski battens vampirically upon his play, first neutralising it then mobilising it as a Trojan Horse for the smuggling of an extremely dubious ideology.

OBSERVING THE OBSERVER

Particularly unheroic, of course, is the position of the observer, and much reflection on Polish-Jewish relations in recent years has concentrated upon the attitude with which Poles may or may not have watched their Jewish fellow-citizens being marched to their deaths. This is the subject of Andrzej Wajda's *Wielki tydzień* (*Holy Week*, 1996), which – although made after the collapse of Poland's socialist government – is of relevance here because of its derivation from a text by Jerzy Andrzejewski written in 1946, and because of the various attempts made to film it before 1989 (an issue discussed in the following chapter on Polish-Jewish relations).

Holy Week evokes the double-bind whereby mere observation provokes guilt, while abandonment of the observer's position catapults one towards death. Wajda himself has said 'it is not a question of the guilty and the innocent but rather that that terrible crime took place before our eyes. That we watched it in a sense, and so did I, though I wasn't living in Warsaw at the time but in the provinces – but I too saw the extermination of that Ghetto after a fashion' (Wajda 1997). The distance between Jan Malecki's household and Warsaw's centre may translate Wajda's own distance during the Uprising and our own temporal one. The very first images broach the theme, as two people later identified as the Jewish Professor Lilien and his daughter Irena watch a dejected group shuffle through a forest, prodded by a German soldier. As the group passes the camera a closer shot reveals the yellow stars on their backs. The camera's move towards the group enacts its attraction upon the Professor, who feels he belongs with them and joins them, ignoring his daughter's stifled, despairing remonstrations. The drastic price of vacating the observer's position becomes clear immediately as he falls and is kicked. The incident glosses the opening title spelling out the German prohibition on leaving the Ghetto, a capital offence both for Jews and for Poles aiding them. By inserting after it a scene originally located much later in Andrzejewski's story, Wajda lays out his theme: what it means to watch a crime, and how people react to the sight in different ways. Irena's frozen observation of the incipient Ghetto rising a few scenes later leaves her oblivious to safety, as nearly hypnotised by the vision, dream and fear of community as her father had been; she has to be bustled into a doorway by her old lover Jan (now married to a Polish girl), who decides to take her home. For all his cowardice, self-doubt, reluctance and mixed feelings – spelled out extensively in Andrzejewski's text – he too crosses the line separating observer from observed and so will finally suffer the fate of the observed and be killed.

Jan Malecki's death is followed by the appearance of motorcycled German soldiers, face-less, impersonal. It is possible that Wajda's perspective on these Cocteau-like 'messengers of death' may be open to description as 'Jewish'. Consider the following eloquent words by Eva Hoffman, herself Jewish, evoking Jewish survivors'experiencess of the Holocaust that swept through their Eastern Polish village of Bransk:

> The German soldiers in Bransk had frightening, hard faces – everyone agrees on that – but they existed at such a remove of power and terror that they were hardly individu-als; they were embodiments of an abstract force … It is possible that the Nazis were beyond hate, transferred to the realm of psychological trauma, of numbing and word-lessness. (Hoffman 1999: 245)

The Poles, meanwhile, the human neighbours, could be hated for their betrayals. If Wajda's perspective is indeed – or overlaps with – a 'Jewish' one then it bridges the festering gulf between the two cultures and shows that the effort to transcend the pre-1989 official state perspective on 'the Jewish question' by filming a pre-1989 text was not necessarily predestined to failure.

Holy Week achieves this by showing the irrevocable separation of Jews and Poles *during a particular period* by the disaster the Nazis visited upon the former. National Socialism may indeed have envisaged an eventual Polish arrival at the same destiny, but 'the Final Solution of the Jewish question' came first. Andrzejewski's early statement of the separating effects of one person's happiness and another's sorrow fittingly furnishes Wajda's final title. The dispar-ity pervades the dialogues of Irena and Jan, the latter's words stumbling repeatedly over the incommensurability of their suffering. Structuring the story around Holy Week renders the gap ironic, tragic and all but unbridgeable, rooted in two communities' divergent readings of the crucifixion of Jesus. Anna, the work's religious conscience, the venerator of a dead Jew's statue in a scene Wajda moves to the film's end, is the closest to Irena, and not just because the women flank Jan as beautiful former lover and plain wife. Anna alone is allowed to recount a loss comparable to Irena's, her family's decimation by the Nazis. Her belief seems to unlock dimensions inaccessible to her pusillanimous husband, and her religious awareness of 'last things' recognises death's ever-nearness. Her ideal Catholicism knows no separation from its neighbour's suffering. Thus to deem her kissing of Christ's image *'quelque chose d'obscène'* (Axelrad 1996: 57), a way of eclipsing the Ghetto's sufferings, is to ignore the work's final focus on Irena's departure into its smoke, as well as the short-circuiting of any facile sublimation by Christ's own Jewishness. The Good Friday end leaves us in a darkness not yet known to precede a resurrection. Wajda's ending, which modifies Andrzejewski's, may be problematic but 'obscenity' is far too strong a term. Here, as in *Korczak*, the last word is that of the intertitle that underlines the limitations of the observer's position: at a certain point images give out, other people pass out of sight. One can only imagine what one cannot see, one's effort aided by the written word, the Andrzejewski text privileged at the end. And ending with the word, beyond graven images, is a form of solidarity with the imagination of the Torah. As so often in cinema, be its allegiances Brechtian or not, the presence of the intertitle is an admonition, the sign of our need to learn – in this case, the Polish need to learn more of the neighbour whose place is now an absence. Only the mind's eye – not that of flesh – can still follow the neighbour separated by her suffering.

POSTSCRIPT: WAR AND TRAUMA – EVERYTHING FOR SALE

It is often stated that certain events are traumatic. Equally often, psychiatrists retort that not all who experience 'traumatic' events are in fact traumatised by them; individual reactions vary. The two statements are not incompatible, of course: certain events may indeed be termed 'traumatising' in the sense that their qualities are such as to make it highly likely that they will haunt participants or viewers; but such haunting is only probable, not certain. It was clearly a highly probable outcome of a war that had killed a third of Poland's population: one sixth of ethnic Poles, and almost all the country's Jews. That is why one can speak of a national trauma: of an event likely to have traumatised most of its citizens, to a greater or lesser degree. But what is trauma, and to what degree is it subject to representation? In this section, I will consider this general issue before examining Wajda's *Kanal*, which is entirely focussed on war, and then – at greater length (since I have considered *Kanal* already in this chapter) – his *Everything for Sale*, in which the triggering trauma of Zbigniew Cybulski's death is imbricated with and summons up other traumas, with war trauma establishing itself finally as the dominant.

Evocations of trauma speak of shock, suddenness and unexpected violence. For Freud, its source lay in the very lack of preparedness that caused its perception as unexpected (Freud 1967, 59–60), a thesis first applied to artistic production in Walter Benjamin's work on modernity, shock and the destruction of experience registered by Baudelaire (Benjamin 1973, 157–202). The traumatised self loses its position of control over and against events, irrespective of whether they unfold at a distance or are felt on the skin as percussion, suction, or force. That force can draw both spectators and participants into a single vortex. If naming comes – if the faculty of language begins to return – it does so in damaged form: with the indirection of displacement, perhaps as the somatic metaphor equally typical of the hysteria to which Freud compares traumatic neurosis (Freud 1967, 29). It may then, in time, much time, float closer to consciousness, becoming the more controlled metaphor that is art, the alternative being simple traumatic repetition in a space beyond control. Whether somatic or aesthetic, the metaphor is bodied forth by the shaping force of an event it also mutes, lest direct contact destroy: in the art of trauma metaphor thus always remains in part a displacement, a naming without naming. Such works are strung out at various points between the event and the discursivity that might name it fully. Viewed metaphorically themselves, they might form bridges to permit the self to limp away from the event. As long as it inhabits the bewitched circle of the horror, however, that self is in need of art that places horror offstage even when it seems to stage it. Such art is afterimage, the hollow container of an aftershock that still reverberates around it. Its metaphorical transposition of the event does not move it from minor to major: it is not the meaning precluded both by the event and the way in which it entered the self, but the next best thing, the only available thing, the fragile suggestion of the possibility of meaning, naming; the possibility that it is part of something with a shape, and hence an ending.

Trauma may be either momentary or it may be a stream of images or blows cataclysmically fused into a moment. As artworks go beyond the minimalist registration of its monumental momentariness and moments, they lay themselves open to accusations of a betrayal that includes self-betrayal, that of their own beginning. Most of Luis Buñuel's *Un Chien Andalou* (1929) can be seen as working away from the piercing shock of its opening, translating the trauma visited upon self and eye into the safer something else of scandal. Much of Wajda's *Everything for Sale* performs a similar operation upon its opening sequence, seeking to extrude it from itself or erase it through the promise of healing proffered by the passage of time. It is surely significant that the artworks most open to such description are those most indebted to surrealism, whose commitment to shock is one to the denial of narrativisation. It is artistic production at its ground or degree zero, the simple reproduction of still unmastered trauma, a lining distended to contain its force; the extreme instance of the idea of inspiration, an explosion blown into a form stretched to the limit. 'Explosion' is no mere metaphor, as warfare is central to trauma. As Graham Greene puts it in *The Ministry of Fear*, pinpointing the relationship between war, the masks of metaphor and the revealingly surreal, '[w]ar is very like a bad dream in which familiar people appear in terrible and unlikely disguises' (Greene 1973: 87). The work's reproduction of the event's molestation may be taken as homeopathic. Its mental repetition and rerepetition may endlessly renew a search for the split second before the horror, which might thus have been forestalled, or continually refuse to believe that the inconceivable could ever have occurred: after all, the evidence for it is the absurdly paradoxical fact that the self has died yet survived. And so, despite Freud's insistence, a wish does indeed inhabit the trauma's repetition: the wish that it had never been (Freud 1967: 31). It feels its way around the event, seeking a crack in its apparent sublime solidity and powerful Otherness, the chink that will point through and beyond it, allow one to enter it and reprogramme it, strip it of the aura of necessity, render it something that always could have been different. At the same time, as the self shuts too late a door blown completely off its hinges, the event's repetition is the next best thing to its naming: numbing; the deadening offered by habit; the placing of a sign as a screen between the victim and the event, its blocking of the event inscribed in its partial departure from it into the sphere of metaphor, even as it remains anchored to it below the surface. The artwork whose logic recalls the dreamwork is Janus-faced, contiguous to and continuous with the nightmare it can thus offer to hold at bay by releasing some of the tension of its repression, preventing the trauma becoming the repressed that can only return amid night-sweats. Name it often enough, the wish says, and the trauma will become unreal, the dissociation absolute: art can promise to hold it ever-captive in its mirror, smoothly sealed in by its lamination and closure, frozen as a fetish. That final release may be postponed indefinitely, though, for art may be as deeply wedded to the possible interminability of analysis as psychoanalysis was, and is, equally symbiotic with the nightmare. Such may well have been the case for such poets as Paul Celan or Sylvia Plath. On the level of the collective, meanwhile, the violence apparently frozen into the force-field of an artwork may thaw out precisely because its conceptualisation as an image has precluded action upon the reality which it metaphorises.

As the artwork proceeds, as it moves beyond repetition of the trauma to insert it into a set of other images to be read as its declensions or as ways of 'placing' and hence displacing it – replacing stammer with pattern, the logic of the aesthetic – it can be seen to betray both itself and its occasion. Film may be particularly prone to this accusation. Ingmar Bergman once described how his works germinated in a single image, and in *Persona* showed a work's emergence from the fascinating, disconnected, disconcerting imagistic stabs walled off from it nevertheless as a pre-credit sequence. Filmic images are themselves, of course, at their heart, a stammer, the twenty three frames' reiterations of what another frame said at almost the same second. The image is a given; artist and work then react to it. It is the shot of which the work is the recoil. The accusations of betrayal become choral whenever such images emerge not from any dark night of artistic solitude, such as Bergman's, but from a collective experience demanding justice, adequation, not just representation. Should such accusations expose the accuser to identification as a member of an unfavoured minority, the chorus may speak *sotto voce*, but it then wounds the artist all the more deeply with the implicit reproach of his relative privilege, that of open speech (gagged themselves, themselves too gnawed by their pain, the members of the chorus do not grasp the extent to which metaphor too is a gag). This occurs, of course, when an artist seeks an audience under a political regime well aware of the extreme sensitivity of his subject matter. Such was the case when Wajda reworked and named the Warsaw Uprising as sheer trauma in his late 1950s film *Kanal*.

Kanal dramatises a collapse of structures of command that becomes in the end a breakdown of structure per se, and hence of the possibility of control. It reverses the method of *Un Chien Andalou* and *Everything for Sale* and whittles narrative away to leave a pile of floating, loosely linked images of hell: partly so as to work existentially towards the dark heart of trauma, partly to indicate the directionlessness of the fighters lost in the sewers, for whom shafts of light are either barred, booby-trapped, guarded by enemy soldiers, or – in the end – revelations of the group's disintegration; but also as part of the delicate political operation of bracketing anything that might provoke official censorship or audience rejection of the work. If it was accused of purveying half-truths about the Uprising, it was as much because it had torn away the popular heroic myths and screen memories that had blanketed its reality (recall Freud's comments on the trauma sufferer's daytime attempt not to recall the event [Freud 1967, 31]) as because it gave hostages to the regime by depicting it as simply futile. In doing so, it displayed the Uprising as an unhealed wound suppurating below the dressing that hid it from sight. No wonder that this Uprising ends up underground, in the site of the repressed still inhabited by the memory of the Home Army, its soldiers haunting the underside of a city whose daylight excludes them: the traumatic reality of memory inscribed in its inaccessibility to consciousness. It returns to that place of inaccessibility at its end, as Zadra, the commander who has lost his platoon, descends back into the sewers, an action that may be read as a symbolic form of the suicide that so often follows survival: the depth to which one's life is interwoven with others' makes their loss finally tantamount to one's own. Their physical death entails one's own psychic one: along with them, the world that would have supported you has been withdrawn. The end of *Kanal* deems survival unbearable; and, by doing so, it sees the war as having inflicted psychic death upon Poland.

Multiple traumas reverberate through Wajda's *Everything for Sale*, some of them obvious, some not. It is surely appropriate that one of its first images should show the director of a film emerging from under the wheels of a train that had seemed to kill him, asking how the shot went, as the whole film will be concerned with the relationship between the seen and unseen – which, here, below the level of the platform, entails horror, as the unseen so often does. The film's founding trauma is signalled by that opening sequence, which would be particularly shocking for Polish audiences aware of the film's widespread trailing as a reaction to the death of Zbigniew Cybulski – often termed Poland's James Dean, and the charismatic hero of Wajda's best-known film, *Ashes and Diamonds* – and recognising the fall under the train as the manner of that death. Even though the man's run and slip are shot from behind, they would also have recognised him – or think they had done so – as an image of Cybulski, the trademark thick-rimmed glasses silhouetted against the moving train seeming to establish the identification clearly. But then the train brakes and although the actor's wife, running up the platform stairs, cries out in horror, the director emerges unharmed to ask how the shot went. Wajda offers a simulacrum of Cybulski's death, as if beginning a drama-documentary, but does so in a way that allows him to turn it inside out to disclose a fiction, which is, of course, all it could ever be. However, it is not the kind of fiction one might expect; not one acknowledging the fictionality of any staging of Cybulski's terrible death, but one about the disappearance of an actor for whom the director figures as a stand-in stunt-man on the first day of the shoot. (The actor in question is clearly of the existential variety that disbelieves in stunt-men.) The focus shifts, as if a frame had suddenly been racked, from Cybulski to the director – and hence to Wajda himself and his relationship with Cybulski, whom he had not used for several years, and who had once said Wajda would miss him. The violence of the shift will be muted and camouflaged, however, by Wajda's casting of someone other than himself as the director, a decision that ceases to seem unexceptionable when one realises that all the other characters are actors performing themselves, with their own names, generating the piquancy of a film à clef. Wajda's statement that Andrzej Łapicki played the director far better than he himself could have done seems to legitimate the casting; after all, he himself was no actor (nor even screenwriter, which is one motive for the film's extensive use of improvisation). He gives no reasons for his original intention of casting Jerzy Skolimowski in this role, though there were surely at least two: Skolimowski's status as both an actor-director (that is, someone on both sides of the camera) and the former husband of Elżbieta Czyżewska, who plays the missing actor's wife. Wajda may well have wished to pair Skolimowski and Czyżewska in order to add extra piquancy, as well as an extra layer of film-reality confusion. He described the casting of Łapicki instead as a recognition that the director had to be someone of his own generation: in other words, a stand-in for himself (Wertenstein 2000: 57).

The mixture of fiction and documentary in that opening sequence sets the tone both for the film and for all Wajda's intra- and extra-textual uncertainties about it. Within the film his then wife, Beata Tyszkiewicz, says he cannot mix reality and fiction like this. Similarly Bogumił Kobiela, a close friend of Cybulski, criticises the director's refusal to make a newsreel-style film about the dead actor, walks out and is never seen again, as he did during the film's making, wanting nothing further to do it. Wajda worried protractedly in interviews about the best form for the film, and was obviously so haunted by the relationship between its fictionality and its non-fiction as to consider either (a) incorporating within it a documentary about its making, shot by Jerzy Ziarnik and called *Na scenie* (*On the Set*) or (b) breaking off the fiction half-way, after the actors have learned of their colleague's death, then inserting a documentary about Cybulski, his wife and his child (Wertenstein 2000: 57–9). Neither proposal would have resolved the question of just what it is that Wajda has done in his opening sequence, and whether or not it was permissible. The whole film reels away from that beginning, both repressing and haunted by it. Viewers themselves may feel very much like its survivors, though the survivor's guilt is entirely projected onto (or, because of what he has done and left undone, taken upon himself by) Wajda, who then deflects it partially onto a director figure played by an actor who – surely not coincidentally – shares his first name.

The film's most evident traumas are those of the viewer and of Wajda, who was surely also in crisis after the disaster of his previous film – usually seen as his worst – *Bramy raju* (*The Gates of Paradise*, 1967). These traumas, however, are but flames playing round the edges of the most visible one, that of Ela, the actor's wife, who is on the verge of breakdown, fearing abandonment. Her intra-fictional trauma is doubled and augmented by the real ones undergone by the actress, Ela Czyżewska herself, who had recently been compelled to leave Poland following the expulsion of her husband, David Halberstam, once the Warsaw correspondent for *Time*, for criticism of the authorities. Returning at Wajda's invitation, Czyżewska was vilified in open letters in the press. One paper – *Walka Młodych* (*Struggle of the Young*) – asked Wajda how he could employ someone who had 'betrayed' Poland. The film gains much of its power from her, and her transformation by her experiences. Thus, in a sensitive profile written in 1989, Jacek Tabecki comments that 'her face in *Everything for Sale* no longer has anything in common with that of a dozen or so months earlier. The expression of this actress, who had only just turned thirty, displays a tragic quality, maturity and bitterness' (Tabecki 1989: 11). There is poignancy in her stated preference for comic roles, for even though she had played many, here it seems wistfully to mark the degree to which laughter had departed her life. If the film's second half does indeed have less impact, as Wajda himself believed, it is surely because she has less screen-time; for the genuineness of her psychodrama – which some critics described as almost exhibitionistic – had underwritten Wajda's own. Meanwhile, Czyżewska may be deemed the most prominent ethnically Polish victim of an ugly persecution whose primary objects were Jewish. For the film was shot in early 1968, in the midst of the notorious anti-Semitic campaign. The trauma of that historical moment – which was particularly great for the artistic community it decimated, sending one person after another into exile – may be the film's least obvious one, but it is surely there, and the Warsaw film coterie's unremitting hostility towards Ela may even be taken (whatever Wajda's intentions) as allegorising a scapegoating the film cannot name: a trauma so close that one cannot even begin to represent it directly, only register the atmosphere's poisoning by its miasma.

In the end, *Everything for Sale* discovers equilibrium in a distilled composite mourning that encompasses Cybulski, Andrzej Wróblewski (Wajda's contemporary, whose paintings and youthful death meant so much to him), Wajda's own generation and generations of defeated Poles before him. Its gravitation towards memories of war and the resistance is apparent in Daniel's quest to discover the truth about the wartime legends generated by the actor, the partial restaging of the vodka-glass scene from *Ashes and Diamonds* and the close-up of the memorial to Poles murdered by the Nazis outside the gallery showing Andrzej Wróblewski's paintings, many of which themselves portray wartime executions. As it does this, the film separates – dissociates – itself from itself, deliberately falling apart: the director asks the interviewer to switch off her tape-recorder before informing her that the actor's death makes continuing the film impossible. This operation of separation requires a doubling both in time and between characters. The doubling of the accident allows the film to redefine the first accident as accidental in the sense of the inessential, which can then be discarded, erased by a re-recording that resembles secondary revision. If the second accident cancels the first, it seems to do so in the name of a conscience that is not acknowledged explicitly. The director's dissatisfaction with his own work – Wajda's with his own film – is displaced by attributing its governing principles to the young assistant director, whose ambition is pilloried as vampirical. In essence, the figure of the director is split, the older one allowed his noble mourning and communion with the dead, the younger one scapegoated. They are both Andrzej Wajda, however, an identity that justifies his non-casting of himself: at this point the psychodrama is in fact expressionist, with different people embodying conflicting urges within the same person, something which would have been obscured had Wajda himself played the director. The figures' identity, even after their divergent decisions about continuing the film, is betrayed by the way the younger director is drawn to the spectacle of galloping horses just as the director had been when visiting the shoot of Jerzy Hoffman's *Pan Wołodyjowski* (1969) – and as Wajda has been throughout his career. Indeed, the final shot of Daniel running with the horses can be seen as alluding to the film Wajda repeatedly voiced his desire to remake, *Lotna,* one of whose first images is of the eponymous horse racing across a field amidst explosions. They are the explosions of World War Two: the earlier, least obvious trauma, to which Wajda's work always returns, the deepest one, of which all others prove in the end to be but echoes.

If *Everything for Sale* is marked by multiple traumas, at their heart lies the problem of representation that has dogged Film Studies, and caused the adoption of trauma theory as a possible way of thinking the simultaneous absence and presence of reference. What is the nature of the relationship between events or states of affairs and their refiguring by an art that is of necessity more than a reflection? If it is oblique, though, do its truth claims become more and more attenuated as the obliquity grows? The problem is particularly acute in film, whose indexical images use imprints of reality as signs and so threaten the dissolution of the sign/signified distinction. The most radical, but absurd, solution would be the Vertovian one that denies fiction a right to exist, insisting on the pre-eminence of non-fiction. Wajda's musings on whether or not he should have included documentary elements show an awareness of the possibility of such an outcome. But since trauma theory describes certain events as both determining and non-susceptible of direct representation, it allows a space for the symbolic act that is art; at the same time, though, it hangs over it an ever-present question mark, a Damoclean sword, as the metaphor can block the light it allows to enter, like a stained-glass window. This position – under a surgical knife that is permanently suspended – is that of Wajda's film, which may thus be described as the perfect object of trauma theory's reflection. Its exceptional nature suggests, however, that trauma theory is less a permanent solution to the aporias of filmic representation than the symptom of a crisis whose tension cannot be sustained for long, be it in the theory or in the works it considers. In the end the knife has to fall as impatience slashes at the dialectical Gordian knot, cutting off the thread of the film, which is then left dangling.

REFLECTIONS FROM THE DAMAGED LIFE:
THE REAL END OF THE GREAT WAR

The deepest rendition of the war trauma Wajda discovers at the bedrock of his generation's psyche is found in a film that encountered little enthusiasm upon its emergence, perhaps because it did indeed come as an emissary from a heart of darkness. It is Jerzy Kawalerowicz's underrated masterpiece, *Prawdziwy koniec wielkiej wojny* (*The Real End of the Great War,* 1957). Like Wojciech Has, Kawalerowicz stood to one side to the Polish School, eschewing the war dramas central to it. *The Real End of the Great War* – with its tragically ironic title – is his sole foray into this area. It shows Juliusz (Roland Głowacki), who returned from a concentration camp four years ago and cannot speak, only repeat a shuffling, circular dance whenever something in his surroundings triggers recollections of baiting camp officers' commands to do this. His wife Róża (Lucyna Winnicka) finds life with him increasingly difficult, his epileptic twitchings horribly overlaying her memory of his whirling, pre-war dance-floor prowess. Only his old housekeeper, Józia (Janina Sokołowska), has sympathy for him, mothering him. Róża loves Stęgień (Andrzej Szalawski), the man she was with when Juliusz returned from the war, but Juliusz's condition has made her feel obliged to stay with him. Still with him physically, mentally she draws further and further away, and when in the end she proposes despatching him to the countryside he hangs himself. For Juliusz at least the great war is finally over.

The rather chilly initial response to Kawalerowicz's film has been seen as a sign of a certain critical helplessness before it (Iskierko *et al.* 1980, 83), and the aesthetic objections may well be explicable only as rationalisations. They include the contention that the expressionist subjective camera in Juliusz's camp recollections represents an excess of art that jars with the rest of the story. Kawalerowicz himself later wondered whether he ought to have shown a developing, parallel story in the flashbacks, or made Róża the central figure (Kawalerowicz 2001: 46–7). Either move, of course, would have deprived the film of its most harrowing feature: its closeness to a mind frozen in trauma. The circle of the dance is the vicious one of a narrative – a life – whose only movement is a downward spiral. There might once have been hope for it though. In the early days after his return Juliusz spoke a little, though the confusion of his speech alienated Róża. The film's significant first image is of her holding shut a door being shaken violently, calling 'darling' and weeping as she tells a silent, unseen other not to cry. The words 'I love you Róża', unspeakable for Juliusz in the present, then echo in her recollection, measuring the distance of the pre-war world where she and Juliusz danced, and he spoke these words. Róża's inability to accept anything other than normal speech reflects her desperate obsession with the normal life she wishes to lead, feels is her right by virtue of her attractiveness (friends comment upon it, and a stranger turns to watch as she passes), but cannot lead with Juliusz. Helpless herself, she drives him ever deeper into silence. Here film and music unite as the only eloquent advocates of the inarticulate. Low angle shots of Juliusz walking the streets show him alone, picked out against the sky, even when people ostensibly surround him, but Róża and Stęgień also often appear isolated in single shots, albeit viewed from a marginally higher angle indicative of their stronger grasp on their identity. Similarly, the music that fuses melancholy and discord in the case of Juliusz speaks also, in more simply melancholy mode, for Róża and Stęgień in their walks and waits among the leafless trees of the autumnal park. And yet hope can tingle and trill in the flute accompaniment to Juliusz's struggle to practise speech in that selfsame park. Meanwhile, the minor key of Juliusz's musical dissonance is rescored in the major in the present when a young couple use loud jukebox music to clear a table for themselves in a café. If discord can persist in the present, then Juliusz is indeed not abnormal, as becomes apparent when magazine pictures of an atomic mushroom crowd jangle the mind of Róża herself, prompting one to wonder whether 'the great war' will ever really be over for anyone. Discord will return again in the present as the traffic noise that accompanies Juliusz's night walk after he has learned of Róża's plan to send him away, and which ends in the final flashback. Expressionism does not just mark the visualisation of Juliusz's memories, but scars the soundtrack – and hence the world – more widely. That is why Juliusz's story does not lie beyond the norm but at one little-understood end of its spectrum.

Just as important as music is another silent form of speech, that of flowers. Juliusz regularly buys carnations for Róża, who does not notice them. When Stęgień brings roses, this emphasises the sense in which he alone truly possesses Róża, whose name is of course 'rose' in Polish. Juliusz – framed beside the roses, trapped with the silent sign of his rival's unspoken superiority – then goes to buy roses himself, only to slip away, pierced by a sense of futility, while the chatty florist's back is turned. Similarly, he manages to scribble that he loves Róża and is not insane, but fails to show her the note. The film's proximity to Juliusz (we alone are directly privy to the causes of his suffering) is deeply disturbing, and one can see why Kawalerowicz might have felt that the focalisation should have been through Róża. Such a shift, however, would have rendered the film even more of the 'case study' as which several of its initial reviewers misapprehended and condemned it (Iskierko *et al.* 1980, 82; Jackiewicz 1983: 134). Moreover, the distance from Róża in fact increases sympathy with her, as we experience her from the yearning, loving position of Juliusz. Juliusz is in fact trapped between two women: the wife unable to access his consciousness and fearful of his apparent, and apparently deepening, abnormality, and the housekeeper who infantilises him as 'Jujulek'. The rhyme between their two names, an apparent concord, is really a telling discord. Wajda's vision of war may be dark, but it breathes an existential glamour, and his protagonists go down fighting, dying with their boots on. A key scene in Kawalerowicz's film, however, shows Juliusz, once an architect, in a building site that has no place for him, holding a feminising shopping basket, lost in dumb wonder: inarticulate, infantilised, feminised, seemingly abnormal, a non-combatant, he is the hero neither of war nor of post-war reconstruction. His struggle is a single-handed one with the inner quicksand into which his experiences have pushed him. Walking like an automaton, he becomes for Róża at moments a figure from a horror film, a grunting Frankenstein-like object of tragic fear and pity. Just as she retreats, weeping, for fear of being sucked in herself, so spectators kept their distance from an unsettling, compassionate survey of interlocking modalities and degrees of grief that also showed the subtle, guilty, craven selfishness that can inform any clinging to normality: it was far too close for comfort to an uncanny home.

The significance of the image of Juliusz's encirclement in the camp in Kawalerowicz's film is underlined by its recurrence – and possible deliberate echo – in Andrzej Wajda's contribution to the *Amour à vingt ans* (*Love at Twenty*, 1962) omnibus film. Zbyszek (Zbigniew Cybulski) has rescued a child from a zoo's bear-pit and been taken home afterwards by the admiring young beauty Basia (Barbara Kwiatkowska-Lass). When her friends visit and begin a game of blind man's buff, his blindfolding plunges Zbyszek into a memory of his wartime near-execution. He falls forward into a bathtub and the friends consider him simply drunk. Zbyszek may fulfil more of the expectations of normality than Kawalerowicz's protagonist, but both men are locked inside an incommunicable experience, both are surrounded, and both find past humiliation prolonged into a present one that also involves sexual emasculation: wartime experience has undermined secure selfhood and sexuality in each case. Wajda himself, however, may find escape by the process of symbolic delegation and projection otherwise known as artistic creation. For if Cybulski is his generation's double, and hence Wajda's, the director has another double in the young man Basia initially forsakes as a cowardly photographer of a scene in which he should have intervened. The boy's youth shows him as the truer double, as Wajda himself was too young to participate in underground fighting. As Zbyszek becomes one with the bear he fended off (as he slumps against the wall, the revellers sing of how well the bear sleeps), he shares its victimhood, and the boy gets the girl in the end. As in *Everything for Sale*, Wajda is doubled in all the main protagonists, whose combination surely issues from a fusion of real failure and fantasised triumph. Perhaps because his author has no autobiographical investment in him, Kawalerowicz's protagonist is allowed no exit from the labyrinth of his pain.

CHAPTER FIVE

WALLS AND FRONTIERS: REPRESENTING POLISH-JEWISH RELATIONS

The identification of Poland with 'the Jewish question' in Western perceptions has been cemented in recent years by Claude Lanzmann's brief for the prosecution, *Shoah* (1985), by the wide attention accorded Steven Spielberg's *Schindler's List* (1994), and by such events as the controversy over the planned construction of a convent and siting of a cross at the Auschwitz I site, and – more recently – the national soul-searching over the atrocity in which Poles burned their Jewish neighbours in a barn at Jedwabne during World War Two (Gross 2001). Within Poland, critics of Poles' treatments of Jews may be viewed as traitors who dirty the nest, while critics without are reminded of the number of Poles the state of Israel deems Righteous Among the Nations for hiding Jews during that self-same war. Coming to terms with this particular past would never be easy, and may not even be possible, irrespective of the obstacles to its exact representation thrown up by the post-war Stalinist regime that had every interest in tarring and feathering Polish adherents of the pre-war, largely democratic order as outdated national-ists and anti-Semites, regressive brakes upon the unfolding of socialism.

There are several obvious points at which one might begin to consider the treatment of Polish-Jewish relations in the films of People's Poland and in the Polish Republic still in its infancy. One might 'begin at the beginning' with *Ostatni etap* (*The Last Stop*, 1948), Wanda Jakubowska's sobering portrait of concentration camp life; with the first film to touch on the subject by Poland's leading post-war director, Andrzej Wajda, *Samson* (1961); or with Wojciech Has's neglected *Sanatorium pod klepsydrą* (*The Hour-Glass Sanatorium*, 1972), a reverie on the work of Bruno Schulz. Another potential starting-point might be Wajda's *Krajobraz po bitwie* (*Landscape After a Battle*, 1970), about the love of a Polish man and a Jewish woman in the imme-diate aftermath of World War Two, whose self-conscious echoes of *Ashes and Diamonds*, Wajda's most powerful and best-known film, indicate the importance he attached to the later work. Yet another might be his *Wesele* (*The Wedding*, 1973), his film of Stanisław Wyspiański's play, where the spirits who invade a *fin-de-siècle* Galician feast are summoned by a Jewish woman.

If I employ a different beginning it is for various reasons. Jakubowska's film is less con-cerned with Polish-Jewish relations than with the solidarity forged between women of various nations through their encounter with the camps' brutality; its subject is not what has come to be known as the Shoah itself. In Wajda's *Samson*, meanwhile (of which more later), the Jew who wanders beyond the Warsaw Ghetto walls, finally coming under the wing of a People's Army unit, is less distinctively Jewish than a cipher of alienation: Jewish homelessness dis-solves into existential isolation. Jakub Gold's step outside the Ghetto is an abstraction from the specificity of Jewishness that transforms him into the archetypal victim – and the abstraction is surely symptomatic of the element of unreality in the work that permits tendentious aggrandisement of the role of the People's Army in the Resistance, ignoring the Home Army. (Although accused of falsifying history in other respects, it is only here that Wajda truly distorts it.)[1] The film is very concerned to utilise the Polish anti-Semitism of the 1930s to validate the Communist cause. Jakub Gold is no Ghetto fighter but battles – when he does so – only under Communist auspices; the effort is typical of Wajda, however, in the desperate existentialism of the plunge into suicidally redemptive action. Has's *Hour-Glass Sanatorium*, for its part, does not so much focus on Polish-Jewish relations as unfold an extended hallucination of the life of turn-of-the-century village Jewry; and although the scene in which the timid protagonist – Jan Nowicki's mediumistic personification of the camera eye – crawls out of a cellar into a pogrom's aftermath was almost cut by the censor, the film having been made so shortly after the government-sponsored anti-Semitic campaign of 1968, its surrealistic self-enclosure makes correlation with reality problematic.

If *Landscape After a Battle* represents a problematic starting point, it is because the focus is less on Jewish suffering than that of the Pole. It is its Polish protagonist, Tadeusz, who has emerged from a concentration camp, while its Jewish one successfully hid from the Nazis. She is merely visiting the new, displaced persons camp Tadeusz inhabits, and her final shooting by American guards while trying to re-enter it is a terrible accident. Moreover, whereas Tadeusz defines himself as Polish first and foremost, Nina rejects her Jewish identity, denying ethnicity. It is the Pole who is obsessed by Nazi-inflicted suffering, not the Jew. Indeed, Nina is far less traumatised than Tadeusz, viewing some of his behaviour as deranged. Wajda's reckoning with Polish nationalism does not address the extent of its responsibility for Jewish suffering. Clearly, this brief encounter makes little attempt to typify Polish-Jewish relations, though an argument in its favour could deem typicality a chimera. Perhaps only if the Tadeusz figure had been Jewish, and the visitor Polish, would Polish-Jewish relations have become central. Insofar as it gives an oneiric allegorical X-ray of late 1960s and early 1970s Poland, it seems both an exoneration and an indictment of Polish attitudes to the Jews: an exoneration, for the intensity of Tadeusz's suffering virtually justifies his rancid self-absorption, and Nina's desire to leave the Polish environment is figured not as an expulsion but as a choice of freedom the Pole himself masochistically refuses, or self-pityingly knows is unavailable to him; but an indictment also, for Nina dies, partly because of that self-absorption, which is a failure truly to recognise the neighbour. This ambiguity renders the film deeply uncomfortable and private, almost self-nauseated, so it feels like a bad dream, curdling in self-involution and self-hatred. It is as if the self-accusation of *Wszystko na sprzedaż* (*Everything for Sale*, 1968) had lost the dynamism, and sense of possible resolution, of the psychodrama and collapsed into a festering melancholia. In *The Wedding*, meanwhile, Rachel's actions, arising out of marginalisation as they do, may indeed bespeak a witch-like power of revenge, but Polish-Jewish relations are themselves marginal to the film's hectic panorama of fin-de-siècle Galicia.[2] The central concern is with Polish Hamletism.[3]

Why then begin, as I do, with a film Wajda made shortly thereafter, *Ziemia obiecana* (*The Promised Land*, 1975)? Not simply because the disjunctiveness of Polish-Jewish relations lies at the heart of the Reymont novel on which it is based, but also because – for all its fusion of the febrile and the academic – the interest in these relations displayed by the film marks the first stirring of a theme to be amplified in subsequent years by the Flying University (those meetings in private flats, hounded by the authorities, at which an unofficial view of the problems of Polish culture and history was developed), and then by Solidarity: the need to claw back from the state the image of a more inclusive pre-war society. Among the things included in that society, of course, had been a large and enormously significant Jewish community. But although certain intellectuals realised that deconstruction of the state's mendacious version of the past also meant critique of the tradition of Polish anti-Semitism, in far too many cases the idealisation of the inter-war period in the popular consciousness did nothing to prevent the recycling of some of that era's stereotypes, including the resuscitation of the ugly bugbear of the 'Żydokomuna' (the phantasmagoria of the Communist Party as a 'Jewish Commune'). It is possible – I will argue – to read Wajda's *The Promised Land* as a seismograph of this contradiction: consciously espousing the liberal intellectual commitment to do justice to the Jews, but unconsciously loath to relinquish the stereotypes guaranteeing a popular appeal Wajda also craves.

Wajda's film, and the foreign reactions it sparked, illustrate an unfortunate feature of so much Polish and Jewish discussion of the two peoples' relations: so fraught have those relations often been that the unreasoning passions intellectuals wish-fulfillingly seek to relegate to the popular consciousness threaten to swamp their own discourse also. This is exemplified by the tone of debate over Poles' treatment of Jews during World War Two by Richard Lukas and David Engel in *The Slavic Review*[4] or the reception of Lanzmann's *Shoah* in terms that saw viewers with reservations dubbed anti-Semites.[5] 'It all begins with a wall', Lech Wałęsa remarked during ceremonies commemorating the fiftieth anniversary of the Warsaw Ghetto Uprising. He was speaking primarily, of course, of the wall the Nazis erected around the Ghetto, but that wall's physical collapse does not preclude the mental persistence of its after-image. Is the mind of a culture a photographic plate, forever scarred by that to which it was once exposed, or can new impressions be made? Just how arduous the assault on the mental wall can be is apparent both in the narratives of the films I will be considering and in the reception accorded those of Wajda in particular. The problem scores *The Promised Land* so deeply that it may serve as the master-text of the portion of the Polish and Jewish story told by some of Poland's best films. Among others, I will also consider, among others: two works by Wajda's close collaborator, Agnieszka Holland, *Bittere Ernte* (*Angry Harvest*, 1985) and *Europa, Europa* (1991); the eighth section of Krzysztof Kieślowski's *Dekalog* (*The Decalogue*, 1989); and finally Wajda's *Korczak* (1990). The fact that Polish directors' most powerful and rewarding treatments of the theme emerge during the twilight of People's Poland – and may even, as in the case of Holland's films, be produced beyond its borders – indicates the selectiveness of official versions of the events of 1939–45. For comparison's sake, though, and also because of the inherent significance of these works, I also include films from the very middle of the history of People's Poland, such as the above-mentioned *Samson,* and the remarkable third section of Stanisław Różewicz's *Birth Certificate,* which complicate the stereotypical view of the period as one unremittingly deep-dyed in anti-Semitism, and one from 1996, Wajda's *Holy Week.*[6] The selectiveness of this brief history of Polish-Jewish relations in Polish cinema is motivated further by a desire to give more than cursory treatment to works of great complexity and richness: only analysis in some detail can begin to do *them* justice.

THE PROMISED LAND: WAJDA'S FAUSTIAN BARGAIN?

Wajda's *The Promised Land* is based on Władysław Reymont's novel of the same title about the polyp-like growth of late nineteenth-century Łódź – a metropolitan Moloch sucking life from the ground and peasants from the soil, its neverending construction's omnipresent scaf-folding continually elbowing passersby into the equally omnipresent mud of the streets. The Fata Morgana of rapid wealth it throws up seduces Karol Borowiecki, a gifted textile colourist, Don Juan and elegant member of the Polish gentry, to cast aside tradition and even excel in the ruthlessness of the robber barons he mimics to succeed. By betraying his *szlachta* back-ground he becomes, as his Jewish friend Moryc Welt remarks, the biggest Lodzermensch of them all. Together with Moryc and the German Max Baum he founds a factory that later burns down mysteriously. Unable to stomach the drudgery of rebuilding he marries the plain, naïve daughter of a German textile millionaire, breaking his engagement with his Polish fiancée. The Positivist programme of national reconstruction through '*praca u podstaw*' ('work at the foundations') succeeds materially but at the cost of moral failure and offers no solace to Polish national pride, being parasitic on prior German achievement. Reymont's version of Positivism would conclude bleakly were it not for the final sentimental *volte face* whereby Karol recog-nises his life's emptiness and determines to imitate the philanthropy of his ex-fiancée.

Julian Krzyżanowski, the great Polish literary historian, once described Reymont's meth-ods as cinematic. He may have been prompted to do so by the play of looks in the Łódź theatre scene, for instance, which does indeed anticipate the shot/reverse-shot alternations of classic film grammar. Thus Wajda's turn to it in the confident early years of Edward Gierek's industrial effort to make Poland rich quick is doubly piquant. (Perhaps unsurprisingly, given the power over Polish criticism wielded by the censor, the period's Polish reviewers do not make the con-nection but seem rather to be caught up in the film's own expansive fervour.) Although Wajda's version diverges from Reymont's in a myriad of ways – some of which I will list – the two major ones concern the plot's reshaping to exonerate Moryc (in Reymont he colludes in the Jewish industrialists' conspiracy against Karol) and the elimination of sources of hope and the possibility of capitalism's self-reform. Indeed, the film could be said to take an almost vulgar Marxist delight in the apocalyptic spectacle of the industrial Sublime, its pulsing score beating out doom to a capitalist world brimful of contradictions.

For one Polish critic, Janusz Zatorski, *The Promised Land* represents a *volte face* in Wajda's career. A series of films that had critiqued the Polish gentry tradition is followed here by a cata-strophist delineation of the suicidal effects of tradition's dismissal (Zatorski 1975). The shifting of the idyllic opening of volume two to the film's beginning makes the subsequent passage to Łódź seem like an expulsion from Eden and corroborates Zatorski's reading. Nevertheless, his salutary interpretation overlooks the contradictoriness of a film that upholds tradition on some levels but subverts it on others. Tradition is undermined, for instance, when the Catholic priest complacently sprinkling Karol's factory confronts its scantily-dressed female workers and appears pompously shocked; when Karol's father fulminates against his son's violation of four hundred years of tradition, becoming the impotent *senex* of melodramatic farce; or whenever images of female nudity obtrude from the work's over-ripe surface. The drum-roll-ing Marxism of the menacing close, where Karol orders troops to gun down striking work-ers, implies the bankruptcy of a ruling class that may have destroyed tradition but itself has no future: whatever future there is lies with the shot worker clutching a piece of red flag in the street. Wajda's perspective is clearly anti-clerical, in an anti-traditional Marxist tradition. A devastatingly succinct early montage juxtaposes louring smokestacks with industrialists' prayers in Polish, German and Hebrew (the order is interesting, suggesting that responsibility for Łódź's perversion of humanity lies with the Poles presented first – which is surprising in the context of the narrative, for which Stach Wilczek, the Pole in question, is only a millionaire in the making): religion and industrialism join hands in exploitation. Nor is Wajda's variety of adaptation exactly reverential, playing so fast and loose with the logic (assuming it may be dignified as such) of Reymont's plot and characterisation as virtually to constitute less an adaptation than a set of variations on his themes. Throughout the film, the currents that maintain tradition criss-cross turbulently with the ones that subvert it.

It is surely an index of the film's contradictoriness that it could both be accused of anti-Semitism and defended as an attempt to drain off the anti-Semitism of Reymont's novel. There is justification for both reactions. In the standard survey of modern Polish cinema Bolesław Michałek and Frank Turaj comment on the accusations:

> something happened that no one expected, least of all Wajda. After showings in Scandinavia and the United States in 1976, *The Promised Land* was charged with containing anti-Semitism by virtue of its negative portrayal of the Jews in Łódź. (Michałek & Turaj 1988: 154)

In rebuttal they argue that:

> the real conflict in the film has nothing to do with nationalities; it has to do with capital and labour. All this was obscured by the allegations. Wajda, whose record of integrity in matters of human rights and any kind of discrimination, whose conduct during and after the political crisis of 1968 with its distinct elements of anti-Semitism, should have made him the least likely to be the subject of such charges, was not given credibility. To this day, against any sensible interpretation of the reality of the thing, the film is thought to be anti-Semitic in Scandinavia and the United States. Interestingly, this is not at all the case in France or Italy, where perhaps Zolaesque realism, with all its candour and completeness, is better understood. (Ibid.)

A defence of Wajda's film on the grounds of its adherence to Zolaesque realism is nevertheless far from compelling. The racist stereotypes permeating Reymont's novel render it anything but an innocent text. And even if one rejects the Adornian argument that Zola's strategies cannot be employed for the production of valuable art 72 years after the novelist's death – after all, whether or not the film is first-rate may well be a separate issue from whether or not it displays prejudice – it is undeniable that an artist working in the aftermath of the Holocaust ought to consider the ultimate effects of the use of stereotype and racial caricature by the fascist regimes of the 1930s and hence be circumspect when approaching a work that employs them. At the same time, insofar as stereotyping is a form of generalisation it is arguably not necessarily pernicious. If, as De Tocqueville argues in *Democracy in America*, generalisation flourishes in cultures addicted to speed, whose members economically pack a maximum of instances into the portmanteau of a single notion, then it is very much part of modernity. (A certain unacknowledged or unconscious mental bombast can result, as in the case of such words – appropriately termed 'loaded' – as 'violence' or 'democracy' itself.) The condemnation of generalisation may itself be a malign generalisation about generalisation, for generalisations conscious of their status as the opposites of particularities they make no claim to absorb are simply economical modes of thought, self-consciously fictive. The same may apply to the stereotype: its insulation from the concrete renders its user's apparent subscription to anti-Semitic beliefs quite compatible with humane treatment of all their Jewish acquaintances (evidence perhaps less of hypocrisy than of the logical separation of the abstract and the concrete, the class and the member). The scapegoat is always already non-existent, and the persistence of anti-Semitism in countries now without Jews may be less paradoxical than it seems (and may not simply indicate ideology's tendency to lag behind actuality). The scapegoat is abstract: no single Jew, or even crowd of Jews, is The Jew – who thus becomes Eternal, tantalisingly beyond reach.

Wajda did indeed reflect on the issue of stereotyping. In an interview given during the film's shooting he stated, 'it can't be the case that if someone is a Jew he cheats, if a German – he's dull but hardworking … I do not intend to present the differences in their characters in this way' (Malatyńska 1974). And so Moryc Welt is no longer the traitor unable to comprehend Karol's willingness to share a financial windfall but, in the words of one critic, 'a fine, loyal and helpful boy' (Poczmański 1975). Zygmunt Kałużyński, musing on why Wajda's 'dogged darkening of moral perspective' lightens here, concludes that often in his films 'the accent of purity' assumes the form of male friendship (Kałużyński 1975b). Although Kałużyński lauds the film's recovery of 'a Jewish culture we had long forgotten about', it does not occur to him that the change in Moryc's characterisation might have been motivated by a desire to avoid anti-Semitic stereotyping. Could this be because the portrayal of all the film's other Jews partakes of the stereotypical? Wajda transforms the novel's pre-eminent Jew, Moryc, but leaves his milieu untouched – perhaps because anti-Semitism is so thoroughly woven into Reymont's novel that its complete removal would have caused the tapestry to unravel. The effect is one of aesthetic inconsistency: as in photomontage, a figure from one space is superimposed upon an incompatible one. A realist figure is pasted onto the background of satire.

The problem arises most clearly in the near-total and verbatim incorporation of two of Reymont's scenes involving Jewish industrialists: Stein's announcement of the death of Victor Hugo, of whom his master has never heard; and the duel of wits between Moryc and Grosglik. In each, the industrialist is buffoonish and grasping, and the roles are played in the style of high theatrical farce. Given the film's thoroughgoing rearrangement of Reymont's chronology, its additions to the story and its shifting and fusion of characters (for example, Grosglik's reasons for preferring Catholicism to Protestantism are distributed between Moryc and Karol; Kessler incorporates elements of Grosglik and even speaks one of Moryc's lines; Max's declaration that he can read Moryc's infamous intentions from his face is placed in the mouth of Moryc himself, and so on), it is all the more surprising that it should have done no more than lightly edit the originals of these scenes. Wajda's transformation of Moryc may indeed have undermined one of the mainstays of Reymont's anti-Semitic argument, but the theatrical showman in him cannot resist these scenes' pointed farce. Their comedy, however, cannot be entirely innocent now – just as one can no longer laugh at the discomfiture of the Merchant of Venice. Paradoxically, while viewers ignorant of the novel may find the narrative at points too elliptical to be fully comprehensible (when Karol complains that Anka, his fiancée, is making a hospital of his home and she refers to a person with broken ribs, the film's omission of the accident at his factory construction site prevents one knowing what she means), those with an awareness of it may find themselves questioning the many arbitrary changes (one of the most glaring being the suicide of Trawiński, who receives a loan from Baum in the novel). Their rationale seems to lie in a will to maximalise contrast, both within and between images. At the same time, the retention of an absurdly large number of the original characters reduces their parts to rapid walk-ons and augments the speed and indirection of a mode of narration that seeks to overpower and bewilder, mimicking the boom-or-bust atmosphere of Łódź itself. It is a narrative style that fuses Welles (the wide-angle lenses) with Eisenstein (the politics, farce and shock-cuts).

Wajda's perspective throughout is relentlessly external. His teeth-baring Borowiecki knows none of the inner struggles of Reymont's and has no hope of the somewhat sentimental redemption the novelist finally proposes. For Maria Janion, Wajda's ending, in which Karol orders troops to fire on striking workers, is an Ensor-like tableau of grotesque marionettes (Janion 1975). Its nightmare quality heightened by the percussive score and the absence of natural sound, it reveals Borowiecki as a waxwork recruit to the capitalist club of the undead. But whereas Janion speaks of Borowiecki in terms of 'the enigma of internal emptiness', for Poczmański the encapsulation within him of all the worst features of capitalism amounts to the character's remystification (Poczmański 1975). Wajda's externalising perspective may even be deemed alarmingly similar to that of Karol who drains the life from everything he touches – Reymont's human machine. And here Wajda's approach is surprisingly close to that of the novel itself, which – for all its idealisation of the self-sacrificing Polish women whose hands workers kiss uninterruptedly – oscillates between condemnation of Karol and an incorporation into the narrative voice of the contempt so often ascribed to Karol: Wajda's naturalism, like Reymont's, is in part crypto-expressionist. Tadeusz Robak notes the film's allegiance to two stylistics, 'one true to reality and one inclined to the pamphlet' (Robak 1975). The inclination towards reality so often deemed the defining quality of film (by André Bazin or Siegfried Kracauer, for instance) did indeed form part of Wajda's motivation for making *The Promised Land*. Speaking of his wish to record nineteenth-century buildings while that was still possible, he emphasised the pleasure of shooting a historical film with the freedom of movement in real locales more characteristic of a contemporary one (Malatyńska 1975), be it in the outlandishly appointed mansions of Piotrowska Street or in textile factories notoriously still using ancient machines. Many reviewers, meanwhile, would stress the educational value of old Łódź's necromantic evocation. Yet Wajda's Łódź is clearly also a dreamlike capitalist City of Dreadful Night, where infernal flames shoot from the soil to consume factories and humanity is mere flesh, orgiastically grasped if female, fed to machines that then spew it forth if male. The insistent wide-angle lenses both provide the space Wajda said was needed by the film's fast-walking, fast-talking protagonists and introduce a sense of vertigo reminiscent of the somewhat meretricious contemporary hallucinations of Ken Russell, whose name often featured in reviews. The distorting lenses' heightening of speed is accentuated by the fast cuts between contrasting scenes, the movement from one to the next the twanging of the elastic space those lenses generate. So precipitously does Mada Muller chase Karol through the family palace that she slides in disarray along its floor.

Although Wajda's reworking of Reymont's novel could have sparked as much controversy as had his version of Wyspiański's *The Wedding*, widespread public ignorance of a work far less central to the Polish literary canon confined controversy to its explicit eroticism.[8] Teenagers lured by the prospect of a Polish version of Bertolucci's *Ultimo tango a Parigi* (*Last Tango in Paris*, 1972) may have voiced their disappointment, but responses by spectators at Warsaw's 'Luna' and 'Palladium' cinemas and Lublin's 'Kosmos' showed that 'the question of eroticism in the film arouses most controversy' (Anon 1975).[9] Magdalena Enke, a pensioner raised in Łódź, praised the work's verisimilitude in other respects but found these scenes irritating. Since their insertion may be read in part as Wajda's defiant assertion of membership of the international film community, of whose recently expanded norms for the representation of sexuality he avails himself, it is ironic that he was unable to foresee some of the international repercussions of his attempt both to tell and to rework Reymont's story of the would-be Polish entrepreneur eaten up by Jews fearful lest his plans for high-quality goods destroy the market for their cheap ones. Perhaps Reymont's story truly could not be redeemed, and Borowiecki's Faustian bargain in a sense mirrored Wajda's own. His international success and Oscar nomination brought him more than he had bargained for.

SAMSON

An alternative beginning to this essay might, of course, as noted above, have been the first sustained address of 'the Jewish question' in Wajda's work, *Samson*. *Samson* is the story of the wartime experiences of Jakub Gold, a Jew who had been imprisoned in inter-war Poland for the manslaughter of a member of an anti-Semitic gang of students that attacked him during his studies at Warsaw University. His neighbour in the next cell is Pankrat, a friendly communist. As war breaks out, a falling bomb liberates the prisoners. During the war, Jakub finds himself trapped outside the wall of the ghetto, seeking shelter in Polish houses. He finds it in the apartment of Lucyna, who herself proves to be Jewish and passes successfully as 'Aryan', an option removed from Jakub by his stereotypically 'Jewish' looks. When Jakub leaves her, rejecting her love, however, Lucyna surrenders herself to the Gestapo. Jakub's next bolthole is with Malina, one of his old prison cell-mates. Malina's death sends him on the run again, and he is taken in by a People's Army resistance group. As their printing shop is raided by German soldiers, Jakub dies defending it, bringing it down on the head of the invaders in a reprise of Samson's revenge on the Philistines.

Samson began its filmic life as a screenplay by Kazimierz Brandys, the author of the original novella, with no director assigned at first. The Script Assessment Commission voiced some doubts about the proposed adaptation, but was generally favourable. Among its members, Krzysztof Teodor Toeplitz said its flashbacks would be *vieux jeux*, unless they followed the practice of Alain Resnais' *Hiroshima mon amour* (1959). Aleksander Ścibor-Rylski both admired Brandys' ruthlessness *vis-à-vis* his own novella and regretted some of the excisions, such as the hero's drunken urination upon the Tomb of the Unknown Soldier. Tadeusz Konwicki saw the curse hanging over Jakub as one of physical strength: 'the issue is not the martyrology of the Jews'. Stanisław Dygat concurred: 'this does not give the impression of a film about the history of a Jew. Everything has been translated into a question of general human suffering, a man's persecution by other men', adding that 'unfortunately there are many works whose upshot is that during the Occupation the Poles were just as dangerous as the Germans. Here one can sense an atmosphere of good-will, and this gives the script a more general, universal character.' Summing up the general approval, Culture Minister Tadeusz Zaorski described Jakub as someone whose face has given him a complex: 'He wants to prove that he's different inside, fuller and deeper than his face can tell, that he is capable of nobler impulses.' In an implication Zaorski either leaves to be read between the lines, or simply overlooks (rather, as both Dygat and Konwicki had failed to notice, the contradiction between the work's 'universality' and its insistence on the importance of Jakub's *looks*) Jakub is seeking to controvert the racist, anti-

Semitic beliefs that (a) there is a 'typically Jewish' face and (b) that Jews are incapable of 'noble' actions (the adjective 'noble' recalling the Polish word for the gentry, the *szlachta*, which felt it had a monopoly upon selflessness) (FN, KK, A-214 poz. 158).

One of Toeplitz's remarks during the discussion raised a question that would be central to Wajda's film: 'Existentialist literature has a great deal to say about man's loneliness, but these issues are not blown up in *Samson*, and perhaps that is not for the best, as the film would be more disturbing and become a more contemporary work' (FN, KK, A-214 poz. 158). The work's positioning with regard to existentialism is indeed an interesting one. Here the casting of the French Serge Merlin is crucial. Initially, Wajda sought a Jewish actor within Poland, but could not find one; he notes how this underlines the devastation of Poland's once-thriving Jewish community. Merlin was recruited through the efforts of Kazimierz Brandys. Given the novella's foregrounding of the status of Jakub's face, which is described as a virtual curse upon him, the question of whether or not to select a 'stereotypically Jewish' actor could have become an awkward one, as choosing such an actor would have suggested the accuracy of the stereotype. Wajda's lack of choice in the matter was probably fortunate, resolving a possible dilemma. For not only does the casting of the 'delicate and short' Merlin (Wajda 2000b: 40) undermine the novella's emphasis on Jakub's strength, diverting the film away from the 'action film' Wajda felt it ought to be; the non-stereotypicality of his face also underlines the work's status as a general, almost allegorically existential declaration of human isolation. That allegorical dimension may clash with the realism of the film, but it simultaneously justifies both its slightly distanced air of stylistic abstraction – read by many critics either as a sign of coldness or that Wajda was nearing the end of a once-fruitful vein of interest in wartime trauma (Mruklik 1969: 52–3; Rhode 1966: 179–81) – and that other distancing element, the mythical title.

Alongside the partial allegiance to existentialism, however, the work retains Brandys' vision of a Polish resistance loyal exclusively to the Communist Party's People's Army, with the majority Home Army nowhere in sight. One could, of course, imagine a scenario even more pleasing to the Party: Jakub might seek succour with the Home Army – many of whose members were indeed anti-Semitic – only to be rebuffed. The absence of the Home Army permits Wajda and Brandys a delicate tight-rope walk between their two constituencies: on the one hand, the Party, gratified by aggrandisement of its own role; on the other, a Polish populace that would react violently against a negative image of the Home Army. Too controversial for easy treatment, the Home Army may well have been bound to be simply airbrushed out.

Samson thus represents an uneasy cocktail of communism and existentialism. The existentialism, meanwhile, lies not just in the (Sartrean) preoccupation with action, commitment and responsibility noted by Barthémy Amanguel (Michalek 1973: 65), but also in the Camusian one with suicide, which is also linked to issues of passivity and feminisation. The work's often tragic irony detaches feminisation from the passivity traditionally associated with it. Of central importance here is the critically ignored parallelism between the work's two acts of suicide: Lucyna's self-surrender to the Gestapo, stating '*ich bin Jüdin*'; and Jakub's final, self-sacrificial hurling of the grenade in the print shop. In each case, the person takes control of an inevitable death. The notion that death is indeed inescapable validates Jakub's assertion that there is a collective fate of the Jews which he, as an individual, has no right to elude. The position of the survivor would be one of guilt, as it has been, alas, for so many survivors who wondered what right they had to elude a death that enveloped so many. (Jakub's escapes thus become postponements of a suicide he is not yet ready to commit – a death with which he has not yet identified in full, as is shown by his escape from a ghetto where he has worked carrying corpses, and over a cemetery wall. The death-drive is a leap into the arms of the collectivity.) Perhaps unsurprisingly in a work entitled *Samson*, feminisation revolves around the question of *hair*. At one point, Lucyna tries to control her fate by dyeing her hair white (the casting of a Polish actress was clearly no problem in this case), while the importance of Jakub's hair is accentuated by his head-band and, of course, the work's title. After all, he is about to become Samson, who recovers his strength as his hair lengthens. Paradoxically, of course, long hair traditionally connotes femininity. Here, however, the femininity is empowered. And at this level, as in that of the casting of Merlin, the work undermines stereotypical representation. Could it be that in fact the face does not matter because what *does* is the hair?

Samson's iconographic use of hair shows it to possess greater subtlety than has been noted generally. Other subtleties pervade its linkage of ghettoisation to a multi-levelled spatial enclosure. The increasing lack of a place for Jakub is apparent not just in the characteristic spaces he inhabits – the prison, the Ghetto, the cellar – but in the recurrent emphasis upon the smallness of the windows through which he peers out. Their frames are continual reminders of the shrinkage of the reality of the larger frame they echo. One of the key dramatisations of this diminution is the memorable sequence of the boarding up of the Ghetto. As plank after plank is added to the fence, less and less is visible of the people huddled behind it, until in the end they disappear. This moment also mobilises the work's characteristic irony concerning the relationship between Christian imagery – and hence Polish experience – and the experience of the Jews. As the boards are nailed to the fence's cross-bars from the edge of the screen inwards, an image of a cross emerges for a while, giving way in the end to a blank array of boards: the link between Jewish and Christian experience surfaces momentarily, then undergoes repression or simple forgetting. The most telling and poignant ironies link the Christian and Jewish stars. When Jakub seeks refuge with Malina, a girl holding a Christmas star opens the door. It recalls the Jewish star imprinted on Jakub's back (a star that transposes the novella's curse of Jakub's face into a new form, one that is culturally imposed, and invisible to its bearer, rather than biologically ineluctable). The connection and irony are underlined as the subsequent scene is shot from behind Jakub, creating a force-field between his coat's star and the multiple stars of the Christmas tree beyond the table. The shooting of Jakub from behind at the film's outset had dramatised the importance of the issue of seeing the face (rather like the presentation of Joan Crawford at the start of George Cukor's *A Woman's Face* [1941]), but it had also breathed a dream-like, mysterious air. That opening verges on the surreal, as the falling leaflets suggest autumn even as one is told it is spring. Jakub's story will soon find itself in the winter in which most of it is played out. The move to winter is also one into a certain abstraction. The seasonal progression matches the tightening of the space around Jakub. In the end, the only place available to him is a death he has to embrace, like the chained Samson. No wonder death can double as the door to an existential freedom that is also the embrace of the collectivity sought by Marxism and identity politics.

BIRTH CERTIFICATE

Another possible starting point for this essay might have been Stanisław Różewicz's moving, self-effacing three-novella study of war's effects upon children, *Birth Certificate*. The weight it accords Jewish suffering is apparent from the triple privileging of the one section devoted it, 'Kropla krwi' ('A Drop of Blood'), which comes last, is the longest, and is the only one in which the film's title object (the birth certificate) figures prominently. Not for nothing did Jerzy Płażewski deem it the most important episode, memorably characterising the entire film as 'a poem told in prose' (Płażewski 1961) (in other words, those of Konrad Eberhardt, 'fundamental matters are played out between the lines' [Eberhardt 1961: 4]). The three sections gradually approach the war's heart of darkness: there are no Jews in the first, a few being marched down the street in the second, but the third follows the wanderings of a young Jewish girl, Mirka, after the clearing of her ghetto. The step-by-step approach testifies to the filmmakers' tact and awareness of the deepening of all suffering as the war proceeded.

'A Drop of Blood' begins in a desolate ghetto courtyard, a few drifting mattress feathers giving evidence of a recent ransacking by the Nazis. Dispassionate and clear-eyed, the camera variously frames the apparently vacant space – as if registering shock, stage by stage, or waiting and checking to make sure it really is empty – before a cover is lifted and a large-eyed, sad girl's face emerges. It is Mirka (the luminous Beata Barszczewska), whom we will follow from now on. Initially she will wander alone through a world whose only sounds are the hostile ones of persecutory German voices. Sound is as important here as Płażewski had noted it was in the first novella (Płażewski 1961): Mirka may be safe where she is, but sound reveals the close proximity of an off-screen reality that is far from welcoming. If all that is safe is the frame, this is perilously little, and Mirka has to be constantly vigilant. Even when she has been taken under the wing of a Polish network that protects Jewish children, outside space remains a source of danger. After all, her current hiding place may be broken up by the Gestapo just as the first one reserved for her had been, before she could arrive there. So she sits inside, looking through the window, watching other children playing. When she was on her own even their childish boisterousness had become a cruel expression of the world's hostility, as their sticks banging on the metal pipe where she slept awoke her, unbeknownst to them. After all, even other children can threaten her, like the peasants met on the open road who force her to kneel and recite the Lord's Prayer to demonstrate her non-Jewishness. Looked after by the simple seamstress Mrs Cieślikowa, and hearing a knock on the door, she asks the lady's husband if the neighbours will give her away. The reply is not entirely reassuring: 'Why? You haven't done anything wrong.' A knock at the door is all the more alarming when she is alone. Just such a knock comes as she has begun to relax and started playing with a doll she has found: the music that represents her lowering of her guard suddenly halts and she hides behind a curtain.

If the world around Mirka is perilous, though, there is little sense that the Poles themselves pose much danger. There are hints that they might do so: one recalls Mirka's fear of the neighbour betraying her, and the doctor's wife taking her by train to a new hiding place cuts short the girl's playful interchanges with the man opposite … just in case. However, what we *see* is a world where Poles provide security and danger emanates almost entirely from the Germans. The absence of *szmalcownicy* – those who blackmailed Jews by threatening to disclose their identity – for instance, corresponds to the reduction of possible Polish threats to a muted, almost buried undertone that is surely a limitation of this otherwise limpid, lucid, moving episode. Although justifiable in terms of the impossibility of engaging all aspects of Mirka's situation in a short film, it is nevertheless uncomfortably close to the official state ideology's focus on German responsibility and Polish martyrology.

Mirka's experience is all the more poignant for the restraint of its registration. The film moves through her story rather as she does through life: uprightly, slowly, as if reality is a minefield, and with a stiffness that suggests the whole body is an unhealed wound, a throbbing bruise. Again and again she appears either in the long-shot that reveals her isolation, or in close-ups displaying her eyes on the verge of tears, her burden of ingrained grief. Różewicz's halting matter-of-factness is similarly resistant to the ease and easiness of tears. Masterfully, he reserves his most powerful effects for the ending, where the birth certificate comes into play with a degree of fearful suspense that puts the viewer firmly in the position of Mirka herself.

The end sees Mirka concealed in a Polish orphanage, equipped with a new identity: that of Marysia Malinowska, a Polish girl whose mother died in childbirth and whose father is an imprisoned Polish officer. This detail, however, carries a musical undertone of the endangered status of even an apparently 'safe' identity, as it recalls the second episode, and its revelation of the Germans' probable treatment of such officers. Shortly after her arrival the orphanage is visited by a Gestapo officer and an official of the racial institute, intent on seeing if it has any new children. A Polish man translates for them, though this reminder of their dependence upon Polish co-operation and of the fact that not all Poles were *dans le vrai*, is slightly muted by the contrast between his behaviour and the threatening expressions of the Germans. They order an assembly of all the children, quickly dismissing the boys. Their decision to inspect the girls more closely arouses all the anxieties our lengthy identification with Mirka has primed us to feel. There is both suspense and a profound moral questioning of the selectivity of film itself, as the Germans pick out a different child, ordering her to walk to the room's end. We may well ask ourselves whether we feel relief – and ought to do so – because Mirka has not been selected. Why should the film focus on any one child, to the detriment of others? Was not what occurred at the ramp in Auschwitz a process of selection? Any dubious relief is short-lived though, as Mirka – lodged as far back as possible, in the second row – is told to come forward. She recoils involuntarily, with only the wall behind her. As the Germans peruse her papers and the Gestapo officer tells the seated racial specialist that '*all diese polnische Papiere sind falsch*' ('all these Polish papers are false'), we are encouraged to fear the worst. We remain fearful as the specialist feels her head, only to hear '*sie hat ausdrückliche nordische Kennzeichen*' ('she has pronounced Nordic characteristics'). She is told to walk a few steps, but her walk towards the other girl in fact separates her from her; her gait also proves her racial origin. Not a drop of German blood should be lost, so this girl should go to a German family or orphanage. The Polish man explains this smilingly to Mirka, as if it were a benediction.

The irony becomes poignant as the work ends by contrasting two faces, rather as Paul Celan's famous 'Todesfuge' ends with the stark juxtaposition of the hair of the German Margarethe and the Jewish Sulamith, and recalling the way in which the film itself had begun with a German inspecting a child: the German's narrowed eyes, wary to the last, despite what he has said, and Mirka staring ahead, her large eyes both stoical and pleading. This child may survive – and the story was in fact based on a survivor's memoirs – but that last impression is one of her piercing isolation. If, as Zygmunt Kałużyński rightfully notes, Różewicz's films differ from others of the Polish School by offering not 'a reckoning with the recent past' but 'an attempt to cleanse oneself, heal, and begin a new life' (Kałużyński 1961), the final question in Mirka's eyes is what sort of life survives in such survival. Will she again ask for poison, saying she did not want to live, as she once asked the Polish doctor who first took her in?

POLISH AND JEWISH ESCHATOLOGIES: *HOW FAR FROM HERE, HOW NEAR?*

As noted above, among the Polish intellectuals of the Flying University the 1970s saw an investigation of the inter-war period that – shocked by the anti-Semitic campaign of 1968 and the ease with which Mieczysław Moczar had tapped undead resentments – was in part fuelled by an idealisation of a lost, more ethnically diverse Poland. One of the first forays into that period was found in *Jak daleko stąd jak blisko* (*How Far from Here, How Near*, 1972) by Tadeusz Konwicki, whose groundbreaking novel *Sennik współczesny* (*A Contemporary Dreambook*, 1963) had already employed a hermetic poetic to evoke his wartime youth in the Vilnius area and who was preoccupied by its amputation from post-war Poland, its thrusting into the underground realm of death and memory. But in Konwicki's work it is a phantom limb that still twitches, with a phantom population that includes many Jews.

Hardly surprisingly, given its title, the film's key formal device is the zoom, which demonstrates how nearness can suddenly become far, the distant can leap into an uncanny closeness. (For the past's disinterment, as Freud noted, is indeed the uncanny, the atmosphere of which hangs heavy in the drifting swathes of Zygmunt Konieczny's brooding music.) That closeness can also be utopian though. The title's foregrounding of the question of camera distance marks the point at which the work's extreme self-consciousness – linked to its male sense of life as riven with shame following military defeat and the continual defeats of the post-war everyday under Soviet occupation – becomes self-referentiality.

Konwicki's very first image is of a Jew suspended horizontally in flight, clouds or smoke playing around him. The camera holds on the Jew. A later image of a Jew hanging from a tree presents him vertically. In each case his flight is arrested in the immobility associated with death. The flames flickering round him are transposed into a blue negative, the aestheticisation of the fantastic serving also to derealise the image into bearability, render suffering – particularly the Jewish suffering so often deemed taboo for Gentile artists – representable. It also shows the mingling of water's blue with fire that is one of the blurred distinctions the hero Andrzej mentions to his father. The ever-burning quality of the flame is emphasised by blue's inability to douse it. The Jew signifies both the East of Konwicki's childhood and, through his burning, the Warsaw Ghetto Uprising. And yet he may not be burning; the vapour billowing round him may be merely cloud. But these clouds in their turn, it later emerges, may indeed be smoke, that of hell, as the image's repetition near the film's end is paired with Andrzej's voice speaking of imagining a Jew thrust into nothingness by devils for his sins. Between reality and the fantastic reference is undecidable: at the film's very end his flight will again be shown in negative, but this time surrounded by red, while the voice-over suggests that he may not be going to hell but labouring towards heaven.

The Jew's point of view is both near and far. Near through his identification with the air and hence with the airborne camera whose alienated, free-associative movement matches that of Andrzej's consciousness; but far because no Pole can dare to speak for Jewish experience. Jewish messianism may in a sense prefigure the Polish one, but a terrible difference separates the fates of the two peoples. The Pole who levitates at the party, his arms flapping as if in recollection of Bogumił Kobiela as the plaster Polish eagle of Skolimowski's *Hands Up!*, only parodies the airborne Jew: he is heard crashing embarrassingly to the ground off-screen the moment after a wide-eyed female spectator had remarked on his rise. And Maks, the dead-alive friend who haunts Andrzej, falls to his death from a highrise. The Polish eagles' wings are clipped.

Andrzej may wonder at one point whether his unknown grandfather was a wandering Jewish merchant, but this is the last option he considers as he reviews a list of possible ancestors, the others being a Lithuanian peasant and a Russian soldier. The depth of his displacement may be seen in his not even entertaining the option of a Polish forebear. It is as if Polishness is the least desirable of identities. His identity is a multicultural one that is also non-identity: of the many rituals the film shows – the ceremonies of marriage and funeral whereby communities affirm themselves – none involve Andrzej himself, and he sets himself against the religious procession his mother follows. This non-identity is of course also split identity, identity bifurcated and spilling out like an egg's yolk, hence the preoccupation with mirrors and their shattering, twins, doubling, substitution and projection. Thus in the case of the notion of messianism Andrzej first notes that he is aged 44, a number he adds is significant for Poles (he refuses to spell out the significance – its use by Mickiewicz, a key figure for Konwicki, and another Lithuanian Pole, to designate Poland's Messiah, though it also adventitiously designates Konwicki's own age at the time) and then declares it potentially as significant as 33 (an age he has outlived – so the messianism is deflated, as are the intimations of apocalypse by their placement in the mouth of the drunken Rura). He finally projects his own messianism onto his ex-wife by accusing her of it. If success in history means becoming its subject rather than its object, obsessive seduction may be a repeated denial of the feminisation of both self and nation (Polska, with a female suffix), a continual effort to place oneself on top in every sense. The Pole has to hold the gun hard, well aware of the danger of losing it and the sense of the self's boundedness it is taken up to establish and maintain. It was, of course, a lesson postwar Israel would determine never to forget.

TRAPS OF IDENTITY: AGNIESZKA HOLLAND

Beginning with her first successful television film, *Niedzielne dzieci* (*Sunday's Children*, 1976), where a couple seek to accelerate the adoption system by buying a baby destined for abortion, Agnieszka Holland's central theme is entrapment. Here, as later, the fundamental trap, the one that always betrays one, is the body itself. It may do so through its femininity (*Sunday's Children, Kobieta samotna* [*A Woman Alone*, 1981], *Angry Harvest*), crippling disability (*A Woman Alone*), Jewishness (the condition of circumcision in *Europa, Europa*) or youth (the many children in Holland's films suffer from what Sartre terms the 'existentially false' position of the child). The theme of biological constraint yields a naturalistic grittiness of style. The scenarios are richest when the different traps interlock, as in *Angry Harvest*, one of whose protagonists is both Jewish and female, or *Europa, Europa*, about a Jew who is also a child.[10] For Holland, Jewishness – and the Polish-Jewish nexus – is of interest as one of the many factors that threaten one's freedom by placing one in the disempowered position of outsider. The yearning for freedom animating her work is what enables her to function within the mainstream of the Polish art of the last two centuries, even as the focus on non-Polish marginal identities and their oppression moves her away from it. In her best films, a powerful and complex dialectic results. It is hardly surprising that the protagonist of *Provincial Actors* should identify so deeply with the hero of Wyspiański's *Wyzwolenie* (*Liberation*, 1903) as to contest a modern director's mindless experimentalism, thereby sabotaging his own attempt to escape the provinces – the setting of so much of Holland's work, and another site of entrapment. (The polemic against experimentalism, meanwhile, reflects Holland's recognition of the degree to which in late 1970s Poland theatrical experiment had become a state-sanctioned freedom pro-moted at the expense of bluntly comprehensible critiques of the regime.) Nor is it surprising that Holland should have filmed a version of the murder of the pro-Solidarity cleric, Father Jerzy Popiełuszko. The priest too is entrapped in the role of non-combative male, one that virtually predestines him to victimisation. Constrained masculinity becomes a problem again in *Europa, Europa*.

Angry Harvest, her first film to excavate Polish-Jewish relations, offers a probing, biting analysis of a multiform quest for release. 'I really wanted to make a film that related to the Holocaust', Holland remarked, one that would be 'a new kind of statement about it' (Anon 1986: 15). Noting elsewhere how her will to make a film about the Warsaw Ghetto had been frustrated earlier by fear and a sense of the difficulty of 'reconstructing with false blood and plastic corpses', she attributed her acceptance of the *Angry Harvest* script to its lack of 'the clichés of SS men with rifles, deportation and concentration camps' (Insdorf 1989: 108). In it release is sought as much by the peasant and would-be priest as by the upper-class Jewish woman he both hides and torments and whose presence torments him. War has elevated Leon Wolny (the surname, 'Free', is ironic): the father of the rich Eugenia once had no time for him, but now he is her protector; the wealthy Jew Rubin kneels before him begging money to emigrate. Kneeling is very important throughout the film: Wolny also kneels before Rosa, the Jewish woman, who becomes both his Madonna and his sex-object. She is the accessible double of, and sacrificial substitute for, the declassed Eugenia, since, for all Leon's satisfaction in his rise in status *vis-à-vis* the latter, he cannot so shake all vestiges of past respect as to seek *her* physical possession. After assaulting Rosa he comments, 'I wouldn't dare do this to Miss Eugenia'.[11] Leon's attraction to Rosa is the sign of his degradation, however, of the sexual desire that prevents entry to the priesthood. If the local priest's sister holds no appeal for him, for all her interest in him, it is not simply because she is less attractive than Rosa but also because for Leon sexuality and religion are incompatible. Since sexuality exists beyond the pale, its ideal object *la belle Juive*: as Sartre remarks, at one level of the imagination of Leon, 'there is in the words "a beautiful Jewess" a special sexual signification ... this phrase carries an aura of rape and massacre' (Sartre 1962: 48). Sexuality's proscription condemns it to find expression only during alcoholic frenzy, the Dostoevskian masochism that flings itself into actions it knows it will regret, apparent power always the prelude to masochistic grovelling, to pleasure in the kneeling mentioned above. Leon is living a double bind: 'please, I'll do anything you want', he tells Rosa as he strives to make love. Sex-object one moment, she is 'Frau Rosa' the next. After Rosa's death (she commits suicide rather than suffer transfer from Leon's now threatened cellar to another hiding-place), unable to deny his desire, he sets the seal upon its aura of degradation by taking up with the servant girl.

Leon's relationship with Rosa is so complex and tortuous as almost to constitute an alle-gorical enactment of Polish-Jewish relations. When he launches the immemorial anti-Semitic reproach, 'the Jews crucified Our Lord', its illogicality – characteristic of the anti-intellectual-ism that nurtures anti-Jewish *ressentiment* – is underscored by her reply that 'Christ was a Jew'. At the end of the subsequent affray she dabs his bloodied nose tenderly and commiserates 'my poor man – what have they done to you?' Insofar as the work is allegorical its theme is the uneven distribution of sexual, racial and class power. Rosa terms Leon 'a good man', and the appellation is more than simply ironic. After all – as many Poles might answer Jewish reproaches – in concealing her he endangers his own life. Cybulkowski's galloping glee at the prospect of obtaining Rubin's orchard clearly appals him. Leon may be read as a composite Protestant and Catholic figure and hence as Holland's metonym for a Christianity as capable of hypocrisy as of self-sacrifice: her use of German (and a German-speaking border setting) not only distances and makes representable issues arguably too sensitive to air in an exclusively Polish production but also splices the self-lacerating sense of sin and unknowable interiority native to so much Protestantism into the mentality of the Polish Catholic peasant. Leon's duality corresponds to the chronic partiality of all his actions: neither priest nor layman, rich nor poor, 'good' nor 'evil', he is always riven, locked in a position inbetween. His sins, those of omission, evoke festering self-discontent rather than the self-evident guilt that cries out for expiation. Consequently a cloud of self-hatred clings to him. Half-truths rather than lies are his stock-in-trade. He may admit that the nocturnal racket above Rosa's cellar was not the German search she imagined, but his failure to state what it truly was – his own drunken rampage – leaves her doubting her sanity. When Rubin's daughter later writes from America, thanking Leon for the sum that ensured her escape and salved his undeclared guilt *vis-à-vis* Rosa and her father, and adds that she has married Rosa's husband, the irony is excruciating. As Leon buries Rosa in the cellar his echo of the death-cry of the Jew he venerates as Saviour – 'my God, why did you leave me?' – emphasises that because his need was for physical as well as spiritual release his deity had to be female. The sun as Rosa saw it, eerily intense because so seldom viewed, shines again in the last shot to highlight the devastating, unbearable fact of her loss.

IDENTITY SUBMERGED: *EUROPA, EUROPA*

In a key moment in *Europa, Europa*, as Solomon Perel and his brother Isaak cross a river while fleeing the Nazi invaders of Poland, a boat from the opposite bank drifts by, laden with Poles in flight from the Red Army. As the boats capsize, Poles swimming for the German and Jews for the Soviet side, Solly's declaration of his own choice of direction is cut short as he sinks. He may end up on the Soviet side, but his identity is always in question. Jewish, but sharing a birthday with the Führer; Komsomol member one day, Wehrmacht mascot the next; despatched to an élite Hitlerjugend academy by Nazis who see him as Aryan (after the war, in a scene the film omits, he would attend their reunion dinner!); mistakenly deemed a war hero by the German platoon that materialises behind him as he tries to return to the Soviet side; saved from execution at the hands of those self-same Soviets by the chance proximity of brother Isaak, who has survived a concentration camp and can identify him – Solly is perhaps even more the chameleon than Woody Allen's Zelig. Is he 'really' Komsomol, German or Jew? Or – as Holland's dry tone might suggest – is he the first postmodern Holocaust hero, a man without qualities? At points he does indeed consciously play with identities: his practice of the Hitler salute before a mirror speeds up into a soft-shoe shuffle. Identities become personae, able to co-exist because each rests on a different ground: the German one linguistic, the Soviet one ideological and the Jewish one biological. Lukács might have described film as permitting humanity to gain a body at the expense of that idealist entity the soul, but in Solly's case – as Holland remarked to one interviewer – 'his penis saved his soul' (Taubin 1991). The circumcised body, the sole constant and compass in Solly's life, dictates his final, post-war move to Israel. It becomes the bedrock of identity. And yet that bedrock is precisely what mainstream cinema cannot show. Solly's voice-over then becomes the desperately needed thread through a labyrinth of deceptive appearance. When he goes underwater that thread slips through our hands.

The gurgling as Solly sinks circumcises his lips. It also censors his words at the behest of what Fredric Jameson would term the political unconscious. To imply that Solly chose a direction would contradict the overall stress on his lack of options. That lack of options renders his Germanic adoption in effect the cross-gender reconjugation of Mirka's in the last episode of *Birth Certificate*. The image of Solly underwater, the film's dreamlike opening, could almost have been inserted here, even though he swam there in Hitlerjugend uniform and was joined by brother Isaak. Does the separation and yet possible relation of these two moments imply that for all his identification with the Soviets, in the unconscious – where opposites meet, as a later dream sequence with Hitler and Stalin dancing together illustrates – allegiances are less clear? The link between water and brotherhood frames the film, which closes with Isaak and Solly passing water in the rain followed by a shot of the real Solomon Perel at a river's side singing in Hebrew, 'How sweet it is to sit surrounded by your brothers.' The suggestion of uterine depths in the first underwater sequence is reinforced by Solly's circumcision a moment later. A child pulls a curtain aside to show the circumcision as theatre, a scene viewed through the glass that is another of the film's leitmotifs.

In the voice-over accompanying these images Solly claims to recall that circumcision, though nobody believes him. The theme of his story's unbelievability recurs at the close, where Isaak counsels against telling it: people will only scoff. Indeed, not until introduced to Holland by producer Artur Brauner did Perel recount it. Holland may preface the film with the caption 'what follows is a true story' and close with the authenticating image of Solly himself, but her ironic laconicism and cutting stress the improbability. Her self-confessed emendations of several incidents heighten the tallness of the tale, for instance by compressing into one event the arrest and interrogation of Stalin's son or bringing Solly together with Isaak after the war, rather than one of his cousins (Anon 1990a).

The most patent improbability occurs near the end. After Solly's lack of Volksdeutsche papers has been questioned he thinks 'only a miracle could save me now' – and a bomb obligingly flattens the administrative building he has just left, making confetti of its records. Holland may show us the bloodied head of his Hitlerjugend comrade Gerd, crushed by fallen bricks, but the wink at the audience occasioned by the promptitude of the 'miracle' short-circuits any sorrow. Something similar occurs when Robert, the gay German ex-actor who discovers Solly's identity but lovingly shields him, dies at his side. Solly's voice-over declares devastation, but the camera rises to a strangely impassive overhead shot. The picaresque epic tone stuns emotion, justifying certain critics' description of the film as a comicbook (Przylipiak 1991). Holland's dryness renders Solly a trickster survivor, fairytale's charmed youngest son, but even as her use of the anti-psychological conventions of pre-novelistic narrative modes smoothes over behavioural improbabilities (it is hard to credit Solly's musing mimicry of the hands on a Jewish headstone a mere moment after the devastating loss of Leni) at the same time it limns the voice-over's agonising with an air of the unbelievable.

As Solly's concluding voice-over tells us that on emigrating to Israel he barely hesitated to circumcise his own two sons, our satisfaction stems less from any sense of Zionist homecoming in the film than from the witty reprise of its starting point. The sight of the real Solly at a river's side cannot but recall Claude Lanzmann's *Shoah*, which begins with another improbable war survivor, Szymon Srebnik, singing on a riverbank. The implication of the echo is not entirely clear, being as likely to entail polemic with Lanzmann as homage to him (after all, his opinion of *Korczak* – whose script was penned by Holland – had been acerbic), and it may perhaps even be unconscious. The real Solly stands like a question mark after the story. Is he also there to show that fictional means can serve a Holocaust story just as well as Lanzmann's painstaking and long-winded devotion to documented 'real time' – with Holland inviting us to rejoice in her own work's difference? There is an inscrutable irony in the fact that the real Solly looks far more stereotypically 'Jewish' than the Marco Hofschneider who has just played him...

In North America critical reception of *Europa, Europa* cast a largely feminist light on a work in which, for a change, a woman director shows a male naked and charts with black humour the dangers of betrayal by one's penis. (Naked males appear in Holland's Polish work also: in *Gorączka* [*Fever*, 1981] a leading revolutionary flees unclothed from recognition at the public baths.) Jim Hoberman (1991) goes so far as to read Holland's direction of combat scenes as an appropriation of male privilege. But whereas a feminist theorist such as Kaja Silverman (1988) links male voice-over to male privilege and potency, Holland uses it to emphasise the fact of Solly's survival: hearing an opening voice-over conventionally assures us that its speaker has outlived the events that follow. The attractive Solly may be favoured by the best-looking girl at the Hitlerjugend academy, but any assertion of potency would betray him.

As often, Holland's protagonist is the insider who is really an outsider. In an early scene, Solly perches naked on the rim of the family bathtub to watch Hitler Youths marching down his hometown street: as one extends his tongue, he does likewise (a moment whose psycho-analytic implications may remind one of the girl with extended tongue in Buñuel's *Un Chien Andalou*). When the window shatters he flees and hides outside in a barrel until his neighbour Kathy brings a Nazi leather jacket to cover his nakedness. (A 'real' moment perhaps more potentially rewarding of dream interpretation than the two actual dreams Holland inserts.) Later he will run naked from the German actor Robert. Nakedness means vulnerability, the danger of being oneself (Robert tells Solly it's harder to play oneself than other people). Solly's vicissitudes suggest that the fluidity and experimental quality of adolescent identity may even become an asset during wartime, when invasions by opposite sides alternately penalise differ-ent identities. Were not the story a real one, spectators might even be tempted to read the film's oneiric quality as marking the wartime incursions as allegorical externalisations of adolescent tensions. If Solly is innocent – for all his transgression of the paternal imperative to remem-ber who he is – it is partly because adolescence insulates him from full responsibility. When Russians capture him in Wehrmacht uniform they deride his claim to Jewish identity, show-ing him victims of concentration camp victims' skulls: if he were really a Jew, they say, this is what he would look like. Solomon Perel never saw himself as a hero; his story denies him both potency and heroism. We may learn early on in the film of his sister's wish to be a boy, but Holland is as it were that sister's sister, underlining the perils of manhood. Among other things she offers a richly ironic response to a Jew's postulate of the theory of penis envy on the edge of an era when the status of Jewish male would hardly be enviable. The sister, meanwhile, might rejoice that Judaism knows nothing of one known as female circumcision.

And what of Polish-Jewish relations? Less important than in *Angry Harvest*, they appear in an acid thumbnail sketch in the Komsomol orphanage, where Solly is the insider, Polish children the outsiders. A female instructor mocks the Poles' Catholicism, taunting them to attempt to demonstrate God's existence by praying for candies to fall from the ceiling. Their fruitless prayer is followed by her own to Stalin, which yields instant results. But the provi-dence that seems to watch over Solly and stage miracles on his behalf (miracles whose deadpan presentation is justified by the voice-over's assurance of his survival) has the last laugh here too, even though this wonder is not on Solly's behalf: a moment later a bomb shatters the roof. Holland is well aware that oppression does not necessarily ennoble the oppressed. Zenek, the fair-haired and genuinely courageous Polish defender of the faith, can also denounce Solly to the Nazis as a Jew. Perhaps there is not one providence but two, with Solly's the stronger, for a truck conveniently flattens Zenek before he can say too much. Since the Polish-Jewish theme is subordinate to the evocation of the deformities of the century's totalitarianisms, it should not be surprising that the film's reception pays it scant attention. The disparity between its complete absence from the Polish reviews I have seen and its partial presence in non-Polish ones may or may not be significant: after all, a reviewer who overlooks it can hardly be accused of repressing the central theme.

The dryness of *Europa, Europa* – modelled, Holland asserts, on Voltaire's *Candide* – may be tonic, but it may also dissipate some of the most searching questions Solly's story can prompt. For Tadeusz Lubelski, for instance, the film replaces the question of the psychological price Solly's conformity exacts with the one 'will he survive?'; and since we know he will 'one watches the film with rather moderate suspense' (Lubelski 1991: 16). Lubelski notes its unevenness and laments the absence of the earlier Holland's incisive analysis of ambiguous motive (ibid.). On meeting the real Solly, Holland may have been struck by his retention of traces of each of his unsentimental educational experiences,[12] but no such reflection is present in the film. Her distance from the material is almost startling, for the uncertainties of Solly's identity recall those of her own, poised between Polish mother and Jewish father (Taubin 1991). (Could the distance be a way of denying that resemblance? Could Holland herself be repeating her father's unwillingness to speak of his Jewishness? [Quart 1988: 239]) The title mirrors that doubleness but also disavows it by stressing Holland's other duality as a director from 'the other Europe' who works in the West. It is ironically appropriate that the German film industry should have been reluctant to term this a German film. German criticism of its melodramatic qualities is something more complex than a simple use of aesthetic categories to mask rejection of unpleasant material, though in some quarters it was precisely that (the snobbishness about 'Hollywood' that dismisses 'foreigners'' right to deal with 'German' matters could also be uncomfortably xenophobic).[13]

Europa, Europa is indeed uneven, being most suggestive when compressed, elliptical and dreamlike. Most oneiric of all are not so much the sequences explicitly coded as dreams as the first ten minutes and the powerful Łódź Ghetto sequence, which merits closer consideration. Told by a dream to search out his family there, Solly takes a tram through the Ghetto. In an echo of his earlier etching of a hastily erased Star of David on the school's dormitory window, he scrapes a hole in the tram windowpane's white paint (it is painted to screen Aryan travellers from defilement by the sight of how the *Unterrasse* lives). The images flowing in and past him are harrowing and hallucinatory, their shadowy edges all the more deathlike for their resemblance to the iris of the defunct silent cinema; and in the parade of faces two of the old people Holland has cast are indeed so emaciated as to recall true ghetto inmates. The fleeting representation of the ghetto – whose images slip through the fingers – solves a problem that would partly vitiate Wajda's *Korczak*: the inevitable theatricality of well-fed modern faces presented as inhabitants of a torture chamber. Solly thinks he sees his mother but cannot be sure. Later he will learn from Isaak that the family died two weeks after the end of his furlough in Łódź. The faces seen from the tram already belong to the dead: the moments shown as present to Solly are uncannily prophetic. And to us they seem remote, unattainable, frozen in another time, as if already past, like Ghetto photographs viewed in the present yet – achingly – animated, as if their inhabitants might yet live. The moment is the one of peering through a narrow aperture that haunts all Holland's films. The boy straining to see through the hole also stands for the filmmaker and for ourselves as we gaze into the past, appalled by our inability to change it and the illusion of presence that feeds the impossible hope that a time-traveller might yet do so. In its fusion of passionate longing and self-awareness, it is the film's most intelligent and most haunting moment.

ODDS AGAINST RECONCILIATION: *DECALOGUE 8*

Polish-Jewish relations are engaged more directly in Krzysztof Kieślowski's *Decalogue 8*, which teases out some of the implications of the commandment forbidding false witness. The eighth in Kieślowski's sequence of ten hour-long television films begins with the interlocked hands of an adult and a child. Darkness is falling, a musical theme that invites naming as Yiddish is playing, we are passing from courtyard to courtyard. The relationship between this prologue and the film's remainder will long be unclear: a cut into bright sunlight and the morning workout of Zofia, Warsaw University ethics professor, reveals nothing. Only much later will the way it haunts the narrative outside which it hovers be understood to represent a wartime trauma's primacy in – and blocking off from – the lives of its protagonists. They are Zofia and Elisabeth, her American Jewish translator. The scene is the only visible trace of Elisabeth's childhood memory of being led to a potential hiding place only to hear the lady she would know as Zofia say she could not accept her, since to do so would entail lying. Elisabeth cannot comprehend the evolution of the Zofia she knows from the woman of that night, and the disparity torments her.

Elisabeth's earlier attempts to confront Zofia with her deed have been unsuccessful. The way a situation now permits this mirrors Kieślowski's existentialist sense of chance's forming and deforming impact upon choice. (Hence Zofia can say that situations release either good or bad in people.) While auditing Zofia's class, where one student has just recounted the dilemma of the female protagonist of *Decalogue 2*, she hears Zofia conclude discussion of whether or not the doctor involved should have allowed an abortion by stating: the important thing is that the child is alive. The comment's implications pull her to the front row, tug her experience from her. It emerges tremulously, and is almost cut short by a disruptive student. The interlude with the student is a suspense device but also more, for it evokes the ease with which the total field of events can frustrate individual intention (a frustration Kieślowski registers at every level of late-1980s Polish life). Zofia will later mention the need to think things through to the end, perhaps because so often they fail to get there of their own accord. Zofia listens agonised, left hand creasing cheek in the posture of Dürer's Melancholia. The telling so drains Elisabeth herself that when all have left she remains seated, no natural noise on the soundtrack, only the opening Yiddish theme.

Things might end there, with Zofia seemingly compromised irretrievably, but the film thinks them through to the end. Haltingly, against enormous resistance – both in the protagonists and in the situations that continue to threaten to derail their encounter – the dark matter is worked through. Zofia offers Elisabeth a lift to her hotel but drives her instead to the primal scene of the courtyard. Elisabeth walks around and then hides. Zofia's inability to find her becomes consternation, and the way the Yiddish theme evokes *her* anguish suggests (in an undertone that may come to naught, since, after all, films privilege images over their sound-tracks) a sharing of suffering and possible arrival at a place where more of the story can be told, in the teeth of the silence hanging between the two women. Soon after, at Zofia's apartment, an explanation will be offered (not a justification, but a complication of the accuser-accused confrontation): the child's transfer was blocked because of fears that the couple due to shelter it were linked to the Gestapo and might betray the underground organisation to which Zofia and her husband belonged. As Oskar Sobański puts it:

We are dealing with a double paradox, a paradox within a paradox. By refusing to lie the film's heroine sentences someone to almost certain death. And yet that refusal to lie … is a lie, a false pretext hiding a noble intention that cannot be revealed: to save many human beings at the cost of a single life. But that is not the end of it: the danger from which these human beings were meant to be saved was also a result of false witness. (Sobański 1990)

Before giving what she terms a banal explanation Zofia tells Elisabeth: 'If you crossed the Atlantic expecting a mystery you'll be disappointed.' But although all is indeed resolved on one level, where a mother-daughter relationship crystallises between Zofia and Elisabeth (the conversation shifts to the second person and Zofia is shot face-on, intimately, from Elisabeth's point of view) it may not be on another level, as the ending shows. This being a Kieślowski film, it is hardly surprising that mystery persists, on another level, rescinding any incipient, almost pat didacticism. On discovering the falsity of the rumour linking the prospective foster couple to the Gestapo Zofia tried to apologise to the man – 'but that is not enough'. Elisabeth's own efforts to address him are stonewalled likewise: a tailor (is it significant for his identification with the Jews that this profession is so often associated with them?), he will not speak of the past, only of making her a dress. Zofia says he has perhaps suffered too much, and Elisabeth terms Poland 'a strange country'. The last image shows him, played by the great Tadeusz Łomnicki, staring through the window bars of his rundown shop at the silent spectacle of the two women beside Zofia's car.

Silence pervades Kieślowski's *Decalogue*: repeatedly events paralyse their protagonists. Yet silence can also reconcile, be sacramental, as when Zofia stands behind Elisabeth, places her hand on her shoulder and Elisabeth clutches it. In remarking that situations bring out either the good or the bad in people Zofia is not exonerating herself: the bad had to pre-exist for the situation's magnet to attract it. She does not think that evening brought out the good in her, and the memory has long tormented her. We do not learn whether or not her saving of many Jews was a later effort to assuage an anguished conscience. As in all Kieślowski's work, choices are fearsomely fraught. Perhaps the sole thread through the labyrinth is the importance of children, that key theme of the sequence.

Although comprised of ten parts and based on the Law given at Sinai, Kieślowski's *Decalogue* does not clearly match one film to each commandment. Several episodes drama-tise more than one – the most obvious being only a starting point – or intersect with the expected one only obliquely. Maria Malatyńska discerns 'a certain arbitrariness in the illustra-tion of a particular commandment' and sees Kieślowski as aiming less at demonstrating 'the Decalogue's continued presence in each of life's situations' than at using it as 'a pretext for consideration of life under the aspect of its helplessness' (Malatyńska 1989). The arbitrariness of the illustration may correspond to the disparity between the protagonists' codes and that of the commandments, and perhaps even between the Polish *Lebenswelt* and that of the Jews. If single episodes can activate multiple commandments, this may also echo the Apostle James' assertion that to offend against part of the law was to break it all. Zofia may be in the dock at first but Catholicism is not. On hearing Elisabeth's story, a student condemns as factitious the reasoning of the couple who refused the child: they could hardly have been Catholic, for the commandment's intent is to forbid false witness *against one's neighbour*. In the published screenplay – though not in the film – Elisabeth says that after many years she became interested in Catholicism. The screenplay also includes a priest's provision of a false identity card for the Jewish child, ending with Zofia telling a priest – one presumes the same one – that the child is alive. The film's omission of these details is more probably motivated aesthetically than ideologically, since Kieślowski was well-known for ruthlessly cutting material alien to the conception that emerged in the editing room. The omissions can result in conceptual gaps that augment the air of mystery the director so values (Coates 1999: 95).

But Jewish and Catholic experiences mingle as well as diverging. I have already mentioned the use of the Yiddish theme when Zofia is distraught at Elisabeth's disappearance. Equally importantly, her unwillingness to use the word 'God' in her work echoes Judaic proscriptions. '*Można nie wątpić nie używając słów*' she remarks, almost untranslatably ('One can be without doubts without using the words'?). The witness figure whose presence throughout the series suggests a pensive recording angel (the camera slides sideways to find him midway through Elisabeth's story) resembles the invariably winged messengers of Christian iconography less than he does the young men who visit Abraham in the desert. Meanwhile, the gaps in the narrative can recall the enigmatic storytelling of the Old Testament, the lack of 'foreground' deemed typical of it by Erich Auerbach. *Decalogue 8* delineates both the possibility of reconciliation and the enormous odds against it. It could so easily not have happened. The final isolation of the tailor, still trapped in his traumas, reminds us of that. A sort of reprise, it shows there are others in need of liberation still.

Perhaps inevitably, the Polish reception of *Decalogue 8* was concerned less with the Holocaust than with its relation to the series as a whole. Those critics who accorded it crucial significance did so less because of its subject matter than on aesthetic grounds, praising its effective screenplay – as did Oskar Sobański – or noting its role as reprise and distillation of the series (Tadeusz Szyma [1990] acutely described its placement as symptomatic of Kieślowski's asymmetrical composition). The story is more an anecdotal instance of severe ethical quandaries than the marker of an historical blank spot calling for *Vergangenheitsbewältigung*. It is nevertheless surely significant that the series should be distilled in this particular story.

KORCZAK: THE HEAVEN THAT DOES NOT EXIST

No survey of Polish films concerning Polish-Jewish relations, however partial, can overlook their foregrounding late in the career of Andrzej Wajda, Poland's most renowned director, in *Korczak*. The interplay between Polishness and Jewishness is dramatised even in the names of its subject, Janusz Korczak being also Henryk Goldszmit. When one of his orphanage children terms him 'the greatest living Pole' and another recalls his Jewishness the first child responds by adding 'and the greatest Jew too'. Only for children, though, can the two groups' relationship be solved by so pleasingly symmetrical a formula. As in *The Promised Land*, the central role belongs to Wojciech Pszoniak, though his Korczak – stiff with horror at the world's abuse of children, suspicious of the adult world that browbeats them, irascibly primed for their defence – is aeons removed from that sunny, mercurial *macher*, Moryc Welt. Since *Korczak* scrupulously avoids any hint of anti-Semitism, its vilification by sectors of the French press deeply disturbed Wajda, who sought to comprehend this reaction as simply due to divergences in viewpoint: 'otherwise I would have to admit that there is racism both on the one hand and on the other. I would not like to think that and do not do so' (Przylipiak 1990). He may deny thinking this, of course, but the thought's very formulation shows the strength of the (successfully resisted?) temptation to do so.

Danièle Heyman, an initiator of the hostile press reaction, wrote of an 'oneiric ending' that was 'particularly revolting' (Heymann 1990).[15] In that ending, the railway carriage bearing Korczak and his orphans to Treblinka becomes uncoupled from the train, halts in a field, and the children emerge in slow motion, processing under the orphanage's banner. Wajda says that the film ended thus so as not to end in the gas chambers: his reticence chimes with the widespread instinct that deems what happened there all but unrepresentable, and is consistent with his realisation that even the most exact recreation of the Warsaw Ghetto could never convey the look of its harrowed inhabitants. Alas, the horrifying force of the excerpts from a Goebbels-sponsored documentary Wajda's film incorporates casts it into the shade. If it renders it less like film than theatre, whose actors are always known to be separable from their roles, it is also a reminder that only the psychological torment Wajda eschews could have brought ghetto expressions to their faces (just such torment has of course engendered many of the greatest film performances – one may think of the vicissitudes of Lillian Gish in some of Griffith's works, or Maria Falconetti's in Carl Theodor Dreyer's *La Passion de Jeanne d'Arc* [*The Passion of Joan of Arc*, 1928] – but the nature of Wajda's subject seems rather to have imbued him with tenderness for his actors and a particular sensitivity to the ambiguity of directorial tyranny; admirably restrained, his apologias do not point this out). Positive reviews deemed the ending poetic and in some cases mentioned the legend, circulating in 1943, that the carriage had indeed become uncoupled, permitting Korczak and the children to escape. The existence of that legend invalidates readings of the ending as a self-indulgent, consolatory flourish: rather, it becomes part of the scrupulous recreation, albeit one that at this point traces the imagination of the past rather than its reality (and unfortunately leaves itself open to misreading by failing clearly to signal the shift to fantasy). In Israel, meanwhile, the image of children bearing a banner with the Star of David could be read as alluding to Israel's persistence, and even to the state's foundation shortly after the Holocaust.

Objections to these closing images nevertheless ignore the statement superimposed upon them, that 'Dr Korczak died with his children in the gas chambers of Treblinka in August 1942'. As often, filmgoers' visual bias can cause an unbalanced response to the mix of media film really comprises. For Wajda's detractors failed to grasp the pregnant clash of image and statement in a fusion of dissonant knowledge and all-but-untenable hope of transcendence. Moreover, slow motion's implied 'this is not really happening' (or 'this is happening in a different sense from the way things normally happen') arguably imbues the ending with an aching wish that escape had indeed been possible. It may even be said to imagine escape appropriately, in the form of a child's fantasy. To object to the suggestion of a possible transcendence simultaneously undercut by the title is not necessarily to speak in the name of Korczak himself, who set aside an orphanage room for children to pray as they wished. To deem it escapist is to overlook something noted by Wiktor Woroszylski: that the stylistics of fairytale had entered the film even earlier, with the children's march out of the Ghetto (Woroszylski 1990: 5). Korczak leads a true children's crusade against the ways of this world, and even as the thought of its terminus sobers us our spirits are strangely exalted, by the power of their dream. To reject the ending as an image of 'children going to heaven' – and hence Christian, unacceptable to Jews – is to traduce its ecumenical poetry, as it represents the hope of transcendence all religions share. Only a misleading binarism can cause 'non-Jewish' to be read as necessarily 'Christian'. Objections to a 'non-Jewish close' are surely further compromised by the half-Jewishness of the scriptwriter, Agnieszka Holland.

If there *are* grounds for criticising the film they lie less in its close than in its general aesthetic weakness. In eschewing the epic an American producer once wished him to make of Korczak's life (a colour production, ghetto scenes reduced to the minimum…), and in shackling himself to scrupulous recreation in monochrome, Wajda denies his own Baroque temperament. Perhaps this is only fitting: the brilliance of *The Promised Land* is as humanly dubious as the work of the Eisenstein on which it draws. Since Wajda had once proved capable of character studies – think of his fine, taut version of *Smuga ciena* (*The Shadow Line*, 1976) – *Korczak*'s weak characterisation and acting surely owe something to the director's age: it has a tired feel and on release was billed as his last film. More crucial still may be the woodenness of Holland's script, whose dogged placement of the words of Korczak's *Ghetto Diary* in characters' mouths smacks of declamatory illustrativeness, devoid of actuality's hesitations. Its failure to distinguish between written and spoken modes lends its truth to Korczak's words an air of falsehood. The acting is often stilted also – one glaring instance being the Nazis' roughing up of Czerniaków. This may be in part the result of Wajda's recorded fear of working with children, never having done so before.[16] (His own formative experiences seem to have been those of war-time adolescence.) The sentimental subplot linking Józef, the orphanage's oldest child, to the blond Polish Ewa is fatally point-making, in TV-movie manner. Scrupulosity so stifles the film that the imaginative leap into the powerful, poignant ending may have been too surprising for the audience to handle.

Another weakness of Holland's script is a certain inconsequentiality, the result perhaps of close adherence to the episodic structure of the diary. The script is strongest at its close and whenever it breathes the irony so pervasive in Holland's own films. A strong irony links the beginning, where Korczak is shown in his radio role of Old Doctor, stating that 'whoever pretends to sacrifice himself for a person or thing is a liar', and the end, where he chooses not to avail himself of an offer of escape. Another is when ex-pupils who have joined the Jewish combat organisation reproach him with founding an educational system that unfits them to fight. (Their reservations echo the critique of Father Jerzy Popiełuszko voiced by his chauffeur in Holland's earlier *To Kill a Priest* [1988].) The film's reception was to be marked by irony of a different, more ghastly kind: mechanical reiterations of the charges of anti-Semitism levelled against *The Promised Land*. If the idealistic doctor-social worker had been a key figure in Reymont's novel, but had not figured in Wajda's brutal apocalypse, *Korczak* makes good the omission by focusing on that character alone, as embodied in Korczak himself. That doctor-social worker had been central to the Żeromski and Prus novels Korczak himself listed among his formative experiences. It is perhaps regrettable that Wajda's film tells us nothing of the earlier Korczak, of the process whereby he became the unyielding defender of children's rights who allowed them to arraign their teachers in his orphanage's court. Because Henryk Goldszmit remained a Polish writer, resisting the lure of Palestine, the director Bolesław Michałek and

Frank Turaj term 'the essential Pole' has every right to tell his story (Michałek and Turaj 1988: 129). One should recall Korczak's own pride in the fact that a generation of Jewish children had learned to read and write Polish from his *Little Review*. Both Korczak and Wajda seek to reconcile Poles and Jews by demonstrating their compatibility within a single person. It is thus fitting that the wall mentioned during the Ghetto Uprising commemoration should encounter another one, erected by Korczak, with an opposite meaning: 'they've separated us from the rest of the world with a wall', he comments, 'so we'll separate ourselves from them' – and he walls up the orphanage windows to shield his children from the horror without.

OBSERVING THE OBSERVER: WAJDA'S *HOLY WEEK*

As mentioned at the outset of this chapter, the identification of Poland with 'the Jewish question' in Western perceptions has been cemented in recent years. Wajda has remarked in an interview that 'as each year passes the West becomes more and more confirmed that the Poles are anti-Semites, as if the Poles as a nation, a society, were actually the ones who helped Hitler commit his crimes – so I think that a voice needs to be heard from our side' (Wertenstein 1995: 29). The difficulty of finding that voice is the subject of this section. For although the issue of Polish-Jewish relations is treated successfully in Holland's intense *Angry Harvest* and picaresque *Europa, Europa*, Holland's German-language films suggest that during the 1980s the issue could be probed by Polish directors only outside Poland. Yet even now, when the theme is no longer taboo within Poland but even fashionable, most reckonings with it are unconvincing, fatally disabled perhaps by the fact that few of the filmmakers involved have more than an academic experience of Polish-Jewish relations (Holland being the exception whose Jewish sense of dislocation – dislocation even from Jewish identity, since her father's Jewishness is not sufficient for her recognition as Jewish, Judaism being matrilinear – helped her survive outside Poland).

In this context Wajda's *Holy Week* becomes of great interest. Written by Jerzy Andrzejewski in 1943, several years before Poland's Stalinisation, though not published until 1946 (in revised form, though Andrzejewski did not say whether the revisions were stylistic or substantial),[17] it was filmed by Wajda in 1996, several years after the socialist state's collapse. Despite the interweaving of Polish nationalist discourse with that of Catholicism over the past 200 years, the link sealed in the coinage *Polak-Katolik* (Pole-Catholic), both Andrzejewski and Wajda replicate the socialist state's post-1956 separation of a reprehensible nationalist discourse from the permissible discourse of Catholicism, an apparent protectiveness of the latter that really protects the state – and themselves – from the opprobrium of seeming to attack it, and which also seeks to deprive the political right of its most powerful ally, the Church. (Wajda's post-1989 Poland, after all, has seen fears of the forging of a theocratic state banning abortion and curtailing freedom of expression.) Andrzejewski's first publications, of course, had been in a 1930s right-wing Catholic weekly, while Wajda's relationship with religious imagery had long been tortured, for the inverted crucifix in a bombed-out church, that justly famous signature image of *Ashes and Diamonds*, embodied existentialist absurdity rather than a Marxist critique of religion's traduction of the creature's sigh of yearning for freedom, and yet also emanated a Buñuelian blasphemousness.[18] Inasmuch as that film both criticised out-of-touch nationalists at home and abroad *and* overturned Christianity's key icon, it served the ends of the socialist state, and Wajda's own later apparent criticism of it in *The Horse-Hair Ring* is partly justified.

Yet even in *Ashes and Diamonds* a part of Wajda is a crypto-nationalist: Maciek Chełmicki may be intellectually in the wrong but our feelings are with him. Whether or not he may be a crypto-Catholic is of course a different issue entirely. Only after 1989 does Wajda feel able explicitly to address the interrelationship of Polish religiosity and nationalism: in *Holy Week* the measure of religion's worth is the humanist one of its ability to promote love of one's neighbour: the most insistently different, little-known, feared and envied neighbour of the inter-war years – the Jew.

Wajda had made several attempts to film Andrzejewski's story. Indeed, Andrzejewski's prose may be peculiarly apt for adaptation; its relative abstraction, its concentration on dialogue and narratorial generalisation, leaving the visual a virtual blank for imaginative completion. Wajda's first, mid-1960s attempt to film the work had been stifled by the official anti-Semitic campaign of 1968, which caused the shelving of a script by Andrzej ewski and Andrzej Żuławski, while a later version foundered on state reaction to Andrzejewski's new-found dissidence, blocking filming of his books. Andrzejewski then sold the rights to the German industry, and Żuławski, Agnieszka Holland and several German directors attempted to mount versions. Wajda commented that before 1989 a story on this subject could have been manipulated to various ends (Wajda 1997), adding that thereafter such manipulation became impossible; and so he began filming it as a co-production of Polish television and Lew Rywin's Heritage Films. His professed aim of simply restating the story's message on celluloid should be borne in mind and respected, since even divergences arguably reformulate the response of the 1940s to fit the 1990s. Thus on the one hand he uses many of the story's dialogues (a fidelity not really marred by slight updating retouches to vocabulary to render the words as realistic to the contemporary ear as Andrzejewski's had once been); while on the other he recognises that the German regulations regarding would-be Jewish escapees need to be spelled out, as occurs in the opening title: Poles harbouring Jews were subject to capital punishment. Similarly, foregrounding the act of observation filmically transposes the story's focalisation around Jan Malecki, whose inner world the story expounds most fully. It is a profoundly self-divided one, riddled with shame and guilt over Jewish suffering and Polish spectatorship. The intensity of the analysis of his reflections suggests elements of self-criticism in Andrzejewski himself, whose irreproachable wartime actions, defending and aiding hidden Jews, left the survivor's guilt unassuaged.

Andrzejewski's work may not be formally cast in the first person, but the dominance of Malecki's consciousness, a clinging, nightmare version of the author's own, imparts a suffocating first-person feel. The Ghetto's suffering appears largely indirectly, as seen by Polish observers, as flame limning the night horizon, or – in a particularly telling detail in Wajda's film – as floating ash staining daytime washing on the line. If Andrzejewski, writing in 1943, could refer early on in his story to a Polish boy devastated by Auschwitz, his face shrunk to a mask, Wajda's omission of him surely takes cognisance of that word's subsequent synonymity with the Final Solution; to mention Polish suffering there too could seem to dilute awareness of the Jewish agony and appear deeply provocative. Even though the boy's *return* might have emphasised the non-return of the Jews and the disparity between the two peoples' fates, that would probably not have offset the possible effect of tactlessness: the detail might have placed the film on a wrong initial footing, while in any case narrative economy permits its replacement by Anna's later mention to Irena of her loss of a brother in Dachau. And when Irena describes the scene of a boy playing in the neighbouring garden as idyllic, Jan simply says 'it seems that way'; there is none of Andrzejewski's unveiling of Jan's memories of the arrest of the boy's parents and the mother's deportation to Ravensbrück. Also excised are the cemetery of Polish war-dead Anna traverses en route to church, along with the controversial reference, apparently in her thoughts (though their fusion with Andrzejewski's own moral reflection renders their status ambiguous) to both the suffering and the 'weight of betrayal' the Jews have borne ever since their rejection of Christ. Instead, she prays, then tells Jan that Catholics should help the Jews.

Wajda's own – male – position may be likened, *toutes proportion gardées*, to that of Malecki himself, whom Andrzejewski distances throughout by using his surname rather than his first name: 'he felt terribly embarrassed and humiliated by her fate, and also by his own helplessness and privilege' (Andrzejewski 1993: 27). A desire to go beyond Polish helplessness – to show as a partial reality the kind of Polish-Jewish communality of which Anna dreams – may be the reason for his stress on the solidarity between Jan's brother Julek and the Jewish insurgents, though the centrality of armed struggle to Wajda's work and film's vocation for the depiction of action may have been contingent causes. Whereas Andrzejewski merely alludes to Julek's action to succour the Jews, Wajda shows him steering young Polish fighters through a breach in the Ghetto wall. Similarly, it is significant that when Wajda shows the carousel turning beside the Ghetto – something often taken as prototypical of Varsovian indifference to its agony and which features momentarily in the background in his earlier *A Generation* – he focuses on Julek and Włodek peering at it in search of a way in. The moving carousel may indicate a certain protectiveness towards Andrzejewski: Artur Sandauer had contrasted its immobility in Andrzejewski's work with the movement famously mentioned in Czesław Miłosz's poem *Campo di Fiori*, and seemed to hint that the former was an inaccuracy serving to palliate Polish guilt (Sandauer 1982: 38–9).[19]

Since Wajda states his intention of simply reproducing Andrzejewski's novella, all omissions and emendations gain in significance. I have already mentioned the important excision of the Polish boy from Auschwitz and the treatment of the carousel. Equally important is the rearrangement of the elements of Andrzejewski's ending. Andrzejewski's final page concerns Irena's curse on the Poles who had cursed her. Falsely accused of causing the death of a child, she curses their children, and her words shock them to retreat and let her pass. Jan Malecki is dead and Anna has already been to church to kneel before her Saviour's image. Wajda, however, presents Irena's departure before these two scenes. His final image of Irena is not of her entering a tram far from the Ghetto but descending from one beside it, then vanishing amidst billowing smoke. Where Andrzejewski's close insists on the retribution awaiting Poles and on Irena's dehumanisation by her experience, Wajda gives an unalloyed image of Jewish suffering. Where Andrzejewski – in quasi-Christian fashion – ends with the Jew as enunciator of an unforgiving moral law often identified with the Old Testament, Wajda's Jew is the stunned victim. And yet in Wajda's work Polish and Jewish suffering are equated by Jan's near-simultaneous death, which is no longer – as in Andrzejewski – the logical conclusion of his moral bankruptcy (his pigeonholing as petit bourgeois doubtless stemming from Andrzejewski's later turn to Marxism and ambivalently echoing the comments of Malecki's murderers). As Wajda shows Jan's death accompanied by Anna's sudden spasm in church (readable as her baby kicking, but also as the death's telepathic aftershock within her body, as in so much cinematic melodrama), the paradox of life's continuance in the midst of death is painfully acute. Andrzejewski's Jan is shot by Poles who have already killed a Jewess: Jan has recognised one of them and so has to die. Wajda shows the killing rapidly, without explanation or the fascists' mocking dialogue over Jan's body. This death is balletic in both book and film, but its accompaniment in Wajda's case by the returning motorcycled Germans, those somewhat cardboard, would-be Cocteau-like messengers of death, makes it seem attributable rather to them than to the Polish assassins. The final intertitle, drawn from an earlier part of Andrzejewski's novella, declares that 'the greatest, most pitiless division is that between the happiness of some and the misfortunes of others'. 'Some' are of course the Poles, the 'others' the Jews. Shared suffering is exceptional.

As Andrzejewski's Irena flees her brief suburban haven, meanwhile, she unleashes the unnerving power of the curse, the evil eye that both responds to and provokes demonisation, the vicious circle of fear, persecution and revenge. Hers is the archetypical position of Jews among Christians, singularised and abstracted into 'the Jew', surrounded by the baiting crowd. The Other's projected mirage provokes persecution. Yet Andrzejewski's ending may be deemed ambiguous, as Madeline Levine has described his work's outrage in general (Levine 1987: 385–99). For although Irena's fate is terrible, so is she, a female version of the stereotypical fulminating Old Testament prophet of doom, fused here with the castrating harpy, which arguably over-rules the suggestion that her fightback may parallel the militancy of the Ghetto. For Wajda, as for Andrzejewski, she is first and foremost the victim of the sexual and class envy personified in Mrs Piotrowska, who resents the attraction she exerts on her husband (the sexuality accentuated by her appearance on the balcony in a nightdress, a detail added by Wajda). But in the last instance, Wajda's Irena is less the victim of Poles than of Germans diagrammatically embodying the malign impersonal historical juggernaut that rolls through so many of his other works. Her resigned, traumatised return to the Ghetto may seem incompatible with the hardbitten determination to survive she voices elsewhere in the film, and in deeming it problematic Catherine Axelrad intuitively recognises it as an addition to Andrzejewski (Axelrad 1996: 57) (Irena's non-recognition by the German soldiers she passes is surely problematic also). Moreover, insofar as Wajda's close shifts the focus from the Polish-Jewish confrontation to the Jew as history's victim, it too is ambiguous and may almost seem to exonerate Poles by arguing that although Poles persecuted Jews the greater guilt lay elsewhere. That may indeed have been so, but emphasising others' guilt may involve failure fully to accept one's own. The image of the character with whom we identify sleepwalking to her doom surely overshadows – perhaps even fails to imagine – the Uprising beyond the ghetto wall. Andrzejewski's work, uncomfortable as it may be both for many Jews and modern readers, is also deeply disturbing to Poles in its accentuation of their responsibility for the neighbour sojourning among them. Wajda's laudably de-emphasises the image of the fearsome Jew, that worthy object of persecution, but it also softens the indictment of Poles – as if in instinctual recognition of the difficulty of admitting guilt in the very public site that is the film auditorium. Irena is threatened by death in the Ghetto, not at the hands of the baiting crowd of compatriots assembled in Girardian unanimity. Meanwhile, Wajda himself has reacted with a mixture of combativeness and amusement to the perhaps slightly automatic accusations of anti-Semitism launched against the film by the French press:

> The accusations are far gentler this time. I don't know what has happened, but perhaps here too people are coming to a deeper understanding. In the end, whatever one says, we in Poland have said something on this subject in several of our films. The French

however have said little of their own adventures during the Holocaust. Let them look to themselves before they set about us. (Wajda 1996)

His aggressive defensiveness suggests that admissions of guilt – be they French or Polish – are more likely when one is allowed to confront one's deeds in the confessional, or in the privacy of one's own conscience, than on the pillory, before others' scrutiny.

By way of a postscript, meanwhile, it may be worthwhile briefly contextualising the work of Andrzejewski and Wajda by juxtaposing it with a Polish reaction to the destruction of the Warsaw Ghetto contemporaneous with that of Andrzejewski, an appeal written by Zofia Kossak. Analysing Kossak's 1943 pamphlet of protest against the Warsaw Ghetto's suppression, Jan Błoński has argued that its interweaving of defence of the Jews with their description, using nationalist terminology, as 'Poland's enemies' should be read in the light of Kossak's own heroic personal efforts to save Jews (Błoński 1994: 8–9). The contradictions, both within the pamphlet and between Kossak's words and her deeds, suggest that in Poland the generation of the image of the Other did not generate a desire to extirpate it. Błoński also notes that priests who had fomented anti-Semitism verbally recoiled from and denounced anti-Semitic acts (Błoński 1994: 9). His remarks suggest that the projected image of the Jew was so necessary to Polish self-definition as partly to protect real Jews, whose suffering at Polish hands never matched what the Nazis visited upon them. Whatever Poles may have inflicted upon Jews, or casually watched them suffer, their lack of the liberating space of 'another country' to cloak their deeds with an invisibility to their loved ones may have forestalled the actual commission of many deeds they may have wished for and imagined, though the short-circuit between imagination and action may also have been an after-effect of the country's paralysis – the weakening of its sense of possible agency – during 125 years of subjection to the surrounding partitioning powers. (The case of Jedwabne – and other massacres led by Poles – is exceptional in connecting imagination and action through a mechanism whose explanation must be speculative in part, as it depends upon factors too complex to be discussed here, though they must include the degree to which members of other villages participated in and even instigated it, and the atmosphere of a bloody carnival outside the normal temporal order.) Since our own post-war societies continue to project the Other and yet also proscribe action against it, the Polish case may be of wider and continued relevance. Is this perhaps why Polish anti-Semitism has been of such widespread interest to contemporary media (who may of course simply have become tired of an over-exploited German variety)? Poland, a land of shifting borders that itself functions as a border (the '*antemurale*') of 'Europe', continues to be a cockpit of modern European identity-formation.

'FOR TO BEGIN YET AGAIN...'

The start of this chapter reflected upon the arbitrariness of beginnings. That arbitrariness is apparent in the way a film my opening survey omitted could have formed an alternative starting point – or furnish a conclusion – for it compacts within itself elements of almost all the films considered hitherto. Aleksander Ford's *Ulica graniczna* (*Border Street*, 1948) should perhaps be placed on one side for more tender, protective reasons: it is a lesser work than the others. Strands of all the other films on Polish-Jewish relations considered here are foreshadowed in it. Its closing clarion call can echo the motif of the importance of a child's survival in *Decalogue 8*, while its very improbability is reminiscent of *Europa, Europa*; the complexity of its etching of Polish attitudes to Jews resembles *Angry Harvest*; the images of children in the Warsaw Ghetto, and the incorporation of newsreel footage, anticipate *Korczak*; and the apocalyptic appearance of the Jew in prayer shawl – a grandfather prays in Hebrew as burning beams tumble round him – recalls Wajda's *The Promised Land*. Moreover, like the 1980s work of Holland and Kieślowski, *Border Street* is not really a product of People's Poland. It stands just before the imposition of the censoring straitjacket Polish cinema would only escape briefly and intermittently, until 1989. (Hence Wajda's more recent *The Horse-Hair Ring* suggests that he may now view even *Ashes and Diamonds* as a tainted presentation of the aftermath of Soviet 'liberation'.) Orthodoxy's onset occurs during the release-time of Ford's film and can be seen dawning ominously in Marian Warszałłowicz's description of its ideological shortcomings: 'it is well known that the material aid the Aryan side provided for the Ghetto fighters came from the workers' camp, from the organisation of the social left – whereas the identity of the people aiding the Ghetto is presented as quite anonymous in this film' (Warszałłowicz 1949: 9) Ford's humanism would come to be deemed problematic. A Jew himself, he had broached Jewish themes in the pre-war cinema and would later be driven abroad by the anti-Semitic campaign of 1968, dying in exile.

Lest the title *Border Street* seem excessively, oppressively symbolic, the narrator begins by stating that the story could have occurred in many streets with other names. Nevertheless, a symbolic dimension is present, contributing to the work's operatic heightening. (For all the ubiquitous ruins, this is not a neo-realist film.) The title is re-emphasised at the end, where the narrator's voice returns to echo the Polish children's feeling that Dawidek can never die, for walls cannot separate people and truth is frontierless. The crossing of ethnic frontiers pervades the film. Good Poles gravitate towards, and are later reclassified as, Jews; malign ones claim German ancestry and toady to the occupiers. The very first sequence suggests an imminent fusion of high and low, the collapse of the conventional markers separating Poles and Jews: the Polish girl Jadzia may take piano lessons on an upper courtyard floor while Dawidek peers through a ground-level window, but the camera's position before their windows connects them by registering their desire to join in the football game outside. Each does so by eluding a custodial adult, with matching childish disasters as a dénouement: the ball's force pushes Dawidek into a water-butt; and when kicked through Jadzia's window it shatters a vase. Although at this point only Dawidek is wet, by the end he, Jadzia and the other boys will all be wading through the sewers.

Education preoccupies Ford's film, something exemplified in the sub-plot with the black German dog. Fredek, son of the anti-Semitic Kuśmirak, points out Dawidek to a German soldier and encourages him to let his dog display its talent for worrying Jews. Once the dog has chased Jadzia and Dawidek into the sewers and a stray German bullet has wounded its paw Jadzia bandages it and tells Dawidek that the dog cannot help biting: it is only doing as taught. Renamed 'Cyclone' the dog attaches himself to her and comes to her rescue, leading her friends to her and Dawidek in a later sewer scene. Truly effective education, however, begins with the parents. Władek's father, a reserve officer in hiding after the Polish Army's defeat, shares the anti-Semitic prejudices of many pre-war Poles. He refuses to take new clothes as a gift from Dawidek's grandfather. But when German soldiers march in, question the old man about the discarded Polish uniform, beat him yet extract nothing from him, the Pole is impressed. The ironic reversal whereby the Jew here conceals the Pole typifies the film's sense of the growing interchangeability of Poles and Jews, as both become victims. Władek's father later tells him that there are Jews like Dawidek's grandfather and Poles like Kuśmirak. Władek's own prejudices, which had turned him against Jadzia when he learned of her part-Jewishness, quickly evaporate.

Although the Germans depicted in *Border Street* have few virtues, they are not the primary objects of Ford's criticism; indeed, their sketch depiction renders them simply a many-headed Invader. Ford's deepest scorn is reserved for Poles who renounce national allegiance and curry favour with the Germans. Kuśmirak, for instance, trims his moustache to match Hitler's, slicking his black hair across, in the Führer's style, on learning of the German triumph. In pidgen German his daughter tells a beer-drinking occupier that she too is one of them – and later they marry. With such a father it is no surprise that Fredek steals the photograph of Jadzia's grandfather from the desk of her doctor father. (The melodrama is a little improbable, it being unclear why Fredek should be perched upon the roof alongside Białek's window. Has his father sent him, or is it a lucky accident? One suspects that it is the melodramatic plot, masquerading as malevolent, cross-eyed Fate, that has sent him.) Reconstituted, its Hebrew dedication translated by an unsuspecting Dawidek, the torn photograph will allow Kuśmirak to blackmail Białek out of his apartment. After despatching Jadzia to the countryside Białek, the assimilated Jew, retires to the Ghetto (the 'handkerchief' with which he waves her farewell is but one of the film's many symbolic details, unfurling into an armband with the Star of David). Fredek will later join a uniformed gang in pursuit of Jadzia. Waylaid and beaten up by Władek, he loses his Nazi armband, and the Jewish one lying nearby is taken for his: a German soldier shoots him as a fleeing Jew. Here Ford's melodrama compromises his humanism, for although the latter would require that Fredek be accorded a chance to redeem himself, melodrama sheds few of its tears over a villain's demise. The other children's shock at the sight of the shooting is the shock any death imparts. Could it be that the imagination *needs* the Other, the scapegoat, so the vanishing of the Jewish Other demands a different one as a substitute?

Separated at the outset, high and low, Pole and Jew, soon become one. The doctor will suffer the fate of the Jews (he now lives *next to* the Libermans, not above them); and Dawidek's uncle Nathan has already fought for the defeated Polish Army (near the film's start he is in as much of a hurry at the barber's as Władek's father – who assumes his call-up papers give him priority – because *he too* is off to the front). Near the end, while fleeing through the sewers, Dawidek, Jadzia, Bronek and Władek encounter armed partisans. (It was surely this scene that prompted Warszałłowicz's objections.) Although warned that the Ghetto is burning the partisans wade towards it just the same. When Dawidek decides to follow them Władek gives him his father's pistol. It is as if the slight 'feminisation' of the Jew that had dictated Dawidek's pairing and paralleling with Jadzia has been dispelled by his grasp of the pistol, bringing him into the sphere of heroic action. The children's conviction that he will not die may seem strange, even objectionable: reactions akin to some French journalists' responses to *Korczak* are clearly possible. It may even seem as if what really matters for the melodrama is the rescue of Jadzia, the Maiden in Distress. The symbolic heightening pervading the film however surely lends the remark the sense that Dawidek survives as a symbol – whatever really occurs – as an emblem of the Jewish people's heroic persistence. This prevalence of symbol over reality is nevertheless another way of describing the defect many reviewers termed a 'lack of authenticity' (Bocheńska *et al.* 1974: 158) It generates the high opera of the closing scenes. *Border Street* is not a great film: formally straitjacketed by theatricality, it is limited conceptually by its depiction of the anti-Semite as necessarily pro-Nazi. Kuśmirak's cosiness with the Nazis carries no hint of the existence of a nationalist anti-Semitism that detests Germans as heartily as it does Jews. But, for all that, the work has integrity and nobility. One can only echo its final hope that the walls between people must fall, that truth has no borders.

POSTCRIPT: THE OTHER AS DOUBLE

I would like to conclude by considering not a film but a single sequence from one: a passage of Jerzy Kawalerowicz's *Matka Joanna od Aniołów* (*Mother Joanna of the Angels*, 1961) which represents perhaps the most intriguing – and baffling – of the images of Polish-Jewish relations thrown up by the cinema of People's Poland.

Some way into the film's second half Father Joseph – the priest charged with the exorcism of Mother Joanna's demons – goes in consternation to the local rabbi for advice. His desire to step outside his closed community of belief may be seen, in retrospect, as the first marker of his incipient insanity, for in confronting the Jew he confronts his own image: the same actor plays both parts. The rabbi addresses him with the intimate second person, and towards the end of their colloquy says, 'I am you, you are me'. The priest having said, 'I have nothing to learn from you', the rabbi echoes this by saying he has nothing to teach him, and concludes, 'I too know nothing'. After leaving, Father Joseph will go to Mother Joanna and, out of love for her, take over her demons. Later still, facing the mirror whose swinging pictures his instability (whose intermittence as it were translates into another key the shot/reverse-shot movement of his encounter with the Jewish double), he accedes reluctantly to demonic persuasions to commit a murder. In doing so, he ensures that the demons remain with him and do not return to Joanna. As so often, encounters with doubles and mirrors betoken borderline states. But why should the double be Jewish? What does this mean? And insofar as it signifies, does it do so only in terms of a projected near-medieval world, or also carry some significance for a People's Poland virtually stripped of all Jews by the Nazis, and yet itself about to expel almost all the few remaining ones in anti-Semitic campaign of 1968?

In terms of the work's understanding of the seventeenth century, the priest's step outside the Church is one into non-existence: *Extra ecclesiam nulla salus*. The rabbi symbolises the Christian's thinking of the unthinkable: 'What if Satan created the world? If God created it, why is there so much evil in it?' Perhaps the rabbi says he has nothing to teach because he represents the unthinkable, nothingness. Is he real though, or just a projection? (Or perhaps even a sign of Christian regression away from the New Testament, the 'fall from grace' mentioned in Paul's letter to the Galatians?) When rising to dismiss the priest, the rabbi lifts a book bearing a cross, a detail that combines with the part's playing by the same actor to underline his status as unrecognised double. He is, on one level, a fantasy of the Jew as one who has nothing to teach the Christian. For a Christian to go to him must indeed be madness. At the same time, the confusion marks the film as partaking of the 1960s art cinema which destabilises reality/fantasy relations.

More important, though, may be the meaning the unrecognised double carries for the costume drama made in People's Poland in 1961. From that perspective, the seventeenth century is dead and gone: the enlightened present can only revisit it to celebrate its freedom from superstition. But what if that present is not so enlightened after all? Were not the majority of Poles Roman Catholics still? The costume drama stages the opacity of the past and the unrepresentability of the present. The past where Jews still exist is only imaginary, as imaginary for Kawalerowicz as it is for his priest, who is thus not really a seventeenth-century priest at all but a contemporary Pole able to imagine 'the Jew' only by casting himself in his role, since he now occupies his place (that this activity is still underway is shown by *Miasto cieni* [*Town of Shadows*, 1996], a documentary in which Poles learn the customs of the Jews who no longer exist in their town of Tykocin). Costume drama establishes the non-existence of the past, whose place is usurped by a present dressing up in new old clothes. It may seem to be dealing with the past, but its real subject is the present. Kawalerowicz's costume drama, like Polish costume drama in general, has a reply to this accusation, however: the reply of all 'Aesopian' art, which seeks to smuggle messages past censors by camouflaging contemporary concerns in exotic or defunct garb; and the audience, meanwhile, adeptly deciphers the reference to the present. So what is the relevance of this particular costume drama to Kawalerowicz's present? The director himself speaks of an opposition to 'the external restrictions placed on man whether these are Catholic or not'. There is clearly more to the film than a simple atheistic denunciation of the Catholic deformation of compulsory celibacy, which renders desire pathological and prone to define itself as demonic. Can this statement be translated into a cryptic diagnosis of the Poles' own enslavement in their Soviet-imposed system? There can be little doubt that Polish readers would have read Kawalerowicz's remark in this way. But is that what the film itself says? It is deeply preoccupied with Otherness, both real and imagined. It shows a society which renders women Other, and hence 'demonic'. But even in the present 'women can be magic' – the witches some would wish to burn at the stake. Does the film encompass a denunciation of Polish society – and not just its political arrangements – which condemns woman to remain Other, with the male masochistically sacrificing himself so she can become a saint? (In other words perhaps, remain at home, untainted by public life?) And what about the image of the Jew? Is his appearance as unrecognised double the sign of a frustrated effort at self-transcendence – with the Pole's effort to break out of the claustrophobic bubble of his homogenised culture, to resurrect its more diverse past, condemned to fail, for that past is no more than a projection? Buried close to the centre of Kawalerowicz's work, the encounter of priest and Jew is its hermetic core, giving the lie to the enlightened pretensions of the costume drama and betraying a deep and unresolved ambivalence regarding the rationalist project's feasibility that may well be the fruit of the collaboration of the more rationalist Kawalerowicz with the modernist Romanticism of Tadeusz Konwicki.

CHAPTER SIX

KIEŚLOWSKI, POLITICS AND THE ANTI-POLITICS OF COLOUR: FROM THE 1970s TO THE *THREE COLOURS* TRILOGY

BEFORE *THREE COLOURS*: MORAL ANXIETY AND THE POLITICS OF DESCRIPTION

Whereas Eisenstein merely reflected an existing revolution, during the mid- to late 1970s Wajda and the X film unit Wajda headed, together with the Tor unit at which Kieślowski worked, helped instigate what Timothy Garton Ash termed 'the Polish Revolution' by bringing into the public sphere depictions of the entrenched abuses of power in Edward Gierek's ripely decaying, failed technocracy, furnishing a key ingredient in the pre-Solidarity ferment. Images of provincial finagling may have seemed merely localised blots on the face of 'real socialism', but the Polish audience enlarged them allegorically into synecdoches of a false totality. But whereas Wajda's description of late 1970s Poland was hyperbolic – rubberised by wide-angle lenses in *Man of Marble* – throughout the decade Kieślowski had pursued a documentary one founded on description of 'the unrepresented world', to use the Adam Zagajewski/Julian Kornhauser phrase that recurs in his statements of this time. In 'Deeper instead of broader', a three-page personal manifesto published in 1981, and written just after August 1980, Kieślowski defined the work he and his colleagues had done in the 1970s:

> For my own part I think that the most important duty of the artist during the 1970s, particularly in my own art, was to describe reality ... Only a reality that has been described can be assessed; and reality cannot be represented outside the bounds of culture. In order to oppose it, to voice alternatives to it, one has to describe it. (Kieślowski 1981: 110)

'Description' has, of course, long been seen as a fundamental characteristic of documentary, and provides the main brief of one of its forms – 'observational' documentary – so Kieślowski's lengthy stint as a documentarist and recurrent returns to the genre during the period of his early feature-making are hardly surprising. But if this is so, what motivates his own move during the 1980s from documentary to the feature-making that was characteristic of 'the Cinema of Moral Anxiety', in which the project of description as the precondition of change was most explicit? Could a feature 'describe' better than a documentary? One might argue that the move to the feature was in fact a rhetorical one, grounded in its ability to assert the *typicality* of quoted behaviour more convincingly than documentary could. The hypothesis seems to be confirmed by Kieślowski's use of an introductory and closing caption to assert its subject's typicality in one of his last documentaries, *Nie Wiem* (*I Don't Know*, 1977), made at the very beginning of the heyday of the Cinema of Moral Anxiety movement. It is surely significant that he feels the need to stress typicality thus, as if it does not go without saying. After all, a figure in a documentary is just one man or woman. The protagonist of a feature, by way of contrast, is either a figure of identification (not just one man or woman but a potential Everyman, representative of you and me) or one of rejection (representative of the They who governed Poland at the time).

The real advantage of the feature, however, is a double one. It solves the problem that haunts Kieślowski's late 1970s work: how to achieve representativeness whilst devoting due attention to the subject's individuality. The two values, each of paramount importance for Kieślowski, were proving incompatible within the documentary form. In *I Don't Know*, a gulf yawns between the experience of this particular man attempting to stamp out corruption in a provincial leather works and the generalisation of the opening and closing caption. A different form of the same problem dogs *Z punktu widzenia nocnego portiera* (*From the Point of View of the Night Porter*, 1977), which was made back-to-back with it. Significantly, Kieślowski's first choice – a Łódź man whose ruminations had appeared in an anthology of diaries – proved an inappropriate camera-subject, being virtually toothless and hence incomprehensible. Marian Osuch, the man finally chosen, was a substitute. Kieślowski reports having deliberately chosen an example 'on the lowest rung of the social ladder … for if this exists on the lowest rung of the ladder, that means it is far more widespread than if we'd looked for it higher up. There are more people on the lowest rung' (Karabasz 1985: 91). A potential aporia emerges, however: if Osuch simply exemplifies a wider phenomenon (Kieślowski comments that the search for a substitute for the first man turned up 'people like him' in every workplace) why single him out? Choosing a fascist or right-wing leader would have been more justified, for such a person would have singled himself out by putting himself forward. Kieślowski's strategy of rejecting a more prominent figure not only matched a post-1960s discourse about 'everyday fascism' but surely also responded, wittingly or not, to the difficulty of locating a self-declared right-winger in a Polish public sphere steeped in the language of socialism. Where socialist discourse is the precondition of advancement, ambitious figures would naturally have recourse to it. Even if they promoted the anti-Semitism central to fascism, as did the onetime resistance fighter, Mieczysław Moczar, they would camouflage it as 'anti-Zionism': not racism, but principled contestation of the policies of the state of Israel. Osuch's low social status, meanwhile, matched the naïveté of the unabashed proclaimer of authoritarian sentiments. Nevertheless, Kieślowski felt a certain protectiveness towards Osuch, refusing to permit the documentary's television broadcast in case it harmed him. Such second thoughts are justified by the way in which Osuch's latent status as near-arbitrary instance of a wider social phenomenon – 'intolerance' or 'the readiness for a fascist philosophy' (Karabasz 1985: 91) – disappears behind his manifest individuality. 'Representativeness' could, of course, be demonstrated through the use of multiple, mutually echoing speakers, as in *Gadające głowy* (*Talking Heads*, 1980), but then their individuality would be sacrificed. Thus although Kieślowski does not explicitly motivate his switch to feature-making in these terms, consideration of the films made during the transition indicate that by so doing he was able to retain two hitherto conflicting values: typicality and individuality.

On abandoning documentary, Kieślowski would film works that would be classified as belonging to 'the Cinema of Moral Anxiety'. His tone and tenor would continue to differ, however, from those of most of the contemporaries whose work would be represented by that half-adequate phrase, the word 'anxiety' camouflaging the violence of dissent, while 'moral' veiled a status as much political as moral in a Polish climate that saw, as Jan Pakulski notes, 'a blending of the political demands with moral postulates' (Pakulski 1990: 44). A truer name, of course, would have encroached perilously evidently on the domain of the PZPR, challenging its 'leading role' in Polish society and arousing extreme suspicion East of the border. During this same period Bolesław Michałek noted the idiosyncrasy of Kieślowski's itinerary (Michałek 1990: 1–3). By refusing melodrama, his Polish features went beyond 'the Cinema of Moral Anxiety', a term Kieślowski professed to detest (Kieślowski 1995: 111), but one that would nevertheless be piquantly appropriate for his later – depoliticised – works. Many Polish viewers, habituated to categorising all worthwhile directors as 'political', read *Przypadek* (*Blind Chance*, 1981) on its belated 1987 release, as primarily political, and hence outdated, missing its philosophico-aesthetic concern with matching different hypothetical lives to contrasting editing styles. This misunderstanding becomes comprehensible nevertheless when one considers the degree to which the work is transitional – as is even *Bez końca* (*No End*, 1985), the first film co-scripted with Krzysztof Piesiewicz. Each is suspended between 'the political' and 'the metaphysical' (understood in terms of the metaphors of distance Tadeusz Sobolewski uses to designate it: as an observation of life's stage 'from the wings' [Sobolewski 1999: 26] or as the view of the 'hidden witness' within us [Sobolewski 1998: 180]),[1] the latter metaphor doubtless suggested by the enigmatic witness figure of *The Decalogue*. The formulations of 'Deeper rather than broader' (Kieślowski 1981: 109–11) are similarly Janus-faced, directed both to his past 'political' (or, as he would prefer, 'social') orientation and to his later apolitical one. Thus, immediately after advocating a form of expression that is concerned rather with the individual than the collectivity, he adds: 'it will be very hard for us to speak of Poland using different words' (ibid.): the point of reference remains national, the individual utterance filtered through the collective 'us'. Just how the interplay of individuality and collectivity is played out can be gauged by considering more closely the two films I have mentioned, *Blind Chance* and *No End*.

BLIND CHANCE: THE DEATH OF THE FATHER

Blind Chance (Kieślowski's most legendary film, which for so many years existed only in rumour, having been pronounced definitively 'shelved' by the authorities) may be described as marrying a near-psychoanalytic 'Western' preoccupation with the effects of the death of the father (with the sense of arbitrariness that afflicts choice in a world emptied of paternal prototypes) to a typically 'East European' reluctance to renounce humanism by invoking such psychoanalytic scenarios as the Oedipal one. This tension renders it one of the richest of all his works, echoing beyond its apparent limitation by the political realia of early 1980s Polish life. The arbitrariness I have mentioned dictates the very form of the film, which gives three different versions of a crucial period in the life of one young man, Witold ('Witek') Długosz. Each version begins like a dream, with the young man running to catch the Łódź-Warsaw train. In the first version he succeeds, becoming a Party activist who suffers rapid disillusion with the Party; in the second, he fails and becomes a dissident; while in the third his failure causes him to stay at home, marry, become a trainee doctor and die in an aircraft explosion. In each case the decision to leave for Warsaw follows the death of his father, whose earlier wish that his son become a doctor loses its force. '*Nic nie musisz*' ('You don't have to do anything') the dying father tells his son through a telephone that seems also to relay a voice from the interior, and so the bereaved son requests a leave of absence from his medical academy's dean.

The father's death frees both son and film from necessity. Its liberation of the son frees the film itself to pursue different styles, each 'life' being edited differently. After the terse, laconic prologue, the life of Witek 1 is shot with a Tarkovskian adherence to 'real time': no time is edited out of any of the sequences in this section, which are shot in long takes. The life of Witek 2 is edited more conventionally, highlighting the 'key' moments in a scene – the ones that advance the dramatic conception – and omitting all else. The final version of Witek's life is edited most conventionally of all, virtually in the no-nonsense manner of a television movie, with point-of-view shots, shot/reverse-shot and so on.

Given the triple framing of Witek's life, it may be wondered whether any particular one represents the 'true' version. With sybilline cunning, Kieślowski himself stated that it should be the final one, because it is the most conventional (private communication 1989). This view has been endorsed by Tadeusz Sobolewski, who notes Kieślowski's lack of condescension towards the conventional, evidenced for instance in his empathy with Antoni Gralak, the protagonist of *Spokój* (*The Calm*, 1976), whose dream is simply of a family and sitting at home before the television (Sobolewski 1999: 22). For Sobolewski, moreover, only the final version is 'real': after all, it contextualises the opening scream, and introduces the death that – as Walter Benjamin might have said – renders the story tellable. In this context, though, it may be worth noting the disparity in the lengths of the stories, each one being shorter than its predecessor: the first lasting 49 minutes, the second – 36, and the third only 21. The brief briskness of the final version might suggest a converse near-contempt for the conventional – or at least a lack of interest in it.

Kieślowski may declare his closeness to the third Witek (Witek 1 and Witek 2 being in a sense fantasies, something signalled perhaps by their polarising placement in opposed milieux), and this Witek's reality may be gauged by the fact that he alone confronts death, but his dying is already intimated in the shadowiness and stereotypicality of his story, the shortest and most conventionally told of the three. The deep irony of its actual primacy would nevertheless be very Kieślowskian. It is certainly the case that the first version occupies the most space in both film and text, standing out further because of the relative unconventionality of both content and style; moreover, it is based on a real case whose fascination for Kieślowski is alluded to in Hanna Krall's novel *Sublokatorka* (Krall 1989: 80–3). The arguments for the pre-eminence of one or another section, however, simply demonstrate the text's shifting to match the varying light cast upon it.[2] It moves as unfixably as a kaleidoscope. Versions one, two and three are related logically as opposites and the excluded middle that is not an option (whence its protagonist's death?). The formula of the opposites and the middle permits the work to close and yet avoid closure, for the three positions generated thereby stand in – *faute de mieux* – for the infinite variety of positions conceivable between opposites: the film-world is a diagram of totalisation, not its (impossible) reality, and Witek is the Everypole who can never be every Pole.

The role chance plays in our lives was frequently emphasised in both Kieślowski's films and many interviews. In *Krótki film o zabijaniu* (*A Short Film About Killing/Decalogue 5*, 1988), for instance, chance carries Jacek and the taxi-driver to their meeting, as a long queue at the Castle Square and a patrolling militiaman cause the former to reject two possible victims, while the latter bloody-mindedly leaves standing the couple who waited while he cleaned his car, then refuses a drunken fare. Moreover, *Przypadek*, which is generally translated as *Blind Chance*, also means 'coincidence'. Of the many chance elements furrowing Witek's life, only one – the missing of the train – is highlighted as decisive. In his case, the role of chance (previously conceivable as a non-determining randomness) is raised to the maximum in this one moment: although he does not know how much depends on it, it determines whether he becomes a communist party member, a dissident or an ordinary, unpolitical man. And yet even as Kieślowski frames his film to aggrandise the role of chance on one level, on another the work's dialectic whittles it away to insignificance. For in each life, Witold Długosz is 'the same' fundamentally decent person. The work's dialectic is more complex than the director's declared intent. Thus although Kieślowski himself frequently stated in interviews that chance governs everything, he – the 'Kieślowski' deducible from the works, an amalgam of the conscious and unconscious – clearly also believed that character remained unaffected by it: the randomness of occurrence merely shatters on its rock. His films thus do not so much expound their maker's existentialism as pose a series of questions to it. The world of pure accident is also one of utter imperviousness to accident. Beneath the flux of absurdity something persists. Is that untouchable bedrock of selfhood perhaps the soul Kieślowski would come to state his interest in filming, its unchangeability established by its persistence through several reincarnations?

By beginning *Blind Chance* with Witek's scream and by deploying opposite scenarios that logically require a middle one to complete and close them, Kieślowski gives his film a structure that preserves it from succumbing entirely to the dictates of chance. As Rudolf Arnheim notes in a passage whose use of a plane's flight as an example uncannily anticipates this film:

> Suppose you watch a straight line growing – a vapour trail in the sky or a black mark in an animated film or on the pad of an artist. In a world of pure chance, the probability of the line continuing in the same direction is minimal. It is reciprocal to the infinite number of directions the line may take. In a structured world, there is some probability that the straight line will continue to be straight. A person concerned with structure can attempt to derive this probability from his understanding of the structure. How likely is the airplane suddenly to change its course? ... The information theorist, who persists in ignoring structure, can handle this situation only by deriving from earlier events a measure of how long the straightness is likely to continue ... Being a gambler, he takes a blind chance on the future, on the basis of what happened in the past. (Arnheim 1971: 16)

Despite its title, the world of Kieślowski's film is structured and hence not one of blind chance. Witold's scream is the logical terminus of Arnheim's 'line'.

However, the world of chance may be represented most fully in *The Decalogue*, for it is only from the viewpoint of an (artist?) demiurge that the apparently random character intersections signify: thus the fact that Romek, the impotent husband of *Decalogue 9*, passes Tomek, the young voyeur of *Decalogue 6*, cements the thematic linkage of the two parts. If the taxidriver cannot know who hurled the rag at him, causality becomes unclear. Consequently, one cannot know what is and is not chance, what actions are and are not purposive. The mask of occurrence does not fall to reveal an individual face. Rather than expressing the impulses of individuals, events simply occur – and so responsibility evaporates. This piquantly echoes the Polish authorities' own news bulletins, whose repeated impersonal verbs served both to deny their own responsibility and to subvert 'bourgeois individualism', but it also helps create what Tadeusz Sobolewski memorably termed the 'solidarity of sinners' (Sobolewski 1990: 91–101) between Kieślowski's characters: where everyone is guilty, nobody is; where no one is guilty, all are. And where this is the case, the judge-penitent of Albert Camus' *La Chute* (*The Fall*, 1956) is likely to come on the scene.

The Fall is a work of enormous significance for Kieślowski. It is alluded to explicitly in the first part of what one might call Kieślowski's 'legal trilogy', which bridges his early 1980s and his final, foreign work: *No End*, *A Short Film About Killing* and *Trois couleurs: rouge* (*Three Colours: Red*, 1994). *No End*, which inaugurates his co-authorship of scripts with Piesiewicz, includes a reference to the interest in Camus' 'judge-penitent' displayed by its main male protagonist, the dead lawyer Antek Zyro. Antek's interest may have lain in his sense of the possibility of himself undergoing the same metamorphosis as Camus' Jean-Baptiste Clamence. Beginning as a defender of orphans and widows, an oppositional lawyer scornful of judges, Clamence had found his own delectation of courtroom rhetoric transforming him into an actor and hypocrite. *His* ability to defend orphans and widows is ironised by *No End*, which begins with his wife's widowing and ends with the orphaning of their son, as she joins him in death. And does a sense of the indecency of courtroom grandstanding dictate the excision of Piotr Balicki's speech from *A Short Film About Killing*? One becomes a judge, as it were, after losing one's innocently self-righteous self-identification with the underdog. Even then, however, self-reproach continues, as if all pretensions to administer justice were accursed. The curse rests most fully on Judge Joseph Kern in *Three Colours: Red* (a film Kieślowski deemed his most personal), who both reincarnates and redefines Camus' 'judge-penitent' Clamence.

In each of *Blind Chance*'s three sections figures who played major roles earlier on are recast – by chance? – in minor functions. The communist old believer Werner, an influential father substitute in section one, becomes a passer-by later on; the priest of section two is glimpsed incidentally at Warsaw airport in section three, about to lead the excursion to France from which the authorities had debarred Witek in an earlier 'life'. In all three sections, however, Witek is 'the same' person. Like the story itself, he is always preoccupied with the degree of coincidence in people's lives (as if he suspected that the life he is leading is merely an accidental variant of an alternative ranged alongside it). In each life he drops to his knees and clutches his forehead in moments of crisis (in version A, after the secret police car has sped away with his girlfriend; in B, when a fellow-conspirator demands the return of the key to the secret printing-shop the militia have discovered; and in C, when his wife announces her pregnancy). The film is profoundly subversive of ideas of destiny (fate belongs in the mythical world of the fathers, whose ending precipitates one into the new, possibly secular world of fortuity). In the process, it subverts the black-and-white notions of character that were so prevalent in a deeply politicised Poland polarised between 'them' and 'us'. In each of his first two lives, Witek is the victim of society's stereotypical division into martyrs and traitors: in the first his girlfriend ostracises him on the assumption that he used his pull as Party member to secure her release from custody; and in the second a colleague assumes that his non-arrest when his conspiratorial cell is breached indicates complicity with the authorities. One can as easily land on one side of the party line as the other. The film's subversiveness extends into a doubt of memory, in the manner of Alain Resnais: the first section shows us a boy bidding Witek farewell before going up a hill to a VW; in the second section we learn the boy's name, Daniel (he is the brother of Werka, with whom Witek 2 has an affair), as well as his identity (he is Jewish). The goodbye preceded Daniel's departure for Denmark as a result of the anti-Semitic campaign of 1968. And yet Daniel says there was no automobile in the scene. Disturbingly, his words extend the principle of arbitrariness into the past, the previously untouched prologue. As they suggest that memory is creative, they also question the cinematic dictum that seeing is believing.

The first we see of Witek is as a child, reflected in a mirror, doing homework; his father says he forms a figure eight as his dead mother did. The presentation of the protagonist as a mirror image would become increasingly typical of Kieślowski's work: it is thus that Antek will appear (reflected in a bookcase) in *No End*, whilst in *A Short Film About Killing* Jacek is first seen mirrored in the glass covering a poster of David Hare's *Wetherby* (1985) in the new section of Warsaw's Old Town. As if drawing conclusions from his move from the documentary to the feature, Kieślowski begins by reminding us that what we are seeing is not reality but an image. But over and above their cinematic self-referentiality these openings suggest that the true life is perpetually displaced. The life we live is governed by coincidence; there is no Platonic form of the true life. Witek's opening scream of 'No!' reverberates with anguish over this realisation. All the works I have mentioned thus seem to be about the loss of the prototype, a theme which may be fuelled by early biographical forces (Kieślowski lost his father when young), but which also reflected his more recent loss of the documentary and his and its love-object, 'reality'. The loss of compelling reasons why one should do one thing rather than another (tell *this* story rather than another one) may also be an argument against apparently irrevocable choice (and so leaving the country, a move so often associated with irrevocable consequences in nineteenth- and twentieth-century Polish history, here has the irrevocability of death). The father, however, has been lost rather than killed, for he is not the locus of power, which actually lies elsewhere. And it was its sense that power lay elsewhere that renders East European cinema still relevant, so bewitchingly accurate a mirror of the era so often described as postmodern, as the crumbling of nationality before the pressure of the world economy defines power as something that continually relocates itself on the far side of continually displaced borders. The knowledge that the cause of the effects we feel is perennially absent pervades Kieślowski's work.

In 1998, more than a decade after the first screening of *Blind Chance*, a written screenplay was published (Krall 1998: 141–77). As might be expected, there are many differences between the text – it being in fact more akin to an independent short story or novelisation – and the completed film: Kieślowski notoriously excised anything shot less resonant on screen than envisaged, as well as welcoming and utilising co-workers' suggestions. In the film, for instance, the text's prologue to Witek's three attempts to catch the train undergoes drastic, riddle-forming abbreviation. The text, in turn, lacks the frame created by Witek's opening scream of 'No'. A subplot with Werka's husband, an airline mechanic, vanishes from the film, as do Witek 2's work with people wishing to see the English faith healer Harris, Werner's argument after Czuszka's arrest in the story of Witek 1, or Czuszka accompanying Witek 1 to the airport – to give only a few examples. The most important difference, however, appears at the very end of the screenplay: as Witek 3 dies, Witek 1 and Witek 2 suddenly stop what they are doing (Krall 1998: 177). Despite the musing, hypothetical mood of so much of the screenplay, Kieślowski does not use the conditional 'would have stopped' but a simple preterite. *Blind Chance* thus becomes very like *La Double Vie de Véronique* (*The Double Life of Véronique*, 1991): like the heroine of that work, Witek exists *simultaneously* in more than one form, each of which is somehow sensitive to the fate of his other (potentially infinite number of?) incarnations. As so often, Kieślowski's films – like Witek's lives – become revisions and re-visions of one another.

NO END: POLITICS OF MEMORY, GHOSTS OF DEFEAT

The opening moments of *No End* densely encode all its future concerns. The first person we see moving is a young man reflected in the glass of a bookcase. The conjunction of the reflection with Zbigniew Preisner's sombre score and the film's first image – an overhead shot of massed candles burning in a cemetery – prepares us to read the blurred mirroring as a metaphor for the young man's condition. The sheer number of candles burning hints that the day is All Souls', a day of collective mourning, and so the subject will be collective, as well as individual, mourning. The voice on the phone the man replaces, saying '*rozmowa kontrolowana*' ('monitored call'), allows us to link this mourning to the martial law General Jaruzelski declared on 13 December 1981. Almost a year has passed, but the depression it brought has not lifted. Since the man, Antek, is played by Jerzy Radziwiłowicz, the iconic hero of Wajda's *Man of Marble* and *Man of Iron*, the carefully assembled images and sounds yield the strong suggestion that this character's afterlife will be that of the spirit of Solidarity. (The initial interest in his hands will prepare us for Ula's later attraction to the tourist whose hands recall his – as if the film is emanating cryptically from her consciousness.) Allegorically Antek's death will stand for that of Solidarity, which was predominantly a movement of the discontented young who, their elders would note, had not known the horrors of war and so did not fear to challenge the Soviet-sponsored authorities. The death of Solidarity is no longer the logical necessity the authorities proclaimed, the sole way out of a crisis, but as unnatural as the demise of the young.

For the man is indeed dead: he sits on the bed and tells us of his fatal heart-attack while starting his car four days earlier. He had been a lawyer in his thirties specialising in the defence of workers prosecuted for strike leadership and membership of the outlawed Solidarity union. His direct address to the camera echoes the ending of Kieślowski's earlier *Amator* (*Camera Buff*, 1979) in which Filip Mosz (Jerzy Stuhr) haltingly recounted the course of his wife's labour and childbirth. There is a suggestion that the one film takes up where the other left off – that in a sense Antek reincarnates Filip. The allusion is a sign that things do not simply end; indeed, in a move that will become increasingly typical of later Kieślowski, the later film amplifies a subsidiary concern of the earlier one (that with memory and the after-life, as the film a man watches of his dead mother in *Camera Buff* resembles a miraculous materialisation of the dead, film itself becoming the *matière de mémoire*).

As this opening sequence continues the camera slides across and behind Antek to his wife Ula, who is lying in bed and clearly cannot see him. An old friend, Tomek, rings from the airport to announce his return to Poland. Ula, still in shock after Antek's premature death, refuses to see him. Throughout the film she will seek to banish the trauma of her loss. She will visit a hypnotist who promises to erase all memory of the person she wishes to forget, but who fails, for Ula has not told him that the person in question is dead and he has no power over ghosts. Perhaps significantly the countdown that ought to bring oblivion ends with an echo of Antek's name, 'zero' recalling 'Zyro': the move away from him is really one towards him. Ula will betray Antek, as she puts it, with an American tourist who picks her up at a bar, though she will then surreptitiously pass the $50 fee to the wife of Darek, the worker Antek had been defending for participation in a strike. (She will seek to pay her dues to Antek by entrusting Darek's case to his mentor, the old lawyer Labrador.) As she uses Polish to describe her distress to the tourist, the non-communicative communication (a way of keeping her problem to herself: '*to jest mój problem*' ['this is my problem']) corresponds to her gradual slide away from the world of the living.

Throughout *No End*, Antek will hover intermittently in Ula's vicinity. His sympathetic presence is announced: by the soundtrack, as if the off-screen, because invisible, stood for the dead; by the solemn, near-sacral near-plainchant of the score; by the eerie silence which descends as he stalls Ula's Volkswagen to prevent it crashing with a bus further up the road. The case of Darek is not the only unfinished business he has to see through. He also has to resolve his relationship with Ula, and the film is in a sense a tale of seduction. The relationship is Kieślowski's central concern, and even as he persists in making political work his withdrawal from it is apparent in the weakness of the depiction of the Solidarity support network and the intensity and inventiveness of the scenes tinged with mystery, such as Ula's passage up the staircase to revisit the hypnotist. Ula's own unresolved, guilt-ridden confusion is apparent from the jealousy she displays on meeting Marta, one of Antek's youthful acquaintances, or from her reaction on discovering among his papers a series of pornographic pictures of herself – taken when she was hard-up – sent him by 'a well-wisher'. Antek had cut the head from each one, an enigmatic action fusing protectiveness and revenge – depersonalising the images so that they become strangely *more* pornographic. As she weeps and destroys them she wonders why he said nothing of them. In the end, she will turn on the gas and, in a closing sequence of enormous power, join him in death. She puts out the rubbish, cuts the telephone line, brushes her teeth (as if preparing to kiss a phantom lover) and tapes her mouth, the last detail both realistic and a shocking, allegorical image of Poland's condition after martial law. The camera advances into the oven and the screen goes black. It then moves back, identifying with the position of the watching Antek as she crouches before the oven. The hiss of the gas is the last uncanny sound to intimate otherworldliness. Ula rises, reflected in the glass of the book cabinet – the recollection of the opening implying rightness in her actions, a sense of a process's fulfilment, two souls' reunification in an alternative world – and strides out of the house at Antek's side. As they move away with measured steps through the blue wintry night we are as devastated and exalted as we are by the endings of Jean Cocteau's *Orphée* (1949), where the emissaries of the Princess, Death, lead her away through the ruins of the Zone, or of *Wuthering Heights*, where dying becomes a mystic marriage.

Since *No End* is deeply concerned with division, it is ironic that the Party's inevitable condemnation and banishment of the film to out-of-the-way cinemas should have been matched by criticism by both the Catholic Church and the opposition. Party hacks, of course, declared it anti-socialist, sex-obsessed and pessimistically opposed to the social reconciliation underway since 1982. The primary Catholic objections, meanwhile, were to its erotic frankness (at one point Ula masturbates and calls Antek's name, as if he is visiting her in spirit; and indeed as she cries out so does her son Jacek, who is dreaming of when he saw his parents make love) and to the dignity it accords suicide. The validation of suicide is bound in with Antek's youthful enthusiasm for Camus, for the figure of the penitent judge, and recalls Camus' statement that the fundamental philosophical question was that of suicide, '*la mort heureuse*'. And yet, despite that, at one point the film even suggests the workings of a Christian providence: as Ula's green Volkswagen leaves behind the horrendous aftermath of the accident from which Antek has saved her, a cross dominates the right-hand side of the screen, as if overseeing her passage. Reviewers in underground publications added criticism of its failure to include a representation of official oppression and of its alleged fence-sitting effort to be – as one put it – 'simultaneously brave and cunningly careful; truthful, but without annoying those who dislike truthfulness'.[3]

The division may be less within Kieślowski, however, than within almost all Poles, broken in spirit by the imposition of martial law. A quotation from Antek's notes on Darek's case condemns the rulers' deliberate division of the country. The collective divisions paralyse the individuals who internalise them. Joanna, Darek's wife, talks of being torn between her imprisoned husband and her father, who brings her *Trybuna Ludu* (the official mouthpiece of the PZPR) to read and parrots the line that describes Solidarity as a union movement fatally hijacked by a band of anti-state politicos. There is no longer any clear way forward: both idealistic defiance and pragmatic compromise reveal their limitations. Characteristically, a song on the soundtrack is entitled 'Dylemat' (Dilemma). So profound is the Polish depression that even after Darek's case has been won and he goes free with the customary 18-month suspended sentence he Joanna and Ula remain in the courtroom dejected, with Antek sitting towards the back, looking on. Kieślowski himself reports that this mood often prevailed at the end of martial law trials: even a successful outcome is deeply depressing to an individual who goes 'free' into a country that is still unfree – a larger prison. The small victory seems insignificant alongside the enormous quenched hopes ignited by Solidarity. For the State's apparent generosity in its sentencing policy reflected both its own, and its subjects', sense that it had won: lenient sentences mocked the outlawed Solidarity's claims to continued relevance. One may remember how, after 13 December, government spokesman Jerzy Urban derided Lech Wałęsa as a man of the past. There can be no unalloyed victory. Labrador may have won his case but he is a man of few illusions and knows it will be his last: partly because a new retirement age has been introduced for lawyers but also because in any case to defend in a political trial is to destroy one's career prospects. Consulting with his client in jail, he remarks on how much he will have to learn to endure in order to survive. Labrador's last previous political case had been in 1952, before Stalin's death. He lost it and his client received a death sentence. In a sense, things may have improved since then: after all, a whole country cannot be executed. Nevertheless after the trial it is Labrador who goes over to Ula and quotes a poem by Ernst Bryll that concludes, 'Lord, assure me that I howl free, although I weep.'

No End situates itself firmly in the tradition of Polish supernaturalist art. The first image is of candles flickering in a cemetery; later Ula will return to Antek's grave on All Souls' Night, her face illumined by the candle's orange light as she reiterates her love for him. Behind Kieślowski's film lie such works as Adam Mickiewicz's *Forefather's Eve* (which revolves around All Souls' rites) and Stanisław Wyspiański's *The Wedding* (in which apparitions seek to stir the somnolent consciences of the wedding guests and mobilise them for an uprising). Their supernaturalism, like Kieślowski's, is partly political in nature: paying homage to the spirits of the dead sustains their original hope for a free and just Poland. Hence Jacek visits the grave of his grandfather, apparently part of the war-time underground. Bearing this in mind, some have argued that the bleakness of the conclusion is merely apparent, contending that it demonstrates the survival of the spirit of Solidarity. The point is surely that Solidarity survives only as a spirit – as marginal, disembodied and painful to recall (as *invisible*) as Antek's spectre. For one survives on the terms Labrador had described to Darek, terms which evoke Antek also (demonstrating the *representativeness* of his fate, that perennial concern of Kieślowski the documentarist, whose work on *No End* itself had begun as an attempted documentary): 'Pretend that you don't exist if you want to remain in this game.' What seems like Solidarity's death may just be its going underground.

The tension in *No End* is that of someone guarding a flame while lighting a candle to the dead. Scene after scene is agonised to the point of near-paralysis; silences hang between characters lost in their thoughts, alien, brusquely separate. One is continually surprised that another scene follows, that two-shots do not vanish entirely amidst the proliferating shots of characters isolated even when conversing – that life and communication do not gutter entirely. As the film nears its end, however, and Ula's identification with and awareness of Antek intensifies, the attitude to the dead comes to resemble Zbigniew Herbert's in his fine poem 'Our fear' ('Nasz strach', 1961): 'Our fear / does not have the face of a dead man / the dead are gentle to us'. At Antek's graveside Ula stares at the camera – that representative of the invisible – and says 'I love you'. The dead offer solace, their felt, unseen presence showing that even after death and defeat something persists. A living death has prepared one to find their company congenial.

Given the theme of co-presence and separation, it is hardly surprising that *No End* displays the glass imagery more thoroughgoingly present in later Kieślowski. Here the glass is primarily that of receptacles of communion: the glass containing the graveside candle; the unnecessary second glass of coffee Ula makes near the beginning; the glass round whose edge Antek runs his fingers as Ula undergoes hypnosis (the strange ringing that results should be added to the repertoire of eerie noises that signal his presence); the empty glass the hypnotist hands Ula when she revisits him; the half-full glass she drops in slow motion – already passing beyond most mortals' time – as she stands in the kitchen near the end. But there is also the glass of Labrador's watch, which falls and breaks as Antek sweeps past unseen, or the shattered windscreen of the car whose crash is seen from a shocked distance like that in *Trois coleurs: Bleu* (*Three Colours: Blue*, 1993). Its final form is the glazed door separating us from the dead whose backs are turned. And since the film also dramatises questions of fidelity, its interest in dogs – also foreshadowing later Kieślowski – is no surprise. A black dog nuzzles up to Antek as he sits unseen on a park bench alongside Ula; it peers into the Volkswagen as she visits Joanna; a dog sits outside as she weeps on discovery of the pornographic photos; and the lawyer who takes Darek's case is named Labrador. The poem he quotes, a wolf's monologue, belongs here also. Various elements will recur in later Kieślowski films, particularly *Three Colours: Blue*, which also begins with a widowing, while Ula's definition of love as she hugs Jacek is reconjugated by Irena, hugging Paweł, in *Decalogue 1*.

The recurrences of the imagery echo the title: there is no ending. No end to the state of misery of which they are part; no end – the viewer has to hope – to the exasperated spirit's capacity to survive. A *dur désir de durer* is embodied in the film's solemn, wary, stubbornly courageous progression, however deep its respect for, and empathy with, Ula's final choice. For in the early 1980s it was Kieślowski alone – rather than his more renowned compatriots, Wajda and Zanussi – who summoned the courage to contemplate the legacy of martial law in Poland. If others preferred to avert their eyes from it, it was because at the time it appeared to be so devastating. For if Solidarity had melted the ice of the cold war, confounding conventional distinctions between right and left, opposing the *soi-disant* socialist state in the name of the socialism that very state repressed, the imposition of martial law precipitated a massive haemorrhage in Poland of hope for the feasibility of socialism. This total divestment from the idea of socialism left stranded the notion of socialist self-criticism, which had provided both a motor and an alibi for the Polish cinema of the late 1970s. In its aftermath, criticism ceased to be reformist and became total, even apocalyptic, and only the strongest spirits had the stomach for it. Kieślowski was clearly such a figure. But it is something greater than Solidarity that Kieślowski mourns, for he recognised that Solidarity embodied it only in part: it is the dream of the ideal represented by Antek. The film is less the incoherent *mélange* of genres several reviewers perceived than the process of one genre's absorption and supersession of all the others. As Ula's yearning takes her beyond this world the political becomes the metaphysical.

IMPLICIT POLITICS: *A SHORT FILM ABOUT KILLING*

A Short Film About Killing – described as Kieślowski's masterpiece by Tadeusz Sobolewski (1999: 28), and his first film to gain tumultous acceptance in the West, winning the Félix (Europe's Oscar for best film) for 1988 – bristles with ironies. They set in as the titles roll: a dead rat in a puddle and a hanged cat dangling before oppressively serried apartment blocks. Varsovians would instantly recognise the irony that juxtaposes the dead animals, evoking an urban inferno, with blocks that in fact contained the apartments of many of Poland's best-known television and film stars: Kieślowski remarked that he had tried to pick one of the best-looking housing complexes. The title itself secretes a deadly irony, as this 'short film' will show how lengthy and arduous is the process of doing a man to death, absorbing approximately eight minutes of screen time. The time it takes to complete the murder's first stage will be marked excruciatingly by the slow-passage of a bicycle along the yellow-lit horizon.

Kieślowski's ironies are not signs of detached, sovereign authorial control but appalling dissonances. They echo in the premonitions of a young lawyer, Piotr Balicki, whose celebration of his graduation to the bar is pierced by a sudden sense that his future will not be as straight-forward as he hopes. As the lawyer celebrates, Jacek, the future murderer, is already drinking in the same café. It is in the scenes of Jacek's wandering around Warsaw – ironically, in its show-case tourist area, near the Old Town – that Kieślowski's film is most remarkable. Jacek traverses a world turned to slime by Sławomir Idziak's green filters, like the drained aquarium street of Joseph Conrad's *The Secret Agent* (1907). He first appears in doubly uncanny form, before a cinema, as a reflection that is also a shadow, in a half-lit world. The partial desaturation of the image – other colours are visible only at its centre – echoes the effect of the tinted band across the windscreen of the taxi whose driver Jacek will kill. As Kieślowski himself notes, the filters obscure non-essential objects in particular (just as his screenplay omits the unnecessary trial) (Niogret 1997: 16). Thanks to the filters one image after another as it were spreads the dirt at the edges of the car window the windscreen wipers cannot reach: the taxi-driver may wash it, but the filters fog it again. And his car window's tinted band is echoed musically as Piotr's girlfriend sits in the café in front of a large green plastic screen, ironically placed centre-screen this time. With its realistic equivalent, the device is never ornamental but suggests – quasi-expressionistically – the closing down of possibility in the murder's world: fatalistically, every image quietly anticipates or recalls the taxi, evoking an inescapably determining primal scene of murder towards which the film descends and from which it only seems to swirl away – until that scene recurs, transformed, in the hanging of Jacek himself. It is hardly surprising that we only learn Jacek's name after his murder of the taxi-driver, as if the deed alone has given him a name, as if – existentially – his deed has defined him completely. The work's expressionistic use of stylisation to evoke Jacek's point of view even allows him to darken the world, identify-ing him as a power of darkness: as he looks back underarm at the Castle Square taxi stand the crooked arm through which he does so blots out the image's edges. Shortly afterwards, filters stretched across the top half of the image darken the sky as the taxi-driver moves off with Jacek as his fare.

At the centre of Idziak's muddied images, only one colour is strongly present: the red worn by a series of girls. This is doubly ironic: girls are unattainable for Jacek, one of whose possible motives for the killing was to acquire a car to take one to the mountains; ironically, Beata, whose recognition of the taxi precedes Jacek's trial, had been ogled and propositioned by the oleaginous taxi-driver. The film's succession of girls in red leads naturally to another red, the blood on the taxi-driver's head. When Jacek covers the bloodied head with a brown checked blanket, he completes the desaturation of his own world by trying to hide the sign of his guilt, to accelerate red's declension into brown. Just as he pulled his head up into the taxi's darkness to escape the look of *The Decalogue* series' recurrent witness figure, he veils the staring face of his victim. (Jacek's unwillingness to be seen is in a sense the precursor of his own death.) The interchange of red and brown in this murder scene formally anticipates the colour-scheme of that other Kieślowski film preoccupied with law and judgement, *Three Colours: Red*. The only girl with whom Jacek is associated in the scenes preceding the murder is a young one in a photograph, in a communion dress, later revealed as his dead sister. She wears white, not the red that is instinct with life, and from the outset we suspect that she is dead: Jacek asks the shop assistant whom he wants to enlarge the photograph, whether photographs can tell one if someone is no longer alive.

Ironies are legion in this densely scripted film. The taxi-driver savours the outlaw qualities of a stray dog, unaware that a human outlaw will kill him (after the murder, Jacek eats the other half of the sandwich thrown to the dog). As Piotr describes law positively as a way of meeting people he might otherwise never encounter, he says this will happen 'if everything goes well': words he applies to his exam, but which follow an image of Jacek and the welling up on the soundtrack of menacing chords. The driver tells Jacek he's driven as far as he'll go, and his words assume a deadly second meaning as the killing begins. (A cutaway to the car's wheels grinding in the mud underlines the futility of any attempted escape.) Jacek's frantic efforts to halt the nightmarishly prolonged blast of the car's horn are ironised when only a horse in a field looks round and then, the moment the horn has fallen silent, a passing train picks up its note (implying the futility of Jacek's activity – for the sound would have been drowned anyway – and that the murder will recur infernally in the mind of its executor); a man selling lottery tickets congratulates the driver on his good luck; and Jacek refuses to let a gypsy read his fortune as he enters the café where the girlfriend of the young lawyer, Piotr Balicki, is reading *his* palm. Jacek's Warsaw is a realm of diabolic coincidence and reversal, a circle of hell.

Jacek's murder of the taxi-driver may seem motiveless, its apparent inevitability the result of the expressionist style and the accumulation of such details as the hanged cat ironically prefiguring Jacek's dehumanisation and hanging or the severed head that is the taxi-driver's good-luck charm – another irony, as it presages the mode of his death. With his fluffy punk hair and denim jacket, Jacek stalks Warsaw like an edgy existential angel of doom. But it is not just the stylistic tour de force that persuades us to accept the experience of the appallingly protracted murder, but Kieślowski's equally important, sombre insistence on the action's status as the logical conclusion of a gratuitous violence in human relations that may well issue from Poland's late-1980s economic decline but which is also something he deems increasingly characteristic of our ever colder civilisation. Whether it be the taxi-driver hooting at a poodle then deliberately leaving would-be clients standing (appallingly rough justice then lands him with Jacek), or Jacek himself telling people at the taxi-stand that his destination is the opposite of theirs, hostility is pervasive. Jacek's action simply discloses its implicit murderousness. It is as if Jacek is the point at which the social chain snaps beneath the overwhelming weight of an oozing evil: who earths it for that society like a scapegoat.

Nevertheless, there are hints of an alternative world linked to the work's children and its idealistic young lawyer, modelled partly on Kieślowski's script consultant on legal matters, Krzysztof Piesiewicz, and surely partly also on Kieślowski himself (he uses his signature-phrase 'nie wiem' ['I don't know'] when motivating his career-choice, while his ironic summary of the putative deterrent virtues of capital punishment anticipates the director's own argument). When Jacek flicks coffee dregs at the café window through which two young girls are watching him, they smile and he smiles back: their reaction transforms his violence into play, and in retrospect it will seem almost as if he has been flinging mud at the image of his sister (throwing earth on her coffin?) and then smiling at her untouchability, the invulnerability of the dead. He looks at her but is separated from her photographic image just as in this scene the glass separates him from the girls. Piotr's exuberance as his scooter weaves in and out of traffic is virtually the sole additional relief in the stalking darkness of the film (the taxi-driver frowns at him). But Piotr's defense of Jacek is useless, its hopelessness daringly embodied in the cut wherewith Kieślowski excises everything between Beata's recognition of the taxi-driver's car and the judge's closure of the trial. Piotr's peroration against the death penalty may be the best the judge has ever heard, but we are not shown it. Piotr's role as secular priest, hearing Jacek's last words in prison, is more important to Kieślowski. But the omission also occurs because his own argument against capital punishment is framed purely filmically. This polemic may be taken as an extension of the critique of fascism in *From the Point of View of the Night Porter*. As Hermann Broch notes, 'a man who campaigns for the abolition of capital punishment loses his interest in magical justice ... With this loss of interest in such magic goes one in the magic-demonic propaganda of the various fascisms' (Broch 1955b: 217). For Broch, writing during the rise of National Socialism in Germany, the abolition of capital punishment would entail a 'leap into the dark' that 'forces men to shut their eyes' (is the darkness pre-existent or caused by those eyes closing?) – but it is the precondition of the open system that is democracy (Broch 1955b: 215–17). In *A Short Film About Killing*, all idealisation of the state becomes impossible as a parallel gruesomeness places individual and state-sanctioned killing on the same plane: Kieślowski does not speak of 'murder' and 'killing' but simply of killing. As militiamen bundle Jacek into the execution chamber, knocking down the curtain, and the man tightening the noose shrieks instructions to his assistant, their frenzy echoes Jacek's earlier realisation of the difficulty of killing a man. In the final, most deadly irony, it is as if the law that has violence at its carefully screened heart, behind the curtains Kieślowski rips away, is itself implicated in the murder Jacek has committed.

Kieślowski suggests several possible explanations for Jacek's deed. There is the need for one of the chronically deprived young to obtain a car (the actual motive in the real case that was the film's point of departure) and hence of youth's revenge upon age. There is the country boy's desire to assert himself in the city whose hostility he reciprocates with a vengeance. Perhaps most mysterious and unconscious of all is Jacek's own death-wish, his apparent search – by means of a murder for which he knows he will die – for a mode of suicide that will not preclude burial in consecrated ground alongside his beloved sister (the suicide motif being first suggested, but not spelled out, by Jacek's visit to a cinema in which *Wetherby* is playing). If Kieślowski neither highlights nor privileges any of these possibilities, it is partly because he wishes to allow for the essential mysteriousness of human actions. Part of that mystery lies in the hints of a possible intersection between these actions and an invisible reality: Zbigniew Preisner's score rises to an agonised crescendo as the taxi-driver moves off with Jacek in his cab; writhing choral voices suggest a dissonant transcendence as Jacek stares at the 'witness' figure who haunts *The Decalogue*. The music re-enters, again with a sense of off-key otherworldliness, as Jacek looks at the bloodied head of his seated, seemingly dead victim and moans 'Oh Jesus'. An entirely mysterious irony, meanwhile, links Piotr and Jacek: as Piotr tells his examining board that as years go by people doubt the meaning of what they do, his head slips into darkness rather as Jacek's will do on passing the witness. There may be a crucial difference – Piotr does not hide in the dark, as does Jacek – but the lighting establishes an enigmatic connection nevertheless, perhaps indicating the sheer pervasiveness (though also intermittence) of the principle of darkness. Kieślowski's refusal of determinist explanation extends to his viewers the freedom Jacek denies himself.

A 'SHORT' FILM

Kieślowski often remarked on the difficulty of finding titles for his works, perhaps because he rejected the most widespread and conventional form of title, which uses a name. His titles are more abstract and conceptual. The only one to mention a person's name – *The Double Life of Véronique* – lures one into expecting one Véronique living two lives (an open one and a secret one) *simultaneously*, while the film in fact both expands and inverts this expectation: what one gets is *two* girls, Weronika and Véronique, living *one* life, which is simultaneous and co-terminous only up to a certain point in time. A title like *Camera Buff*, meanwhile, is descended from the titles employed by the documentarist (*Bricklayer, From the Point of View of the Night Porter*): titles stressing the typicality or representativeness of a protagonist who simply exemplifies a profession. Kieślowski's dissatisfaction with his own titles may reflect a sense of the disparity between the individual life or events filmed and the project of investigating an idea. In the case of *A Short Film About Killing*, whose 'short' is both modest and ironic, a kind of transfer occurs between the words 'short' and 'killing', rendering all the more unexpected the sheer duration of the work's two deaths. In addition to this, Kieślowski employs the idea of the 'short' film given in his title to engender spectator question and suspense, particularly in the film's second half, when the audience knows the end to be approaching, and when language begins to be used extensively – following the near-silent first half – making possible explicit moment-by-moment adjustments in conscious awareness of temporality. Immediately after the verdict has been pronounced, Jacek asks 'is that the end?', and since this is a *short* film we may indeed wonder if it is so. (In the *really* short film that is *Decalogue 5*, meanwhile, the end is indeed closer, and could even come here – after about 55 minutes.) A little later, after the hangman has prepared the execution chamber, he tells the lieutenant 'it's ready', and again the end may seem imminent. But the lieutenant tells the lawyer he can have half an hour with Jacek. Audience members already aware of the film's running time may be tempted to glance at their watches and wonder whether this encounter will take up the film's remainder – as it could well do, since it still has approximately thirty minutes to run when the lieutenant makes this remark, and filmic executions seldom last long. The viewer, perhaps stunned by the earlier appallingly protracted murder (unbearably and ironically *long* in the 'short film'), may even wish to read this announcement as a sign that – despite the expectations aroused by the title ('killing' rather than 'murder' is a category that might be stretched to include execution too) and by the film's genre (the prison execution movie) – the hanging may even not be shown. After all, Kieślowski has already set a precedent for surprise by omitting the trial. Be that as it may, the lieutenant's remark foregrounds the question of time, the insistent ticking away of the clock of a short (young) life in this short film. Later still, the lawyer's dialogue with Jacek will be interrupted by officials asking whether or not he's ready: on the first occasion he says 'not yet'. The interruption is both an alarm clock the text switches off and the kind of momentary suspension of intense encounter Kieślowski frequently employs – to induce suspense, to preserve the scene from monotony or claustrophobia, to evoke a sense of possible and other worlds, to indicate the ease and frequency with which his characters' aims are frustrated. (The principle of such a punctuation goes back to his documentaries, with their analytical subdivisions and occasional lifting of the oppressiveness of their subjects' lives, often with a shot of the world outside, often viewed through a window.) Asked a second time, the lawyer retorts, 'tell the prosecutor that I'll never say I'm ready'. Death always comes too early. The lawyer's position is the one embodied in the title of Kieślowki's previous film, *No End*. Jacek himself may then fling himself to the ground, but there will now be only a brief stay of execution before the short film and his short life are over.

THE DIALECTICS OF DISTANCE

Although Kieślowski's titles distance one, their relationship with the works they head is dialectical, as the camerawork places one *close* to the characters. The images themselves often reiterate that dialectic, counterposing closeness with intervening glass or juxtaposed mirrors. Throughout the works, the camera placement plays out a dialectic of urgency and distance, appeals and their rejection. As a man is chased down an alleyway and beaten up the camera closes in to watch as Jacek observes from a cool distance. It is probably only Kieślowski's consummate alternation between close-up images of the murder and long shots of the car, or the cutaways to other elements around it, that renders this sequence bearable, preventing it becoming utterly overwhelming, not bludgeoning us into insensibility but rather deepening our horror with each return. After Jacek's conviction, the lawyer visits the judge's chambers to ask if another lawyer might have succeeded where he failed. In the shot/reverse-shot interchange between the two men, the camera is closer to the lawyer, evoking and seconding the urgency of his appeal. Since he looks past the camera, the image of Piotr is clearly not from the judge's point-of-view.[4] We then see the judge, seated – protectively? – behind his desk, at a greater distance, and from an angle that suggests the lawyer's point-of-view.[5] The distance shows the judge's capacity to create distance, to mute the urgency of the lawyer's appeal, and it is hardly surprising that the two are then shown together in long-shot, from the end of the judge's chamber: everything is now settled, cut-and-dried. The judge's initial relative smallness corresponds to a diminution of humanity through identification with the judicial killing mechanism, an identification even more apparent in the case of the lengthy sequence of the hangman's preparation: we first see him passing through the prison gate, leaving behind the outside world and his own individual life as he then walks impassively into the distance, shrinking by the moment as he becomes a functionary. Since we are at first unaware of his identity, he seems as impersonal as the doors and windows that clank open and shut with equal impassivity. As the camera registers his preparations, it never draws as close to him as it does to the lawyer: the focus is on his activity rather than his personality, with the implication that the former has extinguished the latter. The ability to distinguish between the two is important for Kieślowski. The lawyer – desperately holding on to the Christian distinction between the sin and the sinner – tells Jacek that the court did not so much condemn him as his deed. But since Jacek himself is to die, while his deed lies in the past and is not available for reinspection (though, crucially, *we* are allowed to reinspect it through its filmic dramatisation), he may be forgiven for failing to recognise the distinction and arguing that to oppose his deed *is* to oppose him. Where the lawyer's position may be deemed Christian, is not Jacek's existentialist? Jacek's surname – Lazar (Lazarus) – poses the question of his final fate, ironically asking if he will ever rise again and noting that (unlike his namesake) he will not do shortly after his death. As Tadeusz Sobolewski notes, the film does not simply hold the murderer at a condemnatory distance: 'we find ourselves as viewers sufficiently close to see in him not the incarnation of evil but a human being stripped of the protective layer that restrains aggression' (Sobolewski 1988b: 8). For Sobolewski, 'the *closeness* of our view of both killings represents a shattering move with aesthetic, ethical and also religious consequences' (Sobolewski 1988a: 83), including the reflection that justice must give way to mercy: a conclusion which 'does not stem from religious presuppositions but from intuition, from the mere manner of looking' (ibid.). The consequences this has for the view of the state meanwhile are – as Broch observes – that it must divest itself of the mystical power of killing in order to demonstrate its humanity to its subjects: 'to make them aware that all human life is inviolable, that no human soul, however depraved, can be excluded from this' (Broch 1955b: 214). If throughout its remainder the film stays closer to the lawyer than anyone else, it is to hug the one sign of life in the dank brown (*non-red*) obscurity of the fearsome, death-dealing space – the valley of death – through which he walks as our harrowed representative.

POLISH CINEMA AND THE QUESTION OF CO-PRODUCTION

The recurrent political oppression of the last two hundred years rendered Westward moves common, even traditional, among Polish artists and intellectuals. The exile's position is, of course, tense and difficult: on the one hand, one may need to leave one's native country to achieve freedom of speech; but, on the other, prolonged absence may sap both the will and – more importantly – the ability to speak for one's countrymen, who may legitimately ask the Conradian question whether the artist is still 'one of us'. Thus when the key Polish filmmakers of the late 1970s – Wajda and Zanussi – took frequent working trips to the West in the early 1980s, they became 'temporary exiles', and their peregrinations testified both to post-martial law oppression and to the fact that the ice that had thawed under Solidarity never regained its old temperature sufficiently to freeze everybody in. The less well-known Agnieszka Holland, meanwhile, was trapped by martial law in a West to which she adapted remarkably well, reaccenting her work to stress its feminist rather than its Polish strain, something perhaps partly facilitated by the way the ethos of traditional 'Polishness' is tinged with a masculinist military virtue her gender made her question. (Perhaps only the tough-minded Kieślowski could have succeeded in making the dark and critical *No End* within early 1980s Poland, but the fact of its domestic production and distribution, albeit unadvertised and in out-of-the-way cinemas, indicated the uncertainty of rulers who would later abdicate entirely.) It is surely significant that whenever possible the departing artists always returned: only sojourn on Polish soil ultimately legitimised their speech to and for the disenfranchised nation. Even Skolimowski sought to set up a Polish project in the early 1980s.

For anyone considering the dynamics of national identity under globalisation and co-production, the case of Central and East European cinema during and after the withering away of state sponsorship and control is profoundly instructive. For individual directors, meanwhile, the demise of *soi-disant* socialist orders meant an evaporation of the availability of the status of political refugee, ending the lineage of Forman, Passer and Polański and turning the East European-US axis into a one-way street travelled by Hollywood producers seeking well-trained, cut-price technicians for works with American stars (thus facilitating the continued payment of those stars' inflated fees). France, the old half-way house for so many Poles, became more likely to be a permanent domicile, especially since to enter the North American cultural sphere often entailed deep marginalisation – as was discovered by Ryszard Bugajski, exiled director of *Przesłuchanie* (*The Interrogation*, 1982), that key Solidarity-era anti-Stalinist text.

Whereas the co-productions of the 1980s had been shot abroad, with directors willingly bearing a Western 'economic censorship' that was nevertheless far less constraining than the native political one, those of the 1990s would be made domestically. The 1989 collapse of the socialist state's film-funding system merely concluded its lengthy tottering. For Poland's key directors of the early 1980s – Wajda and Zanussi – had ventured abroad after the imposition of martial law not just to secure relatively free utterance but also because the native industry's undercapitalisation at a time of spiralling national debt lent it an early openness to co-production. In the process, however, the questions of identity central to these film-makers' earlier works, and to the Polish artist's status as unofficial national spokesperson, often suffered repression: the options open to a Hungarian director like István Szabó, whose 1980s German-language trilogy contributed to the debate on Hungarian identity by tapping the overlap between the then fashionable notion of *Mitteleuropa* and the intellectual afterlife of the Austro-Hungarian empire, were not available to Polish directors. Polish idealisation of 'the West' simply testifies to the country's distance from it (see, for instance, Radosław Piwowarski's feeble *Train to Hollywood* [*Pociąg do Hollywood*, 1987]). Polish filmmakers did not follow the inter-war novelist Witold Gombrowicz and dissect the way local obsession with one's culture's seeming second-class status – particularly *vis-à-vis* the economically more successful West – generates compensatory pride in one's devotion to 'higher things'. The nearest thing to such a dissection was to be found in the early 1980s work of Skolimowski, particularly *Success is the Best Revenge* (1984), where 'revenge' extends to the football field and Poland's famous and unexpected mid-1970s dismissal of England from the World Cup. Such themes, however, hardly promised the large international returns a co-production's outlay demands, and even Skolimowski's low-budget work on Polish themes was financially viable only during the brief heyday of Poland's early-1980s 'newsworthiness'. Nor have native Polish directors interrogated their own idealisation of American culture through appropriation of the road movie, as have Wim Wenders or Hungary's György Szomjas. The major temptation they face when engaged in co-production is thus one of a self-division that may avoid becoming schizophrenia only when consciously thematised – as in Kieślowski's *The Double Life of Véronique*, which devotes only a third of its time to its heroine's Polish incarnation (is such asymmetry also necessary to avoid schizophrenia, indicating greater commitment to one place than to the other?) and then, later, in *Trois couleurs: Blanc* (*Three Colours: White*, 1994). For Polish directors unwilling to follow Kieślowski's lead, however, the question became one of how to find the middle ground upon which both to assert one's national identity and contribute to 'the discourse of others', an issue often resolved by pursuing the investigation of the 'Jewish question' that has sometimes seemed to be the most financially and thematically viable form of the Polish co-production.

AFTER 1989

For many Polish directors, the political liberation of 1989 – which came a mere year after the release of *A Short Film About Killing* – meant disorientation. Old habits of densely encoding meaning for allegorical decipherment by audiences in the know – old chess games and script-margin duels with the censor – had to be discarded. 'The shock of freedom' was the title of Tadeusz Sobolewski's lead article in the January 1992 edition of *Kino* (Sobolewski 1992: 2–3). 'Free from what?' Andrzej Wajda asked a few pages later (Wajda 1992: 3–5). Freedom from what and freedom for what? To make hit-man thrillers in the Western mode, as in the high-concept advertising compositions of Władysław Pasikowski's *Pigs* (*Psy*, 1993)? To burlesque the icons of the recent past, as in Konrad Szołajski's *Człowiek z ... (Man of ...*, 1993), a parody of *Man of Marble* and *Man of Iron* whose chief bugbear is no longer the security officer but that new one, the prurient priest? If, in the twilight of his career, Wajda used his freedom well – for all the aesthetic weakness of *The Horse-Hair Ring* and then, later, the minor status of *Holy Week* – more important may be the manner of its employment by Kieślowski, who, for most late-1980s and early-1990s spectators, incarnated the most vital form of Polish cinema internationally.

If the question of the direction Polish cinema was to take post-1989 conjugated the question 'after politics, what next?', Kieślowski had asked and answered it for himself even before the Round Table talks, in *The Decalogue*, that series of films universalised by its dramatisation of the dissonances between the precepts Moses received at Sinai and harried everyday Polish lives. His subsequent *The Double Life of Véronique* was to be remarkable for reflecting in the double mirror of its Polish and French protagonist(s) the production situation of the work itself. It became a fascinating effort at squaring the circle: at achieving the metamorphosis the audience demanded and the film itself thematised, while also remaining oneself (one rediscovers one's abandoned Polish heroine – both same and other – in a girl from France). Was this the double life of Kieślowski himself?

The Kieślowski of the *Three Colours* trilogy vigorously denied any political intent, his vaporisation of collective subjects matching the existentialism that so profoundly marks his work (his literary preferences being for Dostoevsky and Camus occasionally mentioned in his films). Kieślowski does not portray past or environment as in any way determining but allows characters an existential freedom to make and remake themselves moment by moment. Since Kieślowski's work is more a dialogue with existentialism than its simple exemplification, however, he deems freedom an ambiguous good whose underside is loss. *Three Colours: Blue* links Julie's widowhood to the section's keyword, *liberté*, and in *Camera Buff* Filip Mosz's assistant congratulates him on his freedom after his wife Irka has left him. The definition of freedom is as potentially negative as that of Camus' Jean-Baptiste Clamence, who describes his own 'congenital inability to see in love anything but the physical' (cf. Magda in *Krótki film o miłości* [*A Short Film About Love*, 1988]) and 'faculty for forgetting' as favouring his freedom (Camus 1963: 44), and who links freedom to the death of others (Camus 1963: 50).

Kieślowski's demotion of politics involves its demystification, its draining of the mystery that is the afterlife of the utopia it once embodied. How this is done can be gauged by comparing some moments in *The Double Life of Véronique* with a key moment in Wolfgang Becker's *Goodbye Lenin!* (2003). Even thirteen years after the fall of the Berlin Wall, the latter film stages the valediction to politics as a farewell to Lenin: Christiane, an East Berliner who is recovering from a heart-attack and is unaware of the changes known as the Wende, slips outside alone for the first time, and the dislocations of her notion of everyday GDR life culminate in a helicopter flying past with the broken upper half of a statue of Lenin (an echo, of course, of the famous first moments of Fellini's *La Dolce Vita*). The statue seems to gesture towards her, and the shuddering slow motion registers her transfixed incomprehension. The moment could be designated accurately using Slavoj Žižek's memorable phrase 'the sublime object of ideology'. Christiane senses the shock waves of history rippling across it, but does not realise that what is shaking the ground is an earthquake. This scene can be read as a synthesis of two moments that are widely separated in *The Double Life of Véronique*, one very near the beginning of Weronika's story, one near its end. In the first, a truck bearing a statue trundles incomprehensibly, and unnoticed, down the street of her home town; the indeterminacy of its identity bespeaks a fading interest in the public and political world while also suggesting an uncanny flash-forward from the still-contested Poland of the film's world to the post-1989 one in which statues did indeed come down. In the second moment, shortly before her death, Weronika sees her French double Véronique. As a riot swirls around her, she becomes an Eliotic 'still point of the turning world', its turning rightly likened to a vortex by Žižek, though he ignores the degree to which its intimation of the end of a world is also a slippage into the maëlstrom of a political time-travel (Žižek 2001: 83–4). Weronika turns her back to the massed riot police, having eyes only for the spectacle of her double. The sublime is de-ideologised, just as the political is demystified by the lack of any such emblematic encounter with the fetish that centred East Central European political discourse, the image of Lenin. (That image was, of course, a political fetish in the strictly Freudian sense of the mechanism of fetishisation, which is also one of idealisation, and which disavows and arrests a temporal flow towards trauma: in this case, towards the traumatic aftermath of the death of Lenin, when the Soviet system became Stalinist.) The visionary encounters in the two films resemble one another, femininity and sickness reinforcing the non-agency of the seer. This feminisation of the seer also suggests the openness to the other-worldly that becomes possible when one steps outside the business of life, which is male business. In each case, the moment is marked as one of a hallucination that cannot be integrated into the narrative, as is shown by the fact that neither Weronika nor Christiane asks any questions afterwards. It cannot enter narrative because it lies outside language. To use the terms of an almost-forgotten film theory: the syntagmatic, the horizontal realm of progression, is destroyed by a suffusion of something from above, the (sublime) vertical axis of the paradigmatic. The characters are struck dumb.

The full extent of Kieślowski's demystification of the political only becomes apparent, however, when one juxtaposes these two scenes from *The Double Life of Véronique* with an earlier staging of the spectacle of potency, when Weronika beholds the canted image of a man exposing himself to her. The tipping of the image renders it less sexually explicit and establishes it as a point-of-view shot of the leaning Weronika, who has just suffered a heart spasm, but it also registers the shock it emits and shows the world beginning to fall over. It is thus related to the 'end of the world' imagery of the scene of the riot. The substitution of the man's real penis for the symbolic political phallus – the image of Lenin – demystifies the claims to potency of an image whose fall haunted East Central European cinema in the aftermath of 1989. Splitting what could have been a single scene into three (the appearance of the statue, the man's self-exposure and the dizzying encounter with the double) demystifies it, something underlined by its linkage with the obscene. These three scenes are the three dispersed parts of a shattered monument. The dispersal sets the seal on the demystification.

Kieślowski's earlier move to feature-making, meanwhile, may be seen as a way of freeing his subjects to act in the world rather than reflect upon past action, as they had done so frequently in his documentaries. Paradoxically, in order to achieve this the features mobilise a strategy often associated with documentary, repeatedly *following* the characters. The preferred strategy of the documentaries had been the reverse of this: not the camera behind people, trying to catch up with them, but rather in front of them as they addressed it. Kieślowski trades in the documentary's freedom to allow the subject to look at the camera for the feature's pro-scription of that look, as the characters cease to look out at 'the world' but rather become the world for one another. The freedom of reflection becomes one of freedom of *action*. As is most signally demonstrated in *Blind Chance*, whose protagonist experiences three separate lives yet remains fundamentally 'the same', the political positions they occupy do not affect their essential selfhood. The political discourses of division and contradiction thus become finally irrel-evant.[6] The isolation that feeds the characters' freedom itself flourishes in the delocalised space of co-production. Freedom culminates in a will to rebirth and second life expressed either in self-destructiveness or actual suicide: strategies whose pervasiveness will become apparent in my analyses of the *Three Colours* trilogy.

There is another possible way of describing Kieślowski's itinerary, however: as a movement from realistic depictions of existing varieties of fraternity to evocations of ones that are fantas-tic. This move is not a retreat from the social but itself a form of social criticism: in line with his lament to Urszula Biełous, at the time of *The Decalogue*, that now 'we live separately', he registers the evaporation of unity from social reality. Only magic can conjure it up: the person with whom one is at one lives in another country, and one discovers her existence only after her death; or one's unity with another person is only hinted at (Valentine and Auguste inhabit the same image at the end of *Red* but – as Marek Haltof has noted – look in different directions [Haltof 2004: 144]), and is in any case built upon, and apparently paid for by, the suffering of another (the judge).

The distance Kieślowski had travelled from 'the Cinema of Moral Anxiety' is clearly appar-ent in the first and last films of the trilogy. Nevertheless it can perhaps best be measured through the section of the trilogy that revisits its preoccupations: *Three Colours: White*. For Edward Kłosiński, the cameraman on this film, it constitutes a sort of epitaph for this movement, with which Kieślowski was once associated. Karol is 'a little man, just the kind of person the Cinema of Moral Anxiety dealt with', he says (Kołodziejski 1993: 29). The concern with corruption and the world of shady deals also recalls that cinema, although the context has now shifted from the schemes of Party officials to those of the would-be high-rollers of the early days of post-1989 capitalism. There is a recurrent emphasis on how 'you can buy anything these days' (first said by Karol as he pulls out a gun in the Warsaw metro, then by his chauffeur, who suggests the purchase of a Russian corpse to impersonate Karol). The relationship with the Cinema of Moral Anxiety includes deliberate allusions to its style (as Kłosiński puts it), or rather anti-style, as the movement adopted a deliberately serviceable style that foregrounded issues over aesthetics, and was thus often deemed 'journalistic'. Perhaps only in Wajda's *Bez znieczulenia* (*Rough Treatment*, 1978) does stylenessness become a style in its own right, dry and deadpan. Nevertheless, Kłosiński also describes *White* as seeking to transcend that movement (ibid.). So even though lacking the mixture of lyricism and metaphysics Western viewers had come to associate with Kieślowski by 1994, its distance from the Cinema of Moral Anxiety is hardly surprising given the fact that, as Tadeusz Sobolewski reports, even in 1978 – at the movement's height – Kieślowski had considered it *passé* (Sobolewski 1997: 14). At a film festival in Lower Silesia upon whose jury he sat, his preferred film simply showed a closed door at which someone was knocking. Where the Cinema of Moral Anxiety would take one behind closed doors, unveiling the corrupt mechanisms of power, even at this stage of his career Kieślowski was drawn to an image of Kafkaesque mystery. As Sobolewski notes elsewhere, for Kieślowski – as for Agnieszka Holland – 'it turns out that the unrest did not diminish when Solidarity appeared in the social arena. Both Kieślowski and Holland exploited the season of freedom of 1980–81 to break the bounds of all ideologies in their films. In *A Woman Alone*, in *Blind Chance*, the notion of the system gives way to that of fate' (Sobolewski 1990: 91–2).

TOWARDS 'THREE COLOURS'

What are we but our own mirror images, and where we sit thus together in pairs the third – God – is not far away.
> – Ernst Jünger

In *Blind Chance*, Kieślowski makes of one character three persons. In rendering three 'persons' one character, he abandons binary logic whilst also indicating the impossibility of so doing in the politicised world, as exemplified by early 1980s Poland: only the apolitical third Witek dies. In the third part of the film, Witold tries to juggle three apples and one falls to the ground; it anticipates his own end, Western logic's Aristotelean exclusion of the middle. To speak of Witek as a 'hero' in the same sense as the protagonists of such films as Leszek Wosiewicz's *Kornblumenblau* (1989) or Piotr Szulkin's *Ga-Ga. Chwała bohaterom* (*Ga-Ga. Praise to the Heroes*, 1986) – as does Mariola Jankun-Dopartowa – is to overlook the specificity of Kieślowski's radically hypothetical fictional construction and its effect on traditional notions of individuality (Jankun-Dopartowa 1996b: 145–72). *Blind Chance* may be read as offering the key to all Kieślowski's work: in showing that separate characters are really one, it underlines the theme of brotherhood that runs throughout it, beginning perhaps with *Szpital* (*Hospital*, 1977) (Karabasz 1985: 90), its centrality underlined by its double iteration at the end of his two great series, in *Decalogue 10* and *Three Colours: Red*. To apply the lesson of *Blind Chance* to the other films is to discover triple identities within apparently single figures. The triangle that so fascinates Kieślowski is, of course, the figure of the tragic, of impossible pairing (comedy's geometry, by way of contrast, being the square: two couples pairing off in a world of sufficiency rather than shortage). When Piotr Wojciechowski writes of *Red*, 'the old judge has something of God about him, and something of Kieślowski himself' (Wojciechowski 1994: 49), the critic's shift to the level of symbol and biography dissolves the awkward textuality within which the judge is *also* a judge: not just a pretext for the combined theological and biographical reflection that has been the prevailing note in the best Kieślowski criticism (I am thinking in particular of the essays, reviews and interviews of Tadeusz Sobolewski), but also a character. He is three in one: God, Kieślowski and – last but not least – Joseph Kern (a judge whose fallen status may be indicated by the placement of his handwritten name on the screen *upside down*). Similarly, Alexandre Fabbri – the Maker – is God, Kieślowski (as artist) and a character who betrays Valentine by using her. The functions of the three figures partly overlap but are not identical: their separation means that Kieślowski is not necessarily saying that Alexandre's betrayal of Valentine means that God and the artist also manipulate humanity. In *A Short Film About Killing*, meanwhile, the three elements sometimes intertwined within a single character are separated out. The taxi-driver, Jacek and Piotr are all distinct. But if the spirit of killing clearly animates the first two, may it not also finally begin to surface – appallingly – in the innocent Piotr himself, when he says '*nienawidzę*' (I hate)? With terrible irony, his hatred is as abstract, its objects as arbitrary, as those of the hatred of Jacek and the taxi-driver. And is not killing born of the spirit of hatred, as the Sermon on the Mount reminds us? Kieślowski suggests that perhaps the most dreadful consequence of the killings he has shown us is that they finally cause even Piotr, the film's sole carrier of goodness, to begin to hate. What Sobolewski termed the 'solidarity of sinners' of *The Decalogue* returns with a vengeance as the malign face of brotherhood: that of Cain. A more benign linkage, meanwhile, is found in *Decalogue 1*, where Krzysztof, Irena and the computer all come to say '*nie wiem*' ('I don't know') at one point, as if in solidarity with Kieślowski himself, with his '*je doute, je doute toujours*'.

THE IDEA OF THE TRILOGY

Kieślowski's trilogy is unusual in having been planned and conceived as such from the outset. If the film series termed 'trilogies' were generally only named thus retrospectively (those of Michelangelo Antonioni, Bergman, Satyajit Ray, Wajda) it is because of the double difficulty of, first securing finance for three films, and then of ensuring their release within a period short enough to permit spectatorial recognition of the play of similarity and difference. For although Kieślowski said the films could stand independently of one another, hospitably adding that viewers could watch them in any order, certain continuities (for example, the varied images of the pensioner at the bottle-bank) go astray when the sequence alters. The obstacles to a trilogy's production and proper distribution are compounded by the desired rapid release schedule, which almost inevitably requires its production within an equally short period and may place a near-intolerable physical strain on the director. Thus it is surely significant that all the 'trilogies' mentioned above were made relatively early in their directors' careers. It is probably also significant that all are bunched together in the late 1950s and early 1960s, in the bygone heyday of 'art cinema', when viewers could be expected to return to savour the next instalment in an *auteur* project. These problems of production, distribution and reception – to say nothing of the drain on directorial stamina – make Kieślowski's achievement all the more impressive and exceptional. His subsequent exhaustion and declaration of retirement from filmmaking are hardly surprising.

KEYWORDS AND COLOURS

Kieślowski's many interviews during the release period of the trilogy made it quite clear that it had a double organising principle, revolving around the three colours of the French flag and around the French Revolution's key concepts. Viewers did not have to be very perspicacious to correlate the order of these concepts with those of the colours on the flag. But is there anything *within the films themselves* to reveal the correlation to a viewer unacquainted with Kieślowski's extra-filmic discourse? There are visual clues – marginal, unhighlighted details from the façade of the Geneva Palais de justice. After *Blue* has shown us Julie ascending steps with *liberté* visible at the top, the fuller view *White* gives of the façade reveals another in the triumvirate of modernity's fetish-words – though Kieślowski is wisely chary of extending it mechanically in *Red* to reveal a third word (quite apart from the fact of the inscription's absence from the Palais de justice). And of course *White* includes Karol's peroration on the inequality of justice meted out to Poles in France, its importance emphasised by its previous citation in *Blue*. Giving 'brotherhood' the last word – however inevitable the order of the revolutionary watchwords may have made this – echoes the comic coda of *The Decalogue*'s story of two brothers, and *Red* too is comic in the technical sense of happily concluding Kieślowski's undivine comedy. Yet its *fraternité* also contains *liberté* (the freedom *Blue* had linked to isolation) and *égalité* (here, between people of different ages – including the doubling of the judge by Auguste, who is nevertheless 'more equal' in the sense of happier in the end). Nevertheless, this possible triplication may not be conscious, and to my knowledge neither Kieślowski nor his co-scriptwriter Piesiewicz mentioned it. As for the colour scheme, Kieślowski himself termed it a pretext (one reviewer, Stuart Klawans went even further, declaring it 'blarney'[Klawans 1994: 739]). In exceeding authorial intention, such potential triple reference as the one mentioned above becomes the works' bonus for the cunning of their contrivance, their *Citizen Kane*-like awareness of one word's inadequacy to sum up anyone's life.

As Kieślowski's denial of political intentions would lead one to expect, the title *Three Colours* hides the revolutionary watchwords it ostensibly dramatises. Moreover, as I have noted, only two of its keywords – *liberté* and *égalité* – actually feature in the films, and then only momentarily. They too thus have the status of pretexts, near-invisible axes of the narratives, rather than keys to their reception or self-consciously serious objects of meditation. Northern European associations of blue – the opening colour – with cold and depression, meanwhile, render its pairing with freedom apparently paradoxical, thereby promoting awareness of the arbitrariness of all connotations attaching to both colour and concept. Kieślowski described them as entirely contingent:

> Just because in English – in fact in American – blue is associated with sadness, as in 'the blues', does not mean that it is associated with freedom. Freedom has nothing whatsoever in common with sadness or cold – one could say quite the reverse. Actually freedom ought to be in red, since if we really wished to reflect on what is associated with liberty, what colour flag, it would be with revolution, blood, and so on. But I term it 'blue' for the simple reason that on the French flag – and the film's finance came from France – blue is the first colour. If a different country had provided the finance – Germany, for instance – and I had made it as a German film, then yellow would have taken the place of blue and one would have had 'yellow, red and black'. (Coates 1999b: 170)

Furthermore, he maintained that the colour-concept pairing arose from a misconception on the part of himself and Krzysztof Piesiewicz – the assumption that the French associated their flag's colours with the Revolution's keywords. By the time it had been rectified, the story told by *Blue* had been registered under that title, thus requiring consolidation of its quotient of 'blueness' (Otrębska & Błach [1996] 1997: 292). This consolidation prompts an interesting dialogue of expectations with viewers, who may speculate beforehand on the kind of objects and settings likely to appear in the film – for instance, water (yes: the swimming pool) or sky (no).

Ten years earlier, in the immediate aftermath of the Gdańsk shipyard strike and the Gdańsk and Szczecin accords, Kieślowski had proposed that Polish cinema probe interiors rather than cling to externals. Among other things, this meant removing itself from the politically charged setting of his earlier documentaries and features, the work-places of *Robotnicy '71: nic o nas bez nas* (*Workers '71: Nothing About Us Without Us*, 1972), *Fabryka* (*Factory*, 1970), *Blizna* (*The Scar*, 1976) or *Spokój* (*The Calm*, 1976). This was necessary because

> many subjects that once appeared only in films can now be found in the weekly or daily press, and even in certain TV programmes. If we thought today *just* as we did a few years ago we would have to compete with journalists and publicists in, for example, what might be essentially a race to discover the darker sides of reality, or in works about the social and political activism of the last few months. It is a competition film would be bound to lose, not to mention our complete lack of any desire to participate in it ... Today the truth about the world, which for me continues to be a basic precondition, is not enough. One has to search out more dramatic situations, postulates that reach beyond everyday experience, diagnoses that are wiser and more universal. (Kieślowski 1981: 111)

At the end of the road programmatically announced here comes *Red*, which refigures the colour most widely identified with the movements of twentieth-century politics. The green filters of *A Short Film About Killing* (to say nothing of its girls dressed in red), like the yellow filters of *The Double Life of Véronique*, lead logically to the later explicit address of the status of colour. If the latter in particular points to *Red* it is not just through the presence of Irène Jacob but also because – as Goethe notes in his *Zur Farbenlehre* (*Theory of Colours*, 1810) – 'one can very easily elevate and lift yellow into red, through thickening and darkening' (Goethe 1989: 235). Indeed, it is possible to see Kieślowski's awareness of colour intensifying as early as in *Decalogue 1* which, as Lisa Di Bartolomeo has noted, is organised around an opposition between blue and green (Di Bartolomeo 2000: 47–59). The opposition becomes characteristically complex at the level of that work's two screens: the blue television screen of its beginning and end may be read 'positively', as the preserver of the memory of Paweł, the young boy who drowns, yet also 'negatively', as a graven image. At the same time, although green may radiate from the false deity that is the computer screen, it – like Islamic religious art – displays only words, and so may counter, as well as embody, idolatry. The computer's seemingly miraculous, inexplicable self-activation suggests that a false god need not be an impotent one (unlike the Madonna whose image appears at the work's end, unable to protect the child, perhaps because merely mortal?), for it may even cause Paweł's death through its remote control capability.

HEARING COLOURS: *BLUE*, SOUND AND THE MEANING OF SYNAESTHESIA

Efforts to map the subjective significance of colour may be said to begin with Romanticism and Goethe's anti-Newtonian *Zur Farbenlehre*, which seeks a totality of knowledge by 'thinking science as art' (Goethe 1989: 560). Goethe's constellations of jotted experiences of a series of colours subvert rigid one-for-one associations in a manner arguably reflective of the Romantic aversion to allegory; polemicising against scientific abstraction, he juxtaposes experiences that may not be fully compatible. The emphasis on the concrete and the series anticipates Kieślowski. Indeed, the relations between *Zur Farbenlehre* and the trilogy can be uncannily precise. Goethe's description of red as both dignified and charming, hence equally suitable for age and youth, seems almost to have suggested *Red* 's elective affinity of Valentine and the judge (Goethe 1989: 236–7). Meanwhile, the absence from *Three Colours* of green, the third colour in many tri-colour systems, albeit an inevitable byproduct of the use of the French flag as a point of reference, suits Kieślowski's tense filmic world, its lack of the restfulness so often linked to that colour. (Or is its banishing, despite its association with the '*spokój*' ['calm'] he deeply desired, one of death – as is suggested by the use of green in *Decalogue 1*, as described by Di Bartolomeo, or the green light playing over the concert at which Weronika meets her death in *The Double Life of Véronique*?) Alas, even red – a colour so often linked to vitality – may inscribe the illness that would make this Kieślowski's last film; one may recall a statement elsewhere in the *Farbenlehre* that 'many of the sick, on awakening, see everything in the colour of sunrise, as if through red gauze; this also tends to happen when they read in the evening and fall asleep betimes and waken again' (Goethe 1989: 61). Like the green of the screen of *Decalogue 1,* the colour carries antithetical meanings.

As Kieślowski begins to co-script works with Krzysztof Piesiewicz, the first colour to be highlighted is blue, figuring prominently in the first two joint ventures – *No End* and *Decalogue 1* – and then again in *Decalogue 9* and, of course, *Blue*. A remark by Wassily Kandinsky could have caused the accentuation of blue in the first film in particular: dark blue partakes of 'the deep seriousness of all things where there is no end' (Arnheim 1969: 332). As the cinematic colour of 'day for night', the first seen at dawn, blue signifies the proximity of darkness and dream, those traditional domains of the metaphysical manifestations of interest to 'late Kieślowski'. The frequent association of colour with romanticism, and line with classicism, matches his late statements on the romantic nature of his work (Łużyńska 1995: 3–4). Moreover, since, as Rudolf Arnheim notes, traditional aesthetics identifies line with the masculine, and colour with femininity, it is hardly surprising that the trilogy should privilege femininity too. But whereas Charles Blanc, for instance, had argued that painting could 'fall' through colour 'just as mankind fell through Eve' (Arnheim 1969: 326), for 'late Kieślowski' the values culturally signified by 'femininity' are rather redemptive than deleterious.

Blue is, of course, the story of Julie, a woman who loses her composer husband Patrice and daughter Anna in a car crash, withdraws from life, then returns to it – partly through the work of time, partly because she discovers Patrice's infidelity. In the end, having completed the music her husband left unfinished at his death, she goes to his former friend Olivier, who has long been in love with her. Throughout *Blue*, it is clear that although blue may be the colour of day for night – of the night of so much of the film's early part – it is only the cousin of darkness, not darkness itself. Goethe may describe blue as bringing 'a principle of darkness' with it, and as being 'in its greatest purity … an alluring nothing' (consider the importance the film accords the word 'nothing' – of which more below), but in the end the balance tips away from both purity and negation towards renewed relationship. *Blue* can seem to dramatise Goethe's comment on how the colour's retreating quality invites pursuit (Olivier's of Julie).[7] Julie's combination of blue jeans and black coat shows her hovering between realms of life and death. After she has told Olivier she is coming, her finger presses the score as if to activate the music: a moment later the camera pulls up to the blue lamp above her, abruptly making us aware of blue's virtual absence from the recent scenes, as if its earlier dominance had betokened immersion in the catatonia of Julie's mood, frustrating the *movement* of narrative. Its recurrence functions as a reprise (the visual equivalent of Patrice's 'memento') and, by reminding one of the title, inaugurates the coda, the beginning of the film's end.

In *On Sight and Insight*, John Hull argues that sound – so prominent throughout the film – 'has absence built into it as its counterfoil, whereas sight does not. Sound is always bringing us into the presence of nothingness' (Hull 1997: 146). It is privileged by the fades to black or the intense unhinging of focus as Julie and Olivier compose together and the room blurs for a while. Hull's remarks reinforce one's sense that Julie's periodic entries into pure sound – moments of tuning out of the world – represent a falling out of the world. The flautist who sleeps on the street thus becomes her more self-aware double or admonishing superego when he tells her, as she tries to divest herself of everything, 'you should always hold on to something'. 'Now I have only one thing to do; nothing', she tells her mother, calling friends, love and memories 'traps' (a Kieślowskian keyword that places her very close to her creator). Her mother, echoing the flautist, replies 'you can't renounce everything'. Kieślowski's own drastic editorial shearing away of much of the scripted dialogue clips scenes, identifying with Julie's traumatised brusqueness, non-communicativeness and pain, rendering whatever *is* heard all the more pointed and pregnant.

Hearing's centrality to *Blue* is that of the sensory mode most deeply associated with shock, discontinuity and the experience of being the object rather than the subject of action. It is a hearing of noise – or of music always on the verge of becoming noise, as when Julie slams down her piano's lid or the garbage truck chews up Patrice's score – not of articulate speech: Kieślowski's alterations to the script considerably abbreviate its dialogue. In the modern era, the classical Greek opposition between a seeing derived from the action of the subject (via eyebeams 'extramitted' to strike the object) and a hearing originating in the object (causing airwaves that then strike the ear) persists in the conceptualisations of sight-sound relations by such phenomenologists as Maurice Merleau-Ponty or Hans Jonas: the one sensory register (that of sight) being immediate, the other (that of sound) mediated; the one continuous, associated with space, the other discontinuous and linked to temporality. In the words of David Chidester, 'the perceiver cannot choose to hear something but must wait until something happens in the environment to cause sound' (Chidester 1992: 10). Julie is just such a 'perceiver': action's object rather than its subject. Her self-detachment from the world seeks the contemplative distance more usually associated with the visual and thus seeks – in a sense – to deny the music within her: music's declension into noise corresponds to, and as it were justifies, her will to shut it out. Again and again, however, sounds jab at her from without, well into consciousness from within, forcing and reforging the connection. Nevertheless, the end of suicidal self-contradiction is foreshadowed throughout by Julie's 'hearing' of the colour blue, a synaesthetic confounding of the senses that recalls the *fin-de-siècle* poetics to which the late Kieślowski's 'turn to beauty' is clearly akin, as well as suggesting a supersensory, transcendent mode of perception that justifies and motivates the film's final incorporation of the religious language of St Paul.

Julie's awakening comes when she discovers Patrice's infidelity, the illusoriness of her supposed happiness. As she begins to use Kieślowski's favoured conditional tense, imagining a different past (one *in which she'd known…*), she conceives of a different present also. (In the published script, Julie had used the conditional once, but only to negate it, saying, 'it could even be like this. But it won't' as she watched Olivier sleeping [Kieślowski and Piesiewicz 1998: 31]).[8] Is it significant that the episode's keyword – *liberté* – becomes visible at this point, as she visits the Palais de Justice where Patrice's lover works? Julie may submerge herself in the swimming pool for an agonisingly long time, seemingly seeking death, but she comes up again, coughing – a reprise of her husband's repetition of his joke's punchline ('try coughing now') just after the car crash. Immediately afterwards, she will go to Olivier, her movement reversing the immobility with which she sat waiting on the mattress near the film's start as he entered, rain-drenched.[9] The music heard only in snatches up to this point is doubly privileged, as much of the scene of Julie sharing composition with Olivier slips out of focus, compelling concentration on the notes, which then flower around an imagistic roll-call of the film's characters.

Since Julie's deepest loss in the car crash that opens the film is that of her daughter, children haunt her throughout the film. It is Anna's tiny coffin that she touches on the television screen, and she weeps most convulsively when her name is mentioned during the funeral. To cauterise the grief she seeks an apartment in a building without children; and it is the fact that the mouse in one of its rooms has babies that makes it so hard to kill. But just as she tells Lucille that she put the cat in with the mice, a row of children leap past her into the pool: the question of children – continuing life – will not go away, returning most insistently as she learns of the pregnancy of Patrice's lover. In giving the lover her house she seems to think of the child-to-be, acknowledging it as Anna's half-sibling. She can no longer bury herself in a past and a love she now knows she never really had: rewritten, the past evaporates with no need of the intense effort she had expended to make it do so.

All the energy of that effort – one of repression – now goes free in the remarkable final sequence, where the music heard fragmentarily earlier in the film sounds out, set to the words of 1 Corinthians 13, as Julie and Olivier make love. As they move together, her lips pressed against glass, it is as if they are enclosed in uterine waters that also belong to star-strewn heavens. St Paul's words suggest their enclosure within the embrace of the divine. In the ensuing roll-call of other characters all are similarly enclosed, yet their linkage by the moving camera overcomes the interpolated black frames embodying the nothingness that can only threaten love, not extinguish it. Each is juxtaposed with an image, either of themselves or – as in the case of the hitchhiker – of large faces on wall posters, suggesting the mirrors through which Paul says we see darkly. Most are naked or near-naked, reinforcing a sense of womb-like space and vulnerability. When the roll-call ends, Julie is reflected in an eye (Olivier's), just as earlier her own eye had reflected the doctor as she surfaced after the car crash: the symmetry and circularity signal ending and, through the difference, new beginning.[10] The eye encompasses her, grown as tiny now as a child, metaphorically held perhaps in the mind's eye of God. For if the final reflections crawling across the glass through which she stares emphasise that she is inside, and the earlier part of the sequence has included a blue ultrasound image of Patrice's child pulsing within his lover's womb, is not the implication that she, like all humans, is awaiting birth; that all are children – incomplete, cradled in an amniotic sac? Although Julie and Olivier have moved together, perhaps creating new life, her final separation from him and weeping solitude recall the life that has been, as does the music, whose words may point to a future, a world in which (as St Paul says) we see face-to-face, but which was the last thing Julie and Patrice made together.

In the context of the whole trilogy, *Blue* presents a proleptic miniature of the 'three colours' idea through the three colours of the fades that cross-sect Julie's consciousness and conversations: blue, black and white. The film further anticipates the trilogy's shape in its three-part movement, from initial violence – the violence of all beginning – to the finale that is love: violence and love bookend Julie's intervening blankness and drift. Although Kieślowski himself described the keying of this particular story to blue a matter of arbitrarinesss, motivated simply by blue's primacy on the French flag, his assertion is somewhat disingenuous: to link a narrative of grief and depression to this particular colour inevitably activates thoughts of 'the blues' – the bereft condition of the great black singers who have charted its depths. Perhaps only in the case of *White* is the colour sufficiently recessive to function as the pretext Kieślowski himself terms it. And there too its appropriateness reminds one to trust the teller less than the tale.

INTERLUDE: *BLUE, WHITE,* POLITICS AND POSTMODERNITY

The question of Kieślowski's possible relationship with postmodernism and of the politics of such an orientation has been raised in a sensitive and intriguing reading of *Blue* by Emma Wilson (1998: 349–62). Wilson argues that the film's emphasis on forgetting, forward movement and foregrounded colour effects precipitates a 'postmodern subject', manifesting the depthlessness ascribed to it in Fredric Jameson's well-known description. Nevertheless, she also deems the film 'finally ambiguous' (Wilson 1998: 362), and mentions its possible reading as 'modernist' (Wilson 1998: 356), which for her would make it 'regressive' (ibid.). The possibility of a postmodernist depthlessness also being politically regressive and the question of the degree of continuity between 'modernism' and 'postmodernism' are not considered. Moreover, the determination to assign a political orientation to the work surely frustrates investigation of the ambiguity Wilson rightly mentions – the dialectic of modernism and postmodernism, or (as Goethe would have put it) the co-existence of stimulation and repose within blue. Thus Wilson's conclusion that *Blue* achieves 'a prefiguring of the pleasure beyond the paternal law' (Wilson 1998: 362) may depend on her glaring omission of the all-important text that accompanies the closing music (I Corinthians 13). One may also wonder whether Julie's movement is finally entirely forward and destructive of the past. Does she not *return* to it by completing the score she had sought to destroy – and thus really go forward (to Olivier) by going back?

In *White*, meanwhile, the spirit of the postmodern begins to haunt modernism just as in the early 1990s capitalist commodification departed the black market undergrowth of late-socialist Poland to overrun the country's surface. As it did so, what Marek Haltof has described as a generational change of the guard in the Polish cinema of the early 1980s (Haltof 1995: 25) revealed itself also to have involved an advent of the postmodern. Kieślowski may be described as a mediator of this transition. The ten maxims of the Decalogue or the three watchwords of the French revolution offer only the phantom of modernist totalisation: stories are correlated with them *entirely arbitrarily* – a feature of the works misrecognised by a hostile critic such as Zygmunt Kałużyński, who deemed it mere legalistic ingenuity (Kałużyński 1990). The stories parallel the maxims but never coincide with them in the manner of the modernist renewal of myth through antimyth offered by Joyce, Musil or Kafka. The *petits récits* never graduate into second-order *grands récits*, as their sheer proliferation precludes any single one from achieving such status. The poster for Godard's *Le Mépris* (*Contempt*, 1963) hanging appropriately alongside Dominique's Parisian apartment window as Karol watches from afar also signals the remoteness of the *Nouvelle vague* and Godardian cinematic modernism that employed such cinematic allusions so extensively: a distance both in time and space for Kieślowski, a sign perhaps of his partial self-location (in a double life, one self modernist, one postmodernist) in a modernist cinematic tradition now virtually defunct. Kieślowski's interest in colour also recalls mid-1960s Godard, and when considering how to name the sequence he worried that *Three Colours* might be too Godardian a title – until his producer Marin Karmitz said he liked it. The Godard of a film like *Pierrot le fou* (1965) is fascinated by the spaces between people and objects, and by those people-as-objects – the paintings he sets obsessively against white walls: similarly *White*, the mid-point in Kieślowski's sequence, is the blankness into which its opposed surrounding colours echo. Kieślowski's *Contempt* allusion is all the more appropriate because Dominique's feelings for Karol at this point are ones of pure disdain. The frustration of Kieślowski's original intention of inserting here a poster with a contemporary actress of the Kim Basinger type was, to my mind, a happy accident. Contempt vanishes, of course, when Dominique's partly readable cell-window signals apparently conclude in a wish for remarriage, a ring's pantomimed placement on her finger. *White* may even be read as in part a conjugation of the prolonged scene in *Contempt* in which Brigitte Bardot and Michel Piccoli move back and forth in their apartment among primary colours and under the eye of a female statue: whether wittingly Godardian or not, Kieślowski's interest in colour and the female statue cannot help but recall him.

WHITE: THE ANTI-COLOUR

The dominant colour of *White* is used in a wider range of ways and serves a greater conceptual complexity than the key colours of the other two films. White's presence is more subtle and multiform than that of the other two colours, ranging from the brilliant white of the abstract, sexual climax to off-white and blonde, even becoming an unobtrusively widespread background for action as snow. Kieślowski can play with notions of 'white-and-whiter' and 'whiter-than-white' as he cannot with the other two colours. White is not just a property of objects: Dominique's car may be white, Karol may tumble from his suitcase onto snow, and the rococo statue symbolising Dominique may have its broken nose lovingly reattached with white paste, but white is also resonant as an idea, standing at one point for the problematic represent-ability of sexual climax (the screen explodes into white as Dominique shrieks) as well as the hyper-whiteness of the blonde the would-be gentleman perhaps inevitably prefers. White is the emptiness into which blue and red reverberate, the breathing space that permits incom-patibles' co-existence, holding them together even when they are distant (countries apart). If *Red* concerns relationships (red's warmth) and *Blue* about solitude, *White* may be the riddle that asks when a relationship is not one. Answer: 'when not consummated'? Although linked to purity, white also embodies its opposite: its first appearances are as pigeon excrement on Karol's shoulder and as the toilet where he vomits on leaving the court-room. For Agnès Peck, white is the colour of (Karol's romantic) idealisation of Dominique, which imprisons each in an unfulfillable image of marriage (Peck 1994: 150). The way the wedding is filmed – the camera emerging from the dark church into the sunlight – renders it a form of the 'light at the end of the tunnel' alluded to by Karol's brother Jurek after Dominique's incarceration. (In the script, that motif would have been reflected in the representation of Karol's successful lovemak-ing in the Marriott hotel through a camera's propulsion up a chimney, the spot of light at its summit enlarging precipitously. The obvious sexual metaphor would have extended the theme of height/depth relations whose relation to the work's comedy I consider below.) Certainly, the idea of marriage is the only clearly readable element in Dominique's prison window mime, which ends ('the *end* of the tunnel…'?) with her sliding an imaginary ring onto her finger. Thus the mesh's disappearance as the camera nears her may itself foreshadow liberation. *Within* the film itself the final version of the flashback that inserts Karol may be 'too little, too late', but since *White* is part of a trilogy matters need not end there, and the film does of course have a double ending (the other one concluding *Red*).

White is the second film in the trilogy, after *Blue*, which shows a woman burying herself alive – no longer wishing to live – after her loss of husband and daughter, and before *Red*, about an eavesdropping judge befriended and changed by a young girl. *White* is often described as a black comedy; its jokes often tap an insider's humour. When Karol and Mikołaj buy a company office and the realtor praises the 'particularly attractive view', its inclusion of a shadowy Palace of Culture should amuse any Pole. Stalin's unwanted gift to the Polish nation is itself described as having the best view in Warsaw – less because of its height than because it affords the sole vantage-point from which it is itself invisible. *White*'s generic status as comedy renders it the reversal often situated at the midpoint of a drama, before its final resolution (Kehr 1994: 13), indicating that the trilogy is really one long film in three parts (an expansion of the procedure of *Blind Chance*, which had shown three variants of a man's life, depending on whether or not he catches the Łódź-Warsaw train). It is perversely amusing that the 'black' comedy should be titled *White*, and that Kieślowski himself described the ending as 'happy', for only the second ending given in *Red* is indeed unequivocally so – something Kieślowski recognised when telling Danusia Stok 'you have to see the third film, *Red*, to know that *White* has a happy ending' (Stok 1993: 217). *White*'s visible overlap with *Blue* through Julie's glance into the courtroom may suggest the possibility of *this* film's continuation too, of a coda to the ostensible ending, but one cannot be sure it will materialise. If the work *is* 'comic' it is nevertheless arguably more through this 'happy ending' than its tone, especially since Kieślowski excised a large amount of the material intended to be funny (ibid.). Such 'black comedy' may travel well – becoming a quintessential form of mobile modernity – precisely because it makes no claims to be funny. It may thus be particularly appropriate to a cross-cultural film, which begins by accentuating the travel motif through the suitcase on the airport conveyor belt. Meanwhile, of course, inequality – the systematic inversion of the keyword so relentlessly tracked in the film – is a stock-theme of comedy, which often pairs little men with large ones (or, as in Buster Keaton's *Cops* [1922] or *Seven Chances* [1925], confronts lone individuals with teeming crowds). In *White*, the comic inequality also conjugates the recurrent question of height/depth relations, which usually involve Karol looking up at Dominique or the statue that represents her. This theme becomes blackly comic as the underground in which several scenes unfold becomes the grave for which it stands: six feet under is as low as one can get. On reaching that point, black comedy becomes Beckettian; inequality, a form of liberty.

As the midsection of the trilogy, *White* appropriately points both forwards and back: it is the only section to use both the flashback, one of the key 'violations of classical conceptions of time and space' that identify 'art cinema' for David Bordwell, and the flash-forward (Bordwell 1979: 59–60).[11] The two are visually as well as temporally complementary, for the flashes forward are as visually dark as their meaning is obscure, while the flashback is the overexposed, superwhite image of the wedding. The flash-forwards involve a retrospective decoding that also characterises much of the film's imagery, including even such a scene as the one in which Karol intently observes a funeral near Mikołaj's house: only later do we realise its role in suggesting part of his plot. Similarly, the film's pigeons are at first only realistic details until their association with the wedding flashback causes even a heard delicate flutter of wings to recall Karol's primary aim of securing Dominique (we hear them, for instance, as he purchases the Russian corpse that will stand – or rather lie – in for him). The work's score is similarly anticipatory and reminiscent: when the tentative love theme whose brevity matches that of Karol's potency and which prevails in the early scenes in Paris recurs in the Polish section, it stresses Karol's real motivation, welling up for instance as he runs his finger across a map of the properties procured in the area of the proposed Hartwig/Ikea development. The other theme, an expansive, jaunty tango, first appears on Karol's return to Poland, its confidence anticipating his renewed self-assurance, transposing romantic love into another key.

Generally speaking, Kieślowski uses neither visual flashes forward nor flashbacks, preferring musical anticipation and recollection, so their double use in *White* clearly correlates with its midpoint position. His preference is rather for one life's repetition within another that reworks it, as in *Red* or *The Double Life of Véronique*. The general eschewal of the flashback (the sole exception being found in *Red*, which itself may signal the film's status as self-consciously his last) mirrors Kieślowski's existentialist commitment to the characters' moment-by-moment passage through the world. Kieślowski's suspense always concerns what the character on screen will do *the next moment*, not 'why did this happen?' or 'will he/she/we discover what someone else knows?' This variety of suspense is far-removed from that of traditional fiction and has more in common with that of observational documentary. As noted at the outset, Kieślowski allows characters the existential freedom to make and remake themselves moment by moment.

Perusal of the published script of *White* (Kieślowski & Piesiewicz 1998: 101–98) – its fourth version, Kieślowski told Danusia Stok – is instructive in various ways. The differences between film and script allow partial reconstruction of the criteria whereby Kieślowski deemed material superfluous. Several subplots are omitted, including one with a Polish blonde that would have accentuated the East/West contrast (Karol is interested only in the Western blonde) as well as emphasising Karol's commitment to Dominique (the Polish girl makes unrequited overtures) and to marriage (the Pole is married already). These scenes would have extended the work's discourse on whiteness (a movie poster with a blonde stands beside Dominique's apartment window – Michelle Pfeiffer here, Brigitte Bardot in the film). This subplot was surely the one with Grażyna Szapołowska, excised despite the nice intertextual echo of *A Short Film About Love*, in which she uses binoculars to scan a distant window. Obviously, Kieślowski felt that to duplicate the theme of blondness would have overstated it, while Szapołowska's presence and beauty might have tipped attention away from the Karol-Dominique main plot.

But although many omissions concern arguably superfluous material (Karol's aiding of two robbed Swiss, alluded to in *Red*; his quest for French nationality; the allusions to Van den Budenmeyer; the chauffeur's theft of a computer, and so on), one alteration makes a radical difference. The script sees Karol's successful lovemaking followed by his efforts to halt his unfolding plot against Dominique. He leaves the hotel at what he thinks is 9:30, well in time to forestall its activation at 10:30. While cancelling his airline tickets, however, he learns that the clocks went forward an hour during the night. He re-enters the hotel with the plan already underway, Dominique already arrested. Thus the scripted version shows a simpler Karol: where his observation of the enmeshed Dominique in the film complexly mixes love with vengeful satisfaction, the script's Karol looks on in utter regret.

Other changes instructively illustrate Kieślowski's editing work. Various flashbacks to Karol's first days with Dominique punctuate the scripted courtroom confrontation. All vanish in the film, giving way to the wedding flashback that originally followed it, and which is cued in by the melancholy, hesitant love theme. Its juxtaposition with Dominique's subsequent 'I beg your pardon' – as if she has been lost in *her* thoughts – suggests it may even have been *her* memory, hinting at love's possible subterranean persistence within her. Shifting Karol's vomiting in the toilet from before the court scene to afterwards, meanwhile, gives it stronger motivation. But at least one scene's trimming obscures its meaning. When the film shows Karol spinning his two-franc piece on a table, it is not clear that it is to decide whether or not to accept Mikołaj's commission; it seems like just another instance of his play with it. Kieślowski then replaces this scene's scripted ending – Karol's touching of the alabaster statue – with a flash-forward to Dominique in the hotel room doorway, an image that is also less readable. Only retrospectively, on a second viewing, is it clear that imagining Dominique thus motivates the decision to take up Mikołaj's offer – his fee being necessary to help secure her.

With its accumulation of references to Kieślowski's other works (Coates 1997: 23), the ending of *White* represents an extreme example of the density and multivalence that are perhaps the main reasons why his late works prove so hard to respond to (to 'get') – and hence were often resisted – at a first viewing, the trilogy mechanism being necessary to induce a return to review the works in the light of what went before or came after. The exquisite, strangely beguiling image of Karol's confrontation with the imprisoned Dominique is certainly one of bilateral entrapment, a resolution on the level of image that nevertheless leaves everything narratively unresolved. It is in fact a fascinating compromise between image and narrative: film after film by Kieślowski ends with a figure separated from another by glass, with a frustrated relationship and stasis. Here, however, there is the germ of a possible future narrative, as the camera's approach to Dominique makes the cage before her melt away and her gestures suggest a renewed relationship, though their import for the immediate future ('what will happen *next* ?') is not fully apparent and may leave some viewers frustrated, as was Philip Strick (Strick 1994: 63–4). The ending may in fact be happy for both Karol and ourselves inasmuch as Dominique's prisoner status frees him simply to view her from a distance, relieving him of the problematic requirement of physical transaction, rendering her the cinematic object (his idealism is at home here), him the film spectator. However, there is also the question of the position of the female spectator: as Alicja Helman has suggested, a feminist reading might view Dominique's incarceration as an allegory of female imprisonment in patriarchy (Helman & Miczka 1999: 125). The ending may be taken as the placement at a safe distance of the deliberately frightening, unreadable Dominique of the hairdressing salon scene, where the partial shadowing of her face betokened danger and unreadability. Given Karol's parallel entrapment in legal death, both male and female spectators may be sceptical of Kieślowski's assertion of the ending's 'happiness' (Coates 1999b: 172), and may even recall that an ironic use of the notion had characterised the earlier Kieślowski, the original title of *No End* – which concludes with a suicide – having been 'happy end'. The *really* happy ending for this couple, however – the one found in *Red* – is accompanied by the (happy?) death of a boatload of people.

... the only reasonable divinity – that is, chance.
– Albert Camus

Western culture codes red as the primary signifier of emotion, even emotionality. In interviews concerning his later work, Kieślowski would often term feeling the most important thing, a valuation that may reflect an intellectually sophisticated director's idealisation of the area of his greatest weakness (he often described his films as organised around *ideas*) and motivate his move from the male protagonists of his early films to the predominantly female ones of his French ones. After all, are not women also our culture's conventional carriers of feeling? But the feminisation of Kieślowski's protagonist is two-edged, both the logical conclusion of the male's disempowerment in *No End* (which renders him a ghost) and *Decalogue 9* and *White* (each preoccupied with impotence) and part of an argument that virtues culturally coded as 'feminine' may effectively counteract civilisation's deepening chill. *Red* is multiply inscribed with signifiers of feeling, for it also features Irène Jacob, of *The Double Life of Véronique*, whose discussion in *Kieślowski on Kieślowski* is entitled 'Pure Emotions' (Stok 1993: 172). Red is emotion intensified, appassionata, resistance to the control that is a recurrent Kieślowski motif, from the night porter and the Warsaw central station camera of the documentaries to the puppeteer of *The Double Life of Véronique* and – of course – the judge, Joseph Kern, here. Blood boils and cries for blood, particularly in the upsurge in the body politic known as revolution. Numerous films have finally flown or clutched the red flag, from Eisenstein's *Bronenosets Potemkin* (*Battleship Potemkin*, 1925) to Bertolucci's *Novecento* (*1900*, 1976) to Wajda's *The Promised Land*. Given the late Kieślowski's stated aversion to politics, what will he do with this connotation? The red his ending highlights is a private one, that of the anorak behind Valentine, who has just been rescued from the sea. Several years after 1989, the red Kieślowski shows dominating the Western public sphere belongs not to a Marxism that has all but withered away but to the billboard, that sign of capitalism's all-pervasiveness. Its stronghold may indeed be the Switzerland whose mountains' fairytale hoards have metamorphosed into the untaxed bank accounts modern gnomes guard.

Red, the story of how a girl (Valentine) thaws a retired judge (Joseph Kern) from his misanthropy, is a film of multiple enigmas. At the outset these are the customary ones we assume the narrative will resolve: why Auguste purses his lips in a kiss after hearing the weather-girl identify herself on the phone; why the judge reacts so apparently impassively to his dog's disappearance and accident. But the resolution of such normal narrative mysteries – resolution on the level Noël Carroll terms that of 'the erotetic' – leaves many others still active, particularly the uncanny dislocations and relations between the image-flow and a soundtrack that seems to obey a different temporality. As Valentine first enters the judge's room we hear interference like that on her car's radio just before it hit Rita (the trilogy's motif of music becoming noise – and noise as music). A causal connection may or may not exist. Similarly, a ship's foghorn accompanies Valentine's simulated sorrow at her photo-session (Andrew 1998: 65–6), an aural flash-forward to the ferry sinking of the film's close. Is this precognition – unrecognised, unconscious, perhaps a repressed intuition – or does this moment in a sense *cause* the later one? As in the films of Robert Bresson, effects often precede causes, a dislocation each director links to an intense preoccupation with the soundtrack, the nonsynchronisation of sight and sound: sound-effects precede *seen* causes, both in the short-term – sound draws one's eyes to what one had not seen, as it does the hitchhiker's at the start of *Blue* – and in the long term, as in the examples mentioned above. Sound indicates the limitations of the visible. In an early scene, Valentine picks up a newspaper and looks sad; she then tells the barman at Chez Joseph that she thinks she knows the cause of her slot-machine win. But is it unease at her distant lover's misunderstanding (in another dislocation of sight and sound, we never see his face) or something in the newspaper? Not until the neighbour notes that its photograph resembles her brother do we learn why the paper might have caused sadness, why – in a gesture that replicates Julie's touching of her daughter's especially tiny coffin on the miniature television screen – she touched that photograph. Is it merely a coincidence that Valentine acquires a dog as she begins to appear in the same image as – enter the framed world of – Auguste, another dog-owner? Each element of an image – including its sounds – points enigmatically beyond the instant of its occurrence. Nothing is self-evident, all is in process, and even the final freeze-frame of Valentine, safe on shore after the disaster – an imagistic rhyme in which the earlier photo-session image appears to have been displaced into its *right* place – is as instinct with openness as closure.

The female lead of *Red* is played by Irène Jacob, whose presence inevitably recalls *The Double Life of Véronique*, in which she starred as both the Polish girl who dies and the French girl who 'learns' from her Polish counterpart's experiences. In *Red*, however, the previous life benefits not a female but a male – Auguste, the 'double' of Judge Joseph Kern – and the end's happiness is not stained by the prototype's sacrifice. It suggests instead a utopia of resurrection without the pangs of death (another version of the butterfly transformation of *The Double Life of Véronique*).[12]

The structure of *Red* may be described as derived from its closing moment. During editing Piotr Sobociński accidentally hit the pause button to catch Valentine and a fireman in red behind her and was prompted to say to himself 'This is the key' (Pizello 1995: 71–2). As the film dwells increasingly within the judge's home, the key colour may be said to metamorphose into brown – a rider of the thematics of metamorphosis in general in Kieślowski. Thus Sobociński remarks 'I visualised brown (derivative of red) as the dominant colour', associating it with 'the legal environment of much of the film' (Anon 1994c: 3–4). (Since the only colour forbidden on the set was blue, he comments elsewhere that 'we took away all the jeans from the extras' [ibid.].) The camera's swivelling, magnetic attachment to peregrine red may remind one of that colour's use in Miklós Jancsó's *Fényes szelek* (*The Confrontation*, 1968), while the sight of Valentine's red poster before a *white* traffic light may recall the current prints of *Battleship Potemkin*, whose apparent white flag was once tinted red. We may even suspect Kieślowski of whiting out the red light, like Antonioni painting the streets of *Blow Up*, to eliminate a foreground distraction, until the light changes and does indeed – wittily – become red.

Throughout *Red*, effects of colour, framing and foregrounding engender double vision. The double life of the characters, who exist throughout on a level of (realistic) singularity and one of (fantastic) doubling, is a feature of the film's images also. Image after image oscillates in illusive double focus: red may be simply a component of a scene observed realistically (without the colour filters of some of Kieślowski's earlier films, for instance); but at the same time it is part of *an image in this film*, whose title causes one to highlight and mentally note the key colour. Kieślowski's sowing of *Red* with hundreds of red objects renders the key colour far more prominent even than in *Blue*; yet at the same time it is a continual undertone, never enveloping an entire image (there are none of the fades-to-red of a film like Bergman's *Viskningar och* rop [*Cries and Whispers*, 1972], or the full-screen interpolations of the title colour of *Blue* or *White*): it is as if the *quantity* of red moments compensated a lack of overwhelming *quality*. The presence of these hundreds of objects corresponds to, and is justified by, red's status as a colour that 'stands out'. Its ability to do this means it can foreground itself, without the director needing to flood the screen with it.

And the 'standing out' of this particular colour leads logically to the question of foregrounding. The early sequences in particular cue us to both separate and connect backgrounds and foregrounds. Insofar as our knowledge is as limited as the characters', our look inhabits the foreground, their location and also that of the objects with which they are engaged. But our knowledge also goes beyond the horizon of theirs: we know we are watching a fictional universe where apparent marginalities may prove central. As known characters traverse the backgrounds, we realise that they may later encroach upon foregrounds. Yet we cannot be sure whether, when or how this may happen. We see a little further than the characters, but the surplus of vision is not very enlightening. We do not know *why* the camera foregrounds a slot machine's handle at the same time as Auguste – whose name is still unknown – returns home in the background, though in retrospect (on *second* viewing, in *our* second life) the image may intimate a providential conjunction of endings and beginnings whereby a character's sadness on one level is counterposed (though not balanced, for the germ of the new has not sprouted fully) by its incipient end on another. The coincidence that racks the three slot-machine cherries together is a miniature image of fortune shadowing misfortune, just as ill-luck in love – the result of characters' merely random conjunction – is about to be countered by one that is 'right' ('made in heaven', and/or by Judge Joseph Kern).

The foreground/background dialectic rests on a concern with relations between realities defined (perhaps misdefined) as 'inner' and 'outer'. In these early stages, the two are distinct; thus many images feature looks outward through windows. But the invisibility of glass is one reason why it forms so fragile a border. Later the film will connect inner and outer systematically, becoming fascinated by interiors that open onto exteriors or interiors that are both 'exterior' and 'more interior' – revealed by doors opening inwards in a process of complication. As so often, and on so many levels, Kieślowski's film-work means problematising borders. As the camera accompanies Valentine into Joseph Kern's house, its open door rendering his self-enclosure unconsciously only apparent, the shots through doorways indicate a sense of possibility and arbitrariness: foregrounding the question of framing indicates (that foundational belief of Kieślowski the documentarist) that characters could always have been framed differently – that they are not yet (perhaps never will be) in their proper place. Meanwhile, faces peering through windows sustain an overgrowth of reflections, as if they are not yet fully linked to or looking at the outside, their gaze fixing inscape as much as landscape.

The shots through doorways also dramatise the question of the degree of privacy to which individuals are entitled. Early on, Valentine remonstrates with the eavesdropping judge and declares that everyone deserves a private life. On hearing that a man outside uses a Japanese phone whose wavelength the judge cannot tap, she smiles at the frustration of his surveillance. But the issue is then complicated by the judge's mention of the man's responsibility for most of Geneva's drug-trafficking. He adds that 'we have nothing on him'. This unexpected 'we', speaking in the name of a community that indeed has an interest in monitoring such a man, but from which Kern himself is otherwise outcast, is further justified by the unanimity in the mini-community (the *fraternity*) he and Valentine then form, for the first time: the man deserves persecution, and Valentine vengefully rings an anonymous threat that sends him scuttling for cover. Things are thus less simple than Valentine thinks: she drops a plan to inform a neighbour of the judge's surveillance on seeing the daughter – framed through a doorway – also eavesdropping on her father's homosexual phone sex. The public/private dialectic even embraces the judge's own name. Whereas the cafe 'Chez Joseph' is a public space whose use of a first name affects intimacy, Joseph Kern's house is a private space whose open door – and banks of surveillance equipment – demonstrate privacy's disappearance in the modern audio-panopticon.

Of the three parts of the trilogy, *Red* follows its published script most closely. There are occasional disparities – lines trimmed here and there, moments that differ (Auguste no longer sees Valentine as he emerges from his exam) – but they are only minor. Does the tight fit indicate the deeply personal nature of the script or perhaps mark Kieślowski's enormous weariness as he neared the end of his taxing project, either of which might have caused an unwillingness to change? Few of the alterations deserve mention, though it may be worth noting that Valentine no longer crosses herself on entering the church (like the change of the original title of *The Double Life of Véronique* from 'Chórzystka' ['A Choir Girl'], this deletes any suggestion of religious affiliation in the main protagonist) and that the film omits Marc's realisation of his sister's survival, which would have fitted the *fraternité* theme but have disturbed the final focus on her relationship with the judge – or may simply not have registered well when (or if) filmed. The script makes no mention of the recurrent camera movements, sometimes apparently unmotivated, to pick up glasses or bottles, though it does illuminate one – in the judge's home, to a ball inside a large jar – which is surely the billiard ball he shot into one, mentioned in the script. But the script offers no hint of the rich imagery of redness and broken and unbroken glass, and its lack of any reference to the final red behind Valentine corroborates Piotr Sobociński's account of the (happily) accidental discovery of that key image.

In many respects *Red* is another version of the second life of *The Double Life of Véronique* first suggested by *Blue*, though the echoes with which it is seamed stem from throughout Kieślowski's work. They include the recurrence of Van den Budenmeyer; the resemblances between Auguste and Piotr Balicki in *A Short Film About Killing*; the reappearance of that film's gypsy as the three cherries of Valentine's unhappy love; and the extension of the linkage of betrayal and eavesdropping of *Decalogue 9* (whose music is quoted as an example of Van den Budenmeyer's). The inaccurate weather forecast recalls Krzysztof's inability to calculate the breaking of the ice in *Decalogue 1*. The double life of Irène Jacob in the two films is Kieślowski's most mystical diptych. Where the earlier work sought an image of the soul, the later one maps the interconnections of dreaming, doubling and premonition, and may itself be a dream: Kieślowski himself once suggested, in an interview for *Positif*, that the judge may even not exist (Amiel and Ciment 1994: 28). In his fusion of the fathers and lovers of *The Double Life of Véronique* the judge becomes doubly excluded: neither father (without a daughter) nor lover (he loved another woman). Nevertheless, although Irène Jacob's appearance on both sides of one image in the judge's room, both real and reflected, belongs in the imagistic force-field of the somewhat nightmarish first part of *The Double Life of Véronique* – with its dominance by the dirty yellow Goethe deems unpleasant because sulphuric (Goethe 1989: 232) – in *Red* the fantastic is less explicitly present, more of an undertone. For all their deceptive resemblance, truth and copy, truth and falsity, and reality and image can be distinguished. The true Véronique, the compassionate woman as patron saint of the true image, separates the true judge from his false, fallen, incarnation – the god from the demiurge.

THE LAST JUDGEMENT

Switzerland is a country where very few things begin but many things end.
— F. Scott Fitzgerald

The judge as demiurge, however, is also the brother of Jean-Baptiste Clamence in Camus' novel *The Fall*. Kieślowski's dialogue with existentialism concludes by folding Camus' work into *Red* as an intertext. *Red* suggests that one becomes a judge, as it were, after losing one's innocently self-righteous self-identification with the underdog. Even then, however, self-reproach continues, as if all pretensions to administer justice were accursed. The curse rests most fully on Judge Joseph Kern, who both reincarnates and redefines Camus' 'judge-penitent'.

Jean-Baptiste Clamence, the first-person narrator of *The Fall*, is addicted to judgement, accusing himself in order to be able to accuse others. As he slides from speaking in the first person to speaking of 'us', he ropes all humankind into his plight, and tells his listener: 'I shall listen to your own confession with a great feeling of fraternity' (Camus 1963: 103), piquantly using the keyword of Kieślowski's final film. Like Clamence, the electronic eavesdropper Kern has lost faith in himself as a judge (Camus 1963: 42); he too may like dogs because they are so forgiving (Camus 1963: 90). Like Clamence, he is shielded 'from immediate judgement', isolated as if by 'huge protected lawns'. The wealth that ensures such isolation 'is not quite acquittal but reprieve, and that's always worth having' (Camus 1963: 60). Kieślowski, however, is interested in acquittal. Thus the separation of Joseph Kern from Camus' Clamence – a diabolical John the Baptist who at one point also becomes a 'Pope' – becomes apparent when one considers Camus' ending, which could have been the starting point of Kieślowski's conception. Here Clamence envisages a second opportunity to rescue the girl whose suicide in the Seine he had once heard and ignored (note the importance of sound to Kieślowski's work). Just as Joseph Kern envisages – or perhaps creates – Auguste as his double, at the book's end Clamence imagines his silent listener as a double through whom he himself says, 'O young woman, throw yourself into the water again so that I may a second time have the chance of saving us both' (Camus 1963, 108). Clamence may add, 'it's too late now. It'll always be too late' (ibid.), but Kieślowski projects a temporal doubling that will indeed render this possible: the last image being that of a young woman (Valentine) rescued from drowning. In Kieślowski, penance has an end, escape from the endless concentric circles of the Amsterdam canals that form Clamence's bourgeois hell on earth.

Another pertinent comparison might be with Jean Cocteau's *Le Testament d'Orphée* (*The Testament of Orphée*, 1960), of which *Red* might be a more realistic, less mythical, less explicitly self-referential rethinking. Cocteau's film may be the more self-consciously testamentary of the two, but both he and Kieślowski are concerned with doubling and the undoing of time, something achieved in Cocteau's case through the magical film-reversals that reconstitute the burnt photograph of Cégeste or the destroyed flower, while for Kieślowski it involves the past's reincarnation in a present that profits from a sacrificial rehearsal. In each case, a creator figure (Cocteau himself in *The Testament of Orphée*; in *Red*, the judge) walks alongside his characters. 'You must have a mirror to disappear', Cocteau tells Cégeste; similarly, *Red* marks the judge's disappearance from Valentine's life through his mirroring in Auguste. The judges in *The Testament of Orphée* express their dislike of Cocteau's play with time, perhaps because its resurrectionism threatens the death-dealing regime of punishment. And, as in Kieślowski, the position of judge is accursed: Cocteau asks Heurtebise what has been the punishment for the action he and the Princess took at the end of *Orphée*. 'To judge others', he replies, and says there is nothing worse.

Goethe deemed red the noblest colour because it contained all others, actually or potentially (Goethe 1989: 236), so in closing Kieślowski's trilogy it totalises it; all the main characters can appear at the end. The nobility of the last red, however, is not that of the flame whose upward movement signifies spirituality at the end of so many films but inheres in its regal ability to bestow life. Life's glow frames the face of a woman, in whom life began. The red surrounding Valentine renders her an icon of life and shows the judge to be looking at – back at – life itself. Since Goethe also described a landscape observed through red glass as awe-inspiring because suggestive of the Day of Judgement (Goethe 1989: 237), may it not be significant that the final shot is from a judge's point of view? Kieślowski's last film, *Red*, becomes his Last Judgement. It is passed at the moment at which the light vanishes – as Kieślowski shows it doing twice, once behind a roof, once behind a hillside. Among the many quasi-musical reprises dotting his film is an actual musical reprise of a theme from *Decalogue 9*, which also plays twice – when the judge is alone, like so many of *The Decalogue*'s characters.[13] Shortly after it has first played, he remarks of the people he found guilty that in their place he too would have killed and lied. The Old Testament order of punishment – the old covenant – gives way to forgiveness. In the true equality so absent from *White* '*alle Menschen werden Brüder*': the two plastic cups of Valentine and the judge sit side by side, an equal amount of lousy coffee in each. As at the end of *The Decalogue*, Kieślowski returns to the idea of brotherhood that had animated even an early documentary like *Hospital*. Kieślowski's Last Judgement in fact annihilates judgement.

NOTES

NOTES TOWARDS AN INTRODUCTION

1   An explanation of the form of the reference used for archival sources can be found at the end of this book under 'Works Cited and Consulted'.

2   Andrzejewski 1970: 114. The equivalent page number in the English translation – one the translator describes as severely cut by the publishers – is 79 (George Andrzejevski [sic], *Ashes and Diamonds*, 1962).

ASHES AND DIAMONDS: BETWEEN POLITICS AND AESTHETICS

1   When Andrzejewski has a militiaman describe the deaths of Maciek's victims as the work of 'fascist crimi-nals', Trznadel deems this 'a procedure whereby the author pronounces a certain judgement but seems not to do so' (Trznadel 1988: 237).

CENSORSHIP IN A HALL OF MIRRORS

1   The list of critics viewing the work as incoherent include Zygmunt Lichniak ('Piłat i my', *Słowo powszechne*, 13/2/75); Tadeusz Sobolewski ('Wajda wśród dzieci Chrystusa', *Film na świecie*, 201, May 1975, p. 76); and Janusz Zatorski ('Karnawał na Golgocie', *Kierunki* 18/2/75).

2   See the daily, fortnightly and quarterly files of the Główny urząd kontroli publikacji, prasy i widowisk (Main Office for the Control of Publications, the Press and Spectacle) for the first three months of 1975, lodged in Warsaw's Archiwum akt nowych (Archive of Modern Files). Among the more relevant files are the following daily reports: ZI-050/33/75 (8/2/75) (concerning Kałużyński's review), ZI-050/35/75 (11/2/75) (concerning Sobolewski's), ZI-050/42/75 (19/2/75) (the censored *Polityka* cartoon) and ZI-050/43/75 (20/2/75) (concerning the *Sztandar Młodych* opinion poll).

3   Cf. the German reviewer Gustav Anias Horn, who noted that 'the rubbish dump and Judas' running death are strongly reminiscent of his unforgettable film *Ashes and Diamonds*' (Horn 1972).

WALLS AND FRONTIERS

1   For a rebuttal of the other accusations, see Mirski 1961. Given his own political allegiance, the film's true weakness may be imperceptible to the critic. Even if visible, it is surely not something he would wish to stress.

2   For more on *The Wedding*, see Coates 1992.

3   For several other possible starting points, and a panoramic overview of Polish films on the topic, see Czapliński 1990. Czapliński's survey aim and his article's brevity preclude close analysis of the works

and their internal tensions. Lack of attention to these tensions, however, can prompt an over-dismissive approach to some of the films.

4 For a balanced assessment of the merits of the arguments of the two sides, see Pease 1988.

5 Thus, for instance, Pauline Kael, whose *New Yorker* review began by stating 'probably everyone will agree that the subject of a movie should not place it beyond criticism', found that her careful dissection of the film garnered her an accusation of anti-Semitism from one of the regular reviewers of *The Village Voice*.

6 See Tadeusz Szafar's strictures on omissions in the *History of Poland* (1976) edited by Professor Jerzy Topolski, for instance (Szafar 1983).

7 In Reymont's work, meanwhile, the conflict is primarily one of national groups. 'Polishness' connotes a high culture incomprehensible to money-grubbing Jews; so much so that on realisation of the two cultures' incompatability, a rich Jewish girl in love with a selfless Polish doctor breaks off the relationship. She knows she would never belong in a Polish salon.

8 One poll stated that 80 per cent of spectators had not read it.

9 These scenes were also criticised by Gierek at a Politburo meeting, where he termed them 'pornographic' (Tejchma 1991: 52).

10 Annette Insdorf has analysed the Jew's assimilation to the child in certain films of the 1970s in her *Indelible Shadows: Film and the Holocaust* (Insdorf 1989: 81–97). The assimilation of Jews to the female is analysed in Doneson 1978.

11 Having Leon spell this out is an example of the over-explicitness that mars both the scenario of this film and those of Holland's non-Polish work in general. It may be that working outside a Polish context has deprived her of the belief that her presuppositions can be taken as read, though the difficulty of her Polish-Jewish identity may be a factor also.

12 Solly's identities may conflict with one another on occasions – as when he describes religion as 'the opium of the people' while building a Feast of Tabernacles booth with Robert – but there are no hints of misgivings over their shifts and overlaps.

13 Recently Susan Linville has described the German Film Commission's refusal to classify the film as German as motivated by objections to its vertiginous mixing of genres, to the multiple nationalities involved in the production and to the uncertain identity of Solly Perel himself: 'in effect, lacking pure German bloodlines, *Europa,Europa* came to be seen as the product and expression of a kind of cultural miscegenation, as a film body trying to pass as German, and as an imposter not unlike Solly himself' (Linville 1995: 40–1). The judgement is an unfortunate simplification of Linville's earlier evocation of an overdetermined German reaction: 'though without doubt the German Film Commission, like the German press before it, rejected and criticised Holland's film partly due to a frustrated desire that Germany not again be identified with its fascist past – and especially not with the depiction of an unidealised Jewish youth – rejection of the film was emphatically overdetermined and also reflected anxieties about the nation's present and future' (Linville 1995: 40) Even here, however, the failure to differentiate the Commission's response from that of such an amalgam entity as 'the German press' – many of whose criticisms were far from simply reactionary – is extremely problematic. In likening the undoubtedly objectionable reactions to those of the Freikorps soldiers studied by Klaus Theweleit, however, Linville simply demonises them.

14 See, for instance, his statement in Ciment 1989, in which he stated that '*en accordant trop d'importance a la raison, nos contemporains ont perdu une dimension de la vie*'.

15 It is worth noting that Agnieszka Holland's original script places a scene at Majdanek just before the controversial ending (Holland 1991: 148–9).

16 For all Wajda's praise of his child actors, they give off a sweetish odour of unreality. (One cannot help contrasting the vibrant performance Kieślowski elicits from Wojciech Klata in *Decalogue 1* with the one he gives here as Schlomo.)

17 The changes are generally felt to involve an increase in the number of *dramatis personae* that de-empha-

sises the Irena/Jan relationship. This change was praised by Jan Kott, whom some deem its instigator, as a step towards greater realism (Piasecki 1996). Irena is generally seen as based on Wanda Werten-stein, Andrzejewski's former lover, who survived the war to become one of Poland's foremost film critics, though Andrzejewski himself claimed (to Wertenstein's scepticism) that the prototype had been another woman. Like many novelists, he may indeed have used elements of more than one person.

18 Moreover, visiting such abuse on the image of Christ, rather than that of the Madonna, may also have been self-protective, reflecting Wajda's awareness of her centrality to popular Polish Catholicism (the most influential Polish Catholic radio station in Poland, with an audience of approximately 2.5 million, is called Radio Maryja) – though it may simply, or also, indicate his greater interest in male martyrdom. Not until the close of Kieślowski's *Decalogue 1*, released in 1989, is the Madonna's image attacked, by a bereaved father, though ambiguity shrouds the moment, for the icon's continued tears may reflect his.

19 Sandauer also viewed Andrzejewski's revisions of his own text as indicating manipulation from the outset. He argued that Andrzejewski's emendations sought to make the work more sympathetic to the Jews – whose suffering in the Holocaust was 'particularly close to many representatives of the new author-ities' (Sandauer 1982: 41) – and so ensure its publication. Nevertheless, the passages Sandauer describes as later inserts do not so much increase sympathy for the Jews as reduce sympathy with Malecki, demon-strating 'class consciousness' by ascribing him to that perennial Marxist scapegoat, the much-maligned petit bourgeoisie. Thus any changes served the new regime by 'Marxising' the text, not by rendering it any more philosemitic.

KIEŚLOWSKI, POLITICS AND THE ANTI-POLITICS OF COLOUR

1 Interestingly enough, Zbigniew Preisner – who composed the music for all the late films – identified Piesiewicz as a metaphysician, Kieślowski as a mathematician, and – since music combines metaphysics and mathematics – situated himself inbetween them (Mucharski 1996: 14). *Blind Chance* (like the inex-plicable appearance of the horses during the TV test card in *The Calm*) suggests that the elective affinity with Piesiewicz was rooted in a pre-existing Kieślowskian interest in the metaphysical.

2 For a review of some of the arguments, see Garbowski 1996: 78–9.

3 Józef Drążek, 'Wierzyć w duchy?', in *Kultura niezależna*, October 1985, quoted in Przylipiak 1997: 229.

4 Christopher Garbowski offers some interesting comments on Kieślowski's use of point of view in this and several other scenes from *A Short Film About Killing*, arguing that the camera's alignment with the lawyer's viewpoint serves to evoke the character's 'internal body' (Garbowski 1996: 40–2).

5 Cf. for instance Stok 1993, where he states *inter alia* that 'during martial law, I realised that politics aren't really important' (p. 144) and that 'they're not in a position to do anything about or to answer any of our essential, fundamental, human and humanistic questions' (ibid.).

6 Interviewed by Krzysztof Karabasz, Kieślowski says of *Hospital*: 'This film was not made to tell about the health service or people's terrible suffering. I felt a need to make a film about a certain brotherhood' (Karabasz 1985: 90).

7 See Goethe 233–4. Cf. also Kandinsky (Arnheim 1969: 327) on the blue circle as like 'a snail hiding in its shell', which 'moves away from the spectator', or Arnheim himself remarking that 'a cold person behaves as if he is cold' (Arnheim 1969: 331).

8 By way of contrast, the film reserves the conditional, and the attendant sense of possibility, for the end, when Julie asks Olivier if the photos of Patrice and his lover were in a dossier she almost burned earlier on: had she done so, she would never have known of Patrice's infidelity.

9 The meaning of this reversal is also most apparent if one compares that first scene with the mattress as scripted with its film version. In the script Julie rises to meet Olivier, an action – and activeness – omitted from the completed film, perhaps because of its incompatability with her mood at this point.

10   Is it relevant that before conception a person or thing can be described metaphorically as 'a gleam in someone's eye'? Is it also relevant that in Hindu belief systems blue is deemed a form of protection against the evil eye (the cause perhaps of Julie's initial loss?). For the latter association, see Kulig 1998: 106.

11   The flashforward, that key device of the more challenging film practices of the 1960s, may mark the point at which Bordwell's relatively comfortable 'art cinema' ('classical in its reliance upon psychological causation' [Bordwell 1979: 58]) becomes genuinely modernist. In *White* the flashforwards are verbal as well as visual: remarks like Dominique's reference to Karol's putative revenge as she sets the hairdressing salon curtains on fire, or Mikołaj's question whether Karol sleeps in his case, sow the seeds of future events.

12   *Red* may also be taken as a comment on Nietzsche's cyclical theory of history. Cf. for instance the following remarks in the 'monumental history' section of 'The Use and Abuse of History': 'Ultimately, of course, what was once possible can only become possible a second time on the Pythagorean theory, that when the heavenly bodies are in the same position again, the events on earth are reproduced to the smallest detail; so when the stars have a certain relation, a Stoic and an Epicurean will form a conspiracy to murder Caesar, and a different conjunction will show another Columbus discovering America' (Nietzsche 1910: 19–20). The final clause is also, of course, chillingly Borgesian.

13   *Decalogue 9* may in fact be described as the chrysalis of the entire trilogy: its interest in blue anticipating *Blue*, its subject-matter (impotence) foreshadowing *White* and its concern with aural surveillance anticipating *Red*. The musical reminiscence thus has a many-layered significance.

WORKS CITED AND CONSULTED

ARCHIVAL SOURCES

Archival sources are identified within the text by listing in parentheses the abbreviations for (a) the archive in which they are located, (b) the institution that generated the text, and (c) the file number of the text. Thus, for instance, the Commission for Script Evaluation's discussion of the script for Jerzy Skolimowski's *Ręce do góry!* (*Hands Up!*) would be identified, in parentheses, as FN, KOS, A-330 poz. 1.

1   ARCHIWUM AKT NOWYCH (ARCHIVE OF MODERN FILES) (AAN)
a   Główny urząd prasy, publikacji i widowisk (Main Office of Press, Publications and Spectacles) (GUPPiW)
    For 1975: ZI-050/6/75; ZI-050/8/75; ZI-050/12/75; ZI-050/22/75; ZI-050/24/75; ZI-050/31/75; ZI-050/33/75; ZI-050/35/75; ZI-050/38/75; ZI-050/39/75; ZI-050/42/75; ZI-050/43/75; ZI-050/44/75; Pf-ZI-050/59/75; Pf-ZI-050/64/75; Pf-ZI-050/67/75; Pf-ZI-050/71/75; Pf-ZI-050/73/75; Pf-ZI-050/79/75; ZI-051/3/75; ZI-051/4/75; ZI-Pf-051/6/75; ZI-Pf-051/7/75.
    For 1978: ZI-Pf-052/2/78; ZI-Pf/052/3/78; ZI-Pf/052/4/78; ZI/Pf/052/5/78; ZI-Pf-052/8/78; ZI-Pf-052-9-78; ZI-Pf-052/10/78; ZI-Pf-052/11/78.
    For 1979: ZI-Pf-052/1/79.
b   Naczelny zarząd kinematografii (NZK) (Main Office of Cinematography)
    1/7, 1/8, 1/23a, 1/26, 1/27,1/28,1/29, 1/30,1/31, 1/34, 1/35, 2/12, 4/5, 4/9, 4/14, 4/77.
c   Wydział kultury KC PZPR (Cultural Section of the Central Committee of the Polish United Workers' Party) (WK KC PZPR)
    PZPR 665/18, PZPR 671/14, PZPR 744/3, PZPR 744/4, PZPR 823/59, PZPR 832/71, PZPR 854/83, PZPR 888/13, PZPR 889/49, PZPR 909/65, PZPR 923/2, PZPR 960/122a, PZPR 960/219, PZPR 960/1225, PZPR 987-52

2   FILMOTEKA NARODOWA (NATIONAL FILM ARCHIVE) (FN)
a   Komisja Ocen Filmów i Scenariuszy (Commission for Film and Script Assessment) (KOFiS)
    A-214 poz. 10 (29 Oct. 1952) *Piątka z ulicy Barskiej* (Five Boys from Barska Street)
    A-214 poz. 24 (10 June 1953) (*Przygoda w Mariensztacie*) (An Adventure in Mariensztadt)
    A-214 poz. 18 (28 Oct 1953) (*Przygoda w Mariensztacie*)
b   Komisja Ocen Scenariuszy (Commission for Script Assessment) (KOS)
    A-214 poz. 102 (14 Aug 1958), *Lotna*
    A-214 poz. 186 (7 Feb 1961), *Pierwszy dzień wolności* (*The First Day of Freedom*) (Zespół 'Rytm')
    A-214 poz. 227 (8 Sept. 1961), *Ziemia obiecana* (*The Promised Land*), J. Krzysztoń)
    A-214 poz. 242 (22 Dec. 1961), *Jak być kochaną* (*How to be Loved*)
    A-214 poz. 338 (30 April 1963), *Człowiek z marmuru* (*Man of Marble*)

A-214 poz. 343 (31 May 1963), *Pierwszy dzień wolności*) (Zespół 'Studio')

A-214 poz. 310 (3 July 1964), *Walkower* (*Walkover*)

A-214 poz. 370 (12 Feb 1965), *Chudy i inni* (*Skinny and Others*)

A-214 poz. 393 (14 Sept 1965), *Westerplatte*

A-330 poz. 1 (18 Nov 1966), *Ręce do góry!* (*Hands Up!*)

A-214 poz. 431 (25 Nov 1966), *Słońce wschodzi raz na dzień* (*The Sun Rises Once Daily*)

A-214 poz. 440 (7 Feb 1967), *Słońce wschodzi raz na dzień* (*The Sun Rises Once Daily*)

c Komisja Kolaudacyjna (Commission for Film Approval) (KK)

A-214 poz. 158 (3 May 1960), *Samson*

A-216 poz. 37 (30 Nov 1964), *Rękopis znaleziony w Saragossie* (*The Saragossa Manuscript*)

A-216 poz. 86 (23 June 1965), *Szyfry* (*Ciphers*)

A-216 poz. 92 (21 July 1966), *Bariera* (*The Barrier*)

A-216 poz. 97 (17 Sept 1966), *Chudy i inni* (*Skinny and Others*)

A-216 poz. 128 (24 Aug 1967), *Ręce do góry!* (*Hands Up!*)

A-324 poz. 2 (14 Jan 1971), *Życie rodzinne,* (*Family Life*)

A-324 poz. 7 (30 Aug 1974), *Ziemia obiecana* (*The Promised Land*)

A-324 poz. 9 (22 Dec 1976), *Człowiek z marmuru* (*Man of Marble*)

d Rada programowa (Programme Councils [of the Studios]) (RP)

A-329 poz. 57 (6 Oct 1967) (Zespół 'Studio'; *Dr. Korczak*)

A-329 poz. 63 (23 Feb 1968) (Zespół 'Rytm'; *Diabeł* [*The Devil*])

e Scripts

S-2541 *Popiół i diament* (Erwin Axer)

S-2541 *Po wojnie* (Antoni Bohdziewicz)

S-22143 *Popiół i diament* (Jerzy Andrzejewski and Andrzej Wajda)

S-2379 *Człowiek z marmuru* (Aleksander Ścibor-Rylski)

S-11130 *Korczak* (Bohdan Czeszko)

S-11131 *Dr. Korczak* (Aleksander Ramati)

S-26321 *Korczak* (Agnieszka Holland)

S-9089 *Słońce wschodzi raz na dzień* (Wiesław Dymny)

S-5930 *Słońce wschodzi raz na dzień: nowela.* (Wiesław Dymny)

S-5933 *Słońce wschodzi raz na dzień* (Wiesław Dymny)

f Miscellaneous

Anon. (1953a) 'Wnioski ogólne z dyskusji o filmie "Przygoda na Mariensztacie". A-329 poz. 15.

_____ (1953b) 'Ocena prasowa filmu "Przygoda na Mariensztacie". A-329 poz. 15.

JB [Janina Bauman] (1967) 'Uwagi o scenopisie J. Skolimowskiego "Ręce do góry", Filmoteka narodowa A-330 poz. 4.

Skolimowski, J. (1967) 'Eksplikacja dotycząca retrospekcji w filmie' [*Ręce do góry!*]. Filmoteka narodowa A-330 poz. 5.

_____ (1967) 'Ręce do góry!': Scenopis Filmoteka narodowa A-330 poz. 3.

PUBLISHED SECONDARY LITERATURE

'Abu' (1972) 'Trotz Wajda: Schock blieb aus', *Saarbrücker Zeitung*, 1 April.

A.d. (ed.) (1991) 'Wajda mówi o *Korczaku*'. *Gazeta wyborcza*, 18 January.

Adorno, T. W. (1973) *Versuch, das Endspiel zu verstehen*. Frankfurt a.M.: Suhrkamp.

_____ (1974) *Ästhetische Theorie*. Frankfurt a.M: Suhrkamp.

_____ (1975) *Noten zur Literatur I*. Frankfurt a.M.: Suhrkamp.

_____ (1981) *Noten zur Literatur*. Frankfurt a.M.: Suhrkamp.

Afanasjew, J. (1987 (1970)) *Okno Zbyszka Cybulskiego*. Łódź: Wydawnictwo łódzkie.

'Agnieszka' (1958) 'Twórca "Kanału" Andrzej Wajda kręci we Wrocławiu'. *Gazeta robotnicza*, 19–20 April.

Alvarez, A. (1965) *Under Pressure: The Writer in Society: Europe and the U.S.A.* Harmondsworth: Penguin.

Amiel, V. (1995) *Kieślowski*. Paris: Payot & Rivages.

_____ (ed.) (1997) *Krzysztof Kieślowski*. Paris: Jean Michel Place.

Amiel, V. and Ciment, M. (1994) '"La fraternité existe dès que l'on est prêt à écouter l'autre", entretien avec Krzysztof Kieślowski', *Positif*, 403, September: 26–32.

Anderson, B. (1983), *Imagined Communities: Reflections on the Origin and Spread of Nationalism*. London: Verso.

Andrew, G. (1998) *The 'Three Colours' Trilogy*. London: BFI.

Andrzejevski, G. (sic) (1962). *Ashes and Diamonds*, trans. D. J. Welsh. London: Weidenfeld and Nicolson.

Andrzejewski, J. (1967) *Niby Gaj, i inne opowiadania*. Warsaw: Państwowy instytut wydawniczy.

_____ (1970) *Popiół i diament*. Warsaw: Państwowy instytut wydawniczy.

_____ (1993) *Wielki tydzień*. Warsaw: Cyztelnik.

'Aneks' (1977) *Czarna księga cenzury PRL* (two volumes). London: Aneks.

Anon. (1959) 'Person of Promise', *Films and Filming*, 5/12, September: 17.

_____ (1986) 'Dialogue on Film', *American Film*, September: 13–15.

_____ (1990a) 'Entretien avec Agnieszka Holland', press documentation to *Europa Europa*, Paris.

_____ (1990b) 'Wokół scenariusza "Przedwiośnia" Andrzeja Wajdy. Stenogram z posiedzenia komisji ocen scenariuszy – "Przedwiośnie" Andrzeja Wajdy', *Iluzjon*, 39–40: 34–41.

_____ (1991) 'Wokół scenariusza do filmu "Kanał" Andrzeja Wajdy: Protokół z posiedzenia Komisji Ocen Filmow i Scenariuszy – w dniu 24 I 56', *Iluzjon*, 41: 45–9.

_____ (1994a) 'Uchwała Sekretariatu KC w Sprawie Kinematografii', in T. Miczka (ed.) and A. Madej (asst. ed.) *Syndrom konformizmu? Kino polskie lat sześćdziesiątych*. Katowice: Wydawnictwo Uniwersytetu Śląskiego: 27–34.

_____ (1994b) 'Protokół z posiedzenia Komisji Ocen Scenariuszy w dniu 17 1 1958 r.', *Kwartalnik filmowy*, 6 (Summer): 188–94.

_____ (1994c) 'Colouring the message', *In Camera* (Autumn): 3–4.

_____ (1997) 'Filmy polskie – ankieta "Kwartalnika"', *Kwartalnik filmowy*, 17 (Spring): 4.

Arnheim, R. (1969) *Art and Visual Perception: A Psychology of the Creative Eye*. London: Faber.

_____ (1971) *Entropy and Art: An Essay on Disorder and Order*. Berkeley, LA and London: University of California Press.

Axelrad, C. (1996) 'La semaine sainte: Quelque chose d'obscène', *Positif*, 423 (May): 56–7.

'B.J.' (1993) 'Żegnaj, szkoło Polska', *Film*, XLVII, 13 (April 4): 2–3.

Baniewicz, E. (1994) *Kazimierz Kutz. Z dołu widać inaczej*. Warsaw: Wydawnictwa artystyczne i filmowe.

Bauman, J. (1988) *A Dream of Belonging: My Years in Post-War Poland*. London: Virago.

Bazin, A. (1967) *What is Cinema? Vol. I*, selected and trans. Hugh Gray. Berkeley, LA: University of California Press.

_____ (1972) *What is cinema? Vol. II*, selected and trans. Hugh Gray. Berkeley, LA: University of California Press.

Benjamin, W. (1973) *Illuminations*, trans. Harry Zohn. London: Collins/Fontana.

Bethell, N. (1972) *Gomułka: His Poland and His Communism*. Harmondsworth: Penguin.

Biró, Y. (1983) 'Pathos and Irony in East European Films', in D. W. Paul (ed.) *Politics, Art and Commitment in the East European Cinema*. London and Basingstoke: Macmillan: 28–48.

Błoński, J. (1978) 'Portret artysty w latach wielkiej zmiany', in *Odmarsz*. Cracow: Wydawnictwo literackie, 237–65.

____ (1994) 'Polak-katolik i katolik-Polak', *Tygodnik powszechny* (21 August): 8–9.

Bobowski, S. (1996) *Dyskurs filmowy Zanussiego*. Wrocław: Towarzystwo Przyjaciół Polonistyki Wrocławskiej.

____ (2001) *W poszukiwaniu siebie. Twórczość filmowa Agnieszki Holland*. Wrocław: Wydawnictwo Uniwersytetu Wrocławskiego.

Bocheńska, J., A. Kossakowski, B. Mruklik, I. Nowak-Zaorska, S. Ozimek, D. Palczewska, J. Siekierska, W. Świeżyński, J. Toeplitz, B. Ziółkowski (1974) *Historia Filmu Polskiego* Vol. 3. Warsaw: Wydawnictwa artystyczne i filmowe.

Boczek, E. (1958) *'Popiół i diament'. Nowa Wieś*, 16 November.

Bordwell, D. (1979) 'The Art Cinema as a Mode of Film Practice', *Film Criticism*, 4/1: 56–64.

Borowski, T. (1977) *Wspomnienia, wiersze, opowiadania*. Warsaw: Państwowy instytut wydawniczy.

Brandys, K. (1962) *Samson, Antygona*. Warsaw: Czytelnik.

Bren, F. (1986) *World Cinema 1: Poland*. Trowbridge: Flicks Books.

Broch, H. (1955a) 'Das Böse im Wertsystem der Kunst', in *Gesammelte Werke* Vol. 6. Zürich: Rhein-Verlag.

____ (1955b) *Gesammelte Werke 9: Massenpsychologie*. Zürich: Rhein-Verlag.

Brumberg, A. (ed.) (1983) *Poland: Genesis of a Revolution*. New York: Vintage.

Bukowiecki, L., K. Dębnicki, and M. Radgowski (1958) 'Trzy głosy w dyskusji', *Polityka* (18 October): 9.

Bulgakov, M. (1967) *The Master and Margarita*, trans. M. Ginsburg. New York: Grove Weidenfeld.

Caes, C. J. (2003) 'Catastrophic Spectacles: Historical Trauma and the Masculine Subject in *Lotna*', in J. Orr and E. Ostrowska (eds) (2003) *The Cinema of Anrdzej Wajda: The Art of Irony and Defiance*. London: Wallflower Press: 116–31.

Campan, V. (1993) *Dix brèves histoires d'image: Le Décalogue de Krzysztof Kieślowski*. Paris: Presses de la Sorbonne nouvelles.

Camus, A. (1963) *The Fall*, trans. Justin O'Brien. Penguin: London.

Chidester, D. (1992) *Word and Light: Seeing, Hearing and Religious Discourse*. Urbana and Chicago: University of Illinois Press.

Chvany, P. J. (1967) *'Ashes and Diamonds'*, *Screen Education*, May–June: 57–67.

Chwin, S. (1993) *Literatura a zdrada: Od* Konrada Wallenroda *do* Małej Apokalipsy. Cracow: Oficyna literacka.

Ciechowicz, J. and T. Szczepański (eds) (1997) *Zbigniew Cybulski. Aktor XX wieku*. Gdańsk: Wydawnictwo Uni-wersytetu Gdańskiego.

Ciment, M. (1989) 'Ce qui m'intéresse, c'est l'homme', *Le Monde*, 16 September.

Coates, P. (1992) 'Revolutionary Spirits: The Wedding of Wajda and Wyspiański', *Literature/Film Quarterly*, 20: 2: 133–7.

____ (1996) 'Forms of the Polish Intellectual's Self-Criticism: Revisiting *Ashes and Diamonds* with Andrzejewski and Wajda', *Canadian Slavonic Papers*, 38: 3–4, September–December: 287–303.

____ (1997) 'The Sense of an Ending: Reflections on Kieślowski's Trilogy', *Film Quarterly*, 50: 2 (Winter): 19–26.

____ (ed.) (1999a) *Lucid Dreams: The Cinema of Krzysztof Kieślowski*. Trowbridge: Flicks Books.

____ (1999b) '"The inner life is the only thing that interests me": a conversation with Krzysztof Kieślowski', in P. Coates (ed.) *Lucid dreams: the films of Krzysztof Kieślowski*. Trowbridge: Flicks Books: 160–74.

____ (2002a) 'Dialectics of Enlightenment: Notes on Wojciech Has's *Saragossa Manuscript*', *Comparative Criticism*, 24: 193–216.

____ (2002b) 'Kieślowski and the Anti-Politics of Colour: A Reading of the *Three Colors* Trilogy', *Cinema Journal* 41, 2: 41–66.

____ (2003a) *Cinema, Religion and the Romantic Legacy*. Aldershot: Ashgate.

____ (2003b) 'Wajda's Imagination of Disaster: War Trauma, Surrealism and Kitsch', in J. Orr and E. Ostrowska (eds) (2003) *The Cinema of Anrdzej Wajda: The Art of Irony and Defiance.* London: Wallflower Press: 15–29.

_____ (2004) 'Man of Marble', in P. Hames (ed.) *The Cinema of Central Europe.* London: Wallflower Press, 181–9.

Czapliński, L. (1990) 'Tematyka żydowska w powojennym filmie polskim', *Powiększenie*, 1–4, Rok X: 171–6.

Czeszejko-Sochacka, E. (1981) 'Tamte filmy, tamte lata…'. (interview with Jerzy Lewiński) *Kino*, 16: 9 (September): 31–2.

Czeszko, B. (1977) *Pokolenie.* Warsaw: Czytelnik.

Davies, N. (1981) *God's Playground: A History of Poland in Two Volumes.* Oxford and New York: Oxford University Press.

Demby, Ł. (2002) *Poza rzeczywiścością: spór o wrażenie realności w francuskiej myśli filmowej.* Cracow: Rabid.

Di Bartolomeo, L. (2000) 'No Other Gods: Blue and Green in Krzysztof Kieślowski's *Dekalog I'*, *Studies in Slavic Cultures*, 1 (February): 47–59.

Doane, M., P. Mellencamp and L. Williams (eds) (1984) *Re-Vision: Essays in Feminist Film Criticism.* Frederick, Md.: University Publications of America.

Doneson, J. E. (1978) 'The Jew as a Female Figure in Holocaust Film', *Shoah: A Review of Holocaust Studies and Commemoration*, 1, 1, 11–13; 18.

Douin, J-L. (1981) *Wajda.* Paris: Editions Cana.

Drawicz, A. (1975) 'Afraniusz, Mateusz i inni', *Film*, 3, 5 (2 February): 6–7.

Drozdowski, B., J. Jantos, A. Kossakowski, H. Książek-Konicka, R. Marszałek, E. Nurczyńska-Fidelska, H. Opoczyńska, W. Stradomski, A. Werner, E. Zajiček (1985) *Historia filmu polskiego* Vol. 5. Warsaw: Wydawnictwa artystyczne i filmowe.

Dymny, W. (1967) '"Słońce wschodzi raz na dzień" – fragment scenariusza', *Ekran*, 402 (1 October): 8.

Eagle, H. (1994) 'Polański', in D. J. Goulding (ed.) *Five Filmmakers.* Bloomington: Indiana University Press: 92–155.

Eco, U. (1979) 'The Structure of Bad Taste', in R. Trevelyan (ed.) *Italian Writing Today.* Harmondsworth: Penguin.

Eberhardt, K. (1961) 'Świadectwo dojrzałości', *Film* 16, 42 (15 October): 4.

_____ (1976) *Zbigniew Cybulski.* Warsaw: Wydawnictwa artystyczne i filmowe.

_____ (1967) *Wojciech Has.* Warsaw: Wydawnictwa artystyczne i filmowe.

Eder, K., K. Kreimeier, M. Ratschewa, B. Thienhaus (1980) *Andrzej Wajda.* Munich and Vienna: Carl Hanser Verlag.

Eljasiak, J. (1958) 'Popiół i diament', *Sztandar młodych*, 4–5 October.

Estève, M. (ed.) (1987) *Études cinématographiques: Krzysztof Zanussi.* Paris: Minard.

Etler, E. (1958) 'Popiół i diament', *Odgłosy*, 19 October: 1; 12.

Falkowska, J. (1995) '"The Political" in the Films of Andrzej Wajda and Krzysztof Kieślowski', *Cinema Journal*, 34, 2, 37–50.

_____ (1996) *The Political Cinema of Andrzej Wajda.* Oxford: Berghahn Books.

Falkowski, J. (1958) 'Polonez tragiczny', *Współczesność*, 31 October.

Fik, M. (1992) 'Kilkanaście miesięcy z życia cenzury 1970–1971'. *Dialog*, 37, 8 (August): 134–45.

_____ (1993a) 'Z archiwum GUKPPiW (15 XII 1970 – 31 III 1971)', *Kwartalnik filmowy*, 2 (Summer): 108–12.

_____ (1993b) 'Z archiwum GUKPPiW (V-XII 1971)', *Kwartalnik filmowy*, 3 (Autumn), 181–7.

_____ (1993/1994) 'Z archiwum GUKPPiW (3) (Rok 1972)', *Kwartalnik filmowy*, 4 (Winter): 178–82.

_____ (1994a) 'Z archiwum GUKPPiW (4) Pierwszy kwartał 1968', *Kwarlanik filmowy*, 5 (Spring): 172–80.

_____ (1994b) 'Z archiwum GUKPPiW (5): kwiecień-lipiec 1968', *Kwartalnik filmowy*, 6 (Summer): 217–23.

_____ (1995) 'Z archiwum GUKPPiW (6)', *Kwartalnik filmowy*, 11 (Autumn): 128–35.

Fik, M., A. Friszke, M. Głowiński, G. Herling-Grudziński, J. Holzer, J. Karpiński, K. Kersten, L. Kołakowski,

M. Kula, J. Nowak-Jeziorański, A. Paczkowski, W. Roszkowski, J. Szacki, J. Turowicz, P. Wojciechowski, K. Zanussi (1996) *Spór o PRL*. Cracow: Znak.

Freud, S. (1967 [1920]) *Beyond the Pleasure Principle*, trans. James Strachey. New York, Toronto, London: Bantam.

Fuksiewicz, J. (1967) *Tadeusz Konwicki*. Warsaw: Wydawnictwa artystyczne i filmowe.

Garbowski, C. (1996) *Kieślowski's Decalogue Series: The Problem of the Protagonists and their Self-Transcendence*. New York: Columbia University Press/East European Monographs.

Garton Ash, T. (1983) *The Polish Revolution*. New York: Vintage.

Gawrak, Z. (1959) 'Sprawa dyscypliny gatunku', *Ekran*, 134 (1 November): 7.

Gazda, J. (1997) 'Początek szkoły polskiej', *Kwartalnik filmowy*, 17 (Spring): 16–30.

Gębicka, E. (1998) 'Partia i państwo a kino. Przypadek "Szkoły Polskiej": O ideologicznym stylu odbioru filmów i jego konsekwencjach' in E. Nurczyńska-Fidelska and B. Stolarska (eds) *'Szkoła polska' – powroty*. Łódź: Wydawnictwo Uniwersytetu Łódzkiego: 129–44.

Girard, R. (1977) *Violence and the Sacred*, trans. Patrick Gregory. Baltimore and London: Johns Hopkins Uni-versity Press.

Głowiński, M. (1991) *Marcowe gadanie: komentarze do słów 1966–1971*. Warsaw: PoMost.

_____ (1993) *Peereliada*. Warsaw: PIW.

Godzic, W. (1991) *Film i psychoanaliza: Problem widza*. Cracow: Uniwersytet jagielloński.

Goethe, J. W. v (1989) *Sämtliche Werke*. Münchener Ausgabe, Vol. 10 *Zur Farbenlehre*, ed. Peter Schmidt. München: Carl Hanser Verlag.

Greene, G. (1973) *The Ministry of Fear*. Harmondsworth: Penguin.

Grochowiak, S. (1958) 'Śmierć i dziewczyna', *Walka Młodych*, 26 October: 4–5 (reprinted in *Kwartalnik filmowy*, 17 (Spring 1997): 35–6.

Gross, J. T. (1998) *Upiorna dekada: trzy eseje o stereotypach na temat Żydów, Polaków, Niemców i Komunistów*. Cracow: Universitas.

_____ (2001) *Neighbours: The Destruction of the Jewish Community in Jedwabne, Poland*. Princeton and Oxford: Princeton University Press.

Grzelacki, S. (1967) 'Siedem dumnych dni', *Życie Warszawy*, 9 September.

_____ (1972) 'Próba czasu', *Życie Warszawy*, 8 April.

Guérin-Castell, A. (2000) 'Dwoista forma *Szyfrów* Wojciecha Jerzego Hasa. Prawda do rozszyfrowania', *Kwartalnik filmowy*, 29–30 (Spring–Summer): 42–52.

_____ (2002) 'A film saved from the scissors of censorship', *Comparative Criticism*, 24: 167–92.

Habermas, J. (1998) 'Modernity – An Incomplete Project', trans. Seyla Ben-Habib, in H. Foster (ed.) *The Anti-Aesthetic: Essays on Postmodern Culture*, New York: New Press: 1–15.

Hadiguet, P. (1963) 'Nouvelles cinéastes polonais', *Premier Plan*, 27.

Halecki, O. (1950) *The Limits and Divisions of European History*. New York: Sheed and Ward.

Haltof, M. (1995) 'A Fistful of Dollars: Polish Cinema after 1989 Freedom Shock', *Film Quarterly*, 48, 3 (Spring): 15–25.

_____ (2002) *Polish National Cinema*. Oxford: Berghahn Books.

_____ (2004) *The Cinema of Krzysztof Kieślowski: Variations on Destiny and Chance*. London: Wallflower Press.

Hames, P. (ed.) (2004) *The Cinema of Central Europe*. London: Wallflower Press.

Haraszti, M. (1987) *The Velvet Prison*. New York: Noonday Press.

Harrison, T. (1978) *Living Through the Blitz*. Harmondsworth: Penguin.

Helman, A. (1959) 'Sarmata na płonącej żyrafie', *Ekran*, 132 (18 October): 3.

_____ (1999) 'Women in Kieślowski's late films'. P. Coates (ed.) *Lucid Dreams: The Cinema of Krzysztof Kieślowski*. Trowbridge: Flicks Books: 116–35.

Helman, A. and T. Miczka (eds) (1984) *Analizy i interpretacje. Film Polski*. Katowice: Wydawnictwo Uniwersytetu Śląskiego.

Hendrykowska, M. (ed.) (2000) *Widziane po latach. Analizy i interpretacje filmu polskiego*. Poznań: Wydawnictwo Poznańskiego Towarzystwa Przyjaciół Nauk.

Hendrykowski, M. (1972) 'Realizm i symbolizm *Popiołu i diamentu* Andrzeja Wajdy', *Kino*, 7, 1 (January): 25–8.

____ (1984) 'Styl i kompozycja *Popiołu i diamentu* Andrzeja Wajdy', in A. Helman and T. Miczka (eds) *Analizy i interpretacje. Film Polski*. Katowice: Wydawnictwo Uni-wersytetu Śląskiego: 72–91.

____ (1997a) 'Modern jazz', *Kwartalnik filmowy*, 17 (Spring): 85–96.

____ (1997b) 'Polska szkoła filmowa jako formacja artystyczna', *Kwartalnik filmowy*, 17 (Spring): 120–30.

____ (1999) *Stanisław Różewicz*. Poznań: Ars Nova.

____ (2002) 'Refleksje człowieka medialnego', *Kwartalnik filmowy*, 37–8 (Spring-Summer): 248–60.

____ (2003) 'Uśmiech Stalina, czyli jak polubić socrealizm', *Kwartalnik filmowy*, 41–2 (Spring–Summer): 65–89.

Heyman, D. (1990) 'L'homme de rêve et l'homme de plomb', *Le Monde*, 13 May.

Hjort, M. and S. Mackenzie (eds) (2000) *Cinema and Nation*. London and New York: Routledge.

Hoberman, J. (1991) 'Doing the Nazi', *The Village Voice*, 2 July.

Hoffman, E. (1999) *Shtetl: The History of a Smalll Town and an Extinguished World*. New York: Vintage.

Holland, A. (1991) *Korczak*. Warsaw: Wydawnictwa artystyczne i filmowe.

Hollender, B. and Z. Turowska (eds) (2000) *Zespół Tor*. Warsaw: Prószynski i S-ska.

Horn, G. A. (1972) 'Gegenwart als bloße Dekoration', *Frankfurter Rundschau*, 29 March.

Horoszczyk, A. (1959) 'Wojenko, wojenko…', *Ekran*, 134 (1 November): 7.

Hosking, G. (1980) *Beyond Socialist Realism: Soviet Fiction Since Ivan Denisovitch*, London, Toronto, Sydney, New York: Elek.

Hull, J. (1997) *Sight and Insight: A Journey into the World of Blindness*. Oxford: Oneworld.

Hutnikiewicz, A. (1974) *Od czystej formy do literatury faktu: główne teorie i programy literackie XX stulecia*. Warsaw: Wiedza powszechna.

Insdorf, A. (1989) *Indelible Shadows: Film and the Holocaust*. New York: Cambridge University Press.

Iskierko, A., A. Kossakowski, I. Nowak-Zaorska, S. Ozimek, D. Palczewska, J. Siekierska, J. Toeplitz (1980) *Historia filmu polskiego* Vol. 4. Warsaw: Wydawnictwa artystyczne i filmowe.

Jackiewicz, A. (1956) 'Z ziemii włoskiej do Polski', in *Latarnia czarnoksiężnika*. Warsaw: Filmowa agencja wydawnicza): 148–53.

____ (1958) 'Gdy "Polska wybuchła"', *Trybuna ludu*, 5 October.

____ (1964) *Andrzej Munk*. Warsaw: Wydawnictwa artystczne i filmowe.

____ (1983) *Moja filmoteka: kino polskie*. Warsaw: Wydawnictwa artystyczne i filmowe.

Jameson, F. (1971) *Marxism and Form*. Princeton, NJ: Princeton University Press.

Janicka, B. (1993) 'Kulą w łeb', *Film*, XLVIII (25 April): 12–13.

Janion, M. (1975) 'Wajda i wartości', *Film*, 3, 9 (2 March): 12–15.

____ (1998) *Płacz generała: eseje o wojnie*. Warsaw: Wydawnictwo Sic!.

Jankun-Dopartowa, M. (1990) 'Prawdy żywe kina polskiego lat osiemdziesiątych', *Konkurs* 1: 40–50.

____ (1996a) 'Formy przestraszone ogniem i zapachem krwi. Konteksty kulturowe kina lat 1956–1970', in M. Jankun-Dopartowa and M. Przylipiak (eds) *Człowiek z ekranu: z antropologii postaci filmowej*. Cracow: Arcana: 29–62.

____ (1996b) 'Trzy przypadki bohatera lat 80', in M. Jankun-Dopartowa and M. Przylipiak (eds) *Człowiek z ekranu: z antropologii postaci filmowej*. Cracow: Arcana: 145–72.

____ (2000a) *Gorzkie kino Agnieszki Holland*. Gdańsk: słowo/obraz terytoria.

____ (2000b) *Labyrint Polańskiego*. Cracow: Rabid.

Jankun-Dopartowa, M. and M. Przylipiak (eds.) (1996) *Człowiek z ekranu: z antropologii postaci filmowej.* Cracow: Arcana.

Jeremias, B. (1971) 'Jesus am U-Bahn-Schacht: Der polnische Regisseur Andrzej Wajda filmt in Deutschland', *Frankfurter Allgemeine Zeitung*, 19 August: 28.

'js' (1980) 'Na antenach radia i telewizji. W rocznicę godziny "W"', *Za wolność i lud*, 6 September.

Kajdański, J. (1993) 'Wyprzedaż pierścionków', *Tygodnik Solidarność*: 17 September.

Kąkolewski, K. (1998) *Diament odnaleziony w popiele.* Warsaw: von borowiecky.

_____ (1994) 'Diament w popiół obrócony', *Kwartalnik filmowy*, 6 (Summer): 39–56.

Kałużyński, Z. (1958) 'Morderca z Café de Wąski Spodeń', *Trybuna literacka*, 12 October.

_____ (1961) 'Dziecko, żołnierz i wojna', *Polityka*, 14 October.

_____ (1966) *Salon dla miliona.* Warsaw: Czytelnik.

_____ (1975a) 'Wajda o Jezusie', *Polityka*, 8 February.

_____ (1975b) 'Czarna Łódź kolorowa', *Polityka*, 22 February.

_____ (1976) *Wenus automobilowa.* Warsaw: Państwowy instytut wydawniczy.

_____ (1978) *Demon milionowy.* Warsaw: Państwowy instytut wydawniczy.

_____ (1990) 'Pan z fortepianem', *Polityka*, 21 April.

Kandinsky, W. (1977) *Concerning the Spiritual in Art*, trans. M. T. H. Sadler. New York: Dover Publications.

Karabasz, K. (1985) *Bez fikcji: z notatek filmowego dokumentalisty.* Warsaw: Wydawnictwa artystyczne i filmowe.

Kawalerowicz, J. (2001) *Więcej niż kino.* Warsaw: Skorpion.

Kehr, D. (1994) 'To Save the World: Kieślowski's *Three Colours* Trilogy', *Film Comment*, 30, 6 (November–December): 10–13; 15–18; 20.

Kieślowski, K. (1981) 'Głęboko zamiast szeroko', *Dialog*, 1: 109–11.

_____ (1995) 'Quality Cuts', *Index on Censorship* 24, 6: 110–11.

Kieślowski, K. and K. Piesiewicz (1998) *Three Colours Trilogy: Blue, White, Red*, trans. Danusia Stok. London: Faber and Faber.

Kijowski, A. (1973) *Oskarzony i inne opowiadania.* Warsaw: Czytelnik.

Klawans, S. (1994) 'Three Colors: Red', *The Nation*, December 12: 738–40.

Kołodyński, A. (1993) 'Film biały: epitafium dla kina moralnego niepokoju', *Kino*, 27, 9 (September): 26–30.

Konwicki, T. (1973) *Ostatni dzień lata: scenariusze filmowe.* Warsaw: Iskry.

_____ (1982) *Wschody i zachody księżyca.* London: Zapis.

_____ (2000) *Pamiętam, że było gorąco.* Cracow: Znak.

Kornatowska, M. (1990) *Wodzireje i amatorzy.* Warsaw: Wydawnictwa artystyczne i filmowe.

Koźniewski, K. (ed.) (1958) 'Ankieta: Sto głosów o filmie "Popiół i Diament"', *Polityka*, 22 November.

Krall, H. (ed.) (1998) *Przypadek i inne teksty.* Cracow: Znak.

_____ (1989) *Sublokatorka.* Warsaw: Iskry.

Kruczkowski, L. (1984) *Dramaty.* Warsaw: Książka i wiedza.

'Kryśka' (1975) 'Obiecanki cacanki … komu radość, komu nie…', *Żołnierz Wolności*, February 18.

Krzyżanowski, J. (1971) 'On the History of *Ashes and Diamond* [sic]', *Slavic and East European Journal*, 15, 3: 324–31.

Kulig, A. (1998) 'Barwy samotności w tryptychu Krzysztofa Kieślowskiego *Trzy kolory – Niebieski, Biały, Czerwony*', *Kwartalnik filmowy*, 24 (Winter): 105–10.

Kwartalnik filmowy 15/16 (1996/1997) 'Twórczość Andrzeja Wajdy'.

Kwartalnik filmowy 17 (1997a) 'Kino polskie I'.

Kwartalnik filmowy 18 (1997b) 'Kino polskie II'.

Kwiatkowski, J. (1958) 'Dwie poetyki ("Popiół i diament" po raz drugi)', *Życie literackie*, 2 November: 4.

Ledóchowski, A. (1998) *Ulotne obrazy.* Warsaw: Polska Federacja Dyskusyjnych Klubów Filmowych.

Leftwich-Curry, J. (trans. and ed.) (1984) *The Black Book of Polish Censorship.* New York: Random House.

Lem, S. (1958) 'Felieton apologetyczny', *Zdarzenia*, 26 October (reprinted in *Kwartalnik filmowy*, 17, (Spring 1997): 37–8).

Levine, M. (1987) 'The Ambiguity of Moral Outrage in Jerzy Andrzejewski's *Wielki Tydzień*', *The Polish Review*, 32, 4: 385–99.

Lewis, C. and C. Britch (1986) 'Andrzej Wajda's War Trilogy: A Retrospective', *Film Criticism*, 10, 3: 22–35.

Lichniak, Z. (1975) 'Piłat i my', *Słowo powszechne*, 13 February.

Linville, S. (1995) '*Europa, Europa*: A Test-Case for German National Cinema', *Wide Angle*, 16, 3: 38–51.

Lis, P. (1998) *A jednak się kręci: szkice filmowe.* Wrocław: Towarzystwo przyjaciół polonistyki wrocławskiej.

Lubelski, T. (1990) '"Andrzej Wajda – portret", fragment scieżki dzwiękowej filmu', *Kino*, 25, 4 (May): 20–2.

____ (1991) 'Cztery wcielenia Salomona Perela', *Kino* 25, 4 (April): 14–16.

____ (1992a) *Strategie autorskie w polskim filmie fabularnym lat 1945–1961.* Cracow: Uniwersytet Jagielloński.

____ (1992b) *Popiół i diament*, *Kino*, 26, 9 (September): 20–3; 44–6.

____ (1994) 'Trzy kolejne podejścia', *Kwartalnik filmowy*, 6: 176–87.

____ (1997) (ed.) *Kino Krzysztofa Kieślowskiego.* Cracow: Universitas.

____ (2000) 'Stara i nowa "Ziemia obiecana"', *Kino*, 34, 9 (September): 4–5; 61.

____ (2003) '"He Speaks To Us": The Author in *Everything for Sale, Man of Marble* and *Pan Tadeusz*', in J. Orr and E. Ostrowska (eds) (2003) *The Cinema of Anrdzej Wajda: The Art of Irony and Defiance.* London: Wallflower Press: 30–45.

Łuczak, M. (2002) *Rejs, czyli szczególnie nie chodzę na filmy polskie.* Warsaw: Prószynski i S-ska.

Lukács, G. (1977) *Kunst und objektive Wahrheit*, ed. Werner Mittenzwei. Leipzig: Reclam.

Łużyńska, J. (1995) 'Zawsze robiłem filmy romantyczne' (interview with Krzyztof Kieślowski), *Sycyna*, 22 (24 September): 3–4.

Malatyńska, M. (1974) 'Wejście do "ziemi obiecanej": Rozmowa z Andrzejem Wajdą', *Życie literackie,* 5 May.

____ (1989) 'Dekalog, Kieślowski', *Życie literackie*, 19 November.

Manovich, L. (2001) *The Language of New Media.* Cambridge, MA: MIT Press.

Matuszewski, R. (1958) 'Popiół i diament', *Nowa kultura*, 19 October: 1; 7.

Mazierska, E. (2000) 'Non-Jewish Jews, Good Poles and Historical Truth in the Films of Andrzej Wajda', *Historical Journal of Film, Radio and Television*, 20, 2: 213–26.

Merz, I. (1960) 'Surrealizm czy kicz?', *Film*, 15, 2 (10 January): 6.

Mętrak, K. (1974) *Autografy na ekranie.* Warsaw: Wydawnictwa artystyczne i filmowe.

Michałek, B. (1960) 'The Polish Drama', *Sight and Sound*, 29, 4 (Autumn): 198–200.

____ (1973) *The Cinema of Andrzej Wajda.* London and New York: The Tantivy Press and A. S. Barnes.

____ (1990) 'Kieślowski – odrębne rysy', *Kino*, 24, 2 (February): 1–3.

____ (1981) *Notes filmowy.* Warsaw: Wydawnictwo artystyczne i filmowe.

Michałek, B. and F. Turaj (1988) *The Modern Cinema of Poland.* Bloomington: Indiana University Press.

Miczka, T. (ed.) and A. Madej (asst. ed.) (1994) *Syndrom konformizmu? Kino polskie lat sześćdziesiątych.* Katowice: Wydawnictwo Uniwersytetu Śląskiego.

Miłosz, C. (1981) *The Captive Mind*, trans. J. Zielonko. New York: Vintage.

Mirski, M. (1961) 'Bronię prawdy "Samsona"', *Polityka*, 2 December.

Możejko, E. (2001) *Realizm socjalistyczny: Teoria. Rozwój. Upadek.* Cracow: Universitas.

Mrożek, S. (1983) 'Popiół? Diament?', *Kultura* (Paris): 33–41.

Mruklik, B. (1969) *Andrzej Wajda.* Warsaw: Wydawnictwa artystyczne i filmowe.

Mucharski, P. (1996) 'Do źródeł, pod prąd' (interview with Zbigniew Preisner), *Tygodnik powszechny*, 2 June: 1; 14.

Netz, F. (1984) 'Romans z ojczyzną', *Tygodnik Tak i Nie*, 16 March: 5.

Nietzsche, F. (1910) *Thoughts Out of Season II, Works* Vol. 5, trans. Adrian Collins. Edinburgh and London: Foulis.

Niogret, H. (1997) '"Les coulisses de l'âme": entretien avec Krzysztof Kieślowski', in V. Amiel (ed.) *Krzysztof Kieślowski*. Paris: Jean Michel Place: 66–72.

Nurczyńska-Fidelska, E. (1982) *Andrzej Munk*. Cracow: Wydawnictwo literackie.

____ (1998) *Polska klasyka literacka według Andrzeja Wajdy*. Katowice: Śląsk.

____ (2003) 'Andrzej Wajda's Vision of *The Promised Land*', in J. Orr and E. Ostrowska (eds) (2003) *The Cinema of Anrdzej Wajda: The Art of Irony and Defiance*. London: Wallflower Press: 146–59.

Nurczyńska-Fidelska, E. and Z. Batko (eds) (1995) *Polish Cinema in Ten Takes*. Łódź: Łódzkie Towarzystwo Naukowe.

Nurczyńska-Fidelska, E and P. Sitarski (eds) (2003) *Filmowy i Teatralny Świat Andrzeja Wajdy*. Łódź: Wydawnictwo Uniwersytetu Łódzkiego.

Nurczyńska-Fidelska, E. and B. Stolarska (eds) (1998) *'Szkoła polska' – powroty*. Łódź: Wydawnictwo Uniwersytetu Łódzkiego.

Orr, J. (1998) *Contemporary Cinema*. Edinburgh: Edinburgh University Press.

Orr, J. and E. Ostrowska (eds) (2003) *The Cinema of Anrdzej Wajda: The Art of Irony and Defiance*. London: Wallflower Press.

Ostrowska, E. (1998) 'Filmic Representations of the "Polish Mother" in Post-Second World War Polish Cinema', *European Journal of Women's Studies*, 5: 419–35.

Otrębska, A. and J. Błach (1996) '"Ponieważ są ciągle ci ludzie…": z Krzysztofem Kieślowskim rozmawiali Agata Otrębska i Jacek Błach', *Incipit*, 2, April; reprinted in T. Lubelski (ed.) *Kino Krzysztofa Kieślowskiego*. Cracow: Universitas: 288–301.

Pakulski, J. (1990) 'Poland: ideology, legitimacy and political domination', in N. Abercrombie, S. Hill and B. S. Turner (eds) *Dominant Ideologies*. London: Unwin Hyman: 38–64.

Paul, D. W. (ed.) (1983) *Politics, Art and Commitment in the East European Cinema*. London and Basingstoke: Macmillan.

Pawlicki, A. (2001) *Kompletna szarość. Cenzura w latach 1965–1972. Instytucja i ludzie*. Warsaw: Wydawnictwo TRIO.

Pease, N. (1988) 'New Books on Poles and Jews During the Second World War', *The Polish Review*, 33, 3: 347–51.

Peck, A. (1994) '*Trois couleurs Bleu/Blanc/Rouge*: une trilogie européene', in Michel Estève (ed.) *Krzysztof Kieślowski*. Paris: Lettres modernes: 147–62.

Piątek, J., W. Piątek and S. Zawiśliński (1999) *Kino Krzysztofa Zanussiego*. Warsaw: Skorpion.

Piasecki, M. (1996) 'Dwa "Wielkie Tygodnie"', *Gazeta wyborcza*, 9–10 March.

Piasecki, W. (ed.) (1975) 'Dlaczego oglądamy "Ziemię obiecaną"', *Sztandar ludu*, 16 April.

Pijanowski, L. (1958) 'Zaraz po wojnie – 13 lat!', *Polityka*, 11 October.

Pizello, S. (1995) 'Piotr Sobociński *Red*', *American Cinematographer*, 76, 6 (June): 68–74.

Płażewski, J. (1958) 'Le jeune cinéma polonais: la période de Sturm und Drang alla polacca', *Cahiers du cinéma* 82 (April): 21–33.

____ (1961) 'Poemat i proza', *Przegląd kulturalny*, 12 October.

Poczmański, W. (1975) 'Komu obiecano tę ziemię', *Barwy* , 4.

Polański, R. (1984) *Roman by Polanski*. New York: William Morrow.

Prokop, J. (1994) *Wyobraźnia pod nadzorem; z dziejów literatury i polityki w PRL*. Cracow: Viridis.

Przylipiak, M. (1990) 'Z Wajdą o *Korczaku*', *Gazeta Gdańska*, 21–3 September.

____ (1991) '*Europa, Europa* trochę jak komiks', *Gazeta Gdańska*, 20 September.

____ (1993) 'Było kiedy tylu fajnych chłopców i dziewcząt?', *Kino*, 27: 3 (March): 9–11.

____ (1997) 'Filmy fabularne Kieślowskiego w zwierciadle polskiej krytyki filmowej', in T. Lubelski (ed.) *Kino*

Krzysztofa Kieślowskiego. Cracow: Universitas: 213–47.

Quart, B. (1988) *Women Directors: The Emergence of a New Cinema*. New York, Westport, CT: Praeger.

Ratschewa, I. (1980) 'Interview', in K. Eder, K. Kreimeier, M. Ratschewa, B. Thienhaus, *Andrzej Wajda*. Munich and Vienna: Carl Hanser Verlag: 61–92.

Rek, J. (2003) 'Stalin's Sweet Revenge, or on Some Consequences of Close Encounters Between Film Criticism and Politics. Around Recent Discussions on Socialist Realist Cinema in Poland' (unpublished paper).

Rhode, E. (1966) 'Andrzej Wajda', in *Tower of Babel: Speculations on the Cinema*. London: Weidenfeld and Nicolson: 169–87.

Robak, T. (1975) 'Co odkryli Reymont i Wajda', *Życie literackie*, 9 March.

Różewicz, S. (1967) 'Westerplatte', *Filipinka*, 24 September.

Ruane, K. (1982) *The Polish Challenge*. London: BBC.

Sandauer, A. (1982) *O sytuacji pisarza polskiego pochodzenia żydowskiego*. Warsaw: Czytelnik.

Sartre, J.-P. (1962) *Anti-Semite and Jew*. New York: Grove.

Ścibor-Rylski, A. (1988) *Człowiek z marmuru*. Warsaw: Wydawnictwa artystyczne i filmowe.

_____ (1991) *Pierścionek z końskiego włosia*. Warsaw: Kultura.

Silverman, K. (1988) *The Acoustic Mirror: The Female Voice in Psychoanalysis and Cinema*. Bloomington and Indianopolis: Indiana University Press.

Skorupski, J. S. (1992) *Polski czyścieć*. Poznan: SAWW.

Słodowski, J. (1994) *Rupieciarnia wyobraźni*. Warsaw: Skorpion.

Smosarski, J. (1975) '*Pilat i inni*', *Więź* 3: 139–41.

Sobański, O. (1990) 'Dekalog siedem, Dekalog osiem', *Film*, XLV, 4 (28 January): 11.

Sobolewski, T. (1975) 'Wajda wśród dzieci Chrystusa', *Film na świecie*, 201 (May): 73–6.

_____ (1988a) 'Blisko Kaina', *Odra*, 9: 83.

_____ (1988b) 'Krzysztofa Kieślowskiego "dzieje grzechu"', *Przegląd katolicki*, 25 December: 8.

_____ (1990) 'Solidarność grzesznych: O *Dekalogu* Krzysztofa Kieślowskiego', *NaGlos*, 1, 1: 91–101.

_____ (1992) 'Polskie kino: szok wolności', *Kino*, 26, 1 (January): 2–3.

_____ (1997) 'Twarze Kieślowskiego', *Gazeta wyborcza*, 8–9 March: 14

_____ (1998) 'Świadek życia' in H. Krall (ed.) *Przypadek i inne teksty*. Cracow: Znak.

_____ (1999) 'Ultimate Concerns' in P. Coates (ed.) *Lucid Dreams: The Films of Krzysztof Kieślowski*. Trowbridge: Flicks Books: 19–31.

_____ (2000) *Dziecko peerelu. Esej. Dziennik*. Warsaw: Wydawnictwo Sic!.

Stachówna, G. (1994) *Roman Polański i jego filmy*. Warsaw and Łódź: Państwowe Wydawnictwo Naukowe.

Stawiński, J. S. (1966) *Kanał, Ucieczka*. Warsaw: Czytelnik.

Stok, D. (ed.) (1993) *Kieślowski on Kieślowski*. London and Boston: Faber and Faber.

Strick, P. (1994) 'Trois couleurs: Blanc', *Sight and Sound*, 4, 6 (June): 63–4.

Sulewski, W. (1958) 'Kompleks "101"', *Żołnierz polski*, 12–18 November.

Szafar, T. (1983) 'Anti-Semitism, a Trusty Weapon', in A. Brumberg (ed.) *Poland: Genesis of a Revolution*. New York: Vintage: 109–22.

Szczepański, J. J. (1958) 'Popiół i diament', *Tygodnik powszechny*, 19 October: 9 (reprinted in *Kwartalnik filmowy*, 17 (Spring 1997): 32–4).

_____ (1972) 'Słońce wschodzi raz na dzień', *Tygodnik powszechny*, 14 May.

Szczerba, J. (1995) 'Tragedie wiosenna', *Gazeta wyborcza*, 10 May.

Szyma, T. (1990) 'Dekalog osiem', *Tygodnik powszechny*, 11 February.

Tabecki, J. (1989) 'Elżbieta Czyżewska; nieobecna, usprawiedliwiona', *Iluzjon*, 4: 3–13.

Taubin, A. (1991) 'Woman of Irony', *The Village Voice*, 2 July.

Tejchma, J. (1991) *Kulisy dymisji*. Cracow: Oficyna Cracovia.

Tertz, A. (1960) *On Socialist Realism*. New York: Pantheon.

Toeplitz, J. (1952) '*Młodość Chopina*', *Kwartalnik Filmowy*, 2, 5/6: 116–60.

Toeplitz, K. T. (1958) 'Serce i rozum', *Świat*, 19 October: 7.

____ (1971) 'Z laboratorium do kina', *Miesięcznik literacki*, 12: 71–3

____ (1973) *Wiadomości z tamtego świata*. Warsaw: Wydawnictwa artystyczne i filmowe.

____ (1974) *Próba sensu, czyli notatnik leniwego kinomana*. Warsaw: Wydawnictwa artystyczne i filmowe.

Torańska, T. (1997) *Oni*. Warsaw: Świat książki.

Trinon, H. (1964) *Andrzej Wajda*. Paris: Editions Seghers.

Trznadel, J. (1988) *Polski Hamlet: kłopoty z działaniem*. Paris: Libella.

____ (1990) *Hańba domowa: rozmowy z pisarzami*. Lublin: Wydawnicto 'Test' i Zakłady wydawnicze 'Versus'.

Vale, M. (ed.) (1981) *Poland: The State of the Republic: Two Reports by the Experience and Future Discussion Group (DiP) Warsaw*. London: Pluto Press.

Wajda, A. (1967) 'Destroying the Commonplace' in H. M. Geduld (ed.) *Film Makers on Film Making: Statements on their Art by Thirty Directors*. Harmondsworth: Penguin: 235–40.

____ (1984 [1983]) *Three Films: Ashes and Diamonds, A Generation, Kanal*, ed. and trans B. Sulik. London: Lorrimer.

____ (1989) *Double Vision: My Life in Film*. London and New York: Faber and Faber and Henry Holt, Inc.

____ (1992) 'Wolni – od czego?', *Kino*, 26, 1 (January): 3–5.

____ (1996) Statement to Polska Agencja Prasowa (PAP), *Życie Warszawy*, 9 April.

____ (1996/97) 'Moje notatki z historii', *Kwartalnik filmowy*, 15/16 (Autumn–Winter): 7–21.

____ (1997) Interview before *Wieczór Andrzeja Wajdy*, broadcast in Poland April 26 by Canal+.

____ (2000a) *Kino i reszta świata*. Cracow: Wydawnictwo Znak.

____ (2000b) *Wajda Films*, trans. J. Kozak, E. Krasińska, M. J. Oczko, E. Petrajtis, A. Zapałowski. Warsaw: Wydawnictwa artystyczne i filmowe.

Warszałłowicz, M. (1949) '*Ulica graniczna* film arcyludzki', *Film*, 4, 12 (1 July): 8–9.

Werner, A. (1987) *Polskie, arcypolskie...* London: Polonia.

____ (1990) 'Więcej popiołu', *Kino*, 24, 5 (May): 23–7.

Wertenstein, W. (1971) 'Pod prąd na autostradzie', *Magazyn filmowy*, 16 September.

____ (1991) *Zespół filmowy 'X'*, Warsaw: Wydawnicto 'Officina'.

____ (1995) 'W realizacji – *Wielki tydzień*', *Kino*, 7–8 (July August): 28–9.

____ (ed.) (2000) *Wajda mówi o sobie – wywiady i teksty*. Cracow: Wydawnictwo literackie.

Wilhelmi, J. (1958) 'Tylko historia', *Trybuna literacka*, 19 October.

Wilson, E. (1998) '*Three Colours: Blue*: Kieślowski, colour and the postmodern subject', *Screen*, 39, 4 (Winter): 349–62.

____ (2000) *Memory and Survival: The French Cinema of Krzysztof Kieślowski*. Oxford: Legenda.

Wojciechowski, P. (1994) 'Orzeł, reszka, Kieślowski i Pan Bóg', *Film*, 7: 49.

Woroszylski, W. (1958) 'Tylko popiół?', *Film*, 19 October: 4 (reprinted in *Kwartalnik filmowy*, 17 (Spring 1997): 39– 40).

____ (1990) '"Jestem" Janusza Korczaka i Andrzeja Wajdy', *Kino*, August: 1–5.

____ (1993) 'Pierścionek ze znakiem pytania', *Kino*, 27, 4 (April): 11.

Zajiček E. (1992) *Poza ekranem: kinematografia polska 1918–1991*. Warsaw: Filmoteka Narodowa and Wydawnictwa Artystyczne i Filmowe.

Zanussi, K. (1978) *Scenariusze filmowe*. Warsaw: Iskry.

____ (1985) *Scenariusze filmowe* II. Warsaw: Iskry.

____ (1992) *Scenariusze filmowe* III. Warsaw: Iskry.

Zatorski, J. (1975a) 'Karnawał na Golgocie', *Kierunki,* 16 February.

____ (1975b) 'Mazowieckie Klondike', *Kierunki*, 9 March.

Zawiśliński, S. (ed.) (1994) *Kieślowski bez końca*. Warsaw: Skorpion.

_____ (ed.) (1996) *Kieślowski*. Warsaw: Skorpion.

_____ (ed.) (1995) *Reżyseria Agnieszka Holland*. Warsaw: Skorpion.

Žižek, S. (2001) *The Fright of Real Tears: Krzysztof Kieślowski Between Theory and Post-Theory*. London: British Film Institute.

Żórawski, K. (1972) 'Na miarę greckiej tragedii', *Kultura*, 7 May.

Żukrowski, W. (1969) *Lotna*. Warsaw: książka i wiedza.

Zwierzchowski, P. (2000a) *Zapomniani bohaterowie. O bohaterach filmowych polskiego socrealizmu*. Warsaw: Wydawnictwo Trio.

_____ (2000b) 'Przygoda na Mariensztacie, czyli socrealizm i kultura popularna', in M. Hendrykowska (ed.) *Widziane po latach. Analizy i interpretacje filmu polskiego*. Poznań: Wydawnictwo Poznańskiego Towarzystwa Przyjaciół Nauk: 35–44.